Journeys
Home

Revised & Updated

Journeys Home

Revised & Updated

*The journeys of Protestant clergy and laity
coming home to the Catholic Church
and the Coming Home Network International,
a lay apostolate committed to helping them*

by **Marcus Grodi**
and a host of others

CHResources   Zanesville, Ohio

CHResources
PO Box 8290
Zanesville, Ohio 43702
(740) 450-1175

CHResources is a registered trademark
of the Coming Home Network International, Inc.

Grodi, Marcus C. (March 2, 1952)
Journeys Home Revised / Marcus Grodi

ISBN 0-9702621-6-7

Cover design by Stephen Smeltzer

Contents

Foreword

by Scott and Kimberly Hahn
former Presbyterian minister and wife

Each one of us is on pilgrimage — a journey of faith that leads us closer to the God we love day by day. Some of us received the Faith on our father's knee; others converted to Christianity in the teen years or later. And many of us who began a relationship with Christ outside the Catholic Church could not imagine the riches within the Church that Christ wanted to give us.

Rather than reject the Faith given to us in our youth, we believe we have embraced the fullness that Christ died to give us within the Catholic Church. Now we recognize the mystery where we previously did not know a mystery existed, such as the Eucharist and the other sacraments. Increasingly we appreciate the unity expressed in liturgy, doctrine, and morals through the authority of the Church when previously we had only hoped for basic agreement among our fellow Christians. Daily we harness heaven through the communion of saints when earlier we pictured ourselves much more alone on our journey.

We know from first hand experience that people in full-time Christian service who examine the claims of the Catholic Church have additional concerns and questions beyond those of other seekers. We have walked this rocky road, feeling alone in the midst of never-before-asked theological questions, unthinkable professional consequences, and emotional barriers that alternately separate us from our Protestant past, our possibly Catholic future, and perhaps even each other as a married couple. Consequently, we want to accompany others along this difficult path.

You are about to read excerpts from the spiritual journeys of people whose lives have been transformed through the grace of God in the Catholic Church. The circumstances in which each person discovered the Church—and the doctrines or moral teachings of the Church with which each person wrestled—are as individual as they are. Yet this they have in common: By the mercy of God, they have followed Christ into the Catholic Church, no matter what the cost. Their accounts are invitations to join them mid-journey. Look over their shoulders, as it were, to take stock of their various backgrounds and training in Christian faith, to understand their newfound joy in the Catholic Church, and to be filled with awe at the feet of our Lord for His marvelous work on behalf of each one of us.

God bless you.
Scott and Kimberly Hahn
(authors, Rome Sweet Home)

Acknowledgment

W here does anyone begin to thank all the people God has used in his life—and whom He has used, specifically in this case, to help the *Coming Home Network International* become what it is and this book to come to fruition? I can only mention a few, but for all the rest who have been so patient, merciful, caring, forgiving, and faithful, may God bless you for your loving friendship and encouragement.

First to my parents, Daniel and Dorothy Grodi who not only nurtured me with their love and discipline, but put up with my diverse and too often unsettling spiritual journey.

To the many pastors and priests, Catholic and Protestant, who have been such faithful witnesses to Christ and His Church, including Reverends Elmer J. Melchert, Quentin Battiste, Tom Witzel, Gary Stratman, Tom Cebula, Michael Scanlon, Ray Ryland, Mitch Pacwa, William Stetson, Benedict Groeschel, Augustine DiNoia, Jack Maynard, Don Franks, and the fine Dominican priests at St. Thomas Aquinas, Zanesville. I especially want to thank the Catholic Cardinals and Bishops who have supported our work, including Cardinal George, Cardinal Law, Archbishop Burke, Archbishop Meyer, Bishop Campbell, Bishop Sheldon, Bishop Dudley, Bishop Wuerl, and Bishop Chaput.

A truly *awesome* thanks goes to Mother Angelica and her sisters and brothers whose generous heart and spirit opened the door so I could venture into the unknown world of Catholic television and radio.

To our many supportive friends, Scott and Kimberly Hahn, Steve Wood, Karl Keating, Pat Madrid, Mark Miravalle, Nick and Jane Healy, etc., etc., etc., without whose encouragement and assistance the *Coming Home Network* could never have survived.

To all the fine staff members who have given of themselves for our apostolic work, especially the present wonderful, awesome, immensely gifted, and highly motivated staff: Jim Anderson, Sharon Coen, Jon Marc Grodi, Anne Moore, Laura Nicholson, Rob Rodgers, and Stephen Smeltzer. A special thanks also goes to our faithful *CHNetwork* members, Helpers, and friends in Christ, praise be to Jesus!

To my children, Jon Marc, Peter, and Richard who are a great joy and a proud quiver for an unworthy father.

And now to the one who fills my life with love and meaning, an undeserved gift from God—who is certainly growing in holiness as she patiently offers up all of my foibles—my loving wife, Marilyn.

Sincerely in Christ,
Marcus C. Grodi

Introduction

But when he came to himself he said, "How many of my father's hired servants have bread enough and to spare, but I perish here with hunger! I will arise and go to my father, and I will say to him, 'Father, I have sinned against heaven and before you; I am no longer worthy to be called your son; treat me as one of your hired servants.'" And he arose and came to his father. But while he was yet at a distance, his father saw him and had compassion, and ran and embraced him and kissed him (Luke 15:17-20).

Every single person must go through this same experience of journeying home to the Father. It is slightly or drastically different for each of us, depending upon how deeply into the pigsty we have ventured before we came to our senses. Even if we have been Christians all our lives, having been baptized, catechized, and confirmed in the Church, remaining faithful even up to the present moment, yet the apostle Paul reminds his Roman readers, " . . . all have sinned and fall short of the glory of God" (Romans 3:23).

Each one of us must recognize and confirm our own brokenness. We each must willfully choose to follow Jesus Christ, and then, aided by His grace, we can begin advancing inch by inch along our journey of faith toward holiness and union with Him. As what happened to the young man in the story quoted above, all our heavenly Father needs to see is our contrite hearts, our sincere turning homeward, and He will embrace us with His compassionate, forgiving acceptance.

The book you hold in your hand contains the stories of men and women who have all experienced this loving acceptance from God the Father. These pilgrims have each at some time surrendered their lives to Jesus Christ and, as a result, heard a call to follow Him more completely. Many of these were pastors or missionaries, or their spouses. Others were laymen who, though working in secular jobs, took their calling to serve Christ in the world very seriously.

What is unique about these stories is that each of these faithful disciples discovered, sometimes with great consternation or even horror, that continuing to follow Christ required a journey home they had never anticipated nor desired.

Most of these men and women discovered Jesus Christ in some branch of Protestantism and, therefore, remain eternally grateful to the many faithful Protestant teachers, friends, and family who helped them know Christ and grow in the Christian faith. Yet, in each case, their desire to follow Christ faithfully—to remain faithful to the truth He taught and to the Church He established through His apostles—led them to consider the claims of the Catholic Church.

Many of these men and women came from Protestant faiths that viewed the Catholic Church as the "whore of Babylon" and the pope as the "antichrist." From an early age they were taught all kinds of things about Catholics and their beliefs, sometimes horrifying, repulsive things, that made them wonder whether Catholics could even be saved. Yet, in each case and in uniquely different ways, the Holy Spirit opened their hearts to realize that much of what they had been taught about the Catholic Church was never true. They learned to listen to the voice of truth speaking through history, theology, Sacred Tradition, Holy Scripture, and personal testimony.

Having made this journey from this same background, I realize that any Protestant reader, at this very moment, may be feeling cautious or skeptical, leery to go on, convinced that these men and women have instead been deceived by the prince of lies himself! However, resisting the temptation to jump into long pages of apologetic arguments, let me at least assure you that this is not the case. These stories are told by humble souls who love Jesus Christ, who desire to obey Him fully, and who have denounced completely the devil and his hoard. They have sought to follow the teachings of Scripture, as well as the teachings of the early Church Fathers and the ecumenical councils.

In doing so, they were startled to discover the truth of the Catholic Church and its teachings. In the process, they also discovered that throughout its history, the Church has included not only thousands of saints but also thousands of sinners, lay and clergy. Too often these real but less than perfect followers of Jesus dirtied the fair name of the Catholic Church and gave fodder for the many misunderstandings and exaggerations that have led to so many schisms.

The book you hold in your hand is also unique in another way. It is not strictly a collection of conversion stories, nor does every story contain lengthy, detailed arguments in defense of their conversions. There are other, highly recommended books that accomplish this task, which are listed in Appendix B. Rather, this book also focuses on the formation and ministry of the *Coming Home Network International* and the powerful conversion experiences of its members.

The "Network" was started in 1993 to respond to the needs of the increasing number of Protestant clergy who have been "coming home" to the Catholic Church during the last fifty years. Unlike the hundreds of Anglican conversions that followed the conversion of John Henry Cardinal Newman in the nineteenth century, these modern day conversions are occurring as the result of no single notable precursor nor from any one denomination. Rather, they are coming from every conceivable Christian and non-Christian tradition and for a wide diversity of reasons.

Particularly for clergy, this conversion process requires great sacrifice, including sometimes the loss of family, friends, and vocation. The *Coming Home Network International* provides information, fellowship, and encouragement, as well as financial assistance, for these converts and their families as they become acclimated to the "strange, new world" of the Catholic Church.

I encourage you to read the following with a prayerful and charitable heart. This revised and updated version of *Journeys Home* consists of a compilation of the conversion stories that have appeared in the *CHNetwork's* monthly newsletter.

Part One consists of the conversion accounts of non-Catholic clergy and missionaries. The decision of a Protestant pastor to resign from his pastorate and enter the Catholic Church affects more than himself. It affects his family and particularly his spouse and their marriage. In many cases, the spouses have not shared the same convictions, and marriages have been greatly tested.

Part Two consists of the conversion stories of lay converts. Though their journeys may not have resulted in the loss of vocation or employment, the emotional, intellectual, and relational impacts were equally as challenging.

One key way to help people in their spiritual journeys is to recommend books and resources that answer questions as well as offer profound insight into the Scriptures and the doctrines of the Faith. In Appendix A, therefore, you will find, for your spiritual encouragement, an extensive annotated bibliography, most of which can be purchased through our resource catalogue or from our website: http://www.chnetwork.org

If your are interested in finding out more about the *Coming Home Network International* or in becoming a member, you will find a membership form in Appendix B. You can also check out our website, which also provides access to several discussion groups.

Now as you turn to Part One, I ask that you listen with both your mind and your heart, for here you will hear the whisper and work of the Spirit.

Part One

The Journeys Home of Clergy

Why would Jesus want to throw a wrench into the lives of seemingly contented and effective Protestant clergy and their families? From the beginning of the *Coming Home Network International,* as the membership began sharing their reasons for "coming home" to the Catholic Church, we discovered that our journeys were amazingly similar, though in details very diverse. We, therefore, began sharing our stories as words of encouragement as well as guideposts for others on the way.

The longer, more detailed conversion stories of many of the *CHNetwork's* members, such as the Hahns, Woods, Howards, Rays, and Curries, are available on tape or in book form (see Appendix A for these and other titles). These detailed accounts have provided the spiritual spark for many non-Catholics on their journeys home, as well as rekindled the faith of thousands of life-long Catholics.

The following shorter testimonies, first printed in the *CHNetwork's* monthly newsletter, are collected here for your spiritual encouragement and as a challenge to those who have never openly considered the witness of the Catholic Church.

As you read, please remember that the decisions made by these men and women in Christ were much more compelling and life-changing then, say, having driven Fords all their lives they've now decided to drive Chevys. The decision to become Catholic often means not only the leaving of a familiar religious tradition and culture, but the loss of friends, family, career, and ministry. Therefore, I invite you to read these stories with prayer and charity, as well as an open heart.

What Is Truth?

by Marcus C. Grodi
former Presbyterian minister

I am a former Protestant minister. Like so many others who have trodden the path that leads to Rome by way of that country known as Protestantism, I never imagined I would one day convert to Catholicism.

By temperament and training, I'm more of a pastor than a scholar, so the story of my conversion to the Catholic Church may lack the technical details in which theologians traffic and in which some readers delight. But I hope I will accurately explain why I did what I did, and why I believe with all my heart that all Protestants should do likewise.

I won't dwell on the details of my early years, except to say that I was raised by two loving parents in a nominally Protestant home. I went through most of the experiences that make up the childhood and adolescence of the typical American baby-boomer.

I was taught to love Jesus and go to church on Sunday. I also managed to blunder into most of the dumb mistakes that other kids in my generation made. But after a season of teenage rebellion, when I was twenty years old, I experienced a radical re-conversion to Jesus Christ. I turned away from the lures of the world and became serious about prayer and Bible study.

As a young adult, I made a recommitment to Christ, accepting Him as my Lord and Savior, praying that He would help me fulfill the mission in life He had chosen for me.

The more I sought through prayer and study to follow Jesus and conform my life to His will, the more I felt an aching sense of longing to devote my life entirely to serving Him. Gradually, the way dawn's first faint rays peek over a dark horizon, the conviction that the Lord was calling me to be a minister began to grow.

That conviction grew steadily stronger while I was in college and then afterward during my job as an engineer. Eventually I couldn't ignore the call. I was convinced the Lord wanted me to become a minister, so I quit my job and enrolled in Gordon-Conwell Theological Seminary in suburban Boston. I acquired a master of divinity degree and was shortly thereafter ordained to the Protestant ministry.

My six-year-old son, Jon-Marc, recently memorized the Cub Scouts' oath, which says in part: "I promise to do my best, to do my duty to God and my country." This earnest boyhood vow rather neatly sums up my own reasons for giving up a career in engineering in order to serve the Lord with complete abandon in full-time ministry. I took my new pastoral duties seriously, and I wanted to perform them correctly and faithfully, so that at the end of my life, when I stood face-to-face before God, I could hear Him speak those all-important words: "Well done, good and faithful servant." As I settled down into the rather pleasant life of a Protestant minister, I felt happy and at peace with myself and God—I finally felt that I had arrived.

I had not arrived.

I soon found myself faced with a host of confusing theological and administrative questions. There were exegetical dilemmas over how to correctly interpret difficult biblical passages and liturgical decisions that could easily divide a congregation. My seminary studies had not adequately prepared me to deal with this morass of options.

I just wanted to be a good pastor, but I couldn't find consistent answers to my questions from my fellow minister friends, nor from the "how to" books on my shelf, nor from the leaders of my Presbyterian denomination. It seemed that every pastor was expected to make up his own mind on these issues.

This "reinvent the wheel as often as you need to" mentality that is at the heart of Protestantism's pastoral ethos was deeply disturbing to me. "Why should I *have* to reinvent the wheel?" I asked myself in annoyance. "What about the Christian ministers down through the centuries who faced the same issues? What did they do?" Protestantism's emancipation from Rome's "man-made" laws and dogmas and customs that had "shackled" Christians for centuries (that, of course, was how we were taught in seminary to view the "triumph" of the Reformation over Romanism) began to look a lot more like anarchy than genuine freedom.

I didn't receive the answers I needed, even though I prayed constantly for guidance. I felt I had exhausted my resources and didn't know where to turn. Ironically, this frustrating sense of being out of answers was providential. It set me up to be open to answers offered by the Catholic Church. I'm sure that if I had felt that I had all the answers, I wouldn't have been able or willing to investigate things at a deeper level.

A breach in my defense

In the ancient world, cities were built on hilltops and ringed with stout walls that protected the inhabitants against invaders. When an invading army laid siege to a city, as when Nebuchadnezzar's army surrounded Jerusalem in 2 Kings 25:1-7, the inhabitants were safe as long as their food and water held out and for as long as their walls could withstand the onslaught of the catapult's missile and the sapper's pick. But if the wall was breached, the city was lost.

My willingness to consider the claims of the Catholic Church began as a result of a breach in the wall of the Reformed Protestant theology that encircled my soul. For nearly forty years I labored to construct that wall, stone-by-stone, to protect my Protestant convictions.

The stones were formed from my personal experiences, seminary education, relationships, and my successes and failures in the ministry. The mortar that cemented the stones in place was my Protestant faith and philosophy. My wall was high and thick and, I thought, impregnable against anything that might intrude.

As the mortar crumbled, however, and the stones began to shift and slide, at first imperceptibly but later on with an alarming rapidity, I became worried. I tried hard to discern the reason for my growing lack of confidence in the doctrines of Protestantism.

I wasn't sure what I was seeking to replace my Calvinist beliefs, but I knew my theology was not invincible. I read more books and consulted with theologians in an effort to patch the wall, but I made no headway.

I reflected often on Proverbs 3:5-6: "Trust in the Lord with all your heart, and lean not unto your own understanding; in all your ways acknowledge Him and He will direct your paths." This exhortation both haunted and consoled me as I grappled with the doctrinal confusion and procedural chaos within Protestantism.

The Reformers had championed the notion of private interpretation of the Bible by the individual, a position with which I began to feel increasingly uncomfortable, in light of Proverbs 3:5-6.

Bible-believing Protestants claim they *do* follow the teaching in this passage by seeking the Lord's guidance. The problem is that there are thousands of different doctrinal paths down which Protestants feel the Lord is directing them. And these doctrines vary dramatically according to denomination.

I struggled with the questions, "How do I know what God's will is for my life and for the people in my congregation? How can I be sure that what I'm preaching is correct? How do I *know* what truth is?" In light of the doctrinal mayhem that exists within Protestantism—each denomination staking out for itself doctrine based on the interpretations of the man who founded it—the standard Protestant boast, "I believe only in what the

Bible says," began to ring hollow. I professed to look to the Bible alone to determine truth, but the Reformed doctrines I inherited from John Calvin, John Knox, and the Puritans clashed in many respects with those held by my Lutheran, Baptist, and Anglican friends.

In the Gospels, Jesus explained what it means to be a true disciple (cf. Matthew 19:16-23). It's more than reading the Bible, or having your name on a church membership roster, or regularly attending Sunday services, or even praying a simple prayer of conversion to accept Jesus as our Lord and Savior. These things, good though they are, by themselves do not make one a true disciple of Jesus. Being a disciple of Jesus Christ means making a radical commitment to love and obey the Lord in every word, action, and attitude, striving to radiate His love to others. The true disciple, Jesus said, is willing to give up everything, even his own life if necessary, to follow the Lord.

I was deeply convinced of this fact, and as I tried to put it into practice in my own life (not always with much success), I did my best to convince my congregation that this call to discipleship is not an option but something to which Christians are called to strive. The irony was that my Protestant theology made me impotent to call them to radical discipleship, and it made them impotent to hear and heed the call.

One might ask, "If all it takes to be saved is to 'confess with your lips that Jesus is Lord and believe in your heart that God raised Him from the dead' (Romans 10:9), then why must I *change*? Oh, sure, I *should* change my sinful ways. I should strive to please God. But if I don't, what does it really matter? My salvation is assured."

There's a story about a newspaper reporter in New York City who wanted to write an article on what people consider the most amazing invention of the twentieth century. He hit the streets, interviewing people at random, and received a variety of answers: the airplane, the telephone, the automobile, computers, nuclear energy, space travel, and antibiotic medicine. The answers went on along these lines until one fellow gave an unlikely answer:

"It's obvious. The most amazing invention was the Thermos."

"The *Thermos*?" queried the reporter, eyebrows raised.

"Of course. It keeps hot things hot and cold things cold."

The newspaperman blinked. "So what?"

"How does it *know*?"

This anecdote had meaning for me. Since it was my duty and desire to teach the truth of Jesus Christ to my congregation, my growing concern was, "How do I *know* what is truth and what isn't?"

Every Sunday I would stand in my pulpit and interpret Scripture for my flock, knowing that within a fifteen mile radius of my church there were dozens of other Protestant pastors—all of whom believed that the Bible alone is the sole authority for doctrine and practice—each teaching something different from what I was teaching. "Is my interpretation of Scripture the right one or not?" I'd wonder. "Maybe one of those other pastors is right, and I'm misleading these people who trust me."

There was also the knowledge—no, the gut-twisting certitude—that one day I would die and stand before the Lord Jesus Christ, the Eternal Judge, and I would be required to answer not just for my own actions but also for how I led the people He had given me to pastor. "Am I preaching truth or error?" I asked the Lord repeatedly. "I *think* I'm right, but how can I know for sure?"

This dilemma haunted me.

I started questioning every aspect of my ministry and Reformed theology, from insignificant issues to important ones. I look back now with a certain embarrassed humor at how I fretted during those trying days of uncertainty. At one point, I even wrangled with doubts over whether or not to wear a clerical collar. There is no mandatory clerical dress code for Presbyterian ministers—some wear collars, some business suits, some robes, and others a combination of all. One minister friend kept a clerical collar in the glove compartment of his car, just in case donning it might bring some advantage to him. "Like getting out of a speeding ticket," he once confided with a conspiratorial grin. I decided not to wear a clerical collar. At Sunday services, I wore a plain black choir robe over my business suit.

When it came to the form and content of Sunday liturgy, every church had its own views on how things should be done, and each pastor was free to do pretty much whatever he wanted within reason.

Without mandated denominational guidelines to steer me, I did what all the other pastors were doing: I improvised. Hymns, sermons, Scripture selections, congregational participation, and the administration of Baptism, Matrimony, and the Lord's Supper were all fair game for experimentation. I shudder at the memory of one particular Sunday when, in an effort to make the youth service more interesting and "relevant," I spoke the Lord's words of consecration, "This is My body, this is My blood, do this in memory of Me," over a pitcher of soda pop and a bowl of potato chips.

Theological questions vexed me the most. I remember standing beside the hospital bed of a man who was near death after suffering a heart attack. His distraught wife asked me, "Is my husband going to heaven?" I hesitated for a moment before giving my pat Presbyterian response, as I considered the great diversity of alter-native responses I could give, depending upon whether one were Methodist, Baptist, Lutheran, Assemblies of God, Nazarene, Christian Scientist, Foursquare Gospel, Jehovah's Witnesses, etc. All I could do was mouth some sort of pious but vague "we-must-trust-in-the-Lord" reassurance about her husband's salvation. She may have been comforted but her tearful plea tormented me. After all, as a Reformed pastor I believed Calvinistic doctrines of predestination and perseverance of the saints. This man had given his life to Christ; he had been regenerated and was confident that he was one of God's elect. But was he?

I was deeply unsettled by the knowledge that no matter how earnestly he may have thought he was predestined for heaven (it's interesting that all who preach the doctrine of predestination firmly believe they themselves are one of the elect), and no matter how sincerely those around him believed he was, he may not have gone to heaven.

Moreover, what if he had secretly "backslidden" into serious sin and been living in a state of rebellion against God at the moment his heart attack caught him by surprise? Reformed theology told me that if that were the case, then the poor fellow had simply been deluded by a false security, *thinking* he was regenerated and predestined for heaven when in fact he had not been regenerated all along and on his way to hell. Calvin taught that the Lord's elect will—*must*—persevere in grace and election. If a person dies in a state of rebellion against God, he proves he never was one of the elect. "What kind of absolute assurance was that?" I wondered.

I found it harder to give clear, confident answers to the "will my husband go to heaven?" kinds of questions my parishioners asked. Every Protestant pastor I knew had a different set of criteria that he listed as "necessary" for salvation. As a Calvinist, I believed that if one publicly accepts Jesus as his Lord and Savior, he is saved by grace through faith. But even as I consoled others with these fine-sounding words, I was troubled by the worldly and sometimes grossly sinful lifestyles these now-deceased members of my congregation had lived. After just a few years of ministry, I began to doubt whether I should continue.

Consider the sparrows

I rose one morning before dawn and, taking a folding chair, my journal, and a Bible, went out into a quiet field beside my church. It was the time of day I most love, when the birds are singing the world awake. I often marvel at the exuberance of birds in the early morning. What wonderfully short memories they have! They begin each day of their simple existences with a symphony of praise to the Lord who created them, utterly unconcerned with cares or plans. Sometimes, I'd "consider the sparrows" and meditate on the simplicity of their lives.

Sitting quietly in the middle of the dew-covered field waiting for the sun to come up, I read Scripture and meditated on these questions that had been troubling me, placing my worries before the Lord. The Bible warned me not to "lean unto my own understanding," so I was determined to trust in God to guide me.

I was contemplating leaving the pastorate, and I saw three options. One was to become the leader of youth ministry at a large Presbyterian church that had offered me the position. Another was to leave ministry altogether and go back to engineering. The other possibility was to return to school and round out my scientific education in an area that would open even more doors to me professionally. I had been accepted into a graduate program in molecular biology at Ohio State University. I mulled over these options, asking God to guide my steps. "An audible voice would be great," I thought, smiling, as I closed my eyes and waited for the Lord's answer. I had no idea what form *The Answer* would take, but it was not long in coming.

My reveries ended abruptly when a merrily chirping sparrow flew past and pooped on my head! "What are you saying to me, Lord?" I cried out with the anguish of Job. The trilling of the birds was the only response. There was no voice from heaven (not even a snicker), just the sounds of nature waking from its slumber in an Ohio cornfield. Was it a divine sign or merely Brother Bird's editorial comment on my worries? In disgust, I folded my chair, grabbed my Bible, and went home.

Later that day, when I told my wife, Marilyn, about the three options I was considering and the messy incident with the bird, she laughed and exclaimed with her typical wisdom, "The meaning is clear, Marcus. God is saying 'None of the above!'"

Although I'd have preferred a less humiliating method of communication, I knew that nothing occurs by accident, and that neither spar-rows nor their droppings fall to earth without God's knowledge. I took this as at least a comical hint from God to remain in the ministry.

But I still knew my situation was not right. Maybe what I needed was a bigger church with a bigger budget and a bigger staff. Surely, then I'd be happy. So I struck off in the direction of the "bigger-is-better" church that I thought would satisfy my restless heart. Within six months, I found one I liked and whose very large congregation seemed to like me. They offered me the post of senior pastor, complete with an office staff and a budget ten times larger than the one I had at my previous church. Best of all, this was a strong evangelical church with many members who were actively interested in Scripture study and lay ministry. I enjoyed preaching before this large and largely approving congregation each Sunday. At first, I thought I had solved the problem, but after only one month, I realized that bigger was not better. My frustration merely grew proportionately larger.

Polite smiles beamed up at me during each sermon, but I wasn't blind to the fact that for many in the congregation my passionate exhortations to live a virtuous life merely skittered across a veneer of religiosity like water droplets on a hot skillet. Many said, "Great sermon! It really blessed me!" However, it was obvious that what they really thought was, "That's nice for other people, Pastor—for *sinners*—but I've already arrived. My name's already on the heavenly rolls. *I* don't need to worry about all this stuff, but I sure do agree with you, Pastor, that we've got to tell all the sinners to get right with God."

One day, I found myself standing before the local presbytery as spokesman for a group of pastors and laymen who were defending the idea that when we use parental language for God in communal prayer, we should call him "Father," not "mother" or "parent." I defended this position by appealing to Scripture and Christian tradition. To my dismay, I realized that the faction I represented was in the minority and that we were fighting a losing battle. This issue would be settled not by a well-reasoned appeal to Scripture or church history but by a vote—the majority of votes being pro-gender-neutral-language liberals. It was at this meeting that I first recognized the anarchistic principle that lies at the center of Protestantism.

These liberals (grievously wrong in their scheme to reduce God to the mere functions of "creator, redeemer, and sanctifier" instead of the Persons of Father, Son, and Holy Spirit) were just being good Protestants. They were simply following the course of protest mapped out for them by their theological ancestors Martin Luther, John Calvin, and other Reformers. The Reformation maxim of "I will not abide by a teaching unless *I* believe it is correct and biblical" was being invoked by these liberal Protestants in favor of their protest against masculine names for God. All of a sudden, it hit me that I was observing Protestantism in the full solipsistic glory of its natural habit: protest. "What kind of church am I in?" I asked myself dejectedly as the vote was taken and my side lost.

About this time my wife, Marilyn, who had been the director of a pro-life crisis pregnancy center, began challenging me to grapple with the inconsistency of our staunch pro-life convictions and the pro-choice stance of our Presbyterian denomination. "How can you be a minister in a denomination that sanctions the killing of unborn babies?" she asked.

The denominational leadership had bowed under the pressure from radical feminist, homosexual, pro-abortion, and other extremist pressure groups within the denomination and (though ostensibly members of individual congregations could hold pro-life views) imposed stringent liberal guidelines on the hiring process for new pastors.

When she woke me up to the fact that a portion of my congregation's dues to the Presbyterian General Assembly were most likely paying for abortions and there was nothing I or my congregation could do about it, I was stunned.

Marilyn and I knew we had to leave the denomination, but where would we go? This question led to another: Where am I going to find a job as a minister? I purchased a book that listed the details of all major Christian denominations and began evaluating several of the denominations that interested me.

I'd read the doctrinal summaries and think, "This one is nice, but I don't like their view on baptism," or "This one is OK, but their view of the end times is a bit too panic-ridden," or "This one sounds exactly like what I'm looking for, but I'm uncomfortable with their style of worship." After examining every possibility and not finding one that I liked, I shut the book in frustration. I knew I was leaving Presbyterianism, but I had no idea which denomination was the "right" one to join. There seemed to be something wrong with each of them. "Too bad I can't customize my 'perfect' church," I thought to myself wistfully.

Around this time, a friend from Illinois called me on the phone. He, too, was a Presbyterian pastor and had heard through the grapevine that I was planning to leave the Presbyterian denomination.

"Marc, you can't leave the church!" he scolded. "You must never leave the church; you're committed to the church. It should not matter that some theologians and pastors are off the wall. We have to stick with the church and work for renewal from within! We must preserve unity at all costs!"

"If that's true," I replied testily, "why did we Protestants break away from the church in the first place?"

I don't know where those words came from. I had never in my life given even a passing thought as to whether or not the Reformers were right to break away from the Catholic Church. It was the essential nature of Protestantism to attempt to bring renewal through division and fragmentation. The motto of Presbyterianism is "reformed and always reforming." (It should add, "and reforming, and reforming, and reforming, and reforming, etc.")

I could leave for another denomination, knowing that eventually I might move to another when I become dissatisfied, or I could decide to stay where I was and take my lumps. But then how could I justify staying where I was? Why shouldn't I return to the previous denominational group we Presbyterians had defiantly broken away from? None of these options seemed right, so I decided that I would leave the ministry until I resolved the issue one way or the other.

Returning to school seemed to be the easiest way to take a breather from all of this, so I enrolled in a graduate program in molecular biology at Case Western Reserve University. My goal was to combine my scientific and theological backgrounds into a career in bioethics. I figured that a Ph.D. in molecular biology would win me a better hearing among scientists than would a degree in theology or ethics.

The commute to the Cleveland campus took over an hour each way, and for the next eight months, I had plenty of quiet time for introspection and prayer.

Soon I was deeply immersed in a genetic engineering research project, which involved the removal and reproduction of human DNA taken from homogenized kidneys. The program was very challenging, but I loved it, although compared to the complexities of amino acids and biochemical cycles, wrestling with Latin conjugations and German declension endings suddenly seemed a lot easier.

The project fascinated and frightened me. I relished the intellectual stimulation of scientific research, but I also saw how dehumanizing the research lab can be. Genetic tissue, harvested from the cadavers of deceased patients at the Cleveland Clinic, was sent to our lab for DNA research. I was deeply moved by the fact that this tissue had come from people—moms and dads, children, and grandparents who had once lived and worked and laughed and loved. In the lab, these neatly numbered vials of tissue were just tubes of "stuff," experimental "material" that was utterly dissociated from the human person to whom it once belonged.

I wrote an essay on the ethical problems involved with fetal tissue transplantation and began speaking to Christian groups about the dangers and blessings of modem biological technology. Things seemed to be going according to plan; at least until I realized that the real reason for my return to school was not to get a degree. It was so that I might buy a copy of the local Cleveland newspaper.

One Friday morning, after a long drive into Cleveland, I was eating breakfast and killing time before class, trying to stay awake. Normally I'd squeeze in a little study time, but this morning I did something unusual: I bought a copy of *The Plain Dealer*. As I slipped the quarter into the newspaper machine, I had no way of knowing I had come to a momentous fork in the road. I was about to start down a path that would lead me out of Protestantism. (I suppose if I had known where it would lead, I would have run the other way.) Skimming through, with only nominal interest, I came across a small advertisement that jumped out at me: "Catholic theologian Scott Hahn to speak at local Catholic parish this Sunday afternoon."

I choked on my coffee. "*Catholic* theologian Scott Hahn?" It couldn't be the Scott Hahn I used to know. We had attended Gordon-Conwell Theological Seminary together back in the early eighties. Back then, he was a staunch Calvinist anti-Catholic, the staunchest on campus! I'd been on the fringe of an intense Calvinist study group that Scott led, but while Scott and others spent long hours scouring the Bible like detectives trying to uncover every angle of every theological implication, I played basketball.

Though I had not seen Scott since he graduated in 1982, I had heard the dark rumor floating around that he'd become Catholic. I hadn't thought much about it. Either the rumor was false, contrived by someone who was offended by (or jealous of) the intensity of Scott's convictions, or else Scott had flipped. I decided to make the hour-and-a-half trip to find out. I was totally unprepared for what I discovered.

Much learning hath made you mad!

I was nervous as I pulled into the parking lot of the huge Gothic structure. I had never been inside a Catholic church, and I didn't know what to expect.

I entered the church quickly, skirting the holy water fonts, and scuttled down the aisle, unsure of the correct protocol for getting into the pew. I knew Catholics bowed or curtsied or did some sort of jig-like obeisance toward the altar before entering the pew, but I just slipped in and scrunched down, hoping they wouldn't recognize me as a Protestant.

After a few minutes, when no grim-faced usher had tapped me on the shoulder and jerked his thumb back toward the door— "Come on, pal, hit the road; we know you're not Catholic"—I began to relax. I gaped at the strange but undeniably beautiful interior of the church.

A few moments later, Scott strode to the podium and began his talk with a prayer. When he made the sign of the cross, I knew he had truly jumped ship. My heart sank. "Poor Scott," I groaned inwardly. "The Catholics duped him with their clever arguments." I listened intently to his talk on the Last Supper entitled "The Fourth Cup," trying hard to detect the errors in his thinking. But I couldn't find any. (Scott's talk was so good, I plagiarized most of it in my next Communion sermon.)

As he spoke, using Scripture at each step to support Catholic teaching on the Mass and the Eucharist, I found myself mesmerized by what I heard. Scott was explaining Catholicism in a way I had never imagined possible—from the Bible! As he explained them, the Mass and the Eucharist were not offensive or foreign to me. At the end of his talk, when Scott issued a stirring call to a radical conversion to Christ, I wondered if maybe he had feigned conversion so he could infiltrate the Catholic Church to bring about renewal and conversion of spiritually dead Catholics.

It didn't take long before I found out.

After the audience's applause subsided, I went up front to see if he would recognize me. A throng of people with questions surrounded him. I stood a few feet away and studied his face as he spoke with his typical charm and conviction to the large knot of people. Yes, this was the same Scott I knew in seminary. He now sported a mustache and I a seasonal full beard (quite a change from our clean-cut seminary days), but when he turned in my direction, his eyes sparkled as he grinned a silent hello.

In a moment, we stood together, clasped in a warm handshake. He apologized if he had offended me in any way. "No, of course not!" I assured him as we laughed with the sheer delight of seeing each other again. After a few moments of obligatory "How's-your-wife-and-family?" chitchat, I blurted out the one thought on my mind. "I guess it's true what I heard. Why did you jump ship and become Catholic?" Scott gave me a brief explanation of his struggle to find the truth about Catholicism (the throng of people listening intently to his mini-conversion story) and suggested I pick up a copy of his conversion story tape, which the throng was snapping up in the vestibule.

We exchanged phone numbers and shook hands again, and I headed for the back of the church. I found a table covered with tapes on the Catholic faith by Scott and his wife, Kimberly, as well as tapes by Steve Wood, another convert to Catholicism who had studied at Gordon-Conwell Theological Seminary. I bought a copy of each tape and a copy of a book Scott had recommended, Karl Keating's *Catholicism and Fundamentalism.*

Before I left, I stood in the back of the church, taking in

for a moment the strange yet attractive hallmarks of Catholicism: icons and statues, ornate altar, candles, dark confessional booths. I stood there for a moment wondering why God had called me to this place. Then I stepped into the cold night air, my head dizzy with thought and my heart flooded with a confusing jumble of emotions.

I went to a fast-food restaurant, got a burger for the drive home, and slipped Scott's conversion tape into the player. I presumed I would easily discover where he had gone wrong, before I was halfway home, I had become so overwhelmed with emotion that I had to pull off the highway to clear my head.

Even though Scott's journey to the Catholic Church was very different from mine, the questions he and I grappled with were essentially the same—and the answers he found, which had so drastically changed his life, were very compelling. His testimony convinced me that the reasons for my growing dissatisfaction with Protestantism could not be ignored. The answers to my questions, he claimed, were to be found in the Catholic Church. The idea pierced me to the core.

I was at once frightened and exhilarated by the thought that God might be calling me into the Catholic Church. I prayed for a while, my head resting on the steering wheel, and collected my thoughts before I started the car again and drove home.

The next day, I opened *Catholicism and Fundamentalism* and read straight through, finishing the final chapter that night. As I prepared to retire for the night, I knew I was in trouble! It was clear to me now that the two central dogmas of the Protestant Reformation, *sola Scriptura* (Scripture alone) and *sola fide* (justification by faith alone), were on very shaky biblical ground, and therefore so was I.

My appetite thus whetted, I began reading Catholic books, especially the early Church Fathers, whose writings helped me understand the truth about Catholic history before the Reformation. I spent countless hours debating with Catholics and Protestants, doing my best to subject Catholic claims to the toughest biblical arguments I could find. Marilyn, as you might guess, was not pleased when I told her about my struggle with the claims of the Catholic Church. Although at first she told me, "This too will pass," eventually the things I was learning began intriguing she, too, so she began studying for herself.

As I waded through book after book, I shared with her the clear and common sense teachings of the Catholic Church I was discovering. More often than not, we would conclude together how much more sense and how much truer to Scripture the views of the Catholic Church seemed than anything we had found in the wide range of Protestant opinions. There was depth, historical strength, a philosophical consistency to the Catholic positions we encountered. The Lord worked an amazing transformation in both our lives, coaxing us along, side by side, step by step, together all the way.

With all these good things we were finding in the Catholic Church, however, we were also confronted by some confusing and disturbing issues. I encountered priests who thought me strange for considering the Catholic Church. They felt that conversion was unnecessary. We met Catholics who knew little about their faith and whose lifestyles conflicted with the moral teachings of their Church. When we attended Masses, we found ourselves unwelcomed and unassisted by anyone. Nonetheless, in spite of these obstacles blocking our path to the Church, we kept studying and praying for the Lord's guidance.

After listening to dozens of tapes and digesting several dozen books, I knew I could no longer remain a Protestant. It had become clear that the Protestant answer to church renewal was, of all things, unscriptural. Jesus had prayed for unity among His followers, and Paul and John both challenged their followers to hold fast to the truth they had received, not letting opinions divide them. As Protestants, we had become infatuated with our freedom, placing personal opinion over the teaching authority of the Church. We believed that the guidance of the Holy Spirit was enough to lead any sincere seeker to the true meaning of Scripture.

The Catholic response to this view is that it is the mission of the Church to teach with infallible certitude. Christ promised the apostles and their successors, "He who listens to you listens to Me. And he who rejects you rejects Me and rejects the one who sent Me" (Luke 10:6). The early Church believed this too. A very compelling passage leaped out at me one day while I was studying Church history:

> The Apostles received the gospel for us from the Lord Jesus Christ; and Jesus Christ was sent from God. Christ, therefore, is from God, and the Apostles are from Christ. Both of these orderly arrangements, then, are by God's will. Receiving their instructions and being full of confidence on the account of the Resurrection of our Lord Jesus Christ, and confirmed in faith by the Word of God, they went forth in the complete assurance of the Holy Spirit, preaching the good news that the Kingdom of God is coming. Through countryside and city, they preached; and they appointed their earliest converts, testing them by the Spirit, to be the bishops and deacons of future believers. Nor was this a novelty: for bishops and deacons had been written about a long time earlier. Indeed, Scripture somewhere says: "I will set up their bishops in righteousness and their deacons in faith.[1]

Another patristic quote that helped breach the wall of my Protestant presuppositions was this from Irenaeus, bishop of Lyons:

[1] Clement of Rome, *Epistle to the Corinthians* 42:1-5. Some patristic scholars (e.g. WA. Jurgens and J.A. T. Robinson) date this epistle as early as A.D. 80, though the traditional dating favors A.D. 96. A concise treatment of the arguments for the earlier dating is found in William Jurgens, The Faith of the Early Fathers (Collegeville: Liturgical Press, 1970) vol. 1,6-7.

When, therefore, we have such proofs, it is not necessary to seek among others the truth, which is easily obtained from the Church. For the Apostles, like a rich man in a bank, deposited with her most copiously everything that pertains to the truth; and everyone whosoever wishes draws from her the drink of life. For she is the entrance to life, while all the rest are thieves and robbers. That is why it is surely necessary to avoid them, while cherishing with the utmost diligence the things pertaining to the Church, and to lay hold of the tradition of truth. What then? If there should be a dispute over some kind of question, ought we not have recourse to the most ancient Churches in which the Apostles were familiar, and draw from them what is clear and certain in regard to that question? What if the Apostles had not in fact left writings for us? Would it not be necessary to follow the order of tradition, which was handed down to those to whom they entrusted the Churches? [2]

I studied the causes for the Reformation. The Roman Catholic Church of that day was truly in need of renewal, but Martin Luther and the other Reformers chose the wrong, the *unbiblical,* method for dealing with the problems they saw in the Church. The correct route was and still is just what my Presbyterian friend had told me: Don't leave the Church; don't break the unity of faith. Work for genuine reform based on God's plan, not man's, achieving it through prayer, penance, and good example.

I could no longer remain Protestant. To do so meant I must deny Christ's promise to guide and protect his Church and to send the Holy Spirit to lead it into all truth (cf. Matthew 16:18-19, 18:18, 28:20; John 14:16, 25, 16:13). But I couldn't bear

[2]*Against Heresies* 3,4,1 [ca. A.D. 180], Ibid. Vol. 1, pg. 90.

the thought of becoming a Catholic. I'd been taught for so long to despise "Romanism" that, even though intellectually I had discovered Catholicism to be true, I had a hard time shaking my emotional prejudice against the Church.

One key difficulty was the psychological adjustment to the complexity of Catholic theology. By contrast, Protestantism is simple: Admit you're a sinner, repent of your sins, accept Jesus as your personal Savior, trust in Him to forgive you, and you're saved.

I continued studying Scripture and Catholic books and spent many hours debating with Protestant friends and colleagues over difficult issues like Mary, praying to the saints, indulgences, purgatory, priestly celibacy, and the Eucharist. Eventually I realized that the single most important issue was authority. All of this wrangling over how to interpret Scripture gets one nowhere if there is no way to know with infallible certitude that one's interpretation is the right one. The teaching authority of the Church in the Magisterium centered on the seat of Peter; if I could accept this doctrine, I knew I could trust the Church on everything else.

I read Father Stanley Jaki's *The Keys to the Kingdom* and *Upon This Rock*, and the documents of Vatican II and earlier councils, especially Trent. I carefully studied Scripture and the writings of Calvin, Luther, and the other Reformers to test the Catholic argument. Time after time, I found that the Protestant arguments against the primacy of Peter simply were not biblical or historical. It became clear that the Catholic position was the biblical one.

The Holy Spirit delivered a literal *coup dé grace* to my remaining anti-Catholic biases when I read John Henry Cardinal Newman's landmark book, *An Essay on the Development of Christian Doctrine*. In fact, my objections evaporated when I read twelve pages in the middle of this book. Here Newman explains the gradual development of papal authority: " . . . it is a less difficulty that the Papal supremacy was not formally acknowledged in the second century, than that there was no formal acknowledgment on the part of the Church of the doctrine of the Holy Trinity till the fourth. No doctrine is defined till violated."[3]

My study of Catholic claims took about a year and a half. During this period, Marilyn and I studied together, sharing as a couple the fears, hopes, and challenges that accompanied us along the path to Rome. We attended Mass weekly, making the drive to a parish far enough away (my former Presbyterian Church was less then a mile from our home) to avoid the controversy and confusion that would undoubtedly arise if my former parishioners knew that I was investigating Rome.

We gradually began to feel comfortable doing all the things Catholics did at Mass (except receiving Communion, of course). Doctrinally, emotionally, and spiritually, we felt ready to formally enter the Church. There remained, however, one barrier for us to surmount.

Before Marilyn and I met and fell in love, she had been divorced after a brief marriage. Since we were Protestants when we met and married, this posed no problem, as far as we and our denomination were concerned. It wasn't until we felt we were ready to enter the Catholic Church that we were informed that we couldn't unless Marilyn received an annulment of her first marriage. At first, we felt like God was playing a joke on us! Then we moved from shock to anger. It seemed so unfair and ridiculously hypocritical: We could have committed almost any other sin, no matter how heinous, and with one confession been adequately cleansed for Church admission. But because of this one mistake, our entry into the Catholic Church had been stopped dead in the water.

But then we remembered what had brought us to this point in our spiritual pilgrimage: We were to trust God with all our hearts

---

[3] University of Notre Dame Press, Notre Dame, Indiana, 1989, page 151.

and lean not on our own understanding. We were to acknowledge Him and trust that He would direct our paths. It became evident that this was a final test of perseverance sent by God. So Marilyn began the difficult annulment investigation process, and we waited. We continued attending Mass, remaining seated in the pew, our hearts aching while those around us went forward to receive the Lord in the Holy Eucharist. It was by not being able to receive the Eucharist that we learned to appreciate the awesome privilege that Jesus bestows on His beloved of receiving Him body and blood, soul and divinity in the Blessed Sacrament. The Lord's promise in Scripture became real to us during those Masses: "The Lord chastises the son whom he loves" (Hebrews 12:6).

After a nine-month wait, we learned that Marilyn's annulment had been granted. Without further delay, our marriage was blessed and we were received with great excitement and celebration into the Catholic Church. It felt so incredibly good to finally be home where we belonged. I wept quiet tears of joy and gratitude that first Mass when I was able to walk forward with the rest of my Catholic brothers and sisters and receive Jesus in Holy Communion.

I asked the Lord many times in prayer, "What is truth?" He answered me in Scripture by saying, "I am the Way, the Truth, and the Life." I rejoice that now as a Catholic I not only can know the Truth but can receive Him in the Eucharist.

Apologia pro a final few words sua

I think that it is important that I mention one more of John Henry Cardinal Newman's insights that made a crucial difference in the process of my conversion to the Catholic Church. He wrote: "To be deep in history is to cease to be a Protestant."[4] This one line summarizes a key reason why I abandoned Protestantism, bypassed the Eastern Orthodox churches, and became Catholic.

Newman was right. The more I read Church history and

Scripture the less I could comfortably remain Protestant. I saw that it was the Catholic Church that was established by Jesus Christ, and all the other claimants to the title "true church" had to step aside. It was the Bible and Church history that made a Catholic out of me, against my will (at least at first) and to my immense surprise.

I also learned that the flip side of Newman's adage is equally true: To cease to be deep in history is to *become* a Protestant. That's why we Catholics must know *why* we believe what the Church teaches as well as the history behind these truths of our salvation. We must prepare ourselves and our children to "always be ready to give an explanation to anyone who asks for a reason for your hope" (1 Peter 3:15). By boldly living and proclaiming our faith, many will hear Christ speaking through us and will be brought to a knowledge of the truth in all its fullness in the Catholic Church. God bless you on your own journey of faith!

An earlier version of this article appeared in Surprised By Truth, *Patrick Madrid, ed., Basilica Press, San Diego, 1994.*

Marcus Grodi is the founder and president of the Coming Home Network International. *He is a regular speaker and hosts a weekly live television program on EWTN called* The Journey Home *as well as the Thursday afternnon segment of EWTN Open Line Radio. He contributes articles for several Catholic publications and is the author of the novel,* How Firm a Foundation *(CHResources, 2002). He lives with his wife, Marilyn (see next article), and their three sons (Jon Marc, Peter, and Richard) on a small farm near Zanesville, Ohio.*

[4] Ibid., page 8.

"I Never Wanted to be a Minister's Wife Anyway!"

by Marilyn C. Grodi
former Presbyterian minister's wife

This was the tongue-in-cheek reply I shared at the first *Coming Home Network* gathering in 1993. The statement was definitely true until I met my husband-to-be at the Second Presbyterian Church of Newark, Ohio. Only a few months before, I had returned to the church—I had not been attending any church at all. Here Marcus was the new assistant minister and singles group coordinator.

I was a "baby" Christian struggling to live as one, becoming increasingly aware of my sinfulness as well as my inability to make the needed changes. I was also working in the field of alcoholism as an educator and counselor, and as I sent people to *Alcoholics Anonymous*, I knew I needed a spiritual recovery as much as many of my clients.

A friend in our singles group gave me a verse that made sense but was difficult: "Delight in the Lord, and He will give you the desires of your heart" (Psalm 37:4). So I began praying every day while running or when I'd wake up in the middle of the night. I received counseling from the minister who later married Marcus and me, and during a torturous two years of struggle and backsliding, I desired to turn my life completely over to God.

I was miserable and, for most of my adult life, had been living "my way." I had "looked for love in all the wrong places," so I really wasn't sure I knew how to recognize it when it was available. I became more involved in the church, thinking that teaching high school Sunday school and things like that were reasonable requests from God. But marrying a minister? This was too much to ask.

The string of relationships behind me also made me feel completely unworthy of such a role. I finally prayed the prayer, "Lord, not my will, but Yours; if You want me to be single, that will be fine." Suddenly, I was completely released from a relationship at my workplace that I believe Satan had been using to keep me almost immobile. Soon after, God seemed to take a "two-by-four" to both Marcus and me, and we became engaged.

Three months later, after much reminding from my fiancé that "you are a new creation in the Lord," we were married. (I didn't even have to attend a school for minister's wives-to-be.)

Wow, was married Christian life a rewarding, exciting roller-coaster ride. And with many challenges, too. I became the director of a crisis pregnancy center, and our first child, Jon Marc, was born the day after our first anniversary. Hallelujah, being a mother was the ultimate! Living with Marcus alone has always been interesting. He's always full of creative and sometimes scary ideas. I quickly learned that I need not get overly excited with every new idea. Usually, I prefer things to stay the same.

When we moved from our small country church in central Ohio to a large evangelical congregation in northeast Ohio, I thought, this is it! This active, vibrant church was quite appealing, and with buying a house, my roots were down for at least ten years (or so I thought).

Being a minister's wife was actually quite fun: I was free to do whatever I wanted—teach Sunday school, redecorate the nursery, and develop relationships with many like-minded people. Then Marcus got a bizarre idea. Being restless about his ministry as well as issues in our Presbyterian denomination, he decided to incorporate his science background into his present career by studying bioethics. He left his pastoral position to study full-time while we also began looking at other denominations that might be a better fit. We both had become discouraged about how issues were handled at higher levels of our denomination: abortion, inclusive language, etc. Little did I know how much Scott Hahn's tapes had affected Marcus. Leaving our church was a great disappointment to me and to many in the church—it had only been one-and-a-half years.

Marcus was now driving to Cleveland each day to Case Western Reserve University, while I was caring for our preschooler and newborn named Peter (of all names). Isolation was beginning to take place, since we still lived in our old neighborhood near our church and friends, who didn't understand what we were doing, and neither did I. We were church hopping for a summer while Marcus was not just studying genetics but everything he could get his hands on about the Catholic Church.

Miraculously, we both found ourselves open to the truths of the Catholic Church, and much was making sense that never had before. We had never thought in our wildest dreams about this historic Church, which, at least to me, had always been one of myths and misguided people. Marcus rather quickly came to the point where he felt he could no longer be a Protestant, but neither of us felt that we could actually become Catholics.

When we began attending Mass, it was awful: The parish churches seemed so cold and unfriendly; there were no welcoming Sunday school programs or nurseries for the little ones. The worst part was when we would come to the Sacrifice of the Mass; I would just want to break down and weep or run. Without having dealt with the issue of the Eucharist, I intuitively knew that here was the pivotal difference.

Even though Marcus stated that the kids and I were welcome to continue attending the Presbyterian Church, we did not want to go to separate churches on Sunday mornings. Fortunately, we discovered a parish across town that resembled many Protestant churches: They were a little friendlier, with coffee and doughnuts afterwards, and provided CCD for children (it felt like Sunday school). These rather superficial things actually helped a lot as

I was making the transition into the world of Catholicism. So each Sunday, we would drive tearfully past our old church as we became more convinced about what we might have to do.

Then we ran into a most unexpected barrier. Marcus and I decided we would give the RCIA[1] class a look. But we backed down for two reasons. First, we were not quite ready for the world to know of our leanings toward the Catholic Church, and some of our classmates in RCIA were from our neighborhood. Second, we realized that even if we completed this class, we were at least temporarily ineligible to enter the Church because of a marital commitment I had made in my early twenties.

Well! Maybe here was an issue that would save us from the Church! We never dreamed we would face such an obstacle and angrily thought of many worse sins we could have committed that would not have prevented us from becoming members of the Catholic Church.

After much pondering and prayer, we soon realized that this requirement of obtaining an annulment was yet another great reason for seeking this traditional Church and her teachings. I initially had been attracted to the Catholic Church because it seemed to be the only one that held fast to those things that serve to strengthen and preserve families. Every other denomination had become lax toward abortion, contraception, marriage, divorce, etc.

So I swallowed my pride and took my first big, submissive step, bowing to the awesome power and majesty of the authority of the Church. We really did it together, because Marcus was there, so supportive, at every stage of the process. The annulment process turned out not to be as daunting as I had imagined but rather was a blessing to both of us and our marriage.

Nine months later, after we had moved to Steubenville, Ohio (a pretty good place to learn to be Catholic), we were informed

---

[1] Rites of Christian Initiation for Adults

of the decree of nullity, and within a month, on December 20, 1992, we not only were received into the Church at St. Peter's parish but had our marriage blessed with a re-exchanging of vows and rings. What a joyous occasion we shared with many new friends.

So Marcus isn't now known to many as Reverend. But I'm glad that I was a pastor's wife for a time and am eternally thankful that our entire family is enjoying the riches of the one, holy, Catholic, and apostolic Church.

Originally published in the first edition of the CHNewsletter, July 1993.

Marilyn is the wife of Marcus Grodi (see previous article) and devotes a major portion of her time to the homeschooling of their three sons, Jon Marc, Peter, and Richard.

On Whose Authority?

*by Father Raymond Ryland
former Episcopal priest*

"How can you go into that darkness, once you have known the light?" In deep anguish, my mother-in-law asked my wife and me this question when we told her we were going to enter the Catholic Church.

There was a time when the thought of becoming Catholics would have caused us even greater distress than our news caused her. Now, however, we were near the end of a sixteen-year pilgrimage. We could finally see the Tiber ahead, and we were eager to cross. For many years, we had known ourselves as seekers. Now we realized we were pilgrims. The difference? Pilgrims know where they are going.

Whatever its hidden roots, the "seeking which was a pilgrimage" began not long after Ruth and I married. While the initiative was largely mine, all those years we traveled together: reading, praying, discussing, at times arguing—always just between ourselves. Yet we never walked in lockstep. Sometimes one of us would go ahead and the other would insist on a spiritual rest stop. (I did most of the darting ahead and the chastened retracing of steps.) But we were always together. For that, we are forever grateful.

During much of our pilgrimage, we knew that we were wrestling with the problem of authority. How does one know Christian truth with certainty? We saw with increasing clarity that this issue underlies all the divisions among the thousands of competing Christian traditions. We began to recognize that the issue of authority is at root a Christological question: What has God done in Christ to communicate His truth to the world?

The quest for ultimate doctrinal authority may arise out of psychological need. Some of our friends put this interpretation on our pilgrimage. They seemed to think I was the culprit, dragging my poor wife along on my ill-fated journey. "Ray, we always knew you had a need for the authority and structure you've found in the Catholic Church."

What they said was true. It was true in a far deeper sense than they apparently meant it. With all our hearts, we believe every human being needs the authority and structure of the Catholic Church. In our Episcopal years, Ruth and I grew in our personal relationship with Jesus Christ, loving Him and trying to serve Him. Fairly late in our pilgrimage, we realized that we had accepted Christ on our terms, because we had no other. In every instance of moral decision or of personal belief, we were the final authority as to what we should do or believe. This is the dilemma of all non-Catholics.

The Catholic Church was founded by Jesus Christ and claims to speak for Him under carefully specified conditions. Once the truth of that claim became clear to us, after a long and arduous search, we had no alternative but to submit to the Church's authority. In that submission, we knew we were submitting to Jesus Christ on His terms. No longer were "we" the final authority in matters of faith and morals. This submission is possible only in the Church Christ established and to which He gave His authority.

Looking back over the years, we knew it was the Holy Spirit who long ago had put in our hearts this yearning for ultimate doctrinal and moral authority. It was in entering the Catholic Church that the yearning would know its fulfillment.

The discernible beginnings of our journey lie in my vocation to ordained ministry. The first faint sounds of a call to the ministry came to me in a summer church camp before my freshman year in college. The sounds were so faint that when I entered a college of my denomination, I had no clear vocational focus. I majored in history only because it was my favorite subject. A sophomore course in European history introduced me to details of Catholic teaching. The two textbooks were written by Carleton J. H. Hayes, who was to be the American ambassador to Spain during World War II. (Only recently, I learned he had become a Catholic while a student at Columbia.)

I began to learn about popes and monks and bishops and sacraments and interdicts and penitent kings standing barefoot in the snow. Hayes' books gave far more detail about Catholic belief than the average history book. The Catholic Church was a fascinating subject, but I was not drawn to it by my study then: It was too remote, too utterly different from my Protestant world.

Even though entering the ministry kept coming into my mind, I never thought of asking God to guide me. After all, it was my decision to make, or so I thought. (I thank God that He ignored my ignoring Him!) In my senior year, I decided to enter the seminary at my college.

In that same year came Pearl Harbor. Soon I realized that I could not sit in a classroom while my friends fought a war we all believed was necessary. After graduation, I entered officers training for the Navy. I assumed that if I survived military service and if the attraction to the ministry was valid, the attraction too would survive.

During almost all of my three years in the Navy, I served as a communications and navigation officer on an aircraft carrier in the Pacific theater. We were at sea almost all that time, so in my off-duty hours I read widely and studied in preparation for seminary.

A chaplain on our ship put me in touch by correspondence with his former professor, Robert H. Pfeiffer, distinguished professor of Old Testament at Harvard Divinity School. Pfeiffer very graciously guided my study of his classic introduction to the Old Testament. My correspondence with Pfeiffer and friendship with the chaplain, himself a Harvard graduate, led me to choose Harvard Divinity School.

Ruth and I had been in college together, and we were married just before the war ended. When I was released from the Navy, we moved to Cambridge, Massachusetts, where I enrolled in the Divinity School. I soon learned that some of the faculty and students were Unitarian. Until then, I had scarcely heard the word Unitarian. In my course work, I made a fateful discovery: I, too, was Unitarian. In my college and especially in my Navy years, I had drifted imperceptibly into the Unitarian belief that Jesus was only a great moral teacher, nothing more.

My first theology course was taught by an elderly Dutch scholar with a very impressive name, Johannes Augustus Christopher Fagginger Auer. Without knowing it, I think, he did me a great favor by showing me the superficiality of what I actually believed.

One day, when in a reflective mood, he admitted to us in class, "It's not an easy thing to come to the end of your life and not know whether there's anything beyond death." At that moment, I realized that at most I had only a vague hope that there is something, but no assurance. Ruth had retained the Trinitarianism of her Protestant upbringing, but was not strong in her faith then.

After two or three months of pondering my own situation, I told the dean I had no desire to preach and teach Christianity if what I was learning in class was all there is to Christianity. I must either pursue some other vocation or go elsewhere to inquire further into the Christian religion. I was thinking of transferring to Yale Divinity School.

The dean was gracious and seemed to try to understand my difficulty. Though he himself was a graduate of Yale, he recommended that Ruth and I go instead to Union Theological Seminary in New York. He said that Union was a more cosmopolitan environment than Yale. After a trip to Union and a talk with several faculty members, we decided to transfer there.

Ruth and I lived in the men's dormitory, three floors of which had been given over to married students. We took our meals in the refectory. For three years we ate, slept, drank, and breathed theology. Theological discussion was the consuming passion of everyone at Union. We were immersed in the theological bedlam that is Protestantism—all traditions to some extent contradicting each other with each claiming to be based on the Bible.

Union was indeed cosmopolitan. Dozens of denominations and many competing theological approaches created a lively, fascinating environment. Ardent Barthians argued fiercely with equally ardent Brunnerians; Niebuhrians battled with Tillichians; but everyone, as far as I knew, was Trinitarian. At Union, I heard Jesus Christ powerfully proclaimed. I became a believing Christian, surrendering my life to Jesus Christ, while Ruth's faith in Christ was greatly strengthened.

Amid this bedlam, we thought we heard a voice of theological sanity. We began to learn about the Episcopal Church through one of my professors, who was an Anglican clergyman and a persuasive apologist for his tradition. (Anglicanism is a generic term to designate the Church of England and all its transplanted branches, such as the Episcopal Church in this country.)

The Episcopal Church holds that to avoid theological chaos, Scripture must be interpreted by tradition—in particular, by the tradition of the early Church. Here, we thought, is a church rooted in the past, in historical continuity with the early Church. Its theological approach seemed very sensible. We quickly came to love the Elizabethan language of the *Book of Common Prayer*, the distinctive Episcopal architecture, the Englishness of the Episcopal ethos.

So we became Episcopalians. By this time, I had completed my theology degree and a year of doctoral study at Columbia and Union. Ruth had earned a Master's degree at Columbia while teaching nursery school.

To prepare for ordination and life within the Episcopal Church, we moved to Alexandria, Virginia. I attended the

Episcopal seminary there for a year and worked as a seminarian in a Washington parish. The Episcopal bishop of Washington ordained me to the deaconate and later to the priesthood in the National Cathedral. In Washington I served two parishes, one as an associate rector (pastor), the other as rector. Three of our children were born during our Washington years.

We were happy as Episcopalians, but we became increasingly aware of theological discord within the denomination. Anglicans claim that they have no distinct theology—that their theology is only that of the early Church. But there is widespread disagreement regarding what the early Church's theology was. One distinctive characteristic of Anglicanism is what is called *comprehensiveness*: trying to embrace a wide range of differing and even contradictory theological opinions within one communion.

The longer we lived within the Episcopal Church and the more we studied its history, the more we saw its theological and moral fragmentation. (We deeply regret that in recent years that fragmentation has greatly accelerated.) Initially, at Union, the Anglican claim of comprehensiveness attracted us. Now we saw that term as a euphemism for chaos.

For generations, Anglicans have boasted that theirs is a bridge church. That means they stand midway between Protestantism and Catholicism, partaking of the good features of both and rejecting the bad. I used to remind my colleagues that no one lives on a bridge. A bridge is only a means for getting from one place to another.

A ray of hope did shine on us for a time: a movement within the Episcopal Church (and other Anglican churches) known as Anglo-Catholicism. It is based on what proponents call the branch theory. This theory holds that the original Catholic Church is now divided into three branches: the Catholic, the Eastern Orthodox, and the Church of England. Anglo-Catholics claim that all three traditions are equally Catholic.

Anglo-Catholics believe that theological disarray within the Episcopal Church is caused by Protestant influences. The solution is to adopt Catholic ways in liturgy and (to an undefined degree) in theology. The touchstone of doctrine becomes the Catholic faith of the early centuries—Catholic, they insist, not Roman Catholic.

For half a dozen years or more, we identified with the relatively small Anglo-Catholic movement. I taught my parishioners and anyone else who would listen that Episcopalians are Catholics, not Protestants. During these years, we moved to Texas, where I served a newly formed parish, and three years later to Oklahoma, where I was chaplain of an Episcopal elementary and secondary school. One of our sons was born in Texas and another in Oklahoma.

This Anglo-Catholic ray of hope finally gave out. We recognized that, as a movement, Anglo-Catholicism (like Anglicanism) is essentially, inescapably Protestant. The appeal to the faith of the original Catholic Church, like the appeal to the tradition of the early centuries, is futile. There is no one to say what that faith is, or what that tradition is, or what that tradition says about Scripture.

We had to admit that each individual decides for himself, or chooses a clergyman who will decide for him, what is Catholic and then proceeds accordingly. There is no visible entity to which the Anglo-Catholic can point and say, "That is the Catholic Church to which I belong." That Catholic Church is only an abstraction.

In the nineteen century, John Henry Newman tried desperately for years to convince himself and others that they were part of the Catholic Church. Eventually he recognized that his Catholic Church was only a paper church, existing in the imaginations of himself and other like-minded persons.

Now where to turn?

Like most Anglo-Catholics, we looked on Eastern Orthodoxy with awe—an awe largely born, I later learned, of misunderstanding. The Anglo-Catholic logic regarding Eastern Orthodoxy goes like this: Rome denies that our church is Catholic. (That is, Rome, as well as the Orthodox, reject the branch theory.) Rome, however, does admit that the Eastern Orthodox churches are Catholic. (Today, I know this is incorrect.) Therefore, the Eastern Orthodox tradition is living proof that one can be Catholic without having to be a papal Catholic. We wondered: Is Eastern Orthodoxy the answer to our seeking?

At this stage of our journey, as a chaplain I had summers free. A generous friend and benefactor made it possible for our family to spend several summers at the University of the South in Sewanee, Tennessee. There I studied in the Episcopal graduate school of theology.

In our first summer in Sewanee, a well-known Byzantine scholar offered an introductory course in Eastern Orthodoxy. Ruth and I saw this opportunity for me as purely providential. I found the course and the work on a required research paper to be intensely interesting. I decided the paper should be the basis of a graduate thesis in theology. Our reading and study drew both Ruth and I toward Orthodoxy, but there was ambivalence in our thinking about the Eastern churches. The Orthodox ethos is utterly foreign to Americans. Whatever its ethnic background, an Orthodox church is a very different world to those raised in this culture. How could we, an Okie and a Texan and our five children, ever be truly at home in any of these other cultures?

Increasingly, the essentially ethnic nature of the various Orthodox traditions stood out in our thinking. No other Christian tradition is so deeply rooted in a particular culture as are the several Orthodox churches.

All the Orthodox churches have been ingrown for centuries. None has evangelized any significant part of the world in recent centuries. Their spread to this country and elsewhere has been due almost entirely to the immigration of Orthodox people from their various homelands. Not one of these ethnic churches has demonstrated universal appeal.

Orthodox theologians agree that an ecumenical council is their highest authority. Yet, in over twelve hundred years they have never conducted one, for with no Christian emperor, who can convoke a council for them? If the patriarch of any of the ethnic churches presumed to call for an ecumenical council, he would be opposed immediately as having asserted unauthorized jurisdiction over the other churches.

Most important, Orthodox churches have no real solution to the problem of doctrinal authority. The bishop, they say, speaks for Christ, the ecumenical council is the ultimate authority, and for a conciliar decree to be considered infallible, the entire Church must receive it. However, there is no way of determining whether and when this has happened.

From within the Catholic communion, we now can see other fundamental problems in the Orthodox churches. First, the term Orthodoxy commonly designates the Orthodox churches as a whole. But Orthodoxy and Anglo-Catholicism have this in common: In differing degrees, perhaps, both are abstractions.

There is no entity, no institution to which one can point and say, "There is Orthodoxy." There is no Orthodoxy; there are only separate Orthodox churches. All basically hold the same faith, but they are not organically united. Indeed, jurisdictionally they are divided. In any given city in this country, one may find two or three or more different Eastern churches, each with its own bishop. But where is Orthodoxy? As the Eastern churches gradually separated themselves from Rome, under the influence of powerful Eastern emperors, they became increasingly subservient to the secular authority in their countries. This is the problem of *caesaro-papism*, which has characterized the life of the Eastern churches ever since they began to break with Rome. The Communist secret police's admitted control of the Russian Orthodox Church for generations is only the latest example.

Earlier I referred to the Anglo-Catholic opinion that Rome regards the Orthodox churches as Catholic. This is incorrect. Vatican II documents, for example, always refer to the Eastern Churches, never to the Orthodox Church, and they certainly never refer to Orthodox churches as being Catholic. True, they do have Catholic sacraments and hold most of the Catholic faith, but they are in schism from the Catholic Church.

Again, it was back to the search. We loved the Lord Jesus, we wanted to be in His Church, we wanted to do His will. Where should we look next?

Almost before we dared ask the question one more time, we knew the answer: Rome.

Frequently, in television coverage of baseball games, the camera will focus several times alternately on the pitcher and the catcher, just before the pitcher throws across the plate. The catcher signals for a certain pitch. The pitcher shakes his head, waits for another signal, then another. Finally, when he gets one he likes, the pitcher winds up and delivers.

How many signals from the Holy Spirit dared we turn down? But Rome? Idol-worshiping, power-hungry, priest-ridden, thought-controlling Rome?

From our upbringing and from our seminary training, we had imbibed all the prejudices, all the stereotypes. These, however, had to be put aside. We already knew the outlines of Catholic teaching from our Anglo-Catholic days. Now we admitted to ourselves that we had to listen to the details of Rome's claims. Our reading and discussion resolved most of our objections, which were almost entirely based in misunderstanding.

The last major hurdle between ourselves and submission to Rome was the papacy. We read Newman's *Apologia Pro Vita Sua* avidly and devoured Meriol Trevor's two-volume biography of Newman in large bites. Our journey was much like his, though on a smaller scale. We saw ourselves as pygmies trying to follow a giant. We continually invoked his prayers in our behalf. We received much help from what may be the best single book about the Catholic Church, Karl Adam's *Spirit of Catholicism*.

Sixteen years after beginning our search for the full truth of Christ, we admitted to one another that we had to submit to Rome. Neither of us really wanted to be a Catholic, but God's call was unmistakable. We submitted to His will and eventually to His Church.

We had to keep our decision secret to spare embarrassment to the school of which I was chaplain. Each week for months, we drove to another city to spend an evening in instruction by a Benedictine monk whose friendship has been a rich blessing to us. With his help, I began seeking employment to support our family. We knew that God never leads anyone down a blind alley. We cast ourselves as completely as possible upon His mercy. Then doors began to open, and the way became clearer.

The day we were received into the Church, Ruth and I wanted to have a party in our home. The problem was that we had no one to invite. Our Episcopal friends were either greatly saddened or resentful. We did not know any Catholics. But we had our party: Ruth and I, our children, the two priests who received us, and, Ruth reminded us, the angels and archangels.

On the third day after our family was received into the Church, I went to early Mass in our parish church. As I knelt in the pew after receiving Communion, the words suddenly came to me, half-aloud, in a burst of joy: "Now I'm ready to die!"

For the next seven years, I was a layman in the Church. During that time, we moved to Milwaukee, where I completed course work for a doctorate in theology. Back in Oklahoma, I taught and worked for the diocesan educational department and completed my dissertation. Then came a move to San Diego to join the theological faculty of a Catholic university. While teaching full-time, I was ordained a permanent deacon in the Church and entered law school at night.

Several years after passing the bar, I was preparing to begin part-time practice, which I intended would become full-time after I stopped teaching. Then the Church announced the Pastoral Provision for this country. Under its terms, married Catholic laymen who had formerly been Episcopal clergy were allowed to apply through their bishops for a dispensation from the rule of celibacy and for ordination to the priesthood.

My application was the first to be sent to Rome, though it was not the first one acted on. Thirteen months later, my bishop received a letter from then Cardinal Joseph Ratzinger (now Pope Benedict XVI), telling him the Holy Father (Pope John Paul II) had approved my being ordained. Several months later, after a series of written and oral exams, I was ordained to the priesthood. That was twelve years ago.

Each time I stand at the altar, at least once the thought suddenly comes, "Can this be real? Am I a Catholic priest, offering the Holy Sacrifice?" Then comes that blessed answer: "Yes! Thanks be to God!"

Originally published in This Rock *magazine, January 1995, and then republished in the* CHNewsletter, *September 1993.*

Father Ryland is a former minister of the Episcopal Church. In 1963, he was received with his wife Ruth (see next article) and their five children into the Catholic Church. Twenty years later, he was ordained to the priesthood of the Catholic Church, with a dispensation from the rule of celibacy. Currently, Father Ryland is an adjunct professor of theology at Franciscan University of Steubenville and serves as chaplain of the Coming Home Network *and of* Catholics United for the Faith. *He is a contributing editor of* This Rock *magazine and an assistant pastor at St. Peter's Church in Steubenville, Ohio.*

"I Never Dreamed I'd be Married to a Catholic Priest!"

by Ruth Ryland
former Episcopal minister's wife

In an earlier article, Marilyn Grodi said that she never had wanted to marry a minister anyway. Well, I certainly never dreamed I'd be married to a Roman Catholic priest!

The thirteen years Ray served as an Episcopal priest were exciting, fulfilling years. We had both come from a Disciples of Christ background, and we found the intellectual and liturgical ethos of the Episcopal Church very satisfying. Our five children came along during that period. We loved the people in the various parishes and the school where Ray served. The people were great, good people who struggled along with us to live the Christian life. There were, of course, the usual ups and downs, joys and sorrows of living and serving, but through it all, we felt most blessed by our Lord in all the important ways.

Through these years of study, prayer, and simply living with God's people, we gradually moved to a more "catholic" view of the Church ("low church" to "high church"). There began a search for the historical "roots" of the Church. We became increasingly aware of conflicting views and teachings in the Episcopal Church, not only in doctrinal matters but in moral ones as well. Some teachings were quite heretical. Questions arose: Who was right? Which were the teachings faithful to the Gospel? Who was to say which teachings were true or false? Where was the locus of authority?

When we began to see where the search was leading, we resisted. We did not want to go. We did not want to turn our comfortable life upside down. We did not want to go into the "unknown," into a "foreign land." We loved the Episcopal Church and all it meant to us: the people, the beautiful churches, the grand music, and liturgy. Then there were all the questions concerning how to support our family and about leaving dear friends. (When we entered the Church, we knew not even one Catholic, only the two priests who instructed us.) What about our families who would grieve and be shocked that we had "lost our minds," etc.? Those who have traveled this road know all about the sufferings. And yet, and yet . . . we could hear the insistent beat of the "following feet" of the Hound of Heaven as He pursued, keeping His steady and unhurried pace.

When the Holy Spirit showed us, through sheer grace, beyond the shadow of a doubt that the Catholic Church is indeed the true Church, founded by Jesus Christ Himself on the Rock of Peter, could we say anything but "yes!" to Him? Praised be to Jesus Christ for His mercy and grace!

In 1963, together with our five young children, we were received into the Catholic Church. We had truly come home. In those days, it was rather rare for a Protestant clergyman to take that step. Except for the angels and archangels, we had no one with whom to celebrate our joy. But joy it was and is.

Dear brothers and sisters who are on the Way, or contemplating the Way: the path may be dark for you, the problems seemingly insurmountable, the sufferings great. But if you are looking to Jesus, the Author and Finisher of your faith, you can be certain of this: He will never betray your trust. Trust Him.

Originally published in the CHNewsletter, *September 1993.*
Ruth has been the wife of Father Ray Ryland (see previous article) for sixty years and is the mother of five children.

Delving Deep into History

by Jim Anderson
former Methodist and Lutheran seminarian

The Spirit of God first entered my life on Easter Sunday, April 10, 1955, when, at the age of three months, I was baptized at the Union Furnace Evangelical United Brethren Church.

Reared in Ohio, in a nominally Evangelical United Brethren (later United Methodist) family, I grew up in an environment where neither parent attended church. I was one of those kids who would be dropped off for Sunday school. Afterwards, a neighbor usually would bring me home. The greatest influence on my early faith development was my grandmother Anderson, one of the few churchgoers in the immediate family.

Since I grew up Protestant, Catholicism was not a factor in my life. We did have one neighbor family that was Catholic. The husband would brag about going to Confession before a party to confess any sins he might later commit while having a good time. "You never know," he would say, "what the traffic might be like on the way home."

Our neighbor might have been joking, but how were we to know? We certainly knew he was telling the truth about the parties! I was repulsed by the (mistaken) conclusion that "pre-sin confession" was an accepted Catholic practice.

These warped notions of Catholic doctrine were reinforced when I attended catechism classes in preparation for Confirmation in the E.U.B. Church. The pastor's wife, while teaching us about different Christian denominations, gave the following definition: "Catholics are Christianized pagans who worship statues of Mary."

A basic exposure to the Holy Scriptures at Sunday school enabled my faith in Christ to begin to mature, but only to a point. I understood Jesus as my heavenly best friend. What it really meant for Christ to be my Savior and Lord was obscure.

I wanted to be close to God, but I didn't know how. Every time I watched a Billy Graham crusade on television, I would accept Jesus into my heart again. I knew that the journey began with accepting Jesus, but where was I to go from there?

In the fall of 1973, I enrolled as a freshman at Ohio University in Athens. While taking a course in Western civilization that autumn, an uneasy realization began to grow: the denomination of my childhood lacked any real historic roots.

Christian history, I learned, reached back almost two thousand years. My Methodist heritage was barely two hundred years old. In our Sunday school classes, we only discussed what God had done in the first century. Sometimes there was a comment about His actions in our own church in the last couple of centuries, but even that was rare.

Could it be that the Lord had taken a vacation for sixteen centuries? Of course, such a belief was never voiced by the people. It was just a living, working assumption that we had never questioned—but now I was!

I didn't like the uneasy, precarious feelings these questions produced in me. I was uneasy because I could think of no answer that satisfactorily answered my inquiries. At this time, it was only a faint uncertainty, forming a crack in the wall of my Protestant worldview. Yet little did I know that this uncomfortable feeling would be the beginning of eight years of growing questions and surprising answers.

Sojourn among the Lutherans

The next major step in my spiritual journey was a sojourn among the Lutherans. My introduction to Lutheranism came through my best friend, Brian, who invited me to his church on Easter Sunday 1974. It was here that I first experienced the majesty of the Lord in liturgical worship.

Since up to that time I had attended only Methodist Sunday school, the beauty of liturgical worship came as a very pleasant and unexpected surprise. Sitting in the back pew, I began to wonder whether the pastor had failed to show up. The music had begun, the people were standing and singing, but there was no one up front in the sanctuary. "Where could he be?" I thought.

Then I heard singing coming from behind me and in processed the crucifer, the junior choir, and the senior choir, followed by the pastor. So that's where he was! The Easter liturgy that followed awed me. Methodist Sunday school had taught me that Jesus is my Savior and best friend. This Lutheran liturgy was teaching me the beauty and majesty of our Lord Jesus Christ. He is not only Savior and Friend but also the Lord and King of the universe! The Lutheran liturgy began my training in what it means to worship.

While receiving instruction from Pastor Lueck in Luther's Small Catechism, I remember telling him that I wanted to belong to a church with a heritage and roots deep in history. I told him that my only other option was Catholicism, but because of their idolatry, they could not even be considered. So the Lutherans were my only choice. I became a member of St. Matthew Lutheran Church (a member of the former American Lutheran Church), in Logan, Ohio, on the first Sunday of Advent, December 1, 1974, which was also Communion Sunday.

As a Lutheran, I was learning much about God, Jesus, and the Bible. The Lord, however, had still more in store for me. Upon returning to Ohio University in the autumn of 1975, I saw a course on "Basic Christianity" advertised in OU's student newspaper. This course turned out to be a watershed event in my life.

I discovered that there existed on campus a dynamic ecumenical student faith community called River of Life

Ministries, which accepted me with open arms. River of Life had risen from the ashes of a closed chapter of InterVarsity Christian Fellowship. The student leaders were an interesting ecumenical combination made up of Methodists, a Messianic Jew, an Episcopalian, a Lutheran, and a Baptist.

Even though River of Life was sponsored by Central Avenue United Methodist Church, the group met in the basement of Christ Lutheran Church every Friday night for prayer, teaching, and fellowship. I figured that if they met in the Lutheran church, they must not be too far off base. It was at Friday night fellowship that I was able to deepen my understanding of prayer, Bible study, and fellowship with other Christians.

Having been branded a geek in high school, I had never experienced unconditional acceptance and love from people my own age. I was taken aback at being immediately welcomed as a brother in the Lord by the people of this fellowship group. I basked in the love Jesus was giving me through my newfound friends. All my lasting relationships from college have been with people who attended this fellowship.

Getting to know Catholics

I must confess that I did have a problem with a few of the students who attended Friday night fellowship. Several of them were Catholics. How could that be? My misconceptions of Catholics had not altered greatly over the years.

Some of these Catholic students invited me to a prayer group that met at Christ the King Catholic Student Center. There I was amazed to find a large number of Catholic Christians, and the only statue of Mary was kept in the back corner of the church. "Maybe they don't worship her after all," I thought. At least these Catholics didn't. I soon learned that theirs was a faith based squarely upon Jesus Christ and the apostolic teaching of His Church, enlivened by the Holy Spirit.

At the end of fall quarter, I was invited to attend my first

Catholic Mass. I was aghast! The liturgy was very familiar to me, but there was a major problem. I could not shake the Elizabethan English of the Lutheran liturgy of that time. The Mass was in contemporary English. I had thought I was the one who belonged to the reformed and up-to-date church. Now the Catholic Church seemed more reformed than my own Lutheran church!

Thanks to a well-stocked book table at Friday night fellowship, I began to be exposed to many Christian authors. The one who would have the most lasting effect on my spiritual life was C.S. Lewis. His books were influential in the maturing process of my theology, giving it a solid basis in logic as well as Scripture. My very first book by Lewis was *The Screwtape Letters*. I couldn't put it down. In fact, I sat up all night, finishing it in one sitting! Next on my reading list came *Mere Christianity*. I discovered that a reasoned defense of the Faith could be made with lucidity. Christianity was true, and truth could be demonstrated through logic. Yes, we need to have faith, but our leap of faith need not be a leap into the dark. Lewis answered for me the controversy of faith and works. His analogy of faith and works acting in a person's life as two blades of a pair of scissors made sense to me. *The Great Divorce*, another work by C.S. Lewis, was instrumental in clarifying another Catholic teaching, purgatory. In this wonderful little book, I discovered that the concept of purgatory made perfect sense in light of the just mercy of God. Of course, Lewis' representation of purgatory in the book does not correspond to what the Catholic Church teaches on the subject. He warns that it is only a story, not systematic theology. Yet it still opened me to the possibility of the truth of the doctrine.

Meeting the Church Fathers

In the winter of 1977, a course was offered at the university on the history of early Christianity. Thanks to this course, I was introduced to the early Church Fathers. The class sparked a deep desire to learn everything I could about early Church history and patristic theology.

Going to a local Christian bookstore, I asked if they had any copies of the Fathers. The clerk there didn't know what I was talking about. After some searching in publishers' catalogs, I found I could order copies of texts by the Ante-Nicene Fathers. Thanks to the early Christian writers of the first and second centuries, such as St. Clement of Rome, St. Ignatius of Antioch, St. Justin Martyr, and St. Irenaeus, I learned that many of the doctrines I had always discounted as Catholic, and thus rejected, were in fact taught by the Church of that age.

For example, I had always accepted without question the Protestant doctrine of *sola Scriptura* (Scripture alone), which claims that the Bible is the only source of authority and revelation in the Church. When I read the early Fathers, however, I discovered they taught that the Church was based not on the Bible alone but on Scripture, Sacred Tradition, and the apostolic teaching authority of the bishops (the Magisterium). I discovered statements such as this one written around A.D. 185 by St. Irenaeus, a student of St. Polycarp, who in turn was a pupil of the Apostle John as well as a friend of St. Ignatius of Antioch:

> The Church, having received this preaching and this faith, although she is disseminated throughout the whole world, yet guarded it, as if she occupied but one house. She likewise believes these things just as if she had but one soul and one and the same heart; and harmoniously she proclaims them and teaches them and hands them down, as if she possessed but one mouth. For, while the languages of the world are diverse, nevertheless, the authority of the Tradition is one and the same.[1]

---

[1] Against Heresies 1, 10, 2.

> The true gnosis [knowledge] is the doctrine of the
> Apostles, and the ancient organization of the Church
> throughout the whole world, and the manifestation of the
> body of Christ according to the successions of bishops,
> by which successions the bishops have handed down the
> Church which is found everywhere; and the very complete
> Tradition of the Scriptures, which have come down to us
> by being guarded against falsification . . . [2]

I also discovered that nowhere does the Bible teach that the
Scriptures are the sole rule of faith for the Christian. I deduced
that if such a teaching was not in the Bible and the Church Fathers
taught otherwise, then *sola Scriptura* must be a tradition of man
and not a doctrine of God.

The need for apostolic authority

As a Lutheran, I had been taught that the priesthood of all
believers negated any need for a ministerial priesthood. But
I found that, while not denying St. Peter's teaching that all
Christians are members of a "royal priesthood" (1 Peter 2:9),
the Fathers also insisted on the necessity of apostolic authority
in the Church.

For example, St. Clement, the third bishop of Rome, wrote
to the Corinthian church about A.D. 80: "Our Apostles knew
through our Lord Jesus Christ that there would be strife for the
office of bishop. For this reason, therefore, having received
perfect foreknowledge, they appointed those who have already
been mentioned, and afterwards added the further provision that,
if they should die, other approved men should succeed to their
ministry" (1 Clement 44:1-2). Clement was teaching the doctrine
of apostolic succession! St. Ignatius of Antioch also writes on
this subject:

---

[2] Ibid., 4, 33, 8.

You must all follow the bishop as Jesus Christ follows the Father, and the presbytery [that is, the council of priests] as you would the Apostles. Reverence the deacons as you would the command of God. Let no one do anything of concern to the Church without the bishop. Let that be considered a valid Eucharist which is celebrated by the bishop, or by one whom he appoints. Wherever the bishop appears, let the people be there; just as wherever Jesus Christ is, there is the Catholic Church.[3]

Again, St. Irenaeus writes:

It is possible, then, for everyone in every Church, who may wish to know the truth, to contemplate the tradition of the Apostles which has been made known throughout the whole world. And we are in a position to enumerate those who were instituted bishops by the Apostles, and their successors to our own times . . . But since it would be too long to enumerate in such a volume as this the successions of all the Churches, we shall confound all those who, in whatever manner, whether through self-satisfaction or vainglory, or through blindness and wicked opinion, assemble other than where it is proper, by pointing out here the successions of the bishops of the greatest and most ancient Church known to all, founded and organized at Rome by the two most glorious Apostles, Peter and Paul, that Church which has the tradition and the faith which comes down to us after having been announced to men by the Apostles. For with this Church, because of its superior origin, all Churches must agree, that is, all the faithful in the whole world; and it is in her that the faithful everywhere have maintained the Apostolic tradition.[4]

---

[3] Smyrneans 8:1-2.

[4] Against Heresies 3, 3, 1-2.

The Eucharist

Concerning the Eucharist, St. Ignatius' letter to the church in Smyrna records: "They [the heretics] abstain from the Eucharist and from prayer, because they do not confess that the Eucharist is the flesh of our Savior Jesus Christ, flesh which suffered for our sins and which the Father, in His goodness, raised up again" (*Smyrneans* 7:1). This letter, written in the summer of A.D. 107, was penned by a man who had been ordained by St. Peter and was an acquaintance and student of St. John. And it teaches that the Eucharist is the body and blood of Christ—not that it merely symbolizes Him (as the Methodists teach) or contains Him (as the Lutherans teach).

St. Justin Martyr, writing about A.D. 150, confirms this reality:

For not as common bread nor common drink do we receive these; but since Jesus Christ our Savior was made incarnate by the word of God and had both flesh and blood for our salvation, so too, as we have been taught, the food which has been made into the Eucharist by the Eucharistic prayer set down by Him, and by the change of which our blood and flesh is nourished, is both the flesh and the blood of that incarnated Jesus.[5]

How could these early Fathers have written such things? These writings were so very Catholic! After all, the Protestant faith was supposed to be a restoration of the pure, uncorrupted Christianity of the first centuries.

I could not ignore the fact that Jesus had promised to send the Holy Spirit to His Church and to protect it: "The Advocate, the Holy Spirit that the Father will send in my name, He will

[5] First Apology, 66.

teach you everything and remind you of all that I told you" (John 14:26). "When He comes, the Spirit of truth, He will guide you to all truth" (John 16:13). "I will build My Church, and the gates of the netherworld shall not prevail against it" (Matthew 16:18). "Behold, I am with you always, until the end of the age" (Matthew 28:20).

I figured, then, that I was forced to one of two conclusions. On the one hand, I could conclude that Jesus didn't or couldn't live up to His promises and that the Church was corrupted almost immediately after the last apostle died. On the other hand, I could conclude that the Catholic teaching I was discovering, in the writings of the Fathers, was a valid development of the Church, guided by the Holy Spirit exactly as Jesus had promised. If these teachings were true, they demanded my acceptance in submission to the Lordship of Jesus Christ. I was discovering, then, that if the Protestant position is true, Jesus must have failed to fulfill His promises. *An impossibility!*

Loss of faith among Protestant leaders

During the time I was coming to terms with the Church Fathers, I was also becoming increasingly alarmed at an accelerated abandonment of Christian truth by Protestant leaders I knew. The local Episcopal priest denied both Christ's deity and resurrection. I heard a sermon by a philosophy professor in my Lutheran parish who declared that belief in the resurrection is only pious insurance. He stated that the concept of the resurrection was an accretion from the ancient Persian religion of Zoroastrianism, adopted by the Jews during the Babylonian captivity. It is not, he insisted, an essential element of the Christian faith. During the sermon, the pastor sat beaming his approval.

My friend John, who was attending a Methodist seminary at that time, had encountered a similar lack of faith in church leaders he knew. He complained to me that of his theology professors, only a third accepted the deity of Christ, only a quarter believed in His bodily resurrection, and only one, a Catholic priest, subscribed to Jesus' virgin birth.

I felt extremely anxious being under the authority of a Protestant bishop who didn't believe. Although I knew there were many faithful Protestants in the pews, I found that their leaders were rapidly abandoning Christianity. In the Catholic Church, however, I saw the hierarchy holding firm to the truth of the faith of Christ and the Apostles. I was painfully aware, of course, that many flaky Catholics hold to off-the-wall ideas. But I knew that if I became a Catholic, I would be submitting to the authority of the pope and bishops, whom I saw as powerfully faithful—not to the trendy priests, nuns, and laity.

While reading *Lutherans and Catholics in Dialogue*, the official documents of the Catholic-Lutheran ecumenical dialogues, I became even more disenchanted with Lutheranism. I kept finding myself on the Catholic side in the conversations. Often the Lutherans would say that they agreed with the Catholic teaching but were uncomfortable with the terminology because they believed it had been misused five hundred years ago. All in all, I was having increasing discomfort in remaining a Lutheran.

New convictions developing

By December 8, 1978, my convictions had developed to the point that I could write in my journal:

In the sacrament of the Holy Eucharist Christ, true God and true man, is present wholly and entirely, in His Body and Blood, under the signs of bread and wine. The presence of Christ does not come about through the faith of the believers, nor through human power, but the power of the Holy Spirit through the Word . . . The Eucharist is also the sacrifice of the Church. In it, the Church makes its sacrifice of praise to the Father. At the Eucharist, Christ is re-presented to His Church and the act of the Cross is brought to the present . . . Since the Roman Catholic Church has the longest history, with its roots in the Apostles, and all other Christian denominations have their final origin in it, total unity will not come until all are in full communion with it.

Clearly by this time, the Catholic understanding of the Eucharist had become my own.

The last doctrinal difficulty for me to overcome was Mary. I had no problem accepting her perpetual virginity; I could see how that truth could be deduced from the Gospels. Nor did I have any problem with asking her to pray for us. My problem was centered on the dogmas of the Immaculate Conception and the bodily Assumption of the Blessed Virgin. I just couldn't understand the need for these doctrines. Then it dawned on me: I was being inconsistent. Long before, I had come to believe that the Holy Spirit had given the Church the gift of infallibility in matters of faith and morals. I accepted the infallibility of the teaching authority of the pope. If I accepted the Church's authority, I also must trust God's guidance in all that she teaches. St. Augustine said, "First comes faith and then understanding." So I submitted my prideful intellect, and in time God did grant me the gift of understanding.

In July 1979, I was privileged to spend a month in Europe. I was overjoyed at the possibility of visiting St. Peter's Basilica in Rome, the church of the newly elected Pope John Paul II, the white knight of orthodoxy. When I knelt to pray in the Blessed Sacrament chapel, I felt that this was home. I was in the presence of my Lord in the Church of His vicar on Earth! I belonged here. But why did I remain outside my Father's house? I considered myself Catholic, but I had not yet built up the courage actually to convert because I knew my family would be scandalized. I also was hesitant to approach a priest to tell him I wanted to become a Catholic. The priests I had met had an extremely distant aura about them. They seemed unapproachable to me. So I put off what I knew I had to do if I was to be faithful to the will of God for my life.

Home at last

I entered Ashland Theological Seminary in Ashland, Ohio, in the fall of 1980. My reason for picking Ashland Seminary was that, though it was run by an evangelical Anabaptist denomination, the Brethren Church, it was actually the most ecumenical seminary in Ohio. Over fifty-five denominations were represented in the student body, every group from Quakers to Greek Orthodox. I was interested in being involved in ecumenical dialogue to further Church unity. The Christian cross-section at Ashland would be good preparation for me.

At seminary, I at last came to the conclusion that I had no choice but to join the Catholic Church. Looking at my many and varied fellow students, I realized that Protestantism was like so many boats adrift on the sea without oars or rudders, each claiming theirs to be the only vessel on the proper course.

When I returned to Athens for the summer, I finally told my Catholic friends Andy and Karen that I had to talk to the priest about joining the Church. I met with the pastor of Christ the King Catholic Church during June and July. The big day finally came on July 25, 1981, the Feast of St. James. I made my profession of faith in Jesus Christ and His Catholic Church, and then I received the sacrament of Confirmation. Immediately after my Confirmation, I received the body, blood, soul, and divinity of my Lord Jesus Christ for the very first time as a full member of His Mystical Body, the Catholic Church.

I had arrived home in the Church, but the journey of grace continued. The Lord Jesus had more surprises in store. I continued my studies in Church history at Ashland Seminary. During my senior year, I met Lynn, a Baptist girl from West Virginia, who would soon be my lovely wife. Within a year, she would become the second Protestant student to become Catholic while attending Ashland Theological Seminary . . . but that's another story.

Originally published in the CHNewletter August 2002.
Jim Anderson is the assistant director of the Coming Home Network *with the primary responsibility of assisting non-Catholic clergy on their journeys home to the Catholic Church. Jim and his wife Lynn live in Logan, Ohio. They have four children, Matt, Mary Ann, Krissy, and Andy.*

Catholic Inside and Out

by Dr. Kenneth Howell
former Presbyterian minister and seminary professor

Although summarizing my journey to the Catholic Church is a bit like attempting to put the Internal Revenue Code on a postcard, I will venture to sketch the highlights of this journey. My knowledge of Catholicism in childhood was limited to my father's side of the family, some of whom were devout but most of whom were Catholic in name only. I can remember at times being impressed with the aesthetic appeal of the Catholic Church and having a sense of something greater, but I was completely at a loss to know what that was.

In my late teens (college years), I had a deep sense of the grace of God in my life and loved to read the Sacred Scriptures. I read spiritual literature that stressed the importance of a daily communion with God in the Spirit and found at times an unusual degree of closeness to God, which I can only describe as a gift.

During the late seventies, I attended Westminster Theological Seminary in Philadelphia, Pennsylvania, where I learned the art of biblical interpretation and other theological disciplines. Although I had no interest in the Catholic Church at that time, I do remember being repulsed by the anti-Catholic attitudes of some of my conservative Presbyterian friends. To me, Catholics were misguided, but they were Christian.

In my seminary days, I remember formulating a theological issue that was to play a crucial role in my journey later on. I realized that the only way to justify the splitting of Western Christianity that occurred in the Reformation was to see the Protestant Re-formers as bringing the Church back to its original purity from which it had fallen. This meant that the Protestants were the true Catholics.

In 1978, I was ordained a Presbyterian minister (Presbyterian Church in America) and served two churches while I also obtained a doctoral degree in biblical linguistics. Shortly after my ordination, I was preaching a homily on the unity of the Church and stated that the only justification for the Reformation was that the Catholic Church had left the Gospel. I further said that the demands of unity in the Church, for which our Lord prayed in John 17, required us to do this: If the Catholic Church ever comes back to the Gospel, we must go back to it. Little did I realize in 1978 that I would someday eat my words.

In 1988, my family moved to Jackson, Mississippi, and I began teaching at Reformed Theological Seminary (RTS). I was not even considering the Catholic Church, though two indicators were already present: I had always had a love for the Lord's Supper, and I believed that the Reformed faith was in fact the faith of the early Church—two beliefs that eventually led me to leave the Reformed faith.

Around 1991, I began teaching a course on the Eucharist at RTS that examined the biblical foundations and history of the doctrine in the Church. After two years of teaching this course, I became convinced of the real presence of Christ in the Eucharist and realized that the Calvinist view of spiritual communion was deficient. This spurred me on to study other aspects of Church history, especially concerning liturgy and the patristic period.

From this reading, I concluded two things—first, that Presbyterian worship and a lot of Protestant worship in general had reduced the ancient liturgies to their minimal form. In general, a lot of Protestantism in America represents a kind of reductionism of the Catholic faith. Perhaps the most salient point is that there can be no official worship in the Church without the Eucharist. Even John Calvin seemed to recognize this truth, though most of his followers would not know why he thought this.

The second conclusion involved the "why" part. I have always wanted to know the reasons *why* I must believe something. I had always thought that the Reformed faith represented the teaching of the Scriptures and the ancient Church. When I had to teach the process of biblical interpretation—as opposed to teaching what I thought the Bible taught—I realized that the only way to agree on a proper interpretation of a text is to have a living Magisterium in the Church.

The reason there are so many Protestants who can't agree on what the Bible teaches is that they have no authoritative interpretative body. The analogy in law is, of course, the Supreme Court. The Constitution lying on the table is of no use to anyone, and in the hands of each individual, it might be interpreted in a myriad of ways. So what is needed is clearly an authoritative body of interpreters who can render judgments on which meanings are permissible and which are not.

In sum, I realized that the Protestant faith was not the faith of the ancient Fathers of the Church. The irony of all this is that John Calvin led me to the Catholic Church. Calvin in the sixteenth century wanted to bring the Church back to its original purity from which he and other Reformers believed the Roman Church had departed. So Calvin said in essence: Go back to the ancient Church! But when I did, I found that it wasn't Protestant. So I knew in my con-science that I must leave my Protestant heritage.

My journey during this period was much, much more than intellectual inquiry. Between 1991 and 1994, I met monthly with Father Francis Cosgrove, the vicar general of the Diocese of Jackson, for spiritual direction. It was he who guided me to the Ignatian tradition of spirituality—a very perceptive decision since so much of Ignatian spirituality focuses on discerning the will of God for our lives. In the summer of 1993, I directed my wife in a mini-retreat in the Ignatian pattern using Fr. Andre Ravier's *Do-It-Yourself Spiritual Exercises*. This was the beginning of the end, so to speak.

Another Catholic friend in California paid for my travel and conference fees to attend a *Defending the Faith* conference at Franciscan University of Steubenville in June 1992. Here God had another divine appointment for me.

One day at lunch, I was discussing with the man next to me the theological work of Father Bernard Lonergan, whose writings had helped me understand the doctrines of the Church. A woman in her sixties from Canada was sitting across the table from us. This holy and loving woman joined in the conversation with a theological sophistication that I had not found among Catholic lay people, and I was intrigued. This was to be the first of many contacts with the Catholic sister who has been such an instrument of God in my journey to the Church. She is a cradle Catholic, and my friendship with her was essential in understanding the process of conversion. I think this process can often be distorted if we look at and listen to only recent converts from Protestantism.

What I needed to see was not a zealous convert but someone who had faithfully loved and served Christ her whole life in the Church. This is what Marie Jutras showed me. It was to be her friendship, love, gifts, and prayers that would not only draw me to an authentic Catholic life but also break down some of my wife's misconceptions of Catholicism. Probably more than any single individual, Marie has been God's "sacrament" of love showing me the face of the Savior.

In the summer of 1994, I left my Reformed seminary after six years of teaching. It was quiet and amicable, but they and I knew that I couldn't remain there forever because my views had caused too much of a stir. Theologically, I was probably somewhere between Rome and the Reformation although definitely closer to Rome on many issues (e.g., Eucharist). During this time, I appreciated what had been said in the *CHNetwork* newsletter about using the time we have remaining in a Protestant setting to clear away misunderstandings and misconceptions about the Catholic Church. I endeavored to do just that.

The greatest conviction came when one day I realized that I truly believed it when the priest said, "This is Jesus, the Lamb of God who takes away the sins of the world." Somehow, I knew from that day on that there was no turning back and that becoming a Catholic was just a matter of time. What I didn't know was how much time it would take.

We moved to Bloomington, Indiana, so I could use the excellent research facilities of Indiana University to write a book on the history of biblical interpretation. At the same time, I became good friends with Father Charles Cheesebrough, the pastor of St. Charles Borromeo Catholic Church near the university. This man's patience, compassion, and openness won my heart as I struggled through one of the most difficult years of my life.

I had fully hoped to enter the Church at Easter Vigil 1995, but conversations with my wife and Catholic friends suggested that it would be better for me to wait to see if my wife could join me in that decision.

Then on June 3, 1995, a dramatic event stunned me. An assailant shot me in the neck with a handgun and almost killed me. God miraculously saved my life. Because of the prayers of God's people on earth and the saints in heaven, I was surrounded with angelic hosts from above and human love from below. I learned, as I never had before, that in the moment of our deepest need, God's presence pervades our being.

The people of St. Charles' parish, as well as many other churches in the city, overwhelmed our family with love. This was only one of the many events in the last few years that have taught me the meaning of St. Paul's words, "We always carry around in our body the dying of Jesus so that the life of Jesus may be manifested in our mortal bodies" (2 Corinthians 4:10).

I am so thankful that the Catholic spiritual teachings on suffering are now a part of my heritage as a Christian. Without this under-standing of grace and virtue through suffering, I would not have been able to endure the pains and hurts of my life. I now can say with the apostle, "I rejoice in my sufferings in hope of the glory of God."

For a long time, I was Catholic on the inside while still a Protestant on the outside. For prudential reasons, I was delaying my entrance into the Church with the hope that my wife and I could resolve our differences so that we might join together. God's plans, however, were different. By God's grace and with my wife's encouragement, I was able to enter into complete communion with the Catholic Church on my forty-fourth birthday, June 1, 1996, and received for the first time the body and blood, soul and divinity of my Lord. Praise and honor and glory be to God!

Originally published in the CHNewsletter *Jan-Feb 1996.*

Ken was received into the Catholic Church in June 1996. He serves as the John Henry Newman Scholar-in-Residence of the Newman Foundation at the University of Illinois in Champaign-Urbana, Ill. He is also a member of the board of trustees of the Coming Home Network.

From Sectarianism to the Communion of Saints

by William J. Cork
former Lutheran minister, raised Seventh-day Adventist

On the morning of October 23, 1844, following a long night of eager anticipation, thousands of Americans experienced what has become known as the "Great Disappointment." They had believed that New York farmer William Miller had found the key to understanding and decoding the apocalyptic prophecies of Daniel and Revelation and had determined the precise date of the return of Christ to judge the living and the dead. Now, the sun shining harshly on their rude awakening, they took circuitous routes home through their cornfields to avoid the ridicule of their neighbors. Some could not accept their fate and continued to seek the date of Judgment Day. Others gave up all belief in God. Many turned toward spiritualism or the Shakers.

One group, however, saved face in an ingenious way. They reasoned that Miller had hit on the right date but had misidentified the event. They persuaded themselves that on October 22, 1844, Jesus had entered the most holy place of the heavenly sanctuary to begin a final work of investigative judgment, which would culminate in the blotting out of sins of believers immediately before His return. They did not mind that they alone had come to see this—the rest of the world was "Babylon" and was fallen. Further study led them to adopt the keeping of the seventh day of the week, Saturday, as the Sabbath, and to give up eating those meats declared "unclean" in Leviticus 11. They were encouraged in these conclusions by the visions of a young woman from Portland, Maine, Ellen G. Harmon, later married to James White.

The movement that James and Ellen White midwived through the Great Disappointment became known as Seventh-day Adventism. They no longer set dates, but they still looked for the imminent return of Christ. They believed that great day would be preceded by a time of persecution, directed at them because of their sabbatarianism. The pope had led Christianity away from the biblical faith and had persuaded all Christians to accept Sunday as the Sabbath. Now, in these last days, these Adventists expected the Catholic Church to unite with Protestantism, and together the apostate churches would persuade civil authority to legislate Sunday observance. Those who kept Sunday at that time would receive the mark of the Beast; those who kept the Sabbath would receive the seal of God. And the servants of the Beast would do all they could to put the faithful to death.

This was the worldview in which I was raised. In 1980, I entered Atlantic Union College in South Lancaster, Massachusetts, to begin study for the Adventist ministry. It was a period of theological ferment within Adventism. Australians Desmond Ford and Robert Brinsmead questioned the Adventist views of salvation and the judgment, and California pastor Walter Rea was documenting Ellen White's plagiarism. Many Adventist pastors and seminarians left; some became evangelicals, while others started independent "evangelical Adventist" churches. At the end of my junior year, I made the break myself. Having been raised in a legalistic and sectarian environment, I had two critical issues: the Gospel and the Church. I liked what Ford and Brinsmead were saying about the gospel's message of unconditional forgiveness, but I didn't think forming a splinter movement of a splinter movement was the answer. My study of the Church's history opened to me the continuity of the faith of the ages; experiences with other Christians led me to seek out new and wider forms of fellowship. The Gospel, I came to believe, must create a community of faith in continuity with the preaching of the apostles. It must draw us toward other believers, not away from them.

I could never have made this decision without the influence

of my Adventist professors—even those who never would have dreamed of breaking with the church themselves. My Scripture professors introduced me to form and redaction criticism; this led me to seek the authority of Scripture not in a process of verbal inspiration but in Scripture's transmission in and through a community of faith. Theology professors took us to lectures in Boston to hear such theologians as Wolfhart Pannenberg, Charles Hartshorne, and Langdon Gilkey. In addition, my history professors pushed me continually back to the sources of Christian thought.

My doubts about the truth of the Adventist claims grew, and as a writer (and briefly editor) of the student newspaper, I gave voice to those doubts publicly. In 1983, I finally made the decision to leave. A professor took us to the annual gathering of the Evangelistic Association of New England. Francis Schaeffer was the main speaker. As I gazed upon that diverse crowd of Adventists, Evangelicals, Catholics (in habit and collar), and charismatics (waving their hands), I was overwhelmed by a sense of our unity in Christ and the need to seek fellowship with these brothers and sisters. At that moment, the Adventist sitting next to me poked me in the ribs with his elbow and muttered, "It's too bad these people don't know the truth." That was all I needed. The next day I visited a Presbyterian church in Clinton, Massachusetts, and shortly thereafter, I wrote a letter of resignation to the Adventist church where I was a member.

At this time, however, I had been married for a year. Joy's father is a very conservative Adventist pastor. My "apostasy" shattered him and Joy found herself pulled between us. My own father had become a Christian when I was in high school, and he had become an Adventist himself about the time I went to college. In such emotionally charged surroundings, Joy was not about to even consider leaving—she has remained an active Adventist to this day. My marriage could have been shattered at that time had it not been for one of my professors, to whom I went for counseling. He helped me see that one who undergoes a conversion experience goes through the same sort of grief process as one who is watching a loved one die; and the convert's family and friends go through a parallel process. There will be anger and denial and depression, he warned. And so there was. Knowing its source, however, helped us get through that period.

This emotional upset was one reason that I chose to stay close to Adventism for a while; I felt Joy needed the extra support. I finished my B.A. and accepted a teaching assistantship at Loma Linda University to begin graduate study in church history. My responsibilities there included giving occasional lectures in the undergraduate church history survey and helping to edit a journal of Adventist history.

On Reformation Day 1984, I first entered Trinity Lutheran Church in Riverside, California, a congregation of the Lutheran Church in America. In the Lutheran Confessions, I heard the New Testament Gospel. In the Lutheran liturgy and especially the Eucharist, I recognized the body and blood of Christ and felt connected to the Church of all ages. Lutheranism united for me the evangelical and catholic dimensions of the Christian faith. At this point, however, there was no way I could have considered becoming a ROMAN Catholic; I had too many years of anti-Catholic propaganda ringing in my ears. And yet I was clearly being led on a road to Rome—how else to explain my concern for the church, for liturgy, and for the Eucharist? Ironically, once more Adventist professors were instrumental in nudging me toward considering the Roman option. My department chairman introduced me to John Henry Cardinal Newman's *An Essay on the Development of Christian Doctrine*, had me read the documents of Vatican II, and required that I visit a Catholic church as a class assignment.

Due to financial constraints, Loma Linda was not able to guarantee me scholarship funding for the next year. I began to think it was time to transfer to a seminary. My chairman suggested I consider Gettysburg Lutheran Seminary. He said if I was going to continue in church history, Lutheran scholar Eric Gritsch would be a great mentor. He also introduced me to the book Gritsch wrote with Robert Jenson, *Lutheranism: The Theological Movement and Its Confessional Writings.* This book is a standard work for "evangelical catholics" within the Lutheran churches, for it defines Lutheranism not as the start of Protestantism but as a movement of evangelical reform within the Catholic Church. Its premise is that the Lutheran Confessions are not a constitution to begin a new church but assume Catholic dogma and practice wherever the same is not criticized. This resonated with my own growing understanding of Lutheranism as a *via media* between Rome and the excesses of the Reformed Protestantism of John Calvin and Ulrich Zwingli. But this raised other questions, questions inspired by Newman's *Essay*: Is such a *via media* really possible? If one accepts the Catholic principle of the faithfulness of Christ to His Church through time, will not one be pushed eventually to seek communion with Rome?

I transferred to Gettysburg Seminary in the fall of 1985, endorsed by the Pacific Southwest Synod of the Lutheran Church in America. Joy was regarded with great skepticism by some in the administration. In one of our first conversations, Dean Gerhard Krodel (a former Luftwaffe pilot with a thick Bavarian accent we all loved to imitate) leaned back in his chair and said, "Now, I don't say this myself, but you are going to find yourself in a parish one day and they are going to say to you, 'If you can't convert your own wife, what the hell business do you have preaching to us!' So, what you should do is go down to the bookstore and get a copy of Werner Elert's book, *The Structure of Lutheranism.* It will give you everything you need to convert your wife."

Even apart from such intimidation, the next few years were a busy period. I finished my M.A. in church history the following spring, with a thesis on the abolitionist and transcendentalist Theodore Parker. I continued working on my M.Div., taking some classes through the Washington Theological Consortium at Catholic seminaries. I joined the Army Reserve's Chaplain Candidate program and completed a unit of clinical pastoral education at Walter Reed Army Medical Center. I returned to Trinity Lutheran in Riverside, California, for my internship. In my senior year, I became a member of the Brothers and Sisters of Charity, Domestic, an ecumenical Franciscan community founded by John Michael Talbot. Each of these experiences put me into contact with Catholics, with whom I began to form very close friendships. Knowing what took me to Lutheranism, they continually asked me, "Why not go all the way?" This was echoed in my own heart, but I still was not able to act.

I graduated from Gettysburg in May 1989. I was called to be pastor of the Thompsontown Lutheran Parish in Juniata County, Pennsylvania, and was ordained on June 11. Ten days prior to this, my wife entered the hospital with severe hemorrhaging; our son Andrew was born late that night, two months premature, due to a placental abruption. I began my ministry with him in the hospital for two months.

During my time at Gettysburg, many of us had been concerned about the forthcoming merger that would result in the formation of the Evangelical Lutheran Church in America. We were troubled that those involved in the merger process had decided to put off discussion of theological issues until after the merger. We felt it was becoming just another mainline Protestant church, with no commitment to either Scripture or the Lutheran Confessions.

This confusion was clearly illustrated by my experiences at Thompsontown. This was a two-church parish. Emmanuel, in town, had kneelers in the pews and a hand-carved Tyrolean crucifix over the altar; it used wine for Communion but thought that Communion should be held only once a month. Centre, in the country, was indistinguishable from a Methodist or Reformed church; it used grape juice for Communion and sang evangelical Sunday school songs, but it was a very close, supportive community of faith. Worse, I got sucked into a thirty-year-old conflict between the two and stirred up old jealousies. I exacerbated the situation by defending a more Catholic view of ordained ministry over and against congregationalism.

I resigned after a year. That summer, to gain some healing, I attended a conference for priests, deacons, and seminarians at Franciscan University of Steubenville. I was subscribing to *New Covenant* Magazine and had seen in an advertisement that Father Francis Martin would be one of the speakers. Father Francis was one of the Catholics I had taken a class with in Gettysburg. It was a class on the Book of Romans at the Dominican House of Studies, and I had been very impressed with the way he dealt with the hermeneutical disagreements between Lutherans and Catholics. The worship services and the talks were all inspiring, but I remember most the private conversations.

One day I was talking with some priests about differences between Catholics and Lutherans over the Eucharist. Contrary to Catholic and Reformed misunderstandings, Lutherans have never believed in "consubstantiation." Luther simply denied that Aristotelian metaphysics were useful in discussing the miracle of the Eucharist. He was content to stick with the words of Scripture. At the Marburg Colloquy of 1529, he wrote the words *Hoc est enim corpus meum* on the table. When Zwingli attempted to rationalize their meaning, Luther ripped aside the tablecloth and pounded on the words, demanding, "This is what the Word of God says, and I won't try to get around it."

One question that remains, however, is whether the presence of Christ perdures following the celebration of the liturgy. Lutherans either have said that it goes back to being mere bread (so that one Lutheran church I preached at had no problem throwing the leftover bread to the birds!) or they avoid the problem by consuming all the bread during the liturgy. And yet we had no problem taking Communion to the sick without reconsecrating it!

One of the priests listened to all my objections and excuses and quietly said, "When God gives a gift, He doesn't take it back." That night, when the evening meeting ended, I found myself in a stampede of priests rushing downhill from the red and white tent to the chapel.

"What's going on?" I asked.

"Holy hour," said a priest.

"What...?" I started to ask. But he was long gone.

The chapel fell into hushed silence as the Body of Christ was exposed in the monstrance. Priests fell on their faces. I was speechless. The reality of the Presence of Christ overwhelmed me, and all my objections fell away as I found myself praying, "My Lord and my God!"

Another day that week, I was walking with a priest and we came across another group of priests. After some casual conversation, one suggested praying the rosary. I tried to back out gracefully. A priest (the same one from the other day!) pressed the point. I nervously remembered a quote from Lutheran theologian Gerhard Forde about "not talking to dead people." The priest looked me in the eye and replied, "Don't you believe in the communion of saints?"

The climax of the week for me was a gut-wrenching experience of profound grief and alienation as I sat alone in the pew and the priests and deacons around me went forward to receive the body and blood of Our Lord. We fell on each other's shoulders and cried.

From there, I went on to Arkansas to attend the "Chapter of Tents" of the Brothers and Sisters of Charity at Little Portion Hermitage. One night, they were going to have a "living rosary." I groaned, "Oh, no! Here we go again!" I tried to hide, but Sister Viola saw me, grinned, stuck a candle in my hand, led me to my spot, and said, "You are in the Creed." I thought, "Someone is trying to tell me something!"

The next few months passed in a blur. I did some more Army training, during which Saddam Hussein invaded Kuwait. I spent that fall at Fort Bragg, North Carolina, helping at the 82nd Airborne Division Memorial Chapel.

At Christmas, I was called to be pastor of Shepherd of the Hills Lutheran Church in Montpelier, Vermont. If I could have been a "Catholic" sort of Lutheran anywhere, it would have been here: We re-served the Blessed Sacrament, had weekly Eucharist, "smells and bells"—even a touch of charismatic praise. One of the church's traditions was to use Luther's *Formula Missae* as the order of service on Reformation Day. This was Luther's 1521 revision of the Mass. He had kept it in Latin, with German Scriptures and hymns and a German sermon, but my new parish did it all in English. One year, I suggested doing it in Latin, as Luther had intended. (Contrary to myth, Luther never had a problem with the Latin Mass as such but thought it should be retained as an option.) We used sixteen century Lutheran hymns in English and Scriptures and sermon in English, but the rest was in Latin, in a simple chant setting. This was one of the best-received liturgies I ever did anywhere.

Yet, in spite of all this romantic Romanism, this church was congregationalist in the extreme—in fifteen years it had been successively a member of the Wisconsin Synod, Missouri Synod, AELC (Association of Evangelical Lutheran Churches), and ELCA. It saw no need to participate in the gatherings of the larger church or send money to its national Church body. Not that I blamed the congregation entirely. In 1990, the ELCA published a study on human sexuality that declared that Scripture and church tradition had no answers to contemporary questions on sexuality and that the church must seek its message in an a-historical "radical imperative." I found myself giving up hope that a "Catholic" version of Lutheranism would ever amount to anything other than a sectarian option within a generic old-line Protestant denomination.

I continued dialogue with many Catholic priest friends, especially those I worked with as a chaplain in the Vermont National Guard, and began meeting regularly with the local Catholic pastor "for coffee." I made my permanent profession in the Brothers and Sisters of Charity. I attended other priest's conferences at Steubenville. In 1992, a financial crisis forced Shepherd of the Hills to cut me to half-time, and this provided me with the opportunity to take the action I had been trying to avoid, Hamlet-like, for so long. I entered into dialogue with a Catholic archbishop and with my Lutheran bishop; they felt it best for me to resign at the end of October. My last sermon was Reformation Day. On November 11, 1992, in a private ceremony attended by some priest, deacon, and Franciscan friends, I was received into the Catholic Church.

For the next eighteen months, I was unemployed, with a wife and two children (Aimee was born in March 1992, also premature!). Many Catholic friends obtained financial help for us. A couple of bishops helped me with networking in looking for jobs. I continued to work part-time for the Vermont National Guard, I wrote regularly for the diocesan paper, and got a position preaching Catholic parish missions. I got food stamps and was on welfare for a period. And I wondered whether I had done the right thing. On top of it all, my daughter was diagnosed with a congenital hip dislocation, and we spent three-and-a-half years undergoing repeated hospitalizations to attempt to correct it.

This was a trying time. It gave me a lasting love for St. John of the Cross.

The worst thing, perhaps, was the difficulty of finding a job in a Catholic church. I sent out hundreds of inquiries, got handfuls of responses, and three or four interviews, at which I kept coming in second. I grew angry with the patronizing excuses that people gave for not wanting to hire me: "We don't think it would be just to pay you only twenty thousand dollars a year"; "We don't think it would be fair to your family to move so far"; "Would you accept a janitorial position at $6 an hour, an hour's drive from your house?"

In July 1994, I finally got a full-time position as a director of religious education. I thought at last my struggle was over, but I soon discovered the Catholic Church is not immune from the weaknesses and foibles of human beings. After a year, I found myself caught in the middle of a parish conflict; soon, my wife and children were involved as well. I felt I had really made a stupid mistake and decided that maybe things weren't as bad in Lutheranism as I had imagined. I contacted my old bishop and began the process for reinstatement. I took tests and psychological evaluations and met with committee members, and the committee decided to place me in a kind of second internship. I met with the pastor they wanted to put me with— and discovered he was exactly the kind of pastor I had been, with the same questions and concerns that had sent me to Rome in the first place. I attended a regional retreat of the Brothers and Sisters of Charity in Connecticut, and on my way there it struck me that the stupid decision was not the one that led me into Catholicism, but was the one I was on the verge of making. I had stayed faithful to Christ and His Church through eighteen months of unemployment, and now, after a bad experience in one parish that was caused simply by the normal human strife that is universal, I was ready to throw in the towel and go back. I thought of several Scriptures that touch on that theme and realized that there is no going back: Christ never calls us backward; He only calls us forward. "Further up and further in!" The crisis was past, and some months later, I was offered a position doing Catholic campus ministry at the University of California at Santa Barbara—I felt that the heavens were smiling!

In the years following I continued in campus ministry, and have been for seven years now the Director of Young Adult and

Campus Ministry for the Archdiocese of Galveston-Houston. Evangelization has continued to be a passion; I've been chair of our Archdiocesan Evangelization Commission, and have served on the US Commission for Catholic Evangelization. At the same time, I've learned how to be content as a lay Catholic in the pew. There have been struggles of various kinds, of course, but I haven't seen a return to the past as an answer, partly due to having "settled in," and partly to having had better spiritual directors who have taught me to see those ordinary battles as the primary arena in which we seek holiness. I've grown in my faith, and in my understanding of Catholic teaching and appreciation for those Catholic devotions I once scorned. I had a conversation a few years ago with another convert and remarked, "I've finally gotten to the point where I can pray the rosary and not feel like it is someone else's prayer." He smiled knowingly and said, "I've been in for twenty years, and I think I'm just now getting it."

If I were to summarize the primary reason I became a Catholic and why I remain one, I think the best answer comes from Cardinal Newman's *An Essay on the Development of Christian Doctrine*:

> [W]hatever history teaches, whatever it omits, whatever it exaggerates or extenuates, whatever it says and unsays, at least the Christianity of history is not Protestantism. If ever there were a safe truth, it is this . . . And Protestantism has ever felt it so . . . This is shown in the determination already referred to of dispensing with historical Christianity altogether and of forming a Christianity from the Bible alone . . . Our popular religion scarcely recognizes the fact of the twelve long ages which lie between the Councils of Nicaea and Trent, except as affording one or two passages to illustrate its wild interpretations of certain prophesies of St. Paul and St. John . . . To be deep in history is to cease to be a Protestant.[1]

[1] University of Notre Dame Press, Notre Dame, Indiana, 1989, Pages 7-8

I was a novice church historian when I first read those words, and yet even then I felt their truth. I had already experienced the pull of the faith of the Fathers of the Church; I had experienced the sense of mystical union through the Eucharist and Baptism; I had learned to say "Amen" to the truth in Augustine, the Cappadocians, Francis and Dominic, Thomas Aquinas and Bonaventure, Vatican II and John Paul II. When that priest asked if I believed in the communion of saints, I had to say, "Yes! Of course I do!"

To this day, I believe that Newman's argument remains one of the best reasons to give to a Protestant for becoming a Catholic. As long as Catholic converts try to argue from Scripture to Scripture in a fundamentalist fashion, the Protestant will win the war, if not the battle. For if apologetics is simply a matter of proof-texting, who is to say whether the Protestant or the Catholic twist is the right one?

But step back, and look at the Church of the post-apostolic generation, the period of Clement and Ignatius—a period in which some of the books in the New Testament were being written—and the Protestant must recognize that this was clearly a Catholic Church. Christ promised Peter that upon a rock He would build His Church and the gates of hell would not prevail against it. We've spent so much time arguing about the rock that we've let the main thrust of the text get away from us! Christ promised that the Church would be maintained in faith and purity to the end. Every Protestant ecclesiology demands that we deny this and posit a global apostasy.

Since I became a Catholic, my wife has remained an Adventist, though she has grown in her understanding of and appreciation for my Catholic faith. I talk about this in my chapter in Lynn Nordhagen's book, *When Only One Converts*. I came to realize it is not in my power nor is it my place to try to force her to convert. After all, Catholicism, against Luther and Calvin, has always stressed freedom of the will. The Catholic tradition also insists on the primacy of conscience. Back when the dean at Gettysburg Seminary made his comments about Joy, I had no answer. Later, I thought of one: the fifth article of the Augsburg Confession says that "in order that we may obtain the faith that justifies, God gave the word and sacraments; through these, as through means, God gives the Holy Spirit, who works faith, when and where He pleases, in those who hear the Gospel." I still like that. It says that I am called to be faithful in my witness to the Gospel, and the rest is up to God.

Moreover, He can give us a surprise or two when we do that. A few years after I became Catholic, I got a letter from my brother Jim, a student at the University of Massachusetts. He had joined the Air Force out of high school, spent some time in Japan, dabbled with Buddhism, and then entered UMass to study Japanese. The letter before me began, "You might want to sit down before reading this." I've never gotten a letter like that with good news in it. I sat down. "I've met a Catholic girl. I started going to Mass with her during Advent. I've entered the RCIA. I'm going to be received into the Catholic Church at Easter." The next year, I got a letter from my brother Dan. He had gone to Israel with Youth With a Mission (YWAM), where he had gotten interested in Islam and Eastern Orthodoxy. Then he, too, transferred to UMass. He, too, started going to Mass, then entered the RCIA and was also received into the Church.

My brothers and I have had many chuckles about how we all left Adventism in different directions and found ourselves in the same place. I remarked once, "It just goes to show that 'all roads lead to Rome.'"

Originally published in the CHNewsletter *Jan-Feb 1997.*

William is the director of Young Adult and Campus Ministry for the Archdiocese of Galveston-Houston, Texas. Previously he served as the campus minister at the University of California, Santa Barbara. Before his reception into the Catholic Church, he was a pastor in the Evangelical Lutheran Church in America and a chaplain in the Vermont Army National Guard and US Army Reserve. He has a doctor of ministry degree from the Graduate Theological Foundation, a master of divinity, and a master of arts in religion from the Lutheran Theological Seminary at Gettysburg.

The Gentle Persuasion of Scripture and My Wife

by Paul Key
former Presbyterian minister

I was a child of the manse. My father was a Presbyterian minister and my mother the director of Christian education. I had a good Christian upbringing and after college served as a lay Presbyterian missionary in Caracas, Venezuela. When I returned at the age of twenty-six, I was ready to get married. While studying in an institute in Chicago, I was also actively chasing four Protestant women, all of whom looked eligible. There was one fascinating young lady, however, whom I considered safe to talk with since she was Catholic and therefore obviously not an option.

I still remember the night seated on old chairs in an old building on the west side of Chicago. As Patricia and I were carrying on one of our delightful conversations, I realized all of a sudden that the level of conversation was at a totally different level than I had expected. We began evaluating very rigorously our personalities, our theologies, and particularly the fact that I was planning to be a Presbyterian Minister. I could not imagine her wanting to marry a Presbyterian minister-to-be. But she replied that the Lord had told her this on the very first night we met. (Later, our spiritual director concluded that the Lord had sent Pat to get me. The worst part of this whole process is having to admit to your wife that she was right, but I have a pretty good wife to admit that to.)

After a brief time of testing our convictions, we were married, and three days later, we were both enrolled in the master of divinity program at McCormick Theological Seminary. Patricia completed the whole program, Greek, Hebrew, and all, while also completing thirty-six hours of her undergraduate residency requirements while being pregnant the second year. We raised our first son during the third year, and she graduated second in the class. And since I was not first, I obviously married up.

My wife is very gentle, but when she sees untruth, she goes after it. She gently began explaining to me the biblical foundations for the Catholic Church. She even corrected our Protestant professors in seminary, but we survived and went on into the pastorate.

I very soon got into trouble for all the right reasons: As a good Protestant, I started preaching from the Bible. Our seminary professors had encouraged us to use the ecumenical lectionary, which brought me into contact with all kinds of passages, which otherwise I might have avoided. As a result, I found myself slowly realizing that my wife's claim that the Catholic Church was the biblical Church might be true. Emotionally this was very hard to say, let alone admit to my wife.

Baptists generally consider Presbyterians to be almost pagan and ignorant of Scripture. Since our congregation was near to both an Evangelical Free and a Baptist seminary, we often had seminarians attending worship and Bible studies. I don't like to lose arguments, so to stay one step ahead of their biblical challenges, I kept busy studying Scripture. I rarely lost a biblical argument to these Baptist seminarians, but in the process, I found myself accepting more and more the Catholic understanding of Scripture. Let me give you just a couple of quick examples.

To a Reformed Protestant, the distinctions of *sola fide, sola gratia, and sola Scriptura* are almost the equivalent of the Blessed Virgin to a Catholic. Protestants seemingly worship these three pillars. I once attended a conference where these three great distinctives were posted on an enormous banner in front. When the conference was over, I wondered where salvation by faith alone was found in Scripture. So I began searching and to my dismay discovered that the origins of this phrase came out of Martin Luther's mistranslation of Romans 3:28. The word "alone" is not in the Greek text; Luther added it because, he said, he felt it was to be presumed—but more likely because it was needed to defend his radical reforms.

I also began to study the relationship of faith and works. My evangelical friends said that if you allow works any role in salvation, you are becoming Roman Catholic. But I knew a couple of Scripture passages that seemed to imply this, like Matthew 25:31-46, where the vision of the Last Judgment includes the separation of the sheep from the goats. Here Jesus says nothing about faith and everything about works of love and compassion. I also knew of James 2:14-26, which explicitly teaches that faith without works is dead. I decided to read the entire New Testament and found a plethora of verses emphasizing the importance of works, including Matthew 7:21-23 and 16:27, Luke 10:25-37 and 12:9, John 3:20, Romans 2:1-16, 1 Corinthians 3:8 and 6:9-10, 2 Corinthians 5:10, Galatians 5:19-21, Ephesians 6:8, Revelation 2:23, 20:12, 22:12, and many others.

I was sensing deeply that I was in trouble. I began keeping a list of the places in Scripture where I felt the Catholic Church seemed to be right. When this list reached twenty, I knew I was in trouble. When it eventually reached thirty, I converted. With the eyes of faith since becoming Catholic, that list has grown to over seventy, and it's embarrassing to admit how blind I was. But then I'm getting ahead of myself.

Another area that became overwhelming was the sacraments. Protestants generally teach that sacraments are but empty symbols and do not communicate power. Yet I kept finding Scripture passages that indicated they were intended to contain power. For example, in 1 Corinthians 11:27 and John 6, it is very clear we are talking about the reality of Jesus' body and blood in the Eucharist and not just symbolic ideas. I eventually found passages for each of the seven sacraments that indicated the same thing. From my Protestant prospective, these verses weren't supposed to be in there.

Another associated issue that is particularly difficult for a Protestant to deal with is Eucharistic adoration. As I was getting closer to becoming Catholic, our spiritual director, who was also our referee in marriage, strongly encouraged me to spend some time in Eucharistic adoration. Having never done this, let alone considered doing it, I asked him what one *did* in Eucharistic adoration. He said, "Just talk to Jesus."

Most cradle Catholics may not understand how difficult it is for Protestant converts to do Eucharistic adoration. In a Protestant's eyes, this is out-and-out idolatry. But with a man of my spiritual director's stature, I couldn't escape. So I went into the chapel with my Bible, really irritated but obedient. I decided if this has any validity whatsoever, there must be something about it in Scripture. Turning to the explicit Eucharistic passages, I started reading John 6 and was shocked. Just before the section where Jesus talks blatantly about eating His flesh and drinking His blood, there is a passage that just explicitly calls out to Eucharistic adoration. John 6:40 reads: "For this is the will of My Father, that every one who sees the Son and believes in Him should have eternal life; and I will raise him up on the last day." Now, when do you and I see Jesus? And I have to testify to you that I have found my times of Eucharistic adoration to be incredibly fruitful, insightful times of grace. The entire aspect of the sacraments and the power of the Eucharist in Catholic Tradition have been personally overwhelming.

Maybe one of the strongest areas very central to my own heart that led to my conversion was in the area of marriage and sexuality. We worked hard in my Protestant congregation to build strong Christian marriages. From the pulpit and the classroom we offered lots of Christian formation, Bible study, marriage formation, and marriage enrichment. I became increasingly uneasy, however, as I realized that the resources and foundational concepts I was promoting, though they were Scriptural, tended to be Catholic.

For example, St. Thomas Aquinas taught that the family is an incomplete society needing the state for its support in temporal matters and the Church for its support in spiritual matters. One of the implications of this teaching is that a husband and wife should not expect to carry all the emotional and spiritual weight of a marriage. There is too much going on between a husband and wife—and there was too much going on between Pat and me.

Pat has a strong personality, although she looks very gentle. You just don't want to get her angry. One evening, we were having one of our serious disagreements. I had been preaching this stuff on marriage, saying that every couple needs to have a spiritual director or someone they can have as an impartial, informed third party for difficult times. That night, she looked at me and said, "Why don't you do what you preach?!" Recognizing that she had me, I said OK, and that's how our Jesuit spiritual adviser entered our life.

I found myself casting about looking for wherever I could find truth. Of course, Scripture was most generally present, but when you're living with a Catholic, you look at every other option first. And though Pat was gracious and patient, she also had a good strategy. About once every six months, when I was having a difficult pastoral or maybe counseling problem, she would say "You know, Paul, if you would be Catholic with all the resources of the Catholic Church—spiritual direction, Confession, explicit practice of the sacraments, all the Catholic theology—you would be so much more effective." Now, if a wife says that just once every six months, that is not too much—but over eighteen years, that is thirty-six interventions. I finally avoided the whole issue by getting into a building program.

I thought I could justify to Pat and to myself ignoring all these issues while I was immersed in this building program. Around this time, Scott Hahn's conversion tape was released, and my wife—who never misses an opportunity—obtained it. But with architectural drawings in hand, I said, "I'm not interested," and avoided listening to the tapes for almost three years. After the building program was complete, I truly found myself Catholic and decided I needed a day of personal reflection and retreat.

On October 15, 1991, I drove off to my favorite hiding place along the Mississippi River fortified with a book o Catholic doctrine by Frank Sheed and two sets of Scott Hahn's tapes. After reading a few chapters and listening again to Scott's tapes on "Common Objections" and his series on Mary, I fully realized that all of my biblical arguments had disappeared. It became clear that day that if I remained where I was, I would be compromising, I would be stagnating spiritually and facing spiritual death. When you can see the consequences of your behavior, clearly you have a better chance of making a decision.

So I drove home and said to Pat, "I'm either going to stagnate and die or change," and together we decided that we needed to make some radical changes. I resigned from my pastorate and moved to Steubenville, Ohio, to study Catholic theology and become immersed in the very strong Catholic community. For the entire first week at Franciscan University after listening to Father Mike Scanlan orient the new students, I was in tears because I realized how stubbornly I had been avoiding what I had clearly seen for eleven years. Then at the Easter Vigil Mass in 1992, with my wife and children and friends from the master's program standing up and cheering in the back, I was received into the Catholic Church.

The Lord has truly blessed us. Through gentle leadings as well as with supernatural signs and wonders, He has guided and provided whenever and whatever we have needed. Yes, in this journey we have learned in unexpected ways the importance of the evangelical counsels of poverty, chastity, and obedience. He has humbled me repeatedly, asking that I give up everything — money, position, power, even for long periods my wife and family — all to help me rediscover how much you and I can totally depend upon Him.

After a number of years of study and intense struggles, trying to discern how I might be able to continue to serve the Lord in the Catholic Church, I was hired by the diocese of Lubbock, Texas, as director of evangelization and of their Spiritual Renewal Center.

In the Catholic Church, we have the richness and the fullness of the Tradition, the wisdom of pastoral practice, the wholeness of biblical theology. Now we must prayerfully and charitably help each other learn it and apply it. It continues to be an incredible journey, and I give the good Lord thanks for everything He has done for us.

Originally published in the CHNewsletter *Mar-Apr 1997.*
Paul was a minister in the Presbyterian Church (USA) for eighteen years. Currently he is working as an independent Catholic evangelist giving the spiritual exercises of St. Ignatius of Loyola. Paul and his wife Patricia live in Tyler, Texas.

A Journey Home

by Rosalind Moss
former Jew and Evangelical minister

May He guide thy way, who Himself is thine everlasting end:
That every step, be swift or slow, still to Himself may tend.

As I set out to do the unthinkable—to study the claims of the
Roman Catholic Church—I clung to the prayer above, fearful
that the enemy of our souls would deceive and render me useless
for the kingdom of the Christ I had come to know and love.

I was raised in a Jewish home, one that celebrated many of
the traditions, at least in our younger years. I remember having a
special sense that the one God was our God and that we were His
people. Yet as we grew and went out on our own, much was left
behind. Eventually my brother, David, became an atheist, and I,
perhaps, an agnostic.

In the summer of 1975 (we were now in our thirties), I
visited David. For years, David had been searching for truth, for
the meaning of life, and to know if there really was a God. Many
times, I had thought to myself,

> What makes you think there is such a thing as truth?! . . .
> that there is one thing that is truth? And what makes you
> think you could find it? Wouldn't it be like looking for a
> needle in a haystack? And how would you recognize it?
>
> But even if there was such a thing as truth, and you
> could find it, and you knew when you had it . . . and even
> if the truth meant that there is a God—then what? How
> would *knowing* that make a difference in your life? I
> figured, "I am because of what is. If what is means there

is a God, then therefore I am; if what is means there is
no God, then therefore I am. My knowledge or lack of it
doesn't determine what is, so why know?"

In our conversation during this visit, David told me he had
come across an article that said there are Jews—Jewish people—
alive, on the face of the Earth, who believe that Jesus Christ is the
Jewish Messiah—the Messiah(!) the rest of us were still waiting
for. I'll never forget the shock that went through my system at
that moment. I thought back to all the years we sat at the Passover
table in expectation of the Messiah's coming, knowing He was
the only hope we had. And now David was telling me that there
are people—Jewish people—who believe that He came?!

I said to David, "You mean they believe He was here—on
Earth—already? And n-o-b-o-d-y knows??? The world is not
changed. And He left???!"

Now what? There would be no hope, nothing left. It's insane.
And besides, you can't be Jewish and believe in Christ.

Within three months of that conversation, I had moved to
California and met some of these Jews who believed in Christ.
They didn't just believe that Jesus Christ was the Jewish
Messiah, but that He was God come to Earth! How can anyone
even compute that?

How could a man be God? How could you look on God and
live?!

One life-changing night, I was together with a group of
these Jewish believers, all Christians—all Evangelical Protestant
Christians. They told me that God required the shedding of blood
for the forgiveness of sin, and they explained how, under the Old
Testament sacrificial system, individuals would come daily to
offer animal sacrifices for their sins—bulls, goats, lambs. If it
was a lamb, it had to be a male, one year old, and absolutely
perfect, without blemish or spot. The individual would put his
hand on the head of the lamb, symbolic of the sins passing from

that individual onto the animal. That lamb—which was innocent but which symbolically had taken upon itself the sin of that person—was slain, and its blood was shed on the altar as an offering to God in payment of that person's sin.

I couldn't understand why God would put an innocent animal to death for my sin. It began to get through to me, nonetheless, that sin was no light matter to God. These believers explained further that those animal sacrifices were temporary, that they needed to be repeated, and that they could not perfect the offerer. Those sacrifices pointed to the One who would one day come and take upon Himself, not the sin of one person for a time, but the sins of the entire world, for all time.

And with that, they pointed me to one verse in the New Testament, John 1:29, when Jesus came and John the Baptist looked at Him and said, "Behold, the Lamb of God who takes away the sin of the world!" The Lamb of God—the final, once-for-all sacrifice to which all Old Testament sacrifices point. It shattered me. I couldn't believe what I had just begun to understand. My biggest hang-up was the thought that a man can't be God! But I realized that night that if God exists, He can become a man! God can be anything or anyone He wants to be; I'm not about to tell Him how to be God!

It was not long after that that I gave my life to Christ. And God transformed my life—overnight. I knew little, if anything, about Evangelicalism, or Protestantism for that matter. I had become a Christian. I had a relationship with the God of the universe and a reason to live for the first time in my life. I wanted to take a megaphone to the moon and shout to the world that God is and that they could know Him.

My first Bible study as a new Christian was taught by an ex-Catholic, who himself was taught by an ex-priest. So I learned from the start that the Catholic Church was a cult, a false religious system leading millions astray. For years, I taught against the Catholic Church, trying to help people, even whole families, by bringing them out of such man-made religion into a true relationship with Christ through the only Christianity I knew and believed with all my heart.

It was about a year after my commitment to Christ that David called to tell me that he had come to believe that Christ was God and that, for him, it also meant giving his life to Christ. He was not ready, however, to commit himself to any church (though he had been attending a Baptist congregation). The increasing number of Protestant denominations and splinter groups stood to David as a poor testimony to Christ's words that He would build His church. Where was the unity? How, he would ask, could sincere, born-again, Bible-believing Christians, indwelt, and led by the same Holy Spirit, come out with such varying interpretations of Scripture?

These, and other concerns, led David to the study of the Roman Catholic Church. I was horrified and frightened for him. How could he be a true Christian and buy into that!

It was Christmas 1978 when I visited David again. He took me first to meet the monk with whom he was studying and who I was sure was an agent of the devil on a mission to lead my brother astray. We then went to a midnight Christmas Eve Mass. It was the first time I had ever entered a Catholic church. I sat in shock through the entire Mass and the car trip home. When I could finally speak, I said to David: "It's like it's synagogue, but with Christ!!" He said, "That's right!" To which I answered, "That's wrong!!!!" Christ fulfilled the Law; all that ritual and stuff was done away with. I was sick inside. How could David fall for that? Did he have some hang-up? Was he drawn to the liturgy, to the aesthetics, from our Jewish background? Could he not see Christ as the end to which it all pointed?

David entered the Catholic Church in 1979. Our phone bills between California and New York were hefty over the years that followed. The more he plunged into what I believed was error, the more I devoured what I knew was truth. Having completed the

Bible institute at my church, I entered graduate studies at Talbot Theological Seminary in La Mirada, California, while serving as full-time chaplain of a women's jail facility in Lancaster, California. My deepest desire upon graduation was to be on staff at a local church teaching women, helping them to raise godly families and to reach others with the Gospel.

The God who gives us the desires of our hearts is the same God who brings them to fruition. Upon graduation from Talbot in May 1990, I was called to the staff of an Evangelical Friends (Quaker) church in Orange County, California, as director of women's ministries. Doctrinally, the Friends denomination did not align fully with my beliefs, since they had done away with Baptism and Communion. This particular church, however, under the leadership of a new pastor, of Baptist (and ex-Catholic) background, had reinstituted both for this single congregation within the denomination.

In the fateful month of transition from the jail ministry to that local church, I had time to visit David in New York. It was June 1990. In one of our marathon conversations, David asked, "How is it that Evangelicals don't seem to want to work toward unity? Didn't Jesus pray that we'd all be one?" I saw red. "Yes, Jesus prayed we'd be one, as He and the Father are one, but not at the expense of truth!"

With that, David asked me if I had ever seen the publication sitting on his table titled *This Rock*, which he described as a "Catholic apologetics" magazine. I could not even fathom those two words modifying each other. I never knew Catholics had a defense of their faith—no Catholic ever told me the Gospel. Moreover, I never knew Catholics cared that anyone else should know it.

I took the magazine back with me to California out of curiosity and out of some measure of respect for people who would want others to know what they, at least, believe is the answer to life—even if they are wrong. Inside was a full-page advertisement that read: "Presbyterian Minister Becomes Catholic." There's no way, I thought to myself. I don't care what he called himself or what he functioned as . . . there's no way this "Presbyterian minister" could have been a true Christian if he entered the Catholic Church. How could he have known Christ and been so deceived?

I ordered the four-part tape series of this ex-Presbyterian minister (whose name was Scott Hahn). It included a two-part debate with a professor from Westminster Theological Seminary on the issues of justification (faith alone vs. faith plus works) and authority (Scripture alone vs. Scripture plus Tradition). Hahn's concluding statement summed up two thousand years of Church history and climaxed with the thought that to those who will look into the claims of the Catholic Church and judge the evidence will come a "holy shock and a glorious amazement . . . " to find out that the church which he had been fighting and trying to save people from was, in fact, the very Church Christ established on Earth.

"Holy shock" are the only words to describe what went through me at that moment. "Oh, no," I thought, "don't tell me there could be truth to this." The thought paralyzed me. I couldn't believe what I was thinking—and at such an inconvenient time. In two weeks, I would begin at the new church.

I reread the doctrinal statement of the Friends denomination I was about to enter. It included the story of its founder, George Fox, whose dramatic conversion in the sixteen hundreds filled him with a deep love for God and a zeal to counter the abuses of his day. In his desire that God be worshipped in spirit and in truth, Fox did away with the only two sacraments, or "ordinances," that Martin Luther had left—Baptism and Communion—lest faith be placed in the elements of wine, bread, and water rather than in the God to whom they pointed.

I loved the heart of George Fox, but I believed he was wrong. Baptism and Communion were clearly commanded in Scripture, though I believed they were symbolic. The thought seized me: What if Luther did what Fox did? What if Luther, out of love and zeal for God's honor, also discarded what God intended? My stomach sank as my fear rose. Were my thoughts from God? Were they from Satan? I knew only that, before God, I had to find out what the Catholic Church taught.

During the next two years on staff with the Friends church, I ordered books, tapes, even a subscription to *This Rock* magazine, even though I dreaded the thought of anything Catholic coming to my mailbox. When I told David of my search, he challenged me concerning the doctrine of *sola Scriptura*. "Ros, where does the Bible teach *sola Scriptura*?" The very question annoyed me. I had heard it before and chose to ignore it. "If," I thought, "you truly knew Christ, if you believed Scripture to be the very Word of God, if the Holy Spirit were operative in your life, illuminating and confirming His Word to you, you wouldn't even ask such a question. Why would you have as your focus challenging the authority of Scripture rather than clinging to it as your food?"

He tried to assure me that he did believe the Scriptures to be the Word of God, inspired, inerrant, and authoritative. "But," he asked, "where does the Bible say it is the only authority? And where does Scripture say the Word of God is confined to what was written?"

I ran through several verses of Scripture (2 Timothy 3:16-17, 2 Peter 1:20-21, and others), but none answered his questions. In fact, they posed a further question: "How do we know the New Testament is Scripture? Those verses can refer only to the Old Testament, since the New Testament was not written yet, at least not in its entirety." As I delved into the matter, I came face to face with the fact that the Scriptures nowhere teach *sola Scriptura*.

Without revealing the nature of my search, I asked several pastors and Bible study leaders the same question. No one had an answer from Scripture. Each one came up with the same verses I had already examined. When I countered that those verses really don't teach that the Bible is the only authority, each person reluctantly agreed. "The verse that eludes me at the moment" never came to anyone's memory. "How amazing," I thought. "We are teaching the doctrine of 'Scripture alone,' which Scripture *alone* does not teach! Still, neither does that prove there is another authority!"

But the thought hovered: Evangelicals were teaching a doctrine outside of Scripture while denying that anything outside of Scripture was authoritative. Something was wrong, and if we were wrong about this, could we be wrong or blind about other issues? How is it, I thought, that Protestants accept the canon of Scripture—believing that God, who inspired Scripture, also led by His Spirit chosen men of the fourth and fifth century councils to recognize that which He inspired—and yet discard or disregard what those same men believed about other major doctrines: the Eucharist, Baptism, apostolic succession, etc.? Further, not only in the first four hundred years prior to the completion of the Canon but in the following one thousand years until the invention of the printing press, the faith was preserved, being passed on orally from one generation to the next. Again, how is it that in these nearly five hundred years of Christianity since the Reformation, with the canon in hand and with printing presses galore, the faith has been splintered into thousands of denominations, each with its distinctive and competing doctrines, each "holding forth the Word of life"?

I began reading all that I could, whenever I could, until I knew after two years that I needed to leave my church in California and devote myself to finding out if the Catholic Church was what it claimed to be. I moved to New York and began what turned out to be a two-and-a-half-year intensive and heart-wrenching search. For months, I read every Evangelical Protestant work I could find against the Catholic Church. I wanted to be rescued from the fate of becoming Catholic. To my deep disappointment, I discovered that these authors, for the most part, were fighting something other than Roman Catholicism. They were arguing against what they thought the Catholic Church taught, and it seemed their various understandings or misunderstandings reflected the Protestant perspective from which they came. Archbishop Fulton Sheen's insight became evident:

> There are not over a hundred people in the United States who hate the Catholic Church. There are millions, however, who hate what they wrongly believe to be the Catholic Church—which is, of course, quite a different thing.[1]

Each "discovery" of Catholic teaching led me to reexamine a multitude of Evangelical doctrines. And with every thought that drew me closer to the Church, a sense of death, of mourning, ripped through me as I considered being severed not only from my church in California but also from the only Christianity I had known and loved for eighteen years.

Prior to my leaving California, one very beloved pastor with whom I shared my quest asked: "If there were no Roman Catholic Church, would your understanding of the New Testament lead you to invent Catholicism?" My answer at the time was, "That's what I'm setting out to find out." One year later, I would say, "No, I wouldn't come up with Roman Catholicism, but nor would I any longer come up with Evangelical Protestantism." I had become a Christian without a home. I could not fathom being Catholic, but neither could I return to the Evangelicalism from which I came.

Three books were extremely helpful to me along the way: John Henry Cardinal Newman's *Essay on the Development of Christian Doctrine*, Dietrich von Hildebrand's *Liturgy and*

---

[1] Radio Replies (1938; Rockford, IL, Tan Books, 1979), I:ix.

Personality, and Karl Adam's *The Spirit of Catholicism*. The more I read, the more I began to sense a beauty, a depth, a fullness of God's design for His Church beyond all I had known. On every issue, including those three most famous cries of the Reformation—*sola gratia, sola fide, sola Scriptura*—I came to believe that the Catholic Church was in harmony with Scripture. Yet while everything I read of Catholic teaching and life was drawing me toward the Church, most of what I observed made me want to run from it. Where was the Church I read about? Where was the Church called "home"?

One Sunday, as I sat in the back pew of a Catholic parish I had visited for the first time, I heard the priest say what I had never heard any Catholic say before. At the conclusion of the Gospel message, he said to the congregation, "We need to tell the whole world!" My heart stood still. It was the first time I had sensed a passion for souls from the pulpit of a Catholic Church.

I burst into tears. Since the day I met Christ, I've lived to tell others of Him. I thought: If the Catholic Church is true, why aren't Catholics evangelical?! Evangelical is not a synonym for Protestant. To be an evangel is to be a messenger; it's to reach out to a lost and hurting world to tell them the good news of Christ—that there is a Savior Who came for sinners and Who gives life to all who will come to Him.

I met with that priest, Father James T. O'Connor, pastor of St. Joseph's in Millbrook, New York, at the beginning of March 1995. In two meetings, he helped me immeasurably with some key areas of difficulty, particularly concerning the Mass and the sacramental nature of the Church. I realized soon after that the question of three years before was answered at last: My understanding of the New Testament would not lead me to invent Catholicism, but my understanding now would lead me to embrace it as true to the Scriptures much more than it would lead me to embrace Evangelical Protestantism. Moreover, I knew that, before God, I needed to enter the Catholic Church, which I did that Easter of 1995. I had found the Church called "home."

I'm still a bit awkward. I feel like I've embarked on an enormous ocean and don't quite know how to navigate yet. But I know it's true. It is not doctrinal differences only that separate Evangelical Protestants from Catholics; it's a whole different way of seeing. My entire world has opened up. All of creation has taken on new meaning for me.

I have embraced all of the Church's teachings because I have embraced that Church which Christ Himself established two thousand years ago. It is that Church, founded on the apostles and prophets, the mustard seed grown into a tree, that has preserved and passed on the faith once delivered to the saints; that has stood the test of time through every age, every heresy, confusion, division, and sin. And it is that Church that will stand to the end of time, because it is truly His Body and, in its essence, therefore, holy, immutable, and eternal.

Moreover, gift upon gift, it is that Church that has restored to me the reverence, the majesty, the awe I once knew as a child in the synagogue. I said to David at one point, "I feel like I have God back." How strange a statement from one who came to know Him so wonderfully and truly through Evangelical Protestantism. Yet, in the freedom and familiarity of the Evangelical expression and worship, a sense of the transcendence of God is often lost. It is good to bow before Him.

And yet I have come to see that God, who *is* transcendent, has given us in His Son and in His Body, the Church, more of Himself than I could ever have imagined — not more than Christ, not other than Christ, but the whole of Christ.

Oh, the depth of the riches both of the wisdom and knowledge of God! How unsearchable are His judgments and unfathomable His ways! (Romans 11:33)

As long as God gives me breath, I want to tell the world of such a Savior and of His one, holy, Catholic, and apostolic Church.

Originally published in the first edition of Journeys Home, *1997.*

The initial conversion of Rosalind took her from a fifteen-year business career as a successful executive with corporations to full-time Evangelical ministry, earning a master's degree in ministry from Talbot Theological Seminary. A series of events in the summer of 1990 set her on a compelling course to find out whether the Catholic Church is in fact the Church founded by Christ. She entered the Catholic Church at Easter 1995. Rosalind is now a staff apologist with Catholic Answers.

Our Journey Home

by Larry and Joetta Lewis
Former United Methodist minister and wife

My father is a retired Assemblies of God pastor. My parents had a deep and abiding love for Jesus Christ. Their lives expressed who Christ was.

I vividly remember being awakened in the middle of the night by the sound of their praying—praying for each of the people in their church. Although my parents never spoke in derogatory terms about anyone, including Catholics, many of the ministers I met were not so generous. I heard more than one preacher expound on the evils of Catholicism. For many, it was taken for granted that the Catholic Church was the Great Whore of Babylon and the pope the Antichrist.

I was in my thirties and an ordained United Methodist minister before I met my first nun, Sister Monica Marie. Joetta had taught with her at Ursuline Academy in Dallas, Texas. It was through Sister Monica Marie that Joetta experienced a dynamic encounter with the Holy Spirit. To my surprise, I discovered that this Sister was truly a woman of God. My heart was warmed just by being in her presence. She was totally the opposite of all I had envisioned nuns to be.

My first contact with a priest was in 1996. While working on my doctorate at Oral Roberts University, I met Father Amalor Vima from India. As classmates, we spent a good deal of time together and became close friends. It was in this environment that something happened that would revolutionize my life forever. During a reflective moment in one of our sessions, Selmar Quayo, a Methodist bishop from Brazil, stood and said: "In my country, as a Protestant, I am in the minority. Unfortunately, there is much animosity between our church and the Catholic Church. Many of my people are filled with bitterness toward all Catholics. Yet here, Father Vima is in the minority, and I've seen nothing from his life but the love of Jesus Christ." With tears running down his face, he said, "Father Vima, I want you to forgive me."

I watched as these two men of God embraced. There was not a dry eye in the room. In that one brief moment, my mind began to envision a new possibility—Protestants and Catholics all over the world coming together, embracing in love, and dropping to their knees in prayer.

In this simple act, Selmar Quayo had challenged all of us to become ministers of Reconciliation. My thoughts raced. "Imagine what the Holy Spirit could do if Catholics and Protestants really were one." The words of Jesus flashed through my mind: "If you are offering your gift at the altar and remember that your brother has something against you, leave your gift there in front of the altar. First go and be reconciled to your brother; then come and offer your gift" (Matthew 5:23-24). As I watched the scene unfold, I could almost hear Jesus praying, "May all of them be one, Father . . . that the world may believe that You have sent Me" (John 17:21). I knew at that moment that I must become a minister of Reconciliation.

Years earlier, Joetta and I had ministered at a Southern Baptist church in Tulsa, Oklahoma. After the service, a woman came up to Joetta and asked her if she would pray for her daughter, Regan. She did not want, however, to divulge the specific prayer need. Joetta assured her that it wasn't necessary to know the need because the Holy Spirit would intercede for Regan. For the next year, Joetta prayed faithfully for a young lady she had never met.

At that time, Joetta was working as a technical writer for Thrifty Rent-a-Car. One day, her boss informed her that they had hired a new software trainer and were going to put her in the cubicle across from Joetta's. They asked Joetta to make her feel welcome and to show her around. When the new trainer arrived, she introduced herself as Regan. To Joetta's surprise, here stood the young lady she had been praying for all those months! God was definitely up to something. Joetta and Regan worked as associates over the next seven years. Although they never socialized outside of the workplace, they began to develop a close relationship.

One day in 1995, Regan shared that she and her husband were having problems in their marriage. Kelvin was a Roman Catholic, and she was a Southern Baptist. For several years, Regan attended the Catholic Church off and on with Kelvin, and although he did not feel comfortable in the Baptist Church, he would attend with Regan on special occasions. This arrangement worked until they had children and realized how strongly they both felt about how their children should be raised. To Regan's chagrin, Kelvin was adamant about baptizing and raising their children in the Catholic Church. They were at an impasse when Regan came to Joetta for advice.

Joetta told Regan that a house divided cannot stand and that it was essential that they be in church together. Joetta suggested that if her husband would not go to church with her, she should go to church with him. God would bless their marriage if Regan would submit to the spiritual authority of her husband. Joetta informed Regan of some classes held by the Catholic Church that she could attend, without obligation, to learn about the Catholic faith. Joetta said, "If I were you, I would want to know what my children were going to be taught so that I could counter any incorrect teaching." For Regan's peace of mind, Joetta said, "You go through the program, bring all of the material to me, and I'll give it to Larry so that he can check it out and see if it is scripturally sound."

I never paid any attention to the material Regan gave Joetta, except for two things. One was a newspaper article by a Lutheran journalist discussing Marian apparitions. The author of the article had spoken at Regan's church and told how the Mother of God had been appearing to six young children daily since 1981. Regan was so intrigued that she read everything she could get her hands on. The second thing she gave us was a cassette by a woman who had been miraculously healed at the same apparition site. This experience had so affected this woman, a nominal Christian at best, that she committed her life to serving Christ. I took these items and started to throw them away. On a whim, I stuck them in a drawer instead.

The week before May 25, 1996, Regan told Joetta that she was going to a Marian conference in Wichita, Kansas. She was excited about it because both the author of the article and the woman who had been healed were featured speakers. Regan, however, was bothered by a prayer she had received in the pre-conference material that supposedly would be prayed at the conference. "I would like," she told Joetta, "for you and Larry to look it over and see what you think."

As Joetta read the prayer, all kinds of red flags went up. In almost a state of panic, she brought the prayer to me. It was the Consecration to the Immaculate Heart of Mary. As I read the prayer, the hair on the back of my neck stood straight up. "Immaculate Heart of Mary, I give to you my body and soul . . . " I stopped in mid-sentence. Rage filled my heart. "This prayer is demonic!" I said, "You don't give your soul to anyone but Jesus. Tell Regan she can go to the conference, but whatever she does, she must not pray that prayer." Within three days, something deep within my spirit told me I had made a terrible mistake. Remorse for what I had said flooded my soul.

I decided to take a copy of the prayer to Father Vima. "I don't understand this prayer," I said. "How in the world can you give yourself to Mary in this way?" With a twinkle in his eye, Father Vima gently said, "Larry, have you ever held Joetta in your arms and said, 'I love you, I adore you, I worship the ground you walk on'?" "Yes," I cautiously replied.

"Have you looked lovingly into her eyes and assured her of your complete love and devotion? Have you spoken words like, 'I am completely yours now and forever'? 'All that I am and all that I ever hope to be is yours'?"

I was beginning to get his point. "If the truth were known," I admitted, "I've used those exact words."

"Catholics," he continued, "would never say of Mary, 'We adore you.' We venerate her. We honor her. However, we would never say 'we adore you' because adoration is reserved only for God. It is something we give only to Jesus. We adore Him. He is the King of Kings and Lord of Lords, and there is no one like Him. We believe that Mary, as the Mother of God, loves and cares for us. What we're saying in this prayer is, 'All of me I place in your hands, and I ask you to take me to your son, Jesus.' Mary always points to Jesus."

As I listened to Father Vima, I began to realize how wrong I had been. Two emotions flooded over me simultaneously—shame and joy: shame for my quick assessment and joy at the possibilities that were opening up.

I went home and found the Marian newspaper I had put in one of my dresser drawers and begin to read. As I read what Mary was reported as saying, I was struck by how biblically based her messages were—pray, repent, fast, commit your life to Christ. This was obviously not the work of Satan. I wondered aloud, "Could this really be the Mother of God?" If it were, then what she said was important and worthy of our consideration. One of her more frequent statements was somewhat puzzling: "Pray the rosary every day." Joetta and I knew nothing about the rosary. Perhaps it was time to discover what this prayer was all about.

As Regan was leaving for the Marian conference, Joetta gave her some money to buy a rosary. Their relationship had become strained and sometimes emotionally charged because of Mary, and Joetta felt that if she let Regan show her how to pray the rosary, it would at least keep them dialoguing. When Regan gave

Joetta her rosary, she said, "What's great is that the man who made this rosary lives just outside Tulsa, in Claremore, Oklahoma. If there's ever a problem with the rosary, it is guaranteed."

The more closely that Joetta looked at her rosary, the less she liked the centerpiece. "It looks like an idol. I think I'll call Two Hearts Rosaries and see if they'll exchange it for something else."

"Come on out," the voice on the other end of the line said, "Bob's work is guaranteed, and he will be happy to replace it with something you like." When we arrived, Bob's wife, Johanna, asked Joetta what was wrong with the rosary. "It's the centerpiece," Joetta said, "I don't like the centerpiece." Johanna looked at her quizzically, "What about it don't you like?" "Well, it looks too, you know, Catholic!"

"The rosary," Johanna said, smiling, "is Catholic!"

While Joetta looked at centerpieces, Bob was sharing with me what had happened to them on a pilgrimage to an apparition site in Europe. I yelled at Joetta, "Come in here and listen to this. You won't believe this story!" These were the first real Catholics that we had ever spent any time with, other than Sister Monica Marie and Father Vima.

Bob shared with us how God, through Mary, had transformed their lives. As he told their story, tears rolled down his face. He said he hadn't stopped crying since they returned from their pilgrimage. In his words, his heart "just turned to mush." When they got back, Bob went in and quit his job at Amoco. He was a laboratory technician and had been with the company for over twenty-one years. Not too long after that, Johanna quit her job at Tulsa University. God was calling them to complete obedience and dependence upon Him.

During this time, Bob met a nun who showed him how to make rosaries. Bob decided to make two rosaries: one to thank Mary for leading him to Jesus and one to thank Jesus for saving his soul. The rest is history. All of Bob's rosaries are lovingly hand-made. He sees each bead as a prayer sent out by Mary to convert and bring souls to Jesus. Joetta's and my conversion are the direct result of those prayers.

After our meeting with Bob and Johanna, I was emotionally shaken. As we drove away, neither of us said a word. It was as if we had experienced an epiphany. I can't explain it. I felt as if I had been in the presence of Jesus. Not wanting to go right home, I pulled into a fast-food restaurant to get something to drink. As we sat there looking at each other, tears began to stream down our faces. What was happening to us? What was God asking of us?

Our lives were literally being pushed toward the Catholic Church. Regan had introduced us to the owners of the local Catholic bookstore, so we decided to go there for more information. Lee and Anita lovingly welcomed us and pointed us to exactly what we needed. When we figured our income tax at the end of that year, we discovered that we had spent over $5,000 on books, cassettes, videos, and other materials in search of spiritual truths! We couldn't get enough. We were in Lee's store three and four times a day. "We're here for our Catholic fix." Lee and Anita would just laugh and point us to another book, cassette, or video. It was like an addiction that we couldn't get satisfied. One question just led to another and another. It was a wonderful experience.

We began going to bed later and waking up earlier, trying to jam as much reading into the day as possible. We decided to maximize our time. I began taking Joetta to work and picking her up so that we could read aloud coming and going. I would pick her up for lunch, put a couple of lawn chairs and TV trays in the trunk, and drive to a park so that we could read without interruptions. We took turns—one would eat while the other would read aloud. We did everything together. God was graciously speaking to us together, drawing us at the same pace deeper into Himself.

We read the *Catechism of the Catholic Church* from cover to cover. The Catechism is the greatest systematic theological work we have ever read. Answers to long-sought-after questions were coming like torrential showers.

I remember one Saturday morning in particular. We both woke up about four o'clock in the morning. We sat up in bed, each with a Bible in one hand and a Catechism in the other. I would say, "Joetta, listen to this. This is fantastic. This just brings everything into focus!" Before I would finish, Joetta would interrupt and say, "Larry, wait, wait. Listen to this!" She would then read from a different section of the Catechism. We would read supporting Scripture verses, go to the writings of the Early Church Fathers, and then check a commentary. Before we knew it, it was one o'clock in the afternoon!

We were like sponges. We began to see issues such as the real presence of Christ in the bread and wine, the role of Mary in the Church, prayers to the saints, Scripture and Tradition as authoritative vs. *sola Scriptura*, papal authority, purgatory, and salvation as a process vs. salvation as a completed work in a whole new light. It was like finding all the lost pieces in a huge theological puzzle. The full picture was becoming clear.

The Lord was taking us down two paths simultaneously — one intellectual and the other emotional. We had been praying the rosary and parking ourselves on Bob and Johanna's sofa, asking question after question about Catholic doctrine, tradition, and culture. We asked God to somehow reveal to us if He was drawing us to the Catholic Church, because none of this made any sense to us. We had spent all of our lives in Protestant churches and were quite content in our ministry. We desperately needed to know about the Church to which God was calling us, so three short weeks into our conversion, I prayed this prayer. "Father, if you are drawing us into the Catholic Church, I want a sign, and I want it big."

Several days later on our way home from a short trip to Dallas, we witnessed the largest, most vivid sun either of us had ever seen. It went from horizon to horizon, and we thought we were going to drive right into it—an indescribable array of colors: orange, red, and pink. It was magnificent, so much so that our young grandson, who was sleeping in the backseat, sat up and said, "Grandpa, Grandpa, do you see that? Isn't it beautiful?" As brilliant as it was, we could look right at it.

As the sun went down, we put in a cassette tape by Dr. Scott Hahn and continued toward Oklahoma City. As I looked into the night sky, I prayed again silently, "Oh, God, if you're drawing us into the Catholic Church, give us a sign, and please make it big!"

At the same time, unknown to me, Joetta was staring out the passenger window, silently praying, "Blessed Mother, if you're real, we have to know beyond a doubt." Suddenly, I heard Joetta gasp and say, "Oh, my, Larry, Larry, look!" As I looked to the right, I saw what looked like a chain of stars falling in slow motion at a downward angle from right to left. Just before the stars reached the horizon, they shot straight up and then fell back toward the earth again, falling right in the center of the highway. Usually a falling star shoots downward and moves so quickly you don't have time to tell anyone about it. We were speechless, because we both saw it! Finally Joetta broke the silence, "You did see that, didn't you?" We were both visibly shaken.

I put in a cassette by Catholic singer Dana in which she sings through the rosary, and for the next hour and thirty minutes, we prayed the rosary with her. We finished just as we reached the exit road going toward our parsonage. As we turned under the freeway and went up over a little hill, there, sitting on the road in front of us, was the most beautiful, enormous, vivid quarter-moon we had ever seen. Like the sunset, it seemed to literally sit in the middle of the road and extended as high into the sky as we had seen the sun. For two-and-a-half miles, we watched in total silence.

As we turned into our driveway, the moon disappeared. "Joetta, what does all of this remind you of?" "Revelation, chapter twelve," she said: " 'A great and wondrous sign appeared in heaven: a woman clothed with the sun, with the moon under her feet and a crown of twelve stars on her head.' " At that moment, we knew not only that the Holy Spirit was bringing us to the Catholic Church but that Mary was leading the way.

Two months later, Joetta and I knelt in a small chapel on the University of Tulsa campus and prayed the prayer of Consecration to the Immaculate Heart of Mary. Our love for her is without bounds. I had been afraid that she would somehow take away from my love for Jesus, but what I found was that my love for Christ has deepened beyond measure. Truly, our cup runs over!

On September 12, 1997, I surrendered my ordination papers to Bishop Bruce Blake of the United Methodist Church. In doing so, I laid down thirty years of Protestant ministry to become a Catholic. To many of my colleagues, this seemed a horrible mistake, but to Joetta and me, it was "coming home."

In January 1998, we made a pilgrimage to Rome to symbolize our desire to place ourselves under the authority of Pope John Paul II and the Roman Catholic Church. In March, we made a pilgrimage to a Marian site in Eastern Europe to thank the Blessed Mother for bringing us into the Church. And finally on Easter Vigil, with great anticipation, Joetta and I were received into full communion with the Catholic Church. This was the culmination of a twenty-three month, life-transforming odyssey. Thank you, Mary, for loving us home.

Originally published in the CHNetwork Journal *Jan-Mar 1998.*

Larry Lewis had a master of divinity degree from Phillips Theological Seminary and had been a doctoral candidate at Oral Roberts University, where his doctoral research was on Catholic apologetics. Larry passed away in January 2004. Joetta currently lives in Tulsa, Oklahoma. They have three married daughters and five grandchildren.

Searching For Authority

By Christopher Dixon
former United Methodist minister

For nine years, I served the Lord Jesus Christ as a United Methodist pastor in New Jersey. For five of those years, I had no thought of being anything else. I had a growing church, I was happy in my denomination and pleased with my prospects, and I was satisfied.

I believed that denominations were not only inevitable but good. Since Christians would always disagree about their beliefs and practices, having different denominations kept them from fighting. I didn't believe that visible or doctrinal unity was necessary for the Church. At the same time, I insisted strongly on my own beliefs, which were defined largely by Wesleyan orthodoxy, and believed strongly that churches needed to teach doctrinal truth (which I still believe). The Christian faith was what it was, and the big things were not up for grabs.

I had been a lifelong Protestant, but I didn't grow up with a strongly defined religious identity. Until I was seven, my parents were active Methodists, but when we moved to Schenectady, New York, my mother (a nurse) worked every weekend and my father was never again involved with any church. I think the infighting common to Protestant congregations gave him a distaste for church life. But my brothers and I were sent to Sunday school at the nearest church, Calvary Orthodox Presbyterian. There I received an excellent grounding in the Bible and a Christian faith that I never lost (although my practice of it was inconsistent until I met my wife, Pat, in college).

From my days at Princeton Theological Seminary, I believed in the authority of the early Church to speak definitively on the content of the Christian faith. I had no doubt that the Councils of Nicaea and Chalcedon, for instance, spoke with the authority of the Holy Spirit. What I had not thought about much was what happened to that authority in the centuries since. I suppose I had the idea that it stayed in the Catholic Church (having nowhere else to go) until the Reformation and then made a lateral move to the Protestants. Nor was I concerned that the bishops at Nicaea who insisted on the divinity of Christ also insisted on His bodily presence in the Eucharist. The apostolic faith is all of a piece, but I did not know that yet.

Another important experience at seminary was reading John Henry Cardinal Newman's *Apologia Pro Vita Sua*, his story of how he converted from Anglicanism to Catholicism by searching for the "Catholic tradition" in the Church of England. I had never thought much about tradition and authority; I took it for granted that different churches have different beliefs and that it was just a matter of personal preference as to which church one belonged. Newman, however, described a church that commanded assent, whose beliefs and visible form were both grounded in the teaching of the apostles. I longed for such a church. I was transfixed and, as Newman discovered that the Catholic tradition was found in the Catholic Church, I couldn't find any flaws in his argument. I wondered whether I ought to become Catholic.

Pat's response to this was, "I don't want to hear that! You came here to become a Protestant minister. I want to have children, and I don't want any more changes!" At that point, I wasn't prepared to pursue the issue myself, either. The matter was dropped — not resolved, but put aside — though I brought a rather High Church approach to Methodism.

After my graduation and I was into my pastorate, I began to have questions about the basis of my denomination. John Wesley intended Methodism to be a spiritual renewal movement within the Church of England, not a separate church. He had an Anglican view of the Church, sacraments, and ordination (though he was not always consistent). His successors, however, did not, and though they kept many of the externals, there was nothing with which to replace Wesley's view. The result was a church with a somewhat sacramental appearance but little sacramental theology, with strong central authority and no doctrinal authority, with an ecumenical emphasis (at least with other liberal Protestant denominations) but suspicion of any attempt to define what Christians must believe.

For years, Pat had felt something missing in her relationships with the churches we'd been part of without knowing what she wanted. She thought it came from wanting children, and then the isolation of being a new mother with my being gone so much as a pastor. This came to a head in 1992 and 1993, when tensions with some in the congregation left her feeling totally cut off from the church and wishing desperately that she could belong to some other church. I didn't want to consider—"You can't do that! I'm the minister!" It was not a helpful response, but then it's hard to cope with the fact that the minister's job is tied to his wife's spiritual community.

I was right in believing that my wife and I ought to be one religiously, but I asked myself: Just what was it that we needed to be one in? Was there any reason for Pat to be Methodist except that I was the minister? If there wasn't, why was it so important to me? What is the Church, anyway? What holds it together? What reason could I give anyone for belonging to my church? I realized that I couldn't give any reason except preference. There was no relationship between our church and our faith.

Practically speaking, we didn't define the Church theologically: people belonged to a church because their family went there, or they liked the worship service, or each other, or the pastor. But that was not enough. We both realized that we wanted (actually Pat had wanted for a long time) a Church that had a claim on us even if it didn't make us happy, whether we liked it or not—where the Church was more than a preference. We wanted a Church with authority, a Church that was necessary. Part of the historic faith of the Church was that the Church didn't create itself and that its authority came from God, not men.

No denomination can claim that, because none can claim to be more than an association of like-minded Christians. Wherever the lines are drawn, it's a purely human creation; a group of people gets together and says, "We are the Church." If a denomination has a strong theological foundation (for example, the Orthodox Presbyterian Church where I attended Sunday school as a boy), it at least has a reason for being separate: teaching the truth according to its beliefs. But where there is no strong theological foundation, the denomination becomes nothing more than an administrative body and the congregation becomes an ingrained social habit.

My convictions about the Church crystallized more than they ever had. The Church was meant to have unity in structure and faith, and both were necessary. Unless it was united in faith, there was no reason to be united in structure. If the Church couldn't claim to tell me what is true, why should I give it my loyalty? If I had to figure it all out for myself, why would I need the Church? (Which, indeed, is the situation of many Protestant denominations: since they don't claim to be necessary, people don't believe they are necessary.) I realized that the nature of the Church went along with its beliefs. If the Church was to teach with authority, it had to have authority in its being. That couldn't be given by a denomination. Either it existed in the whole Body of Christ together, with visible unity giving shape to spiritual unity, or else it couldn't be found at all.

It struck me quickly that only two options avoided drawing arbitrary lines: congregationalism (in which each gathering of Christians could decide its own beliefs) or Catholicism, which claimed a principle of unity that brought everyone in. Congregationalism, however, seemed both unscriptural and unhistorical. Jesus said, "Where two or three are gathered in My name, there am I in the midst of them," but that didn't define the whole nature of the Church. If it did, there would have been no great disputes, no councils, and no commonly held faith. The Council of Nicaea meant more than the National Council of Churches. Only the Catholic Church truly represented visible and doctrinal unity. The alternative to Catholicism was doctrinal chaos and no unity. The Reformers had decided according to their own judgment which parts of the Catholic faith to keep and which to reject. Their followers continued the process of revising, and then the results were codified as revealed truth. The authority of the Catholic Church was simply replaced by the authority of Martin Luther or John Calvin. In the liberal denominations, the fall was even worse; the principle of revealed truth was replaced by theological pluralism, the absolute belief that there are no absolute truths. Yet in both, the Church's authority was replaced by the individual's, and the visible church became nothing more than a collection of individuals.

The result was worse than each church believing something different: It was a milieu in which it didn't matter what a church believed, in which no teaching needed to be definitive and in which the idea of necessary belief seemed offensive.

Some Catholic friends who knew what was going on with us came back from a conference at Franciscan University in Steubenville, Ohio, and gave us a tape of Scott Hahn's conversion story. Its effect on us was electric: He addressed the issues we were wrestling with rationally and biblically. Our beliefs were rapidly becoming more Catholic. We read *Humanae Vitae*, found it thoroughly convincing, and began Natural Family Planning. We were attracted by the Catholic Church's pro-life stand; our denomination was incapable of taking any strong position on this basic moral issue. We considered marriage indissoluble. We recognized the pope as the earthly head of the Church; indeed, we soon found events in the Catholic Church more relevant than events in Methodism. We now had no doubt that Christ is truly present in the Eucharist in the Catholic Church, but I knew it wasn't the same thing in Protestantism. (Indeed for a period I found it difficult presiding at Communion in my church. I felt I was pretending.)

To Pat and me it now seemed essential that we belong to a church that was founded on religious belief and wasn't afraid to teach it. When the *Catechism of the Catholic Church* appeared in 1993, we thought, "Wouldn't it be great to belong to a church that can teach the truth like that!"

It would take a while, however, for near the beginning of this time of change, more change happened. I was sent to another Methodist church in July 1993, and we were expecting our third child. I had to support my family, and in any event, I knew I needed clearer convictions than I had at that point. But I also knew that I would never find the solidity or consistency of belief in Methodism that I wanted.

There were also doctrinal issues that needed to be resolved. The Virgin Mary was the most difficult, but there were others. At the heart of them all was the infallibility of the Church, for if the Catholic Church was really what it believed itself to be, then its teachings had to be true. I had to learn to subordinate the sovereignty of my judgment to the voice of Christ in the Church.

I investigated all these things, but as long as I was in the ministry, I didn't feel that I could do more. Pat had more freedom, and with my encouragement (for spiritually she was left high and dry, and I would have urged any parishioner to go where her faith led her), she went to a wise and sympathetic priest, Father Joseph, for instruction. For Pat, it was like water in a thirsty land. Within months, she had no doubts at all. I was delighted; she would be there to welcome me into the Catholic fold herself. In December 1995, she became a Catholic. Our daughter Lisa received her First Communion the next fall.

I knew I couldn't stay in the United Methodist Church forever; my beliefs wouldn't allow it. I was feeling the strain of not being able to act on my beliefs. By now, I had found others on the same path. Jeff, another Methodist minister whom I hadn't seen in years, heard of my interest in Catholicism from a Presbyterian pastor we both knew. "I hear you're thinking of swimming the Tiber," he said when he called, and we began meeting for lunch. Jeff was even closer to conversion than I was, and he became Catholic in the summer of 1995. I found encouragement in meeting others who had converted and in cradle Catholics. Brian, the local Baptist minister, and his wife, Phyllis, had become good friends of ours. Phyllis became Catholic shortly before Pat. Then Brian did. People in town were getting suspicious.

In March 1996, I attended a Catholic men's retreat at Arnold Hall in Massachusetts, where I realized that nothing further needed to happen before I could convert. I fully believed the Catholic faith already. I didn't need any clearer light than I had—indeed, it couldn't be clearer.

With another baby due in July, a conversion, career change (to what, I didn't know), and relocation were not an option that summer. But I knew I couldn't delay much longer. In the meantime, Father Joseph introduced me to his friend Monsignor James McGovern, who was seeking someone to work in adult education, Confirmation training, visitation, and various other responsibilities at the Church of Our Lady of Good Counsel in Moorestown, New Jersey. Pat and I discussed this possibility and reached an agreement. In June 1997, I delivered the last sermon from my pulpit.

A month later, when Bishop John M. Smith of Trenton, a successor of the apostles, received me into the Catholic Church, I became fully united to the only church that I believed could teach with complete authority. To this day, in the voice of the Church I (still) hear the voice of Her Lord.

Originally published in the CHNetwork Journal *Apr-June 1998.*

Christopher served as a United Methodist minister for nine years. He was received into the Catholic Church in 1997. He is now teaching history at Ivy Tech Community College in Kokomo, Indiana.

Affirming All Things

By Dwight Longenecker
former Anglican minister

American Gothic

Taking dramatic steps of faith runs in the family. In the eighteenth century, my ancestors left Switzerland for the new colony of Pennsylvania to find religious freedom. The two Longenecker brothers were Mennonites—members of an Anabaptist sect so strict that they were persecuted by John Calvin.

Seven generations later, my side of the family had left the Mennonites, and I was brought up in a Bible Christian church. Like many churches in the sixties, our independent Bible church was a strongly evangelical and conservative group of Christians who were disenchanted with the liberal drift of the main Protestant denominations in the postwar period and set off to do their own thing.

That same independent movement included the foundation of a fundamentalist college in the Deep South by the Methodist evangelist Bob Jones. So after the war, my parents and aunts and uncles went to study there, and it was natural for my parents to send my siblings and me there in the seventies. In the heart of the so-called Bible Belt, Bob Jones University incongruously mixes hollerin' hell-fire fundamentalism with grand opera and a famous gallery of fine religious art. BJU gave Northern Irish firebrand Ian Paisley his honorary doctorate and brands even Billy Graham as a liberal.

The religion in our own home was simple, Bible-based, and balanced. Like our Mennonite forebears, there was a quiet simplicity and tolerance at the heart of our faith. We believed Catholics were in error, but we didn't nurture hatred toward them. At BJU, the tone was different. There the Catholic Church was clearly the "whore of Babylon" and the pope was the Antichrist.

Anglican Orthodoxy

Ironically, it was at BJU that I discovered the Anglican Church. We were allowed to go to a little Episcopalian schism church named Holy Trinity Anglican Orthodox Church. The church was founded by a bishop whose orders—an Anglican bishop later told me—were "valid, but irregular." He had been ordained by a renegade Old Catholic as well as a breakaway Orthodox bishop.

Along with some other disenchanted Baptists and Bible Christians, I went to the little stone church and discovered the glories of the Book of Common Prayer, lighting candles, and kneeling to pray. I was taken with the experience, and after searching for God's calling in my life, I decided to be an Anglican priest. I had studied English literature and visited England a few times and thought it would be perfect to minister in a pretty English village in a medieval church.

I wrote to the evangelical Anglican J.I. Packer, and he suggested a few English seminaries. Oxford was the Mecca for devotees of C.S. Lewis, so when the opportunity to study at Oxford came my way, I jumped at the chance and came to England for good. After theological studies, I was ordained and a life of ministry in the Anglican Church opened up.

The Affirmative Way

This whole period was a time of great growth and learning. Often it is the little bit of wisdom that makes the most impression. I will never forget a little quotation from the great Anglican social commentator F.D. Maurice I came across while I was studying theology. He wrote, "A man is most often right in what he affirms and wrong in what he denies." After the negative attitude of American fundamentalism and the cynical religious doubt that prevailed at Oxford, Maurice's statement was like a breath of fresh air.

It was sometimes tempting to feel guilty about leaving the religion of my family and upbringing. But with Maurice's viewpoint, I increasingly felt the Anglican riches I was discovering were not so much a denial of my family faith as an addition to it. So I took Maurice's dictum as my motto, and whenever I came across something new, I asked myself if I was denying or affirming. If I wasn't able to affirm the new doctrine or religious practice, I wouldn't deny it—I would simply let it be.

So when a Catholic friend in the United States suggested I visit a Benedictine abbey, I took her advice and made arrangements to go to the one closest to Oxford—Douai Abbey. There I found a world as alien to evangelical Anglicanism as Oxford was to Bob Jones University. The monks impressed me with their sense of solemn self-mockery. Here was a sense of touching a Christianity far greater and wider than I had yet experienced.

St. Benedict the Balanced

My link with the Benedictines continued after I was ordained and went to serve as an Anglican curate. I made my annual retreat at Quarr Abbey on the Isle of Wight, just off the south coast of England. I read about the history of monasticism and felt drawn to the Benedictine Way.

There seemed to be a balance, a simplicity, and a profound spirituality that echoed back to the simple sincerity of my Mennonite ancestors.

Just as I was about to visit Quarr Abbey for my annual retreat, a friend brought me a rosary from Walsingham. I had never touched such a Catholic artifact, but F.D. Maurice's wisdom touched me, and I thought, "If so many Christians pray this way, who am I to deny it?" So I bought a book about the rosary and learned how to pray it. Any ideas of accepting the Marian dogmas were out of the question. I substituted different glorious mysteries that were more Christ-centered. My five Biblical glorious mysteries were: Transfiguration, Resurrection, Ascension, Pentecost, and Second Coming. Despite my individualism, another window was opened and something new affirmed, for I found that the rosary grew in importance and I started to receive great graces through the prayers of Our Lady.

When my curacy was finished, I had three months free and decided to hitchhike to Jerusalem. So with backpack and a pair of sturdy shoes, I headed across France and Italy, staying in various religious houses along the route. I found my journey went best when I fit in with the monastic routine. So I would begin a day's journey with Mass and the Divine Office in one monastery, say my Anglican office while traveling, and then arrive at the next monastery in time for Vespers, the evening meal, and Compline.

The pilgrimage to the Holy Land also took me further into Christian history. Part of the appeal of being ordained into the Church of England had been to leave the modern subjective church of Protestant USA and find deeper roots in the history and faith of Europe. Suddenly, traveling through France, Italy, and Greece to Israel, I was immersed in a religion obviously older and deeper still than Anglicanism.

The Benedictine houses put me in touch with roots of faith that were deeper and more concrete than I imagined could exist. Although I realized my views were becoming "more Catholic," I didn't fight it. I wanted to "be right in what I affirmed."

The Apostolic Ministry

I had been ordained for about six years when my dream came true and I went to be vicar of two beautiful old churches on the Isle of Wight. By this time, I was not an Anglo-Catholic, but I did regard my ministry in a very Catholic way. I knew we were separated from Rome, but I considered my ministry to be part of the whole Catholic Church. Despite the formal separation, I thought of Anglicanism as a branch of the Catholic Church and prayed for the time of our eventual reunion.

My pilgrimage to the Catholic Church had—for the most part—been intuitive. I simply adopted the Catholic practices that seemed suitable, and when it came time to question certain doctrines, I looked at them and made every effort to affirm and not deny. This mind-set brought me almost unconsciously to the very doorstep of the Catholic Church. What I said to some friends who were considering conversion was true of me as well—I was more Catholic than I myself realized.

It was the Church of England's decision to ordain women as presbyters that helped clear my vision. Suddenly, things became crystal clear. Female priests were not the problem. Instead, it was what the General Synod's decision-making process revealed about the true nature of the Church of England. The key question was: Is the Anglican Church a Catholic Church or a Protestant church? If she wishes to be considered Catholic, then she does not have the authority to ordain women as priests. But if she is Protestant like all Protestant groups, she may indeed take the decision to ordain women as ministers. So when the General Synod made the decision, I was in a quandary. Everything within me said a Catholic church could not make such a decision on its own. Yet I hated taking a negative position about anything. According to my motto, I was rejecting women priests and was wrong to do so.

Then Father Leo Avery, the late abbot of Quarr, gently pointed out that greater affirmations often include smaller denials. In other words, you can't have everything. Choices need to be made. Rejecting women priests was merely the negative side of affirming something greater—the apostolic ministry. And affirming Catholicism had to include the denial of those things contrary to Catholicism.

Affirming All Things

The next few years were a terrible time of indecision. By now I was married and we had two young children. I hadn't trained for any other career, and if we left the Anglican Church, there seemed nothing but an uncertain future. One Sunday evening, I went to Quarr Abbey for Vespers and Benediction. As the monks chanted, I agonized over the decision to leave the Church of England.

"But I only wanted to serve you in the ancient Church in England!" I cried out to the Lord.

As the incense wafted heavenward and the monstrance was lifted, the still small voice replied, "But *this* is the ancient church in England." Then the struggles ended. My mind was made up, and in the autumn of 1994, my wife and I began our course of instruction with Father Joe McNerny at Quarr.

There was grief at losing our home and church, but at the same time, we received a tremendous welcome from our new Catholic friends. It was during this time that Keith Jarrett—the secretary of the St. Barnabas Society—offered friendship, help, and encouragement as he has done for so many who have taken the same step. Once we were received, the St. Barnabas Society continued to be there with practical advice and financial assistance.

As we went through our instruction, I not only read the documents of Vatican II but did further reading in the Apostolic Fathers. Day by day, I discovered that all the things I had come to affirm intuitively were part of the great unity of the Catholic Faith. When I became an Anglican, I felt my Bible Christian background was being completed. Now as we prepared to be received into the Catholic Church, I realized that I could still affirm everything my non-Catholic friends and family affirmed. I simply could no longer deny what they denied. F.D. Maurice's little snippet of wisdom had brought me across the Tiber, and in becoming a Catholic, I was affirming all things and denying nothing that was true.

Our reception took place in a quiet service one February evening in the crypt of Quarr Abbey Church. That night, all was harvest. There, as the monks sang their ancient and moving plainsong and we were finally received into full communion, the simple faith of my Mennonite forebears, the Bible Christians' love for the Scriptures and the ancient beauties of Anglicanism were all gathered together and fulfilled in a new and dynamic way.

Originally published in the CHNetwork Journel *Jul-Dec 1998.*
Dwight is an American who has lived in England for over twenty-five years. He holds degress in English and speech, and a degree in theology from Oxford University. A former Anglican priest, he and his family entered the Catholic Church in 1995. Dwight works as the Southwest District organizer for the St. Barnabas Society—the Coming Home Network's *English counterpart. He is also active as a Catholic writer and broadcaster. Dwight along with his wife, Alison, and their four children (Benedict, Madeleine, Theodore, and Elias) live in Chippenham, England.*

Returning Home

By Rick Ricciardi
former Assembly of God minister

It is strangely ironic that as I recall the events that led me back to the Roman Catholic Church, the words "I was raised Roman Catholic" come to mind. I wonder how many times over the course of twenty years I have said those words, usually at the beginning of a personal testimony or introduction. I also wonder how many times I have been on the receiving end of those words.

In many of the Evangelical Protestant or fundamentalist churches of today, more than twenty percent of the members or regular worshipers can say the words "I was raised Roman Catholic." At banquets or meetings, I recall many times sitting around a table, attempting to meet and learn about the other people sitting with me. Inevitably, someone would say those words. Heads would start nodding seemingly everywhere, and the smiles would begin. Additional words weren't required, because each of us understood.

We had escaped from a church that we believed taught works for salvation and tradition over Scripture, and had never told us about having a personal relationship with our Lord. Each of us would say, "We never heard the Gospel until we began to attend . . . " such and such church.

Now, after being away for over twenty years, I understand what the Catholic Church truly teaches about works in relation to salvation. I understand not only the need for Tradition but also how it acts as the glue in the foundation of our faith. To my shame, I am now aware how week after week for twenty-two years, I had heard the Gospel read and preached at Mass but I never listened to it. "They hear, but they do not understand." Lord, forgive me.

For most Protestant denominations, their specific or unique theological emphases have been formulated only over the past hundred years, some more, many less. Usually, each group was formed after splitting away from another group over a particular theological, doctrinal, biblical, or moral issue that was debated and then either implemented or rejected. So often, at least it seems to me, each newly formed denominational group leaves something behind in the process. I think the Reformers would be shocked to see how the denominations they founded have evolved in their ever widening theologies.

Catholic New Testament theology covers nearly two thousand years. The consistency and depth of teaching within the Church should be something to be marveled at, not criticized. Unfortunately today, even in the Catholic Church herself, we find priests, religious, lay teachers, and organizations who do not follow the teaching of the Church, which only leads to more confusion among lay Catholics as well as non-Catholics. Can there be any question as to why many lay Catholics don't know their faith?

To Christians of other traditions, the Catholic Church, especially the Mass, seems strange or antiquated. It's not until one takes the time to learn and begin to understand what the Church truly teaches that one sees that much of what is practiced, both in obedience to Sacred Tradition as well as in cultural Catholics' devotions and customs, is based on what was delivered, taught, and practiced in the first centuries of apostolic Christianity. The Jewish roots of the early Christians can be clearly seen in these traditions.

On the other hand, most Protestant denominations have been established rather recently, with their own traditions being based on what their first-generation Protestant leaders and members practiced.

The specific tradition that I recently left, the Assemblies of God, was formed in 1914. Most of the first generation have long since passed on, leaving the second generation to hold true to what was then established. The third and now fourth generations, many coming from other Christian traditions, are questioning why things are done the way they are. The second-generation people are fighting to bring the denomination back to the roots they inherited, while the third and fourth generations are pushing to change in ways that seem important to them and their families. All of this has happened in the twentieth century. When you contrast the changes made in less than one century in this one new Christian tradition with the consistency following twenty centuries in the Catholic Church, it should make you pause.

Who would have thought fifty years ago that some mainline Protestant traditions would be considering, and in many cases accepting, abortion, same-sex marriages, and homosexual clergy?

Once again, the Catholic Church, in spite of the attempts of dissident groups whose motives are often suspect, has remained consistent in its call to all Christians to remain faithful to the faith and teaching that have been handed down, from generation to generation, for nearly two thousand years.

My Wandering Begins

When I was twenty or twenty-one, I began indulging in some heavy drinking and experimenting with drugs, and I almost entered a marriage that would have proven disastrous. Why? I don't know. God, however, was faithful, even though I most certainly wasn't.

A string of circumstances led me to a Southern Baptist church in Louisiana. Those circumstances became the bulk of my testimony whenever I would joyfully tell how I "became a Christian." Today, as I look back, I am very grateful for how God worked in my life to open my heart to His love and grace. Now, however, my conclusion is different: He saved me, but He saved me from me.

At this small Southern Baptist church, I found people who cared for me, loved me, and shared their lives with me. Outside of my own family, I never realized people acted this way. Many nights I would be at one of their homes, sitting at the kitchen table and asking questions about the Bible. They always had time for me.

There I discovered Jesus in a way that was totally different from what I had experienced as a Catholic, and I believe this is one reason why Catholics leave the Church. I don't mean to oversimplify this, but I think what draws many away is hearing clear, directive, confrontational preaching for the first time—not a short homily demanding little or no response but a thirty, forty, even sixty-minute sermon, which fully develops a scriptural text into a practical application that leads to a climax requiring a "Yes!" or a "No!" This is why, I believe, so many "born-again" ex-Catholics say they had never heard the Gospel before. What they are really saying is, "I was never put in a position to say 'yes' before." At least this was true for me.

But there is another aspect, found in most Evangelical Protestant churches, that is also important: the feeling of involvement. In the Southern Baptist church I began to attend, there was Sunday school followed by the morning service. In the evening, there was another time of teaching called Training Union, followed by the evening service. On Wednesday, there was midweek service. On Thursday, there was visitation to the people who had visited the church on Sunday or who recently had moved into the area. Throughout the week, there were Bible studies and committee meetings. With all of this you begin to feel involved, to feel needed—that you are "somebody."

I have learned that the same opportunities for involvement have been there all along in most Catholic parishes. There are many things going on, ministries to be involved in and therefore ways to feel you have something to offer. But I wonder how many former Catholics, now so heavily involved in their new Protestant churches, made the same efforts to be involved in their former parishes? More than attending weekly Mass, I mean. How many taught religious education or worked with the teens, college students, singles, young married couples, widows, converts, those who are grieving, those who are in need, etc.?

In April 1974, I became a Baptist, joining the church I had been attending. I preached my first service at a youth revival in June of that year. I remember working for days on that sermon and being so nervous when the day finally came. I arrived at the church early and sat anxiously in the first row. With my back turned to the congregation, I had no idea how many people were entering behind me. When it came time for me to preach, I approached the pulpit and turned to see a church absolutely packed. I had never seen the church that full before.

In spite of my heart pounding and my knees shaking, I began a one-hour sermon that probably included every piece of Bible knowledge I had accumulated since April. Anything and everything I had ever heard was in that message. At the end, I gave an altar call, and a teenage girl came forward and gave her life to Christ. It was one of the most exciting nights of my life, and I knew I was where God wanted me.

While helping with the youth group, I met a young woman named Jeannie, and within months we knew God was calling us to be married. I discouraged any of my family from attending our December wedding. This of course was just another "hurt" in a long list of "hurts" that I would cause for my parents. The excuse I gave was that the wedding was in Louisiana, a long way from my parents' home outside of Chicago. There were still six siblings living at home, so it would have been very difficult and expensive for them to come.

But the real reason I persuaded them not to come was because I was embarrassed by them—not by them personally but because they were Catholic. In my heart, I truly wanted them to be there with me, especially my mom and dad, but I didn't want to introduce them to my new church family. My anti-Catholic feelings were starting to emerge. I was beginning to enjoy my new zealousness, and I didn't want to be challenged by two Catholic Christians.

I enrolled in a Bible college, and for the next few years, my anti-Catholic views, and at times my hatred for the Catholic Church, were the dominant part of my life. I had just enough knowledge of the Catholic Church to be considered an "expert" by many of my fellow Bible college students but not enough to be able to discern the errors that I was hearing about the Church.

From 1974 to 1985, I served in several Baptist churches in Louisiana, Washington state, and California. I was always involved in lay ministry and church leadership. I served in pulpit ministry, preaching when the pastors were on vacation or ill. I also taught Sunday school classes as well as adult Bible studies.

When we moved to Arizona in 1985, my wife and I took the opportunity to join an Assembly of God (Pentecostal) church. We remained there until April 1997, when I finally resigned my positions as deacon and secretary/treasurer of the board of directors.

My Heart Starts to Turn for Home

I think the beginning of my restlessness with the Protestant form of worship—basically prayer, a greeting, singing, announcements, an offering, more singing, more prayer, a special song either by the choir or an individual or group, a message, and finally some opportunity to respond to the message—was the realization that this was all about "going to get something." If the songs weren't the ones I liked, it could ruin the whole service for me. Participating on the leadership team, we always tried to make sure the emphasis was on worshipping God regardless of how we felt. But so often it still came down to how we felt. I believe this is the source of the standard line, "I'm not being fed."

Without knowing it, I was beginning to think there had to be a better way. I remember talking to the pastor shortly before I announced I was leaving, and he admitted that he felt under much pressure—that he was carrying the service on his shoulders. He didn't want it that way, but he felt like he was performing.

Then in the spring of 1996, my family began preparing for our first visit in ten years back to my home near Chicago. I am the oldest of nine children—six boys and three girls. Most of my brothers and sisters were small children when I left home at the age of nineteen, so I didn't know them very well, and the thought of seeing them became an ever-increasing problem. I was the only one who had left home, and I was the only one who wasn't Catholic. Over the years, I had always found excuses to avoid returning, and by now my anxiety verged on paranoia.

The reason for this particular trip home was the wedding of my brother Paul to his fiancée, Katherine. I had missed many of my brothers' and sisters' weddings, but this time, my dad insisted that all of his sons be in this wedding.

Paul and Katherine were graduates of Franciscan University in Steubenville, Ohio, where Paul had received an M.A. in theology. I remember thinking, "What a sap! He spent all that money and time earning a degree in Catholic theology. I'll bet they didn't open the Bible once during the whole two years he was there."

We arrived a few days before the wedding, and of course, everything was in chaos. I made a point of stealing some time alone with Paul to discuss his education and to convince myself he was really a Christian. During our discussion, the subject of Mary came up. We talked about the different doctrinal beliefs about Mary that Catholics must hold, and at first I thought he was kidding. This had to be a joke that he had been saving for months to spring on me. Then I realized he was serious. Thoughts flew through my mind. My brother isn't a Christian! Two years at that school, and he thinks Mary is equal to Jesus!

Initially this discussion only led to anger, but slowly I began thinking again about the Catholic Church. These thoughts weren't things I cared to share with anyone, but slowly over the days before the wedding, God began softening my heart.

As far as I was concerned, the wedding rehearsal was a disaster. I wouldn't cooperate by bowing before the altar as I came down the aisle. I goofed off the whole time, making jokes about everything the deacon was saying or trying to do. I was a total distraction to those around me. That was the first time I had been in a Catholic church for a long time, and I thought it was all a joke.

The morning of the wedding was an exciting, beautiful day. I had gotten over all the fears and apprehension of seeing my brothers and sisters, not to mention relatives that I hadn't seen in twenty years. I was even looking forward to seeing everyone at the reception afterward.

At the church, I began seeing people whom I never thought I'd see again. We laughed and told stories, amazed at how years could vanish in moments. We gathered in the church and waited for the bride to arrive.

I noticed that my brother Don was acting as if he wasn't feeling well. He started to get anxious for fear of disrupting the wedding, which made him feel worse. We tried to calm him down, but he kept getting worse. I put my hands on his shoulders and prayed for a healing touch and calmness to come over him. It was the first time I was able to do "my thing" around all these Catholics.

Praying for my brother helped me to focus on the wedding, to think about God, and to make a commitment to Him that I would take the upcoming ceremony seriously. When Katherine arrived, the wedding began. In a few minutes, I would begin a journey that I never thought I would take.

My Journey Home

I was enjoying the wedding Mass, looking around, making eye contact with cousins who had arrived late and who appeared just as excited to see me as I was to see them. I was feeling at home, very comfortable in a very strange place. When it came time for Communion, I did not intend to go forward to receive, but I sure wanted to. Being in the wedding party, I was sitting in the front row. To my surprise, after the priest gave Communion to Paul and Katherine, he came straight to the wedding party in the front row. I was second and was caught off-guard. When the priest came to me, obviously assuming that I was Catholic, he said, "The body of Christ" and I instinctively said "Amen" and received the Host.

I knew (and know) that I should not have done that. But the moment I received the Host, something happened in my heart—I instantly believed in the real presence of Jesus. It seemed so "right." Why did I ever doubt this? A hunger was born inside of me, and a need to rediscover the Catholic Church began.

Without making a big announcement—"I am rethinking the Catholic position"—I began reading books and magazines, listening to tapes, anything I could find at my parents' home. Eventually I found a copy of *Pierced by a Sword*, a novel by Bud Macfarlane Jr. The title was intriguing, and the book cover surprised me. Here was a Catholic novel dealing with the end of this age, something I had become quite "informed" about as an Assembly of God Christian.

As I read, it I thought, "But where's the Antichrist?" There was no mention of a temple being rebuilt or any talk about the Rapture. There was a lot of talk about Mary, but what did she have to do with the end times?

I also struggled with the novel's main characters. How was I going to accept or believe that God might use characters who drank and smoked? Not just a little—a lot! Even the priest in the story drank and smoked, and yet he was portrayed as a good priest. This was too much for my Assembly of God scruples to handle. "Christians don't drink or smoke, and if they do, they sure don't do it where they can be seen."

In *Pierced by a Sword*, the author intersperses information and statements from the many reported visitations or apparitions of Mary. He also slips in a lot of Catholic theology and philosophy. I kept saying, "Where is this guy coming up with this stuff?" I probably threw the novel down six times, each time saying something like, "I've got better things to do than read this."

But I finally became absorbed in the book. I couldn't stop reading it. I was getting up early, staying up late, trying to have some quiet time or find a quiet place to finish this book. Nothing else mattered; I had to finish this book.

In the end, it was a story of hope. It particularly helped me understand the Catholic teaching on the communion of saints, which in just a few months would prove to be an unexpected comfort. I probably could have picked up any number of other books lying around that also could have affected my life. But God, who understands me better than I do myself, knew which one I needed to pick up and read.

Returning Home

If I had just read that book and left it at that, I would have returned to Arizona and never thought again about becoming Catholic. My heart, however, was driven to take another step. After our vacation, I wrote to Bud Macfarlane Jr. to tell him about the impact of his novel on my life. In addition to an autographed copy of *Pierced by a Sword*, Bud sent me a copy of *Surprised by Truth* by Patrick Madrid, a book of testimonies of Protestants who had come home to the Catholic Church. This I devoured. I had no idea there were other Protestants who not only were thinking about becoming Catholic but who actually had become Catholic.

One of the wonderful ways that God encouraged me during this difficult time was in the way people would make contact with me. I was reading *Surprised by Truth*, and happened to finish the chapter written by Marcus Grodi, the founder and president of the Coming Home Network International. The very next day, when I returned from lunch and listened to my messages on my answering machine, there was a message from Marcus saying how Bud had given him my name. Even more than a great story, God used *Pierced by a Sword* to bring people like these Catholic brothers into my life. It started a chain of events that in many ways was miraculous.

Beginning in the fall of 1996, Bud and Marcus became my support team by telephone, mail, or e-mail. Their wisdom, along with a ton of tapes by Scott Hahn and other great teachers—which I had purchased or borrowed and listened to multiple times—along with a great deal of research and prayer eventually brought me to a crisis point. I had to announce my resignation and my return to the Catholic Church. If I did not, I was being disobedient.

One thought, I believe, really helped to speed up my return home. When I heard Jeff Cavins—a former Assembly of God pastor and then host of the *Life on the Rock* program on the Eternal Word Television Network (EWTN)—speak about living a life of rebellion during his years away from the Church of his youth, I knew exactly what he meant. Our stories were different, but this mindset of rebellion, I believe, is true not only for me but for a whole generation of former Catholics.

I had been limited in my ministry, my relationships, my joy, because I was in rebellion. Once I understood this, accepted it, and began to experience true repentance, my joy began to return and my days away from the Catholic Church were numbered.

Jeannie and I began the RCIA classes at our local Catholic parish in June 1997. On Saturday afternoon, August 9, I made a general confession—my first confession in at least twenty years. Then on Sunday, August 10, I received the Eucharist, legitimately.

On Saturday, November 22, 1997, I had the privilege of watching my wife and her RCIA class make a profession of faith and receive the sacrament of Confirmation, and then First Holy Communion. We were now able to receive the sacraments together as husband and wife.

So much has happened in such a short time. There were many times during this process that I became discouraged and wanted to forget about it. "Do I really want to walk away from this ministry for which I have devoted years of preparation?" However, each time I doubted, God would send someone, usually someone I didn't know, often over the Internet, who just felt led to write me a letter sharing their story or to offer encouragement. For all of you who made contact with me, thank you. God has truly continued to bless my wife and me as we stepped out, leaving many years of ministry and friends behind, but filling our lives to overflowing with new friends, brothers, and sisters in Christ.

I had the privilege of serving under some godly men during my years away from the Church. These men provided friendship, wisdom, and many wonderful memories. These were close friendships with men that I loved and still do. Each time I had to say goodbye, I felt as if my heart was being torn out of my chest.

Today I have fallen in love with the Catholic Church. When I think back to the words, "I was raised Roman Catholic," I can only say, "Thanks, Mom and Dad—I love you."

Originally published in the CHNetwork Journal *Jan-June 1999.*

Rick is a revert with a past. Catholic, Southern Baptist, miscellaneous Baptist, Pentecostal, and finally Catholic again. Rick and his wife, Jeannie, live in Mesa, Arizona, where he works for Boeing on the Apache helicopter program. They have two grown children, James and Joanna.

Logic and the Foundations of Protestantism

by Father Brian W. Harrison
former Presbyterian minister

As an active Protestant in my mid-twenties, I began to feel that I might have a vocation to become a minister. The trouble was that I had quite definite convictions about the things that most Christians have traditionally held in common—the sort of thing C.S. Lewis termed "mere Christianity."

I had had some firsthand experience with several denominations (Presbyterian, Anglican, Lutheran, Methodist) and was far from certain as to which one (if any) had an overall advantage over the others. So I began to think, study, search, and pray. Was there a true Church? If so, how was one to decide which one?

The more I studied, the more perplexed I became. At one stage my elder sister, a very committed Evangelical Protestant with somewhat flexible denominational affiliations, chided me with becoming "obsessed" with trying to find a "true Church." "Does it really matter?" she would ask. Well, yes, it did. It was all very well for a lay Protestant to relegate the denominational issue to a fairly low priority among religious questions: Lay people can go to one Protestant church one week and another the next week, and nobody really worries too much. But an ordained minister obviously cannot do that. He must make a serious commitment to a definite church community, and under normal circumstances that commitment will be expected to last a lifetime. So clearly that choice had to be made with a deep sense of responsibility, and the time to make it was before, not after, ordination.

As matters turned out, my search lasted several years and eventually it would lead me to a destination I at first never suspected. I shall not attempt to relate the full story but focus on just one aspect of the question as it developed for me — an aspect which seems quite fundamental.

As I groped and prayed my way toward a decision, I came close to despair and agnosticism at times as I contemplated the mountains of erudition, the vast labyrinth of conflicting interpretations of Christianity (not to mention other faiths) that lined the shelves of religious bookshops and libraries. If all the "experts" on truth — the great theologians, historians, philosophers — disagreed interminably with each other, then how did God, if He was really there, expect me, an ordinary Joe Blow, to work out what was true?

The more I became enmeshed in specific questions of biblical interpretation — of who had the right understanding of justification, of the Eucharist, Baptism, grace, Christology, Church government, and discipline, and so on — the more I came to feel that this entire approach was a hopeless quest, a blind alley. These were all questions that required a great deal of erudition, learning, competence in biblical exegesis, patristics, history, metaphysics, ancient languages — in short, scholarly research. But was it really credible (I began to ask myself) that God, if He were to reveal the truth about these disputed questions at all, would make this truth so inaccessible that only a small scholarly elite had even the faintest chance of reaching it? Wasn't that a kind of gnosticism? Where did it leave the nonscholarly bulk of the human race? It didn't seem to make sense. If, as they say, war is too important to be left to the Generals, then revealed truth seemed too important to be left to the biblical scholars. It was no use saying that perhaps God simply expects the non-scholars to trust the scholars. How are non-scholars to know which scholars to trust, given that the scholars all contradict each other?

Therefore, in my efforts to break out of the dense exegetical undergrowth where I could not see the forest for the trees, I shifted toward a new emphasis in my truth-seeking criteria. I tried to get beyond the bewildering mass of contingent historical and linguistic data upon which the rival exegetes and theologians had constructed their doctrinal castles so that I could concentrate on those elemental, necessary principles of human thought which are accessible to all of us, learned and unlearned alike. In short, I began to suspect that an emphasis on logic rather than on research might expedite an answer to my prayers for guidance. The advantage was that you don't need to be learned to be logical. You need not have spent years amassing mountains of information in libraries in order to apply the first principles of reason. You can apply them from the comfort of your armchair, so to speak, in order to test the claims of any body of doctrine, on any subject whatsoever, that comes claiming your acceptance. Moreover, logic, like mathematics, yields firm certitude, not mere changeable opinions and provisional hypotheses. Logic is the first natural "beacon of light" that God has provided us as intelligent beings living in a world darkened by the confusion of countless conflicting attitudes, doctrines and world-views, all telling us how to live our lives during this brief time He has given us here on Earth.

Logic, of course, has its limits. Pure "armchair" reasoning alone will never be able to tell you the meaning of your life and how you should live it. But as far as it goes, logic is an indispensable tool, and I even suspect that you sin against God, the first Truth, if you knowingly flout or ignore it in your thinking. "Thou shalt not contradict thyself" seems to me an important precept of the natural moral law.

Be that as it may, I found that the main use of logic in my quest for religious truth turned out to be in deciding not what was true but what was false. If someone presents you with a system of ideas or doctrines that logical analysis reveals to be coherent— that is, free from internal contradictions and meaningless absurdities—then you can conclude, "This set of ideas may be true. It has at least passed the first test of truth—the coherence test." To find out if it actually is true, you will then have to leave your logician's armchair and seek further information. But if it fails this most elementary test of truth, it can safely be eliminated without further ado from the ideological competition, no matter how many impressive-looking volumes of erudition may have been written in support of it and no matter how attractive and appealing many of its features (or many of its proponents) may appear.

Some readers may wonder why I am belaboring the point about logic. Isn't all this perfectly obvious? Well, it ought to be obvious to everyone, and is indeed obvious to many, including those who have had the good fortune of receiving a classical Catholic education. Catholicism, as I came to discover, has a quite positive approach to our natural reasoning powers, and it traditionally has its future priests study philosophy for years before they even begin theology. But I came from a religious milieu where this outlook was not encouraged and was often even discouraged. The Protestant Reformers taught that Original Sin has so weakened the human intellect that we must be extremely cautious about the claims of "proud reason." Martin Luther called reason the "devil's whore"—a siren that seduced men into grievous error. "Don't trust your reason, just bow humbly before God's truth revealed to you in His holy Word, the Bible!"—this was pretty much the message that came through to me from the Calvinist and Lutheran circles that influenced me most in the first few years after I made my "decision for Christ" at the age of eighteen. The Reformers themselves were forced to employ reason even while denouncing it, in their efforts to rebut the biblical arguments of their "Papist" foes. And that, it seemed to me, was rather illogical on their part.

Logic and the Sola Scriptura Principle

Thus, with my awakening interest in logical analysis as a test of religious truth, I was naturally led to ask whether this illogicality in the practice of the Reformers was perhaps accompanied by illogicality at the more fundamental level of their theory. As a good Protestant, I had been brought up to hold as sacred the basic methodological principle of the Reformation: that the Bible alone contains all the truth that God has revealed for our salvation. Churches that held to that principle were at least "respectable," one was given to understand, even though they might differ considerably from each other in regard to the interpretation of Scripture. But as for Roman Catholicism and other churches that unashamedly added their own traditions to the Word of God—were they not self-evidently outside the pale? Were they not condemned out of their own mouths?

When I got down to making a serious attempt to explore the implications of this rock-bottom dogma of the Reformers, I could not avoid the conclusion that it was rationally indefensible. This is demonstrated in the following eight steps, which embody nothing more than simple, commonsense logic and a couple of indisputable, empirically observable facts about the Bible:

1. The Reformers asserted Proposition A: "All revealed truth is to be found in the inspired Scriptures." However, this is quite useless unless we know which books are meant by the "inspired Scriptures." After all, many different sects and religions have many different books, which they call "inspired Scriptures."

2. The theory we are considering, when it talks of "inspired Scriptures," means in fact those sixty-six books that are bound and published in Protestant Bibles. For convenience we shall refer to them from now on simply as "the sixty-six books."

3. The precise statement of the theory we are examining thus becomes Proposition B: "All revealed truth is to be found in the sixty-six books."

4. It is a fact that nowhere in the sixty-six books themselves can we find any statements telling us which books make up the entire corpus of inspired Scripture. There is no complete list of inspired books anywhere within their own pages, nor can such a list be compiled by putting isolated verses together. (This would be the case (a) if you could find verses like "Esther is the Word of God," "This Gospel is inspired by God," "The Second Letter of Peter is inspired Scripture," etc., for all of the sixty-six books and (b) if you could also find a biblical passage stating that no books other than these sixty-six were to be held as inspired. Obviously, nobody could even pretend to find all this information about the canon of Scripture in the Bible itself.)

5. It follows that Proposition B—the very foundation of all Protestant Christianity—is neither found in Scripture nor can be deduced from Scripture in any way. Since the sixty-six books are not even identified in Scripture, much less can any further information about them (e.g., that all revealed truth is contained in them) be found there. In short, we must affirm Proposition C: "Proposition B is an addition to the sixty-six books."

6. It follows immediately from the truth of Proposition C that Proposition B cannot itself be revealed truth. To assert that it is would involve a self-contradictory statement: "All revealed truth is to be found in the sixty-six books, but this revealed truth itself is not found there."

7. Could it be the case that Proposition B is true but not revealed truth? If that is the case, then it must be either something that can be deduced from revealed

truth or something that natural human reason alone can discover without any help from revelation. The first possibility is ruled out because, as we saw in steps 4 and 5, B cannot be deduced from Scripture, and to postulate some other revealed extra-Scriptural premise from which B might be deduced would contradict B itself. The second possibility involves no self-contradiction, but it is factually preposterous, and I doubt whether any Protestant has seriously tried to defend it—least of all those traditional Protestants who strongly emphasize the corruption of man's natural intellectual powers as a result of the Fall. Human reason might well be able to conclude prudently and responsibly that an authority that itself claimed to possess the totality of revealed truth was in fact justified in making that claim, provided that this authority backed up the claim by some very striking evidence. (Catholics, in fact, believe that their Church is precisely such an authority.) But how could reason alone reach that same well-founded certitude about a collection of sixty-six books that do not even lay claim to what is attributed to them? (The point is reinforced when we remember that those who attribute the totality of revealed truth to the sixty-six books, namely Protestant church members, are very ready to acknowledge their own fallibility—whether individually or collectively—in matters of religious doctrine. All Protestant churches deny their own infallibility as much as they deny the pope's.)

8. Since Proposition B is not revealed truth nor a truth that can be deduced from revelation nor a naturally knowable truth, it is not true at all. Therefore, the basic doctrine for which the Reformers fought is simply false.

Calvin's Attempted Solution

How did the Reformers try to cope with this fundamental weakness in the logical structure of their own first principles? John Calvin, usually credited with being the most systematic and coherent thinker of the Reformation, tried to justify belief in the divine authorship of the sixty-six books by dogmatically postulating a direct communication of this knowledge from God to the individual believer. Calvin makes it clear that in saying Scripture is "self-authenticated," he does not mean to be taken literally and absolutely. He does not mean that some Bible text or other affirms that the sixty-six books, and they alone, are divinely inspired. As we observed in step 4 above, nobody ever could claim anything so patently false. Calvin simply means that no extra-biblical human testimony, such as that of Church tradition, is needed in order for individuals to know that these books are inspired. We can summarize his view as Proposition D: "The Holy Spirit teaches Christians individually, by a direct inward testimony, that the sixty-six books are inspired by God."

The trouble is that the Holy Spirit Himself is an extra-biblical authority as much as a pope or council is. The Third Person of the Trinity is clearly not identical with the truths He has expressed, through human authors, in the Bible. It follows that even if Calvin's Proposition D is true, it contradicts Proposition B, for "if all revealed truth is to be found in the sixty-six books," then that leaves no room for the Holy Spirit to reveal directly and nonverbally one truth that cannot be found in any passage of those books, namely, the fact that each one of them is inspired.

In any case, even if Calvin could somehow show that D did not itself contradict B, he still would not have succeeded in showing that B is true. Even if we were to accept the extremely implausible view represented by Proposition D, that would not prove that no other writings are inspired, and much less would it prove that there are no revealed truths that come to us through tradition rather than through inspired writings. In short, Calvin's defense of biblical inspiration in no way overthrows our eight-step disproof of the *sola Scriptura* principle. Indeed, it does not even attempt to establish that principle as a whole but only one aspect of it—that is, which books are to be understood by the term *"Scriptura."*

The schizoid history of Protestantism itself bears witness to the original inner contradiction that marked its conception and birth. Conservative Protestants have maintained the original insistence on the Bible as the unique infallible source of revealed truth, but at the price of logical incoherence. Liberals, on the other hand, have escaped the incoherence while maintaining the claim to "private interpretation" over and against that of popes and councils, but at the price of abandoning the Reformers' insistence on an infallible Bible. They thereby effectively replace revealed truth by human opinion and faith by an autonomous reason. Thus, in the liberal/evangelical split within Protestantism since the eighteenth century, we see both sides teaching radically opposed doctrines, even while each claims to be the authentic heir of the Reformation. The irony is that both sides are right: Their conflicting beliefs are simply the two horns of a dilemma that has been tearing at the inner fabric of Protestantism ever since its turbulent beginnings.

Reflections such as these from a Catholic onlooker may seem a little hard or unyielding to some—ill suited, perhaps, to a climate of ecumenical dialogue in which gentle suggestion rather than blunt affirmation is the preferred mode of discourse. But logic is of its very nature hard and unyielding; and insofar as truth and honesty are to be the hallmarks of true ecumenism, the claims of logic will have to be squarely faced, not politely avoided.

Originally published in the CHNetwork Journal *Jul-Dec 1999.*

Father Harrison, OS is currently teaching theology at the Pontifical University of Puerto Rico in Ponce. He writes frequently on matters of liturgy and canon law.

In Celebration of My Ignorance

By Thomas Hickey
former "Scofield Bible" Baptist minister

"I am a former Protestant minister." The words sounded as if someone else had spoken them. I was in the office of the pastor of the local Catholic parish. At that moment, I realized that my whole life was defined in terms of what I used to be. A silent wave washed over me: I used to be employed; I used to be a homeowner; I used to be confident and focused.

Let someone else figure out authenticity. I had given heart, soul, mind, and strength to trying to make *sola Scriptura* work. That pivotal doctrine of the Reformation proved to be a cruel mistress, seducing me with the promise of a pure and spotless Bride that never materialized. The pursuit of this phantom had occupied the best years of my life and drained the life right out of my family.

My Fruitless Quest for Unity

Up to this time, no one had ever mentioned Catholicism. The Catholic Church was the one thing that we always knew was not the true church—the only concept on which all Protestants agree. Although I had not voiced it but to two or three people, I had canceled my quest for the true church at the point of acknowledging the immense success of the Catholic Church as an institution. History has an air of infallibility to it—what happened, happened. I had to admit that one church had been in existence for two thousand years, unlike ours. Fifty years would be an old church for us.

Ironically, it was this recognition of our lack of history that had launched my quest many years earlier. It disturbed me that the longer any Protestant denomination stayed in existence, the farther it strayed from my touchstone—the Scriptures. They would all begin at some point to deny the authority of the Bible, never offering anything better in its place. So, filled with many admirable good works but bereft of any moral authority, they all predictably failed to find moral grounds for opposing abortion, for example. Among the Protestant denominations that had not lost their bearings, I could find the same tendencies beginning to crop up in the largest ones. In addition, we had turned worship into a circus. So, I was consigned to the smaller denominations. There I was shipwrecked by the principle that if you want to stay pure, you have to keep splintering. But you can't sail a toothpick. I found denominations as small as six churches splitting.

Finding a true expression of the church was like a puzzle always before me. It bothered me that I couldn't piece it together. I am not really a cantankerous or divisive person, but at times in my life I have been both. Our Lord's prayer in John 17 fueled my frustration. I believed the church Christ prayed for was a church of inclusion and unity founded on truth—the Word of God. I knew from this prayer that there was only one Church. But when I faced the multitude of churches around me, I had no way of identifying any one of them as more authentic than any other. That was because I had excluded Catholicism and Eastern Orthodoxy from the list. And mixing them all together was both a practical and theological impossibility.

I was left with a masochist's delight—a puzzle that couldn't be solved. Oh, the misery I could have spared myself if I hadn't been so hardheaded! I concluded that the only way for Christians to unite was around the Word of God, which I took to mean the Bible, even though the New Testament wasn't written at the time Jesus prayed the words of John 17. I turned this into a principle that I followed scrupulously: The only reason for not worshipping with another church was deviation from the Bible. I never allowed personality, preferences, styles, or history to be the basis for division in my mind. We were dealing with the authority of the risen Christ and His infallible Word. Thus if there were different confessions of faith that kept churches apart, someone had to be wrong. If I could not clearly state where another church had denied the Word of God, it would be sin not to worship with them.

The Frustration of a Sincere Conscience

I can say this now, but at the time I could not see what a perfect recipe for frustration I had concocted for myself. On the one hand, I had to become an expert on other churches' deviations from the Word of God; to avoid the sin of schism, I had to make them be the sinner. On the other hand, I at least had to tacitly declare that my church did not deviate. Thus, I became condemning and self-righteous, which I despised in others but could not see in me.

My frustration grew as I found no one else in ministry willing to face this dilemma. None of my colleagues seemed to understand that if we were not the authentic church, then people's souls were at risk. I was haunted by a thought I kept locked in a closet in the back of my mind: I was supposed to be telling people how to get to heaven. If I didn't have the proper authority, or if I misdirected people, they would have every reason to blame me for their perdition (or their increased purgatory, I can say now). This was the Protestant doctrine of *sola fide* rattling its chains in my soul. I was ministering in churches that constantly reassured their congregations that the one time they walked down the aisle of their church to "accept Jesus" was all they needed to be certain of heaven. Needless to say, those looking for that kind of consolation found other churches to attend. Mine never grew.

Born on the Wrong Side of the Ocean

Looking back, I see my life in a metaphor of a man born on the wrong side of the ocean. He senses a deep, unspoken longing in his soul for a safe harbor on the far side of the ocean. Some distant Irish ancestors had perhaps brought their children to be baptized by St. Patrick with a prayer that their family might live forever in the blessings and comfort of Mother Church. My grandfather left Patrick's church and eventually became a colonel in the Salvation Army. But God's faithfulness extends to a thousand generations. In His providence, He had my parents baptize me in the Methodist Church. The liturgy of those early years left me with a profound God-consciousness. And the Father was faithful to His Word when He sent the Spirit of God to stir my heart during my first years of college. The Baptists recognized this stirring and led me to an experience they called "getting saved." They baptized me again because—they said—my first one didn't count. Then they put a Scofield Bible in my hands, which I devoured.

The Scofield Reference Bible is the largest-selling study Bible in the history of the world. Its effects are deadening in three regards. First, it orients the Christian toward an expectation of Christ's return very, very soon, and thus there is no long-term outlook. Second, it relegates the Church to a temporary "parenthesis" in the plan of God. And third, it associates the Antichrist with Catholicism. Perhaps for this reason, the one church in the world big enough to deal with its errors has chosen to be silent.

Here I must ask a very pointed question to all Catholics—in love and friendship. But the question needs to be asked: Where were you? I am not pointing fingers or blaming anyone. Forgive me this question; I mention this merely as a demonstration of the wounds I bear in following the path of Christ. It would be understandable if these wounds had come from Christ's enemies. But they came from His shepherds. The error of Scofield was taught to me by pastors and Bible scholars. Where were you? I could have been spared over thirty years of aimless tacking back and forth across the entire ocean, only to see my family swept away in the end. All kinds of evangelical Christians were there when heaven was awakening me to my need of salvation. Catholics were there too. But they were silent. The Spirit of God is ever at work; it is we who are asleep.

I even took a class on Church history at the state university I attended. A Catholic priest very well known on the campus taught it. I really thought I knew more than he did. The priest was oblivious to the spell I was under; we couldn't communicate. The introduction to the Scofield Bible says that C.I. Scofield studied arduously all the systems of theology present in the world and verified that the system of thought contained in his notes was indeed the historic faith of the Church. That, of course, was a lie. I have taken comfort recently in Augustine's *Confessions* in which he chides himself for the foolish and ignorant doctrines of the Manicheans he followed so avidly.

Bishop Ambrose understood Augustine's errors, could communicate with him, and eventually won his heart and his intellect for the kingdom of Christ. I have found few Catholics today who understand how extensive and damaging are the errors taught in the best-selling study Bible in the history of the world. Perhaps one of the reasons is that Scofield's doctrine has mutated into a thousand different forms, none of which use Scofield's name. Worse, I have found some Catholics who seek to imitate this and wish to incorporate some of this error as well. God help us.

Nobody Told Me

Listen to me! When God woke me up in college and I began searching for Jesus and rest for my soul, all the Baptists could give me was a book. Thankfully, it was the New Testament. All the while, right across the street from my dormitory was a Catholic church. I was desperately searching for Jesus, and He was present in the Tabernacle fifty yards away from me. NOBODY TOLD ME! I can't say that I would have listened, but I can say that nobody told me that Jesus was there. In fact, my anti-Catholic bias, picked up from the pages of the Scofield Bible, left me with the impression of Jesus sitting outside the Catholic Church on the curb, alone and forlorn, while the worshippers gathered inside.

I didn't have to launch out across the ocean in a leaky boat with no map. But I did. I left that unvisited tabernacle far behind, took a wife, went to seminary, took my first church, started our family, and began my restless wandering. I loved the church, and I got that from the pages of Scripture. Surprisingly, the Baptist seminary I attended emphasized quite strongly the primacy of the local church with Christ as its head. But already, in my first ministry, I began to realize that the authority of Christ was not present in that church. We left that denomination and tried an independent work, mostly composed of Catholics who left their church in the charismatic renewal of the seventies. Those poor souls had never been instructed in their own faith. They left Jesus in the Tabernacle to go wander in the desert. We met in a picnic shelter in a state park every Sunday to sing new songs and learn the doctrines of C.I. Scofield under the guise of teaching "just the Bible." During that time, I had the opportunity to work full-time and minister part-time, but after five years, I was restless and irritable again. Somewhere, there had to be a real church.

How could I find my way home when those who were already there didn't stay? How could I find the life-giving food my soul craved when those who had dined on it despised it?

Running Too Hard

I created a tumult by leaving that church in the park in the hands of the elders (I never was one) to attend a church that had just welcomed our oldest daughter into its inaugural first-grade class. No one understood what my soul needed. I certainly didn't. The new church was part of a fellowship of churches with a statement of faith devoted to Scofield's teaching, so I was happy. I was even happier when, in a strange set of circumstances, that church called me to be its pastor. After five years of hard work, the school grew; the church did not. I was frustrated.

That kind of frustration multiplied, as did my listening for faint whispers of whatever was missing in my ministry. Our denomination had an aggressive missionary ministry around the world, including France. We met some of the French missionaries, considered whether our gifts and talents would be better used over there, and even made a visit to explore the possibility. My Scofieldism was still intact, and all the prophecy preachers I trusted agreed that the Church would surely, surely be whisked off the Earth before the year two thousand. What better place to spend our last years on Earth than right in the heart of Antichrist's ten-nation confederacy taking shape before our very eyes in Europe? That was at least one of my reasons for being interested. As silly as it sounds, I can assure you that this doctrine has millions under its sway. It would be difficult to estimate how many zealous missionary endeavors are fueled by this kind of thinking.

We cross an Ocean

Laura always had more common sense than I did, and so she always listened with a yawn when I began lining up the prophetic "signs of the times." But this time it was Laura who said, "Yes, let's go to France." So we did. Trauma. Turmoil. Upset. Confusion. Uprooting my children and throwing them into a whole new world really hurt them, making it impossible for them to ever trust me again. We all eventually adapted, and all of us would go back if we could. We all loved our six years in France. But we lost the Lord's face. When I saw my children thrown to the wolves in French-speaking schools, there was no amount of consolation or prayer that would touch them. They learned to turn their hearts to the same degree of stoniness they found in their classmates. As their Dad, I couldn't even go in at night to tuck them in and pray with them.

That move cost too much. I couldn't pray any more. I studied and taught, but my private devotional life dried up. My hope was that the Rapture would come as predicted, and then my children would forgive me. But Jesus didn't come. I was lost. I really was. I initiated theological conflicts with my colleagues, thinking that fidelity to our statement of faith was the way to restore order to our lives. I could no longer live with authority that had deceived me.

What were we doing there anyway? France is a Catholic country, n'est-ce pas? Once again, I have to say that, though I met some very vocal Catholics who tried to defend their faith, they simply didn't know enough of what they believed to make an impression. And they certainly didn't know what I believed to be able to counter it. The closest I got to understanding a Catholic was once in a conversation with a devout man lamenting the fact that some modern priest had not baptized his infant son because, the priest said, it is better to wait until he can profess faith. The baby fell sick, and the priest did not arrive in time. The father was weeping as he told me his baby was not born of the Spirit. I tried to console him by saying that the Bible does not teach that an infant is born again through Baptism (for such we believed). In exasperation, he replied, "Well, that may not be what the Bible teaches, but it is what my Church teaches!" He knew where authority lies. I did not. How sad that I spent six years in a land full of empty church buildings that were little more than museums. Woe to the shepherds who do not watch the flock!

Scofield Unmasked

While in France, I met the author of the only comprehensive biography ever written on C.I. Scofield. It seems Scofield was incapable of writing the notes that bear his name, and the origins of those notes remain shrouded in mystery. It is clear, however, that this system of thought was devised near the end of the nineteenth century. I say this to my immortal shame: Woe unto shepherds when they feed the sheep doctrine invented yesterday! As I shared my discoveries with my colleagues in ministry, I was stunned to find that they didn't care. Our whole statement of faith was based on Scofield's system. Perhaps they sensed the upheaval I would experience as I began to extract myself from its influences. They simply didn't want to face it.

I needed time to sort it all out and discover just what I did believe, what—or whom—I could trust. Our work in France was done, and we were due for a year back home, after which we could report for a new mission elsewhere in France. Our oldest daughter was ready to enter college, and the others would follow shortly after her. We made the decision to return home permanently. I considered stepping out of the ministry but knew that the theological questions would not go away. I hoped to find a small church in our denomination where I could devote time to extensive study and rethinking. We found such a church and began to face the same trauma we had faced in moving to France—reverse culture shock. Our girls were rootless and alone as they faced the challenges of American life and culture. As their dad, I was changing so much that they decided to tune me out. I kept my public preaching and teaching within the bounds of our statement of faith, but I knew that a crisis was coming. I tried to develop a business on the side so that I might have something to support me when it hit.

This was change number four for my family and the biggest trauma I had ever faced. My world was shaken. I felt betrayed by men I had trusted to teach me the Word of God. I didn't know how to approach the Scriptures. The issue of authority was now a wide-open question. I began reading everything and anyone, some of it quite novel and bizarre. But, of course, I read no Catholics. They were the enemy. The question spurring me on was "Who has the authority to speak for God?" I had to conclude from the very apparent evidence: anyone, absolutely anyone. Anybody can start a church; anyone can get on the radio or TV and speak in Jesus' name.

My Wittenberg Door

I had painted myself into a corner. Our denomination was composed of autonomous churches voluntarily cooperating in a fellowship that we insisted was not a denomination. There was no hierarchy, no central authority, only voluntary organizations formed from the churches to accomplish various tasks such as foreign mission work, education, or the planting of new churches. We had groups of pastors in a region that met in what we called a ministerium. This group had no authority over the churches. Though we would examine a man for ordination, for example, it was his own local church that ordained him. Each church owned its own property and incorporated independently of any other authority.

I raised certain questions in our ministerium concerning our statement of faith, a woefully inadequate document that essentially said, "We believe the Bible, and the Bible teaches this . . . " followed by fourteen headings (not explained) of what we believe. I had hoped to initiate a district wide study of those headings that I believed were not taught in the Bible. Not even the terminology could be found in the Bible. I realized that a study of these things could lead to my resignation, but I hoped to help others rethink these things in order to avoid the damage created when they are taught and believed.

I should have known better. I was too weary in mind and spirit, though. My mind was constantly racing in those days as I studied some new aspect of my quest and had to make room for it in my theology. I was constantly shifting everything, because one new doctrine affects all the others. I felt like my mind was one of those puzzles with sliding tiles and one empty spot that allows you to shift everything around to get a picture or a message. I was shuffling those tiles frantically in my mind, night and day, trying to put it all together. I prepared a document for my colleagues, outlining my concerns. But it was too pointed, too critical, and too intimidating. I should have foreseen their reaction. They simply wanted to know if I believed our statement of faith. No study. Very little discussion. I said no. They said, "Then you must resign."

I was imbued with the spirit of Martin Luther at this point. I said, "I do believe what our statement of faith affirms in its one opening statement, that the Bible alone is our source for all doctrine and practice. I do believe the Bible. But I do not believe the Bible teaches some of the fourteen points listed, and I can demonstrate that to you." They again asked me to resign. I was perverse enough at this point to realize that one reason they wanted me to resign was that they had no authority to take any action. I pressed my point. "No," I said. "I will not resign, because I want you to go on record as saying that all fourteen articles of our faith are taught in the Bible."

What I had hoped to accomplish is not at all clear in my mind. I suppose it was a bit of a martyr complex. It had taken me over twenty-five years to get to that point and I wasn't going to turn back. I had the full support of the leadership of my church, as I kept them posted on all the proceedings. I fasted for several days and went to face my sentence. The ministerium met and determined that they would have to remove me from the list of approved ministers in our denomination. I smiled inwardly because I knew that no such list existed. They could not, and in fact did not, revoke my ordination. But I got the point. They threw me out.

The House Collapses

As this incident was reported by others, I had been "defrocked." That was not true, but had I known this was how it would be viewed, I would have simply resigned. I think. I cannot speak for my state of mind at that time.

The congregation of my church then had to decide to ask me to resign or leave the fellowship. I offered my resignation, arranged a business meeting of the congregation, and invited officials from the ministerium to come address the meeting while I left town. The church overwhelmingly voted to leave the fellowship, which they were perfectly free to do in the voluntary association we had. Once again, the telling of the tale was worse than the act. Word was that I "stole" the church from our fellowship. It is difficult for a Catholic to understand the structure of independent, autonomous churches in denominations like ours. But the congregation owned that church, and at the end of the ordeal, they still did.

Had I exercised better judgment, however, I would have resigned and moved on, if for no other reason than the rest I needed. I now found myself at the head of a congregation eager to learn what I had been unable to teach them up to that point. In addition, I wanted to find a new denomination for us to join. We finally settled on the Reformed camp of Protestants because they at least had historical roots back to the Reformation. This camp included all the various Presbyterian denominations. History was becoming important to us. Here I absolutely ran out of gas. Mainline Reformed denominations were already straying far from the Bible as their authority, and that left me with the disgruntled, the divisive, the self-righteous, and the confused Reformed and Presbyterian pastors, most of whom were trying to form new denominations. I finally settled on a medium-sized Presbyterian group that had its problems but would give us some identity and sense of history.

It was about this time that I flipped the switch. I wanted to lead our church into this denomination and then resign. I didn't know where I would go, but I was aware of a curiosity—how do those Catholics keep themselves together in one group and not lose their moral identity? For example, they are unquestionably the most pro-life institution in the world, yet they also did more than anyone on Earth to help those who had had an abortion. What was probably more amazing is that this church maintains the fervent loyalty and devotion of those who disagree with these positions.

Now I'll Listen, Lord

I joined Toastmasters in an effort to open up new vistas. Someone there heard me speak and gave me a tape with a witness I would recommend to anyone. He said, "Tom, I think you will really appreciate this. I realize it could be offensive, and so I will never mention it again. However, if you like it, I have several other similar ones." It was Scott Hahn's testimony, a man who went through every contortion I had gone through in Protestant theology. At any other point in my life, I would have thrown the tape away because it was Catholic, but the Lord's school of discipline had finally softened my hard head enough to listen. I couldn't refute anything he said. That meant I would have to study more. I asked for the rest of the tapes and was stunned to hear the testimonies of several former Protestant ministers who had converted to Catholicism.

The tapes and my accompanying reading addressed what had been gnawing at my sanity for a couple of years—the issue of authority. I had upset the comfort zone of everyone around me by simply going through every aspect of our church life and asking, "Who authorized this?" The typical reply of "the Bible" was beginning to be unmasked for the ruse it was. An open Bible on a pulpit authorizes nothing. It takes a person to read it and then authorize some form of action. I was beginning to see that we probably had a thousand different voices in the Protestant world authorizing various doctrines and practices in the church, all from the same Bible. What we did was pick the voice we thought best expressed the intent of the Scriptures. I was haunted by the conclusion that was forming in the back of my mind— everything we did was self-authorized. In the end, it was my individual decision that said, "The Bible says we must do this."

Scott Hahn addressed this issue head-on. The Reformation doctrine of *sola Scriptura* says that the Bible is the sole source of authority for faith and practice. The only problem with that idea is that it is not taught in the one place it should be taught—the

Bible. Hahn made that very clear, and I was ready to hear it. But what was left? Could it possibly be the unbroken tradition of apostolic authority established by Christ Himself? That authority loomed before me now. I knew that I could not do what Scott Hahn had done. He studied every last doctrine and document, consulted with the best anti-Catholic scholars he could find, and finally concluded that the Roman Catholic Church was the one true Church. That approach seemed to me to be more of the self-authorizing route I was trying to abandon.

I saw myself more in the role of the Roman centurion asking for a healing in his household (Luke 7:1-10). His doctrine and understanding were probably woefully inadequate. All he needed was the source of authority. Jesus commended his faith as greater than all the scribes in the land. My white flag had already been hoisted. I wanted to surrender to an authority greater than myself. I would conform my belief to this authority and not the other way around. To my great surprise, when I first attended a Mass, I found the words of that centurion forever memorialized in the Liturgy of the Eucharist as the congregation responds to the invitation to come to the Lord's Supper: "Lord, I am not worthy to receive You; only say the word and I shall be healed." Thus before I ever attended my first Mass, I was emotionally converted. But emotional conversion is not adequate. I needed to actually meet with Catholics and attend Mass and study and pray. For the first time in my life, I was willing to do it.

A Strange Welcome

In my metaphor of the man born on the wrong side of the sea, I could now see that I had often sailed past the harbor I was looking for because the harbor was Rome. At times in my journey, I would hear the distant call of her voice, but as I sailed our ship in that direction, I would recognize it was Rome and pass it by, only to wonder why the voice faded. Other times, I would see the light of the blessed port I sought and head in its direction, only to overshoot it and see its light fade. What I didn't know was that I was tacking across the ocean, zigzagging ever nearer to my sought-after harbor. Each time I passed it by, I was actually closer. Finally, I could smell her sweet fragrances and wondered why they faded as I passed by the one place I knew was not my destination.

Scott Hahn's tape brought me to the shore. Shoals and crashing surf had beaten my ship to splinters, but I was like a mad Captain Ahab, determined to meet my destiny. I finally understood that all I sought for was present in the nearest Catholic Church. Jesus was there in the Blessed Sacrament, watched over by a successor to the Apostles with authority to absolve my sin. Overwhelmed, weary, beaten, guilty, forsaken, and hungry, I drove to the nearest Catholic parish. I made an appointment to see the pastor. There I met a man who, in an attempt to encourage me, said all the wrong things. He scoffed at the idea that he was in the line of succession from the apostles and told me other things I pray he has since reconsidered. I forgave him. I told him that he could be a drunken homosexual and I didn't care, because I knew he had the authority I was seeking.

Once again, my greatest deterrent to finding my way home came from within the Church, not without. God forgive us. I had found the pearl of great price, and it has cost me everything. This priest's confusion wasn't going to deter me. I started attending Mass at his parish. But I sought out other help from someone who could understand why I had crossed the ocean to come home.

Tangible, Visible Authority

I was at a Mass once where a deacon was going to read the Gospel. Before he was permitted this responsibility, he bowed his head before the priest, who blessed him and authorized him to carry out a task that tens of thousands of Protestants perform without batting an eye. To me, the image was clearly speaking of authority. The deacon had to be authorized by the priest to even read the Gospel. The priest is authorized by the bishop, to serve in his place, so to speak. Bishops are appointed by the pope as successors to the Apostles. There was the authority I was seeking.

Another incident I observed will further illustrate this. I had begun the practice of visiting as many different Catholic Masses as I could, even though I could not partake of Communion. One Sunday, I took a seat in a church and watched the usual reverence of worshippers arriving early to kneel in private prayer before the service began. I saw a young mother come in with a babe in arms and a three-year-old son trailing behind. The boy seemed to be watching everything but his mother as she found a seat a few rows ahead of me. She knelt at the end of the pew, in reverence of the presence of Christ in the Tabernacle. As she rose to make her way down the aisle, her son arrived, and not knowing any different, he knelt as he had seen his mother do. I was genuinely moved. Where, in this world, does anyone learn respect and reverence for anything? The authority present in a Catholic church brought a toddler to his knee, even though he didn't know why. All he knew was that there was some reason to kneel in a Catholic church. I thought about the hundreds of evangelical churches in which I had worshiped and in which there was nothing worthy of such respect.

I knew I was coming home. I knew I was seeing something I had longed for all my life. Sometimes I could smell the bouquet of the Communion wine. How had I lived all my life without it? How could I live any more without it? I was already beginning to lose the ability to communicate with old friends. As an Evangelical Protestant, you define home as a place without repetitious prayer, without images and statues, without prayers to saints, without devotion to Mary, without priests, without an altar, without purgatory, penance, and confession. When you break free of that and begin searching for a home with all those things, you are left with almost nothing but arguments. I didn't want to argue. Neither did anyone who knew me before. They simply didn't want to encourage me to go down this path. I had to go alone.

A Warm Welcome

I felt like the prodigal son who grew tired of eating with the pigs. I was going home. I called Monsignor Laurence Higgins and explained that I was a Protestant minister seriously considering converting. He cleared a space for me on his busy schedule and met me with a broad smile and arms wide open as I walked into his office. Earlier I had met with Father Philip Scott, who had his entire religious order pray for me. Through Monsignor Higgins, I was introduced to Bishop Thomas Larkin. It took all three of these men of God to keep me in one piece while taking classes, working at nights, and trying to find a new vocational direction for my life. During this time, I found great solace in the Mass, even though I could not partake of the Eucharist. I learned to pray the rosary, and would frequently take time to sit before the Blessed Sacrament in any church I happened to pass.

When most of the dust had settled, Bishop Thomas Larkin took me through a condensed RCIA program and arranged a private Mass for me to be received into the Church. On May 14, 2002, on the Feast of St. Matthias, I was welcomed into the one, holy, Catholic, and apostolic Church. When this seventh change came—into the Catholic Church—I was all alone. Except I wasn't. Monsignor Higgins sponsored me, and Father Philip Scott concelebrated in this holy feast where I first tasted what my soul had ever longed for—the body and blood, soul and divinity of our Lord Jesus Christ. I had earlier attended an Easter Vigil. It was the first time I had ever heard the Litany of the Saints. That tune is ever in my head. I am not alone. I never was. And I never will be. I am home.

Home

Home. It is what drives the Pacific salmon to turn away from the vast waters of the ocean to head inland. Sensing a call to spawn where she was spawned, she will brave peril, danger, difficulty, and exhaustion to answer that call. Once she starts her journey, she will never know the help of her natural element. Upstream, always upstream, she will struggle mile after mile against swift currents that at times become raging torrents. She will brave them all and then somehow summon the strength to jump time after time up spills of water, defying the waterfalls. She is driven by something unseen to arrive at all costs at her destination, the place of her origin, that place on Earth that nurtured and sustained her first days of life.

The call of home is that powerful. On the day I was received into the Church, I stood with my hand surgically pinned together after a recent fall. I had a mountain of medical bills as a result and no steady employment. I had no title, position, or honor. I was a divorcé, prevented by Church law from marrying again. I was still emotionally bruised, still weary from my journey, still confused about my future, still hurting from my ordeal. The timing couldn't be worse. It was that dreadful time in 2002 after the Pope John Paul II's urgent meeting with the American cardinals and before the conference of bishops in June. The news was full of stories about abuse, corruption, cover-up, and scandal in the Church I was joining. As her flaws were uncovered, I was transfixed by her beauty. There was not a happier man on Earth.

Our Lord told a parable about a man who found a treasure hidden in a field. He sold everything he owned to buy the field. He was a wise man. I was a fool. He willingly sold all he had. I had to have everything stripped from me to realize the value of the treasure in that field. Anyone who reads this, please understand. I have not lost anything. I have only gained. What the world sees as a little round wafer of wheat, I recognize as a treasure worth more than everything else I have. As long as I live, I will ever praise my God for loving me enough to chase me into His kingdom.

A Final Plea

I do not share this story to magnify any heroic effort on my part, for there is no heroism here except for the man of Calvary, God in human flesh, willing to taste death for our redemption. I relate my journey to instruct others about the vast and treacherous distance that separates those who freely dine at the Lord's Table from those who seek to satisfy themselves on something less. I hope to encourage others to make the same journey I made, only more willingly. I also hope to assist good Catholics everywhere to never cease in their labors to invite all men everywhere to this wonderful feast of love. There is no price too high, no sacrifice too precious, and no demand too great for the privilege of dining at the table where Jesus comes to us in the Eucharist.

Originally published in the CHNewsletter *May 2003.*

Tom was first a Baptist minister and finally a minister in the Nicene Covenant Church. He was received into the Catholic Church in May 2002. He now runs the Office of Evangelization and Adult Formation for St. Ignatius of Antioch Catholic Church in Tarpon Springs, Florida.

A Search for Truth

By Father Steven D. Anderson
former Charismatic Episcopal minister

My heart was pounding as I walked into the small café to meet with my bishop in the Charismatic Episcopal Church. In this meeting, in February 1999, I planned to inform Bishop Fick of my intention to come into full communion with the Roman Catholic Church. I was nervous and concerned about how he might take my news. I knew that making this announcement would produce in me a certain sense of finality. But I did not fully understand the depth of emotion this would touch. Welling up and overflowing inside me was the excitement that after all these years of searching for truth, I had found a great treasure. I was certain I was ready to become Catholic, and this brought a profound peace that carried me through the variety of emotions connected to such a drastic conversion.

Truth: *"I am the Way, the Truth, and the Life.*[1]

Mike McCaughna was a great friend during elementary and middle school. We were unbeatable in neighborhood football, had sleepovers, and got into a lot of mischief. Mike was a Baptist preacher's son. It was during our friendship, in the early seventies, that I began to question my faith in a good way. I was Presbyterian, but I liked visiting Mike's church as a boy because the singing was more upbeat, the preaching was more energetic, and they had altar calls. People would walk to the front of the church to give their life to Jesus. (I still do this at every

[1] John 14.6

Mass!) When I was fourteen, I prayed that Jesus would come into my heart and life, and I gave myself to Him. When I was sixteen, I received the baptism in the Holy Spirit in a dynamic, unquestionable way. My faith and hunger for the Scriptures came alive as never before. While this brought a power to live a more vibrant faith, another experience led me to fine tune my faith.

Like so many before me, when I was sixteen, I thought I really knew it all. And being newly filled with the Spirit, I was eager to talk about it. In a disagreement about the Bible one evening, Ray Scherf, a wonderful elder of our church, said something that became a driving force in my faith walk and will for the rest of my life. In the middle of our debate, he paused and said, "Steve, don't ever be afraid of the truth." I find it fascinating how something that simple stayed with me. But it was like a word from God. From that day on, I was committed to pursue the truth, even if it meant moving in a direction that made me uncomfortable.

The Bible: "All Scripture is inspired by God" [2]
The Holy Spirit has been the dynamic in my life—the *dunamis* or power. My journey was always for truth, and the Holy Spirit would lead me into all truth, as I studied the Bible and the writings of the early Church fathers. I imagine that if I could see in the spiritual world, I would see tracks in the ground where my heels have been dug in for the last twenty-some years. The Holy Spirit would consistently challenge me to believe every truth in the Bible.

Beginning with my spiritual re-birth of faith at sixteen, I experienced an insatiable desire to read the Bible. After two years with a steady diet of Spirit-filled prayer, Bible study, tape series, and retreats, I discerned that God was calling me to be a pastor in the church. So in 1977, I transferred to Oral Roberts University

[2] 2 Timothy 3:16

to study the Bible and prepare to be a pastor. I was determined to guide God's people into truth, not dead religion and with the Sprit's help, I would find that truth in the Bible.

I focused my studies on the Bible, and especially enjoyed learning Hebrew and Greek because they would be important tools for my quest. I remember my excitement when I reached the level where I could take classes that actually read books of the Bible in these original languages. One part of being scholarly was to research all the great Bible scholars and theologians through the ages, listen to their interpretations of a Bible passage or topic, determine the strengths and weaknesses of each argument, and then write my conclusions. This was like an intense and exciting mission to sift through the great mysteries of the Bible and discover once and for all the truth of the Holy Scriptures.

Like all great human missions, however, I encountered a problem. My determination in the Spirit remained strong, but my excitement was became checked by what I discovered in my pursuit of truth.

The first thing I realized was that I was not the first to attempt this noble task. Great men of faith before me had learned Greek and Hebrew and studied the Scriptures in detail. The problem was, however, their great scholarship not withstanding, they all came up with different opinions, even those from the same theological or denominational backgrounds. It became apparent how each scholar's theology, experience, agenda, and culture influenced his or her interpretation of the biblical text. As a result, I gradually realized that my search for truth was a more complex struggle than I ever expected, and overcoming my own biases would make this an even harder quest.

Pursuing truth in the Bible is a great endeavor. However, for me as a Protestant, the Bible itself raised many concerns, verses that we referred to as "hard passages." All too often, these passages taught things contrary to what we believed based on other Scriptures. We would set these aside, up on the shelf so to speak, until we either came across a definitive answer or until we "get to heaven." In heaven, we planned to ask Jesus what these verses truly meant. What I didn't expect to discover was how clear the Bible would become once seen through the eyes of Catholic Tradition, and this began twenty years later, at a private dinner with a Protestant brother.

Dinner with Dave: "They examined the Scriptures daily to see if these things were so"[3]

Dave was a preacher in a Bible-believing denomination. He seemed genuinely troubled that I would become Catholic after believing in the Bible alone as the source of my faith and in faith alone as the key to eternal life. We agreed to meet for dinner at a local Big Boy restaurant for a friendly discussion. I let Dave set the agenda for our discussion by asking if he could tell me his most pressing concern about the Catholic Church. That was easy—the Catholic Church, he said, undermined the Word of God by its man-made tradition. Jesus had rebuked the Pharisees for this same thing. We agreed to discuss this particular issue at dinner.

I asked Dave if he would be comfortable preaching that *"a man is justified by works and not by faith alone"* (James 2:20). We discussed how this was the only place in the Bible where the words "faith alone" appeared together, and I was surprised when he said he would never preach this in his church. I challenged him to consider that the doctrine of "faith alone" is a man-made tradition from the Reformation and is refuted in the Bible. I also challenged him to consider that his tradition undermined this Bible verse.

Dave began to question me concerning important verses he thought Catholics did not believe. He asked if I believed Ephesians 2:8-9 which said, *"For by grace you have been saved by faith, and it is not from you; it is the gift of God; it is not*

---

[3] Acts 17:11

from works, so no one may boast." Yes, I certainly believe that. Catholics fully believe that *"it is by grace that we are saved, and again it is by grace that our works can bear fruit for eternal life"* (*Catechism of the Catholic Church*, No. 1697). We thank the Holy Spirit in us for bringing us to faith, and we thank Jesus, who lives in us, for continuing to do good works through us. To God be the glory! Many of my Protestant friends did not know the official Catholic teaching about grace and good works.

We followed this pattern through many different places in the Bible. The verses I shared showed how the Catholic teaching on Baptism, Tradition, and the Eucharist come directly from the Bible.

Baptism:
- This prefigured baptism, which now saves you. (1 Peter 3:21)
- He saved us . . . through the bath of rebirth and renewal by the Holy Spirit. (Titus 3:5)

Tradition:
- Therefore, brothers, stand firm and hold fast to the traditions that you were taught, either by an oral statement or by a letter of ours (2 Thessalonians 2:15).
- I praise you because you remember me in everything and hold fast to the traditions, just as I handed them on to you (1 Corinthians 11:2).

Eucharist:
- The cup of blessing that we bless, is it not a participation in the blood of Christ? The bread that we break, is it not a participation in the body of Christ? (1 Corinthians 10:16).
- 'I am the living bread that came down from heaven; whoever eats this bread will live forever; and the bread that I will give is my flesh for the life of the world.' The Jews

quarreled among themselves, saying, 'How can this man give us his flesh to eat?' Jesus said to them, 'Amen, amen, I say to you, unless you eat the flesh of the Son of Man and drink His blood, you do not have life within you. Whoever eats My flesh and drinks My blood has eternal life, and I will raise him on the last day. For My flesh is true food, and My blood is true drink. Whoever eats My flesh and drinks My blood remains in Me and I in him. Just as the living Father sent Me and I have life because of the Father, so also the one who feeds on Me will have life because of Me. This is the bread that came down from heaven' . . . Then many of His disciples who were listening said, 'This saying is hard; who can accept it?' . . . As a result of this, many of His disciples returned to their former way of life and no longer accompanied Him (John 6:51-66).

Dave admitted that he did not believe what these Bible verses were plainly saying. In the end, his tradition of faith alone and the Bible alone would undermine his desire to believe every truth written in the Word of God. I know, because I had been there. Where does it say in the Bible that if we simply label a verse a "hard passage" we can ignore it and we do not have to believe it? Dave continued to raise some verses he thought Catholics do not believe. But every verse he introduced is believed within the Catholic tradition. I was almost surprised by the outcome: Protestant tradition, not Catholic tradition, would sometimes undermine the Word of God. I no longer struggled with hard passages. The Bible, which came alive for me by the Holy Spirit, truly is a Catholic book. My Catholic faith was strengthened. I was able to believe all that the Bible teaches.

Apostolic Tradition: "They devoted themselves to the teaching of the apostles"[4]

At Oral Roberts University, my excitement was growing about a class that was coming up. Being raised Presbyterian

(Reformed) and having become Charismatic, I had a class coming up that was taught by a man who was Reformed and Charismatic. Dr. Charles Farah taught Systematic Theology III, and the class was devoted to integrating these two parts of my spiritual formation. When he became ill, Dr. Williams, an Eastern Orthodox convert, took the class, but he changed the area of focus. Instead of studying Reformed and Charismatic theology, we got a steady dose of early Church Fathers with an Eastern Orthodox twist. Many of us were quietly outraged. Dr. Williams seemed to convert two or three seminarians each year to the Eastern Orthodox Church. We had the Bible. We had the Spirit. Why were we learning our faith from a man who valued a religion of dead ritual?

Catholic from the Start: "I will build My Church"[5]

One of the Church Fathers we read was Justin Martyr who wrote around 140 A.D. Justin was interesting because his writing includes the earliest description of a church service. This was great! This would be proof in writing that the Church was a simple Bible-believing, Spirit-filled worshipping community. I dived into the reading with tremendous anticipation. What would it say? I was shocked. I remember hearing myself saying, "Look how fast they fell away from the faith!" I then sensed the Holy Spirit warning me, "No Steve, it is you who are two thousand years removed from the Apostles." I read it again with an open mind. The first recorded church service had all the elements of the Catholic Mass. This was difficult to accept, but I still had a way out. The Episcopal liturgy resembles the Catholic Mass. My prejudice against Catholicism ultimately meant that I would become Episcopal first.

---

[4] Acts 2:42

[5] Matthew 16:18

Unity: *"Complete my joy being of the same mind"*[6]

A second Church Father would change my life. Irenaeus was bishop of Lyons, France, from 180 to 202 A.D. He was the disciple of Polycarp, bishop of Smyrna, who was the disciple of the Apostle John. The historians I read were somewhat uninterested in Irenaeus, because they said he added nothing new to the development of Christian theology. Aha, my interest was piqued. A bishop in the second century who taught nothing new, but authentically passed on the apostolic faith. Irenaeus himself contends that his teaching is the very teaching of the apostles. One of his books was even titled *Proof of the Apostolic Preaching.* Then he wrote the most fascinating thing. In another of his books, *Against Heresies*, Irenaeus challenged his readers not to take his word alone but to go to any of the bishops of any of the churches in his day because **they are all teaching the same thing.** Tears came to my eyes. I said, "Not anymore, Irenaeus, today we all tend to teach our own thing." I began reading everything this faithful bishop had written, looking for the true faith that was held with one mind at the beginning of the Church.

The Pope's Authority: *"You are Peter, and on this rock I will build My Church"*[7]

Then came the most amazing statement of all. I had been taught that Pope Gregory the Great was the one who first claimed universal authority for the pope in the sixth century, but Irenaeus proved this wrong. He was explaining to his reader how he could easily list the apostolic succession of every bishop of every church in his time. But to do so would require too much space in his book. He decided he would give only the apostolic succession of the bishop of the Church of Rome. Why? Because, he said, everyone had to agree with that church because of its

[6] Philippians 2:2

[7] Matthew 16:18

"pre-eminent authority." The authority of the Church of Rome went back to the teaching of the apostles! My eventual decision to come into full communion with the Roman Catholic Church was influenced profoundly by St. Irenaeus. To my delight, Irenaeus' writings were steeped in biblical references. He was a remarkable bishop who was faithful and wholly committed to one thing: passing on the apostolic tradition he had received from Polycarp, who had received it from John, who had lain on the bosom of our Lord Jesus Christ.

The Eucharist: "Do this in memory of Me"[8]

All the earliest writers gave a special importance to the Eucharist. The *Didache*, Justin Martyr, and especially Ignatius of Antioch gave instructions and directions concerning the Eucharist. Eucharist was the center of the early Church's worship. The question I had was whether to emphasize the words "This is My body" or "Do this in memory." Was the Eucharist always understood to be the body of Christ, or was the Eucharist originally just a memorial? What I came to understand was that the biblical use of "memory" was much more than merely recalling a past event.

When the Jews in the Bible, who lived a thousand years after the time of Moses, would remember the great events of the Exodus, they spoke as if they were the ones actually there. The ritual remembering connected them to the event. When Jesus commands, "Do this in memory of Me," he intends that we relive the Eucharist in a way that we actually participate in the original once-for-all sacrifice of Jesus Christ two thousand years ago. This is the reason Paul says, "The cup of blessing that we bless, is it not a participation in the blood of Christ? The bread that we break, is it not a participation in the body of Christ" (1

---

[8] Luke 22:19

Corinthians 10:16)? "Do this in memory of Me" and "This is My body" are two sides of the same coin!

Jumping In: "And immediately they left their nets and followed Jesus"[9]

"Don't they know what that means?" my dad exclaimed as he dialed the phone. It was 1974, and he was calling a family whose teenage son was dating a Catholic girl! As a boy, I listened to my dad explain the many dangers of the Catholic Church. I would not be able to become Catholic easily. Much of my seminary training involved anti-Catholic apologetics. Evangelism Explosion trained me to evangelize and even provided the tracts and technique for evangelizing Catholics because they did not believe in faith alone. These kinds of things created a deep bias in me. I was carrying significant emotional baggage that resisted becoming Catholic.

Throughout my life, I had studied the Bible and now I had found it to be Catholic. Church history was Catholic. Tradition was Catholic. Because of this journey for truth, I had become Catholic in faith and worship style, but I was not in communion with the Catholic Church. Why? I decided to explore the possibility of coming into full communion with the Catholic Church.

What About Mary: "Most blessed are you among women, and blessed is the fruit of your womb"[10]

My wife, Cindy, and I would talk almost every day in the fall of 1998. What about Mary? What about the pope? We went through every issue quite thoroughly and we took our time. Though I was committed to finding the truth, I loved being the pastor of the wonderful people at Church of the Resurrection. There was no hurry. Looking back, I imagine that I looked at

[9] Matthew 4:20
[10] Luke 1:42

every issue so closely because we did not want to leave Resurrection. What would being Catholic mean for us? What would it be like to be Catholic? Ultimately, I needed to be honest.

Someone once told me that if you want to know what Israelis think, don't ask Palestinians. To find out what Catholics truly believe about Mary, I could no longer be honest if I only asked anti-Catholics. I read the *Catechism of the Catholic Church*. Catholic teaching is very clear. The faithful are to worship only God, and Catholics worship God as Trinity—Father, Son, and Holy Spirit. Catholics use the words "adore" or "adoration" for worship but the words "venerate" or "veneration" with reference to the respect and honor that is appropriate for human beings. Catholic teaching forbids the worship of Mary, but Catholics venerate her as the mother of Jesus, Who is fully God and fully man. Catholics also ask Mary to intercede for them to her Son Jesus Christ. This teaching is clear and consistent.

Some people very close to me said, "I do not care what the Catholic Church teaches; when I look at those people, I can plainly see they are worshipping Mary." Sounds like Archie Bunker saying, "Don't bore me with the facts. I've already made up my mind." In all fairness, even if someone wrongly did worship Mary, this does not mean Catholics worship Mary any more than the Pentecostal who reads his horoscope means Pentecostals believe in astrology. Both people act contrary to the clear teachings of their church. Catholics honor Mary (and Scripture), who proclaims in the Bible: "from now on will all ages call me blessed." And in the same way Protestants ask friends to pray for them, Catholics ask their friends in heaven to pray for them. They are a great cloud of witnesses!

Others ask, "Why don't Catholics go directly to Jesus, who intercedes perfectly for us in heaven?" But, strangely, at the same time, they belong to the Intercessors Prayer Group at their Protestant church. It is common for Protestants to ask someone to intercede for them in prayer. Why won't they ask those who live closest to the Lord in heaven to intercede for them in prayer? Talk about an untapped prayer resource.

One day, Cindy was praying in the car, asking God about the Immaculate Conception of Mary. Until that time, Cindy did not believe it. In her prayer, God revealed the reasons for this great truth. She came home excited to tell me about how the Holy Spirit had revealed to her the reasons for the Immaculate Conception. I was in shock. I got out the Catechism and read back to her almost word for word what she told me. I had just finished studying in the teachings of the Catholic Church the very words she had heard in prayer. I kidded that it must be nice not having to study.

When we realized we were Catholic, we quit protesting against the Catholic Church. Obviously, the word Protestant is a reference to the five hundred year protest against the Catholic Church. This culture of protesting is so strong with some that one of the Charismatic Episcopal Church teachers coined the phrase "Romaphobia." Many Christians will not believe or practice something just because Rome does. I realized that the abuses that existed in the Church in the Middle Ages were corrected a long time ago. It was in the Charismatic Episcopal Church that I realized how much we Protestants had thrown out the baby with the bathwater.

Infant Baptism in the Bible: "This promise is for you and for your children"[11]

Just before I was ordained a priest in the Charismatic Episcopal Church in 1995, I had to struggle with my position on infant baptism. The CEC baptized infants, and I needed to be one hundred percent sure I believed in it, too. In Peter's first sermon on the day of Pentecost, he said to them:

[11] Acts 2:39

Repent and be baptized, every one of you, in the name of Jesus Christ for the forgiveness of your sins; and you will receive the gift of the Holy Spirit. For the promise is made for you and to your **children** and to all those far off, whomever the Lord our God will call *(Acts 2:38-39)*.

Many who do not believe in infant baptism claim that the word "children" here refers to descendants, not necessarily their children alive at the time. So I let the Bible determine how the word "children" would be interpreted. I looked in the Greek to see what word was used in this verse. The Greek word is *teknon*. I studied every place that it was used in the New Testament. In every single case, it means a person already born. *Teknon* never means a potential person. It could mean "descendant" in the sense of a person being a child of Abraham, but in every instance, that person was always already born. A descendant of Abraham not yet born is called the "seed" of Abraham.

This distinction between a "child" meaning someone already born and "seed" meaning someone not yet born is consistently followed. This is especially true in the Gospel of Luke and the Acts of the Apostles. Therefore, the "children" in Acts 2:39 must have been born already. They were "children," not "descendants." Baptism is for children! This helps interpret verses in which a person and his whole household were baptized.

In Colossians 2, baptism is compared to circumcision. Circumcision was performed on children born into the covenant, and on converts and their children, too. Children were always included in the Old Testament covenant and were marked by the sign of the covenant. How discouraging if children could not be baptized, the mark of the New Covenant? Interestingly, a study of the New Testament era reveals that Gentile converts to Judaism were washed in a ritual bath—their children, too! The words that were spoken over them in this ritual bath are remarkably similar to the words used in the New Testament to describe Baptism and its effects.

Baptism in the Early Church: "Let the children come to me, and do not prevent them"[12]

The Church Fathers who address infant baptism all attribute it to apostolic tradition. Some misleadingly teach that Tertullian, the first of the Fathers to speak of infant baptism, was against it. What they failed to mention was that he wanted everyone, not just infants, to wait until they were near death so they would not abandon their faith after baptism. He acknowledged that infant baptism was the early practice, but those who abandoned the faith later in life scandalized him. Interestingly, I was told that a recent study showed that a higher percentage of people baptized after the age of reason fall away from their faith than those baptized as infants. I wondered why we were not taught the whole truth.

The first Christian to describe the baptism of people of various ages was Hippolytus, around 210 A.D. He instructs the faithful to baptize the little ones first. If they can speak for themselves, let them do so. If they cannot yet speak for themselves, then let a parent or sponsor speak for them. Then baptize the men, and last the women. Hippolytus claims that this is the tradition that was passed down from the Apostles. "Believer's baptism" that required all children to wait until the age of reason, I learned, was never practiced for those children who grew up within the Church until the Reformation, fifteen hundred years after the fact. Any early Christians who delayed Baptism for their children, for any reason, were firmly rebuked for denying this grace-filled sacrament to the infants. What a tremendous joy it has been for me to baptize many little ones into the New Creation in Jesus Christ.

---

[12] Matthew 19:14

Conversion: "We have given up everything and followed you"[13]

Coming into full communion with the Roman Catholic Church in 1999 brought a great sense of fulfillment. Conversion, though, always has two sides. Those who have gone through conversion know this. I was certain I would become Catholic. I was uncertain what becoming Catholic would mean to all the cherished friendships I valued as a priest in the Charismatic Episcopal Church. Peter once questioned Jesus, saying, "We have given up everything and followed You. What will there be for us?" Jesus responded, "Everyone who has given up houses or brothers or sisters or father or mother or children or lands for the sake of My name will receive a hundred times more and will inherit eternal life" (Matthew 19:27,29). So, all wrapped up together, I experienced the excitement and joy of gaining such a rich Catholic faith with the potential of losing many of the people I loved the most.

The convocation of the Great Lakes Diocese of the Charismatic Episcopal Church in 1998 provided a good opportunity for people to get to know their diocese. Those who attended from my parish, Church of the Resurrection, were astonished to hear our Bishop introduce me to the diocese with such favorable words. He said that he loved all his priests, but that I was like a son to him. I genuinely felt this same close bond. Now, I wondered, could our bond endure this important change in my life?

As we gathered, we were amazed to discover so many others who had been on the same journey. At one time, each of us had thought that he was the only one who believed in the Bible, the power of the Holy Spirit, and the sacraments and liturgy all at the same time. The Charismatic Episcopal Church was a brand-new denomination of like-minded men and women attempting to recover and balance these three strands we felt essential to

---

[13] Matthew 19:27

the Christian tradition—the Bible, the power of the Holy Spirit, and the sacraments and liturgy. We were committed to growing in the truth, and it took courage to break from our previous faith traditions and ministries to walk in this new convergence of three streams.

Those closest to me were my church family at Resurrection. Four years earlier, in the spring of 1995, it all began when my wife and I had dinner with a couple in Brighton, Michigan. They were former Episcopalians who were looking for the same expression of the Christian faith that we had in the Charismatic Episcopal Church. Soon after this dinner, we began to meet with five other families of like mind. In June, I was ordained to the transitional deaconate, and within a few months, others had joined with us to become the founding members of the Church of the Resurrection. On September 15 in the same Mass, we were received as a mission parish, and I was ordained a priest.

Each year for a couple of years, the membership of Resurrection doubled until we leveled off. We grew together. Everyone participated according to his or her gifts, and I grew to be the pastor and father of a family knit together in love. As was the developing custom of the Charismatic Episcopal Church, my wife and I planned to be at Resurrection for life.

When we left in 1999, the profound depth of grief and loss was overwhelming. Those we were closest to in the parish and diocese seemed to cut us off. Perhaps they felt hurt, abandoned, or betrayed. For many, conversion has some very real costs. Peter and Jesus remind us of this. Weeping on my bed from my personal loss, I said to Cindy (who sat graciously beside me), "No one will ever know what this was like." But people do know. My personal conversion contains many common elements that others have experienced. In the same way, I suspect that my personal reasons for coming into full communion with the Roman Catholic Church will speak to some of those courageous people who are going through this same process.

The most difficult step in my journey, however, was meeting in that café to inform my CEC bishop of my decision to become Catholic. He was sympathetic; even admitted that he would become Catholic, too, but he knew that cannon law would prevent him being the pastor of a church. He was a pastor and could not give it up. The thought of not being a priest was devastating to me, too. I suggested that only he could know how tough my decision really was. Maybe they would not let me be a priest, but they would allow me to be obedient. He had another concern. I could appreciate the rich treasure of the Catholic faith and leave so much to gain it, he said, but other Catholics would not have this same appreciation of their faith. They would walk out of the church from the Communion line, he said; they would not even wait for the blessing. When I finally came into the Catholic Church, I watched after Mass on Sundays. Some would take Communion and leave immediately, but most returned to their pew and most of these knelt to pray until Communion ended. Most Catholics who attend church do appreciate their faith.

My journey of truth will always continue, but my journey for the true Church has brought me home. Cindy and I have never looked back. Many of our former parishioners and diocesan friends have been restored to us. Some have even joined us in full communion with the Roman Catholic Church. Remarkably, the priest who replaced me at Resurrection has become Catholic, too! We did not give up any of our faith. I am still a Bible Christian. I am still a Charismatic. Ultimately, I kept what I had and added to it the fullness of the Catholic Faith that has been guarded faithfully, in an unbroken line, from the time of the Apostles and Jesus Christ. Moreover, I have learned, grown, and been enriched from the faith walk and wisdom of many saints who have loved Jesus with all their hearts, minds, and strength for almost two thousand years.

202   *Journeys Home*

Originally published in the CHNewsletter *August 2003.*

Fr. Anderson, a former Charismatic Episcopal priest, was received into the Catholic Church on Easter 1999. He was ordained a Catholic priest in June 2003. He lives with his wife Cindy and their three sons (Austin, Steven, and Christian) in Grand Blanc, Michigan and ministers at Holy Family Catholic Church.

The Spiritual Journey

By Don and Ruth Newville
former Assembly of God minister

Ruth and I were born into Protestant families, raised in the church, and saved at an early age. Eventually I was ordained as an Assembly of God minister, and we served eight years in missions, five of them in Africa. Our desire has been to please God in all we do. We have sought Him and served Him wholeheartedly. We never dreamed, therefore, that there would come a time when we would decide that we could no longer continue in the Protestant ministry or even remain Protestant. Even though we were a mere three-years short of retirement, we had decided to give up our ministry and means of support to join the Catholic Church.

Why would anyone in his right mind want to do that? In the pages that follow, I will try to show you that what we did was God's will for us. My hope is that it will spark your interest to study these matters further.

I should have been born in a log cabin, but it burned down the year before I was born. My parents were small time dairy farmers with lots of kids. The ninth of eleven, I was born on July 9, 1940. By age fourteen, I was saved, baptized, and confirmed. I graduated from high school in May 1958. My career goal was to enter the ministry in our Evangelical United Brethren denomination. I enrolled at Wisconsin State College in Eau Claire because I heard they had a good pre-seminary course and it was close to home.

In my second year of college, I met Ruth. She was American Baptist, a seriously committed Christian, who wanted a good

Christian husband. We fell madly in love and were married on May 28, 1960. Before I proposed, however, she had to agree to go with me wherever God would lead us, even to Africa if necessary. She gladly agreed. Forty-two years later, she still agrees.

In June 1968, I graduated with a master of science in social work. I had specialized in administration and supervision, and I worked in those kinds of positions for many years thereafter. The first of these was in Milwaukee. There we found our EUB pastor from six years earlier. He had transferred to a small United Methodist church near our new home. The EUB had merged with the Methodist Church to become the United Methodists.

In June 1971, we moved back to our home area, where I took a social work supervisor position in a rural county. We wanted to get our three children away from the evils of the big city. I kept that job for nine years, and we raised our children on a farm.

A neighbor lady invited us to the nearby Lutheran church, and we became active members. We liked the pastor and the people. One Sunday afternoon, our three children were baptized. We thought Marie was still too young, but since Lutherans baptize infants, we went along with it. Spiritually, however, I still didn't know what to believe. The Lutherans had a liturgy, which was a new experience for us. They read their prayers. We had been taught that prayer should be spontaneous, but their doctrine was biblical enough to satisfy our Evangelical beliefs about Jesus.

Another event, three years later, would seal the deal. Our Lutheran pastor became Spirit-filled and invited another Lutheran to preach in our church. He taught about the Holy Spirit and prayed for people to be baptized in the Spirit. This was all new to us, but it was in our own Lutheran church, all very orderly, and nothing like what we had heard about Pentecostals. On the last night, Ruth, our teenage son, and I went up for prayer and received the Holy Spirit. It was an event that changed our lives.

After becoming Spirit-filled, my old call to the ministry resurfaced. Could it be we were still supposed to be in ministry?

I explored seminaries. My Lutheran pastor gave me information about Luther Seminary in St. Paul, Minnesota. I considered the United Methodist seminary. I visited a Pentecostal school in Anaheim. I thought about Oral Roberts University. None of these seemed right.

In June 1980, Ruth and I visited a Bible school in Tulsa and attended its Sunday night service. That night we became convinced that God had called us to missions and that we should attend the school's two-year missions program. Ruth and I made an application the next morning and a few weeks later, we were accepted. We resigned our jobs and community positions, listed our farm for sale, rented a Ryder truck, and moved to Tulsa. So now, where should we go to church? What could be a reliable guide? We decided that a church pastored by a graduate of our Bible school would be a safe bet. We found one and started attending. It wasn't quiet and orderly like our Lutheran church, but they had the Spirit. They were independent and answered to no one. We soon left for another congregation and then another, all the while searching for truth and authority.

Some fellow graduates of the Bible school and members of our church were moving to Hawaii to plant a Faith Church. We had heard that Hawaii, despite its great attraction for tourists, was a very dark place spiritually. They asked us to join them. So in January 1983, we made our first visit to Hawaii. The couple we followed there attempted to start a church, gave up in a few weeks, and soon returned to Oklahoma and got divorced. We were finally cured of independent churches.

I was convinced we needed a church that had some structure and a firm belief system. It could not be everyone making up his own belief system. I thought an older, established church would be better, but not so old that it had grown cold and unspiritual. We started attending the First Assembly of God. The Assemblies had a history of more than seventy years, a long time in Pentecostal circles.

Over the years, I engaged in many ministries at First Assembly of God, including prison ministry, Communion deacon (the big task here was to fill eighteen hundred little cups with grape juice once a month), van deacon, counselor, teacher, and board member. After our children left home, we spent most of our non-working time in these various ministries.

In 1992, I decided to apply for licensing by the Assemblies of God. The denomination accepted my Bible school courses, much to my surprise. I had to complete a couple of correspondence courses, but in April 1993, I was licensed to preach. In early 1994, our interim pastor asked me to teach for three months at an AOG Bible school in Uganda. When we returned home, we were asked if we would return for a two-year term. We agreed, and in December 1994, we left our jobs, sold our condominium and car, gave away many things, and moved to Uganda.

In Uganda, we were troubled by the great diversity of Christian teachings. Ugandans were struggling so hard to recover from years of civil war. Instead of working together, each Protestant group was promoting its own particular brand of the Gospel. Some of my Bible school students were United Methodist, and they seemed just as holy as the Assembly of God students. Yet, the two church groups could not work together. In April 1999, we felt we had done what we could in Uganda and moved back to First Assembly in Hawaii. The Hawaii District of the Assemblies of God ordained me at its district council the week we arrived. It could have been done a few years earlier, but I was out of the country.

During one of our annual visits to America, in March 1998, I began to read stories by converts to the Catholic Church. Our Lutheran son had joined the Catholic Church after marrying a Catholic. He had studied long and hard before converting and I was still looking for something more than I was finding in the Assemblies, so I was open to learning why he had switched churches. We attended Mass with him and his wife. While I knew nothing about Catholic doctrine, other than the usual Protestant misconceptions I had picked up, I was drawn to the liturgy. I thought it was beautiful and full of God.

One of the books in my son's large collection was *Born Fundamentalist, Born Again Catholic* by David B. Currie. It was the story of the author's spiritual journey to the Catholic Church. He carefully explained the doctrines and why he agreed with them. This book unsettled me. Curie's spiritual background was similar to mine in many ways.

On my next visit, I read *Rome Sweet Home* by Scott and Kimberly Hahn. I had never heard of them before, but their book affected me. *Surprised by Truth,* edited by Patrick Madrid, really did surprise me as I read many conversion stories by people who I thought should have known better. I was beginning to have serious doubts about my AOG faith, but nevertheless, I faithfully continued in my ministry.

When we returned to the States in 1999, we once again had television and even cable. I discovered Eternal Word Television Network (EWTN). Mother Angelica, founder of EWTN, impressed even Ruth, who until this time had ignored my inquiry into the Church. On EWTN, I also discovered the *Journey Home* program, where a former Protestant pastor, now Catholic convert, Marcus Grodi, interviews other converts. The first time I saw it, I knew in my spirit that my Protestantism was in trouble. I don't remember who his guest was, but those guys had something I needed. I discovered that the Internet had mushroomed while we were in Africa and I found the website of the *Coming Home Network*, an organization established to aid Protestant clergy and laity in their exploration of the Catholic Church. Posted on its website are many conversion stories, and I read them all. Another feature was an e-mail discussion group, and I soon joined it. After lurking for a while, I dared to ask some questions, but I used my middle name. I wasn't ready to have my church know about my inquiry, and I didn't know who might be reading the list.

One of my first questions to the group was about praying to the saints. I had been taught that we cannot, and should not, talk to the earthly dead who are now living in heaven. God is against that, and besides, how could they hear us? There is no telephone hookup. Someone answered that the Holy Spirit conveys the prayers from us to them. Now, how could a good Pentecostal argue with that? Certainly, if God can hear us, and the Holy Spirit is God, and God is everywhere, then why can't He tell the residents of heaven what our prayer requests are? And if we can ask believers here on Earth to pray for us, as we all do, then why not ask those in heaven to do the same? I thought of it as God's e-mail system, with the Holy Spirit as the moderator.

This concept of praying to the saints opened the door to understanding requests to Mary. After all, who would be in a better position to intercede for us than the mother of Jesus? Since she was always close to Jesus during His earthly ministry, certainly she would be close to Him now. Just as she asked Him to solve the problem of the wine at the wedding feast, so now she would ask Him to meet our needs. He would grant His mother's request just as He did then.

In the spring of 2000, I taught a course at a Bible school in Hawaii. The course was "Twentieth Century Pentecost." In studying the Pentecostal movement that I had been involved in for almost twenty-five years, I discovered great instability. Each leader had his or her personal belief system. They fought bitterly while forming hundreds of nondenominational denominations. There was great fervor, many conversions, and healing miracles. But it always seemed to end in fights and confusion.

Then, in the fall of that year, I taught a course on the nature and character of God." The text we used was quite a theological study and quoted many early Catholic Church writers. I not only learned about the nature and character of God but some history of the Church as well. It moved me closer to Catholicism. Still studying about the Catholic Church, watching EWTN, and participating in the *Coming Home Network* discussion list, I was increasingly impressed with the doctrinal stability, morality, and authority of Catholics.

Visiting our son again in August 2000, I read and reread some of his books. He and I discussed the issues, and together we attended Mass and the Catholic charismatic prayer group. One by one, my objections to the Catholic Church were being answered. For the first time we discussed converting. Ruth wasn't in favor of it and said if I converted, I would probably be going to church alone. I was not in favor of that.

In June 2001, we decided to resign our position in Hawaii and return to our home state of Wisconsin. During the weeks between our resignation notice and leaving our church, Ruth went off to our son's home in Florida for the birth of our second Catholic grandson. While there for one month, she did some Catholic reading for the first time. She chose *Rome Sweet Home*. Reading the Hahns' story, she decided that if I converted, she would also. She didn't want to be spiritually separated as they had been.

However, while I was still finishing up in Hawaii, First Assembly prevailed upon me to return to Uganda for at least six months. I had left there in March 1999 and visited in March 2000 and January 2001. I knew the need was great and no one else was available to go. So after moving the family back to Wisconsin, we somewhat reluctantly returned to foreign missions.

I bought *Surprised by Truth 2* by Patrick Madrid and brought it along. While there, I read it through twice and Ruth read most of it. Fifteen people tell their stories in this book. Some were former Catholics who returned after years as Protestants. Others were lifelong Protestants. They each tell how God drew them to the Catholic Church and explained many of the doctrinal issues. To my surprise, the Internet had improved greatly in Uganda and it was possible to receive the *Coming Home Network* e-mail discussion list. It provided daily discussions of issues that concern potential converts. I also brought along the *Catechism of the Catholic Church* and read it all the way through. This book contains the official Vatican-approved beliefs of the Church. I had bought it a year earlier and had read parts of it. I was surprised to find that the basis of the teaching was the Apostles' and Nicene Creeds that I had learned way back in Confirmation and had reaffirmed at the end of my Bible school training. In Hawaii, I took notes from the Catechism and preached a series of sermons on the Creeds. Nothing in the Creeds conflicted with our Assembly of God beliefs. The Catechism is well presented and easy to follow. Hearing what Catholics themselves had to say about what they believed was much different from hearing the Protestant version of what the Catholics believed.

Settling back in Uganda, I was distressed by the problems in the churches that we had left behind. Without consistent leadership, much of what we had left in place had fallen apart. The other Protestant churches in the area were experiencing many disputes about doctrines, and great error and corruption were rampant. New little churches were springing up everywhere. Each one was right in its own eyes and better than the others. With my almost-Catholic eyes, I saw a fragmented, confused group of churches all competing with each other for members and money. It was not a pretty sight. Nevertheless, the Gospel and love of Jesus does go forth, and some souls are saved from the fires of hell. But I could see that there had to be a more lasting, more effective way. I noticed that the Catholics had a large church on each end of our town while there were over sixty little Protestant churches. Now I was beginning to understand why.

During our inquiry into the Catholic Church, we were looking for the whole truth and nothing but the truth. To our dismay, we discovered that Protestants have lost or purposely discarded several major benefits of the New Covenant. What the Catholic Church had recognized as truth was re-evaluated by the protesters, who had to make things fit their new "each one is his own authority" belief system. Who gave them the authority to overrule the Church Fathers? As I studied these, I could see no valid reasons for discarding these truths.

Authority was the biggest issue. From childhood, I have witnessed bitter wrangling over doctrines and morals among church members. Once the issue of who has the authority to decide these things is settled, everything else falls into place. Who should make decisions in the Church? Who can be trusted to do it right? Such questions have plagued me for a long time. I began to see that Peter and the other apostles had been given the authority to run the Church, and that they had passed this authority on to their successors. I found great comfort in that. From the very beginning, as shown in the book of Acts, the Apostles made decisions on the issues and sometimes held councils to assist in the process.

I had chosen the Assemblies of God because it was at least seventy years old and well established. It had wavered little from the views of its founders. Now, however, I had found a church that was nearly two thousand years old and had still not wavered from the views of its Founder, Jesus.

I had been taught that Communion was a memorial service and that the elements were only symbolic. Now I learned that the Catholics believed what Jesus said about eating His body and drinking His blood. They believed that the consecrated elements are literally His body and blood. They call it the *Real Presence*. I studied this issue very carefully in the Gospels and Epistles. I could see no reason not to believe what they said. I felt we were missing a great deal by not believing it.

As I studied the other six sacraments, I found the same thing. Catholics believe that in Baptism, Confirmation, Communion, Marriage, Anointing of the Sick, Penance (Reconciliation), and Holy Orders, God imparts His grace to us. These powerful gifts had been omitted from my previous belief system, and I could discover no good reason why. I felt cheated by our Protestant forefathers.

Removing books from the Bible was another maneuver the Protestant Reformers had used to ensure that the Bible supported their new beliefs. Although certain books had been approved as part of the Old Testament canon in the Church councils for more than a thousand years, suddenly the Reformers decided that these books were not as inspired as the others and threw them out. Again, on whose authority did they do this?

Trying to understand the role of Mary and the other saints was difficult. However, once I understood the difference between veneration and worship and between asking the saints to intercede for us and asking them to directly do things for us, I had no more trouble. I discovered they are not worshipped but are respected and honored and held in high regard. Only God is worshipped.

The rosary interested me, so I bought a little book and started praying it on occasion. I discovered the rosary was made up of Scripture verses and a prayer request. So in saying it, we are simply reciting Scripture and praying. During the recitation of the Hail Marys, we are asked to meditate on the life of Jesus and recall what He did for us. Even a good Protestant ought to be able to do that. It is all Scripture. After coming back to Uganda in October 2001, Ruth and I started praying the rosary together every morning.

Purgatory was another thing missing in my Protestant beliefs, so I had to find out what Catholics really believed. I especially liked what the Catechism had to say about it in paragraph 1030: "All who die in God's grace and friendship, but still imperfectly purified, are indeed assured of their eternal salvation; but after death they undergo purification, so as to achieve the holiness necessary to enter the joy of heaven." The idea of purifying made sense to me. I have known many believers who died with major flaws still in their lives. Surely they would want to be purified before coming into the full presence of God—I know I will!

We wanted to attend Mass to become familiar with it, but we felt we couldn't in Uganda or Hawaii. Explaining it to our church would be a bigger job than we cared to undertake. We didn't want to bring confusion to an already confused people. So we just shared the Gospel and the love of Jesus with them.

By late November, we were quite certain we would both join the Catholic Church upon our return home from Uganda. We would give up our mission work and my Assemblies of God ordination, which meant giving up our only means of support as well. I informed my church in Hawaii that I would be resigning and that we were "seriously considering joining the Catholic Church." I wrote a long letter to them and our close friends and relatives explaining our reasons. We thought the church might relieve us of our duties immediately, but instead they pleaded with us to stay. We agreed to complete our six-month commitment but stood firm in our resolve to move on after that. God had called us to this mission field, but now He was calling us home. We were eager to see what He has in store for us there.

In 2002, Ruth and I were received into full communion with the Catholic Church with its vastness, unity, and diversity. We knew there was dissent within it. We did not expect to find perfection. The forces of hell have attacked the Church all through the centuries, but Jesus said they would not prevail, and they have not and will not. Therefore, we expected to find the Church that Jesus Himself had founded, and we are grateful to be accepted as a part of it.

Leaving our church and ministry behind was not easy. We served the Lord with gladness in our Protestant churches — at First Assembly for twenty — and have no regrets. We wish to thank our parishioners and God for all they did for us. We gave our time and money, but the church gave much more than that to us in return. With sadness, we left First Assembly and our churches in Uganda. They loved us, and we loved them. We continue to thank God for them and pray that He will continue to bless them because they earnestly desire to do His will. May God bless all those who have helped us on our journey.

Originally published in the CHNewsletter *November 2003.*

After thirty-five years of missionary work in Africa andd Hawaii, Don and ruth were received into the Catholic Church in the fall of 2002. They are now active in lay ministry in their parish in Altoona, Wisconsin.

"The Land was Broad, Quiet, and Peaceful"

By Gerald and Jennifer Tritle
former Presbyterian minister

Throughout our spiritual journey, Jennifer and I always seemed to be advancing in one direction while our Christian friends were reverting to others. When we left the Charismatic movement for modern Evangelicalism, our friends were becoming Pentecostal. When we transitioned to the Reformed Presbyterian Church, our friends were migrating to modern Evangelicalism, and when our friends and acquaintances deserted Rome for Protestant Evangelicalism, we joyfully went to Rome.

I was born in Springfield, Ohio, into a line of Lutherans whom I can trace to sixteenth century Germany. Baptized and confirmed into the Lutheran Church, I worshipped with my grandparents and parents in this liturgical and sacramental environment until I reached age seven. My parents then quit attending church services, and we ceased discussing religion in our home. When I was twenty-two years old, a zealous Evangelical Christian presented the Gospel of Jesus Christ to me. Enlightened by the Holy Spirit, I consciously embraced Christ as Lord and joined the Assemblies of God, a Pentecostal denomination. I devoured the Sacred Scriptures and Pentecostal theology and ultimately, while maintaining my business vocation, became a lay minister. I never desired to become a full-time minister, but wanted instead to help build up the church, living out my faith as a layman.

Three years later, I transferred from the Assemblies of God to an independent Charismatic church that I believed was more aligned to the Scriptures' presentation of the early Church in polity and theology. From these experiences, I came to appreciate the Charismatics' respect and zeal for understanding the Scriptures. I also grew to pursue a right, authoritative church polity and an understanding of God's covenant with man. On the other hand, I became disenchanted with the Charismatics' errors of dispensational theology, a pietistic and pessimistic outlook on life and culture, and a discipleship that produced ascetic, self-absorbed believers who focused continually on their own psyches.

Jennifer's relatives, on the other hand, immigrated to America from Italy during the 1940s. Originally Catholic, they quickly converted to Protestantism, joining the Christian Church of North America (an Italian Pentecostal church). Her family's spiritual journey over several years included attending Nazarene, Free Methodist, Calvary Chapel, and Evangelical Free churches. Jennifer was baptized at age ten, but by age twenty, after having witnessed years of church infighting, pastoral immorality, and doctrinal immaturity, she became disillusioned with organized religion. The Holy Spirit intervened when she was twenty-one and opened her eyes to see that the Scriptures were the standard for faith and life and God required obedience to them.

Jennifer and I met in 1986, when I was on a business trip to California. We were married in Ohio in 1988 where in our marriage ceremony we vowed to love each other and dedicate ourselves to serving and blessing Christ's people, His church. On our honeymoon in Gatlinburg, Tennessee, we met a noted Reformed scholar who was ministering in a local Charismatic church. He taught us the glory of church history and her saints, the errors of dispensationalism and the need to train one's children diligently in the faith. We resonated with his message. It launched within both Jennifer and me a great desire to seek and know and enjoy the righteousness, peace, and joy in the Holy Spirit—the Kingdom of God—to which the Scriptures refer in Romans 14:11. God had graced us to seek the blessed land wherein, according to 1 Chronicles 4:40, the children of Israel found rich, good pasture in a land that was broad, quiet, and peaceful, i.e., the Church. We had not yet found this land, but upon our return to Springfield, Jennifer started her new job as a clinical therapist working with male juvenile sex offenders. Her associate in this work and his wife, the Whites, were a lovely, peaceful, and knowledgeable Catholic couple.

Within a few months of our marriage, Jennifer and I mutually agreed to save money so that the following year we could take a sabbatical to attend a Charismatic Bible school in East Texas to deepen our understanding of the Scriptures and the Kingdom of God. Our spiritual journey to date had left us without assurance that we were interpreting God and His will for our lives correctly. We were desperate to know God and His way, a desperation that to our friends seemed overly zealous and somewhat foolish. By the end of that sabbatical year, God had answered more of our prayers regarding His Kingdom: To put it bluntly, He had showed us through our experience at the Bible school that the undisciplined and subjective nature of the Charismatic church was misguided. We saw that it lacked unity with the broader Church; it was substandard in theology and devoid of any historical roots before the early 1900s.

On our last day in Texas before returning to Springfield, we visited a bookstore where we found several volumes by Reformed Presbyterian and Christian Reconstructionist authors. The store manager was the wife of a minister who would become one of our Reformed Presbyterian mentors. We purchased $200 worth of books that would, over the subsequent months, root us in the history of the Church, in the theology of the creeds and confessions, in the knowledge of the Kingdom of God, and in the doctrines of the broader Protestant church. Jennifer and I were so distracted by all that God was teaching us that we never considered that we were entrenched in an irrational Protestant bias. We were not consciously bigoted against Catholicism. The thought of embracing Catholicism simply never occurred to us. Sadly, most of the Catholics we knew were cynical and unknowledgeable about the Church and the Scriptures.

After returning to Springfield in 1990, Jennifer and I had no church affiliation, having left the Charismatic movement. Instead, we led a home Bible study group in which we studied the Scriptures, the Westminster Confession of Faith, and Schaff's *History of the Christian Church*. Eventually our group concluded that we needed to join the Presbyterian Church. We were extremely attracted to its polity of elder rule, its Reformation-based theology (much of which is grounded in the Scriptures) and its historical roots—all elements that are missing in Evangelical Protestantism. Confused by the existence of hundreds of Presbyterian denominations and thousands of church congregations, we called upon our mentor in Texas for help. He belonged to the Reformed Presbyterian Church in the U.S. (RPCUS), but counseled our Bible study group to join the Orthodox Presbyterian Church (OPC), which we all did in 1992.

We thought that our journey into the broad land was accomplished. We had found more of the Kingdom of God than we had ever known: spiritual authority, enthusiastic preaching of the Scriptures, and the organized and visible church in all of her, we believed, orthodox glory. The Reformation cries of *sola fide* and *sola Scriptura* were faithfully taught, and we took church membership vows to honor those tenets.

Unbiblical ecclesiastical traditions were nixed, so we thought. Our three children—Jedidiah, Josiah, and Sarah (ages thirteen, nineteen, and nine respectively, as of this writing)—were baptized in the OPC. Three years later, I became a ruling elder, and the following year I began to train to become a minister in the Orthodox Presbyterian Church. In 1997, I earned a master of divinity degree from Greenville Presbyterian Theological Seminary, the most conservative seminary servicing the OPC. My studies were steeped in church history, the ancient Greek and Hebrew languages, and the development of theology, and these, along with my extra historical and ecclesiastical studies with Jennifer, broadened our theological and ethical outlook. By reading the Early Church Fathers, the creeds and confessions, and the *Catechism of the Catholic Church,* I began learning a great deal about Catholicism.

Jennifer and I were exhilarated by all we were learning, and our zeal infected many of our lay brethren in the church. Delighting in God's will, we were forming intimate fellowship with many families who seemed fervent for the faith. In addition, I taught a series from the Book of Ecclesiastes that changed Jennifer and me to this day. From that book, we learned that we did not need to be overly righteous or religious about life (Ecclesiastes 7:16). We could relax and eat, drink, and be merry while submitting to the fear of God and the keeping of His commandments (Ecclesiastes 12:13). We realized that God did not require us to be able to split every doctrinal hair in order to please Him. We assessed our lives and agreed that our journey to date had made us overly narrow theologically, too legalistic, too pietistic, overly critical of others and other churches, anti-Catholic (although we believed that there were Christians in the Catholic Church), and devoid of a zeal to perform good works out of a warm heart of love. We saw ourselves becoming what we did not want to become and what we clearly saw in the Scriptures that Christ detested.

We repented thoroughly to God. Christ, we realized, was not as concerned about what exactly we believed as He was concerned about our charity toward all of mankind. The parables that we had studied about the sheep and the goats and about the poor and the needy were illuminating our minds and correcting our thoughts.

We realized that God would be just as pleased whether I was serving others in my business vocation or in full-time ministry. In addition, each day we were feeling more and more the need to burst out of the fetters that our elders had placed on us. We were serving the church twenty to thirty hours per week and were exhausted. They were merciless about giving us any reprieve. In addition, we were feeling the need to be OUTSIDE of the church's four walls to serve Christ and to build our own lives: to serve in a soup kitchen, to bake for the neighbors, to provide free tutoring for a child, to enroll our children in community affairs, and to pursue creative ventures. Verbally and nonverbally, the elders communicated to us their displeasure with our newfound liberty and trajectory.

We subsequently made a collaborative decision not to pursue a pastorate in the OPC. This was the beginning of sorrows. In 2000, not having found a suitable congregation to join and yet equipped with the qualifications, ministerial experience, sponsorship, and desire to begin a less legalistic and more merciful Reformed church in Springfield, we joined with our mentor minister in the RPCUS to begin pastoring a new church: Springfield Reformed Presbyterian Church.

The OPC that we left learned of our new congregation and the sponsoring RPCUS denomination. Though Springfield had no Reformed church, and though the nearest OPC church was about thirty-five miles away, the OPC church feared that their parishioners would travel that distance to Springfield to partake of a former elder's ministry. The RPCUS graciously requested that the OPC allow the Springfield church to come into the RPCUS without incident. The OPC, after much discourse, refused to do so. Because of this, our church became a member of the Association of Free Reformed Churches.

Although our church seemed free and clear of the most sectarian portions of Presbyterianism, we were beginning to note that these several judicatories were doing "what was right in [their] own eyes" (Judges 21:25). Not only was all of this an example of disunity, but my family also had to bear my verdict of excommunication, a result of a humiliating and public church trial. The judgment of excommunication means that that session of elders ruled me an "infidel" or an "unbeliever" to be shunned. Families and friends with whom we had spent countless ministry and friendship hours no longer spoke to us, fearing punishment if they disobeyed the elders. Nearly ten years of relationships and emotions were annihilated. We were ousted and ostracized because we failed to adhere to what the OPC defined as the Protestant ministerial tradition. Nevertheless, we ministered, published, worked, and persevered for nearly four years at Springfield Reformed Church.

Our church grew, and we served our community. We urged the flock to be rich in good works. Eventually, however, as we witnessed the continued disunity and hateful infighting among many members of the Reformed community locally and nationally, Jennifer and I began to become disenchanted with Reformed Presbyterianism and Protestantism altogether. A crisis point in our spiritual journey home had arrived.

While teaching a series on the justification of the saints to my church, I returned to my studies of the doctrines of Protestantism and the Catholic Church that I had learned in seminary. Several theologians seeking Protestant and Catholic dialogue had sparked my consideration of the legitimacy of Roman Catholicism. While poring over Protestant and Catholic dogma, I lost my theological moorings. I began to vacillate back and forth between wanting to remain Protestant and wanting to join the broad fellowship of Roman Catholicism, which I saw as "deep in Scripture, deep in tradition, and deep in history" (a quote from the *Coming Home Network* Website, which I had been perusing). At first, I would spend days holding to Protestantism and minutes holding to Catholicism. Then I would wake up Protestant in the morning and become a convinced Catholic at night. I was angry that my spiritual journey had come to this major confusion. My poor wife, while waiting for me to land, longed for our family to be rightly planted and rested in Christ's church. She would have continued in our church if I had desired it, but she did not want me to continue ministering as a pastor if I was so frustrated and unhappy.

Eventually we came to some rational conclusions. First, Jennifer and I realized that Protestantism was not honest, as it purported, with all of the Scriptures regarding justification by works (such as James 2:24). As a result, we concluded that *sola fide* was now out. I also found that the Scriptures themselves were a part of Church (i.e., Catholic Church) Tradition and even spoke of the reception of Church Tradition. This made the phrase *sola Scriptura* not only unscriptural but unethical. So, *sola Scriptura* was out too. Moreover, Church Tradition and Sacred Scripture compose the "deposit of faith" handed down to us by the Fathers. My eyes were opened to the fact that Protestants reject the pope in favor of establishing their own smaller popes (Independent churches) and curia (Presbyterian churches).

Furthermore, I was deeply frustrated that Protestants, no matter how large their denomination, were unable to work out theological or ministerial unity among themselves, to the detriment of the growth of the entire church. Their pursuits of what has been called the "narcissism of small [doctrinal] differences" will be their collective doom. Along with every other Protestant pastor or bishop, I would always be relegated to reinventing the wheel of polity and ministerial infrastructure. How, in this divided and schismatic enterprise called Protestantism, could I ever work to minister effectively to those in Africa, Croatia, or Cincinnati for that matter?

Finally, I saw and understood that, according to St. Peter's words recorded in Acts 10:34-35, God accepts WHOEVER fears Him and works righteousness. The Roman Catholic Church teaches and lives this. The Protestants tack on theological particulars that go beyond what God Himself requires.

I pondered the major reforms of Roman Catholicism since the sixteenth century. I began to acknowledge the fervent love for

Christ and His Word exhibited by the Catholic Church. I wanted a unified, international, and historically legitimate Church that embraced the historic creeds and confessions. I believed in Trent over against the Reformed Creeds and I realized that I was no longer fighting the ecclesiastical wars of the sixteenth century.

We contacted our Catholic friends, the Whites, to tell them of our decision. They eventually became our sponsors into St. Teresa Catholic Church back in Springfield.

Our transition to Roman Catholicism was emotional and difficult but ultimately healing. I drafted a letter to my presbyter, my original mentor, stating my intentions to demit the ministry of the Springfield church and join the Catholic Church. My plan was to continue preaching for six weeks so that I could help the parishioners transition to other churches, including the Catholic Church, should any desire to do so. Within one evening, the presbyter called each parishioner and told them that I, now an "idolatrous papist," was defecting to the "Sicilian pit" of Rome and was not worthy to be their pastor for a single day longer. This devastated the congregation and me. Given that I was obviously fired, I visited my own church one more Sunday, trying to explain my transition to Catholicism and offer my help. The weeping among the congregation was great—and brief. The crying turned to anger and name-calling within but a few days. The church dissolved fourteen weeks later. Even though I lost church income, I had kept my professional job and thus avoided problematic entanglements and financial difficulties while making this transition.

In November 2003, my family joined our parish's RCIA and CCD classes, and during the 2004 Easter Vigil, Jennifer, my three children, and I were confirmed into the Catholic Church and partook of our First Communion. The pain and wounds notwithstanding, God, through much tribulation, had driven my family out of harrowing trials and into the broad and blessed land of His Catholic Church.

Though we knew the pleasant and unpleasant episodes of Catholic history, we embraced Christ and the Church because it is His Church. We now know the blessedness of the faith once and for all given to the saints; the rightly administered and real presence of Christ in the sacraments; the legitimate Church polity and clergy whose origin comes from the Apostles; and the joy of worshipping with unified Christians from every tribe, tongue, and nation. In fact, we are now preparing to minister on our RCIA team, to provide premarital counseling to engaged couples, and to teach our parish's youth group. We now, without doubting, finally have the assurance that we know God, His will, and His Church, and this is a most blessed estate in which to be. We diligently sought the Kingdom of God, and, as He promised in Sacred Scripture, we found it (Matthew 6:33; 7:7).

We understand what the online edition of the *Catholic Encyclopedia* means when it says, "The convert, beside and beyond his knowledge, must have sufficient strength of will to break with old associations, old friendships, old habits, and to face the uncertainties of life in new surroundings. His sense of duty, in many cases, must be of a heroic temper." Although we embrace a greater breadth and number of friends today, we are sad about the loss of those friends and associations that were apparently based only upon mutual agreement on small theological differences.

Were the non-Catholic beginnings of the journey a tremendous waste of time and resources? Not at all! Our Reformed instruction rightly taught us that nothing happens apart from God's sustaining and governing love over all of His creatures and over all of their actions. Our journey thus far was God's decretive will. Ours was to love and to obey His Word as it was revealed by the Holy Spirit to us at each step of the way. We kept seeking after His Kingdom and praying for His wisdom. We trusted God to direct our steps providentially, through circumstances and the like, to where He would have us. The tribulations were a sanctifying part of the journey. As St. Paul stated:

> [N]ot only that, but we also glory in tribulations, knowing that tribulation produces perseverance; and perseverance, character; and character, hope. Now hope does not disappoint, because the love of God has been poured out in our hearts by the Holy Spirit who was given to us (Romans 5:3-5).

In reflection, life in Protestantism for us was difficult, fractured, and somewhat hopeless. The cost of transitioning to Catholicism was small when compared to the glorious joy that my family and I are now experiencing at home and serving the Lord in the Catholic Church.

Originally published in the CHNewsletter *October 2004.*

Formerly a minister in the Reformed Presbyterian Church, Gerald is now a proposal manager with BTAS, Inc. He also teaches at Urbana University and is a disk jockey. Gerald, his wife, Jennifer, who is a substitute teacher, and their three children (Jedediah, Josiah, and Sarah) were received into the Catholic Church at Easter 2004, in Springfield, Ohio.

Part Two

The Journeys Home of Laypeople

Though the initial reason for the formation of the *Coming Home Network International* was to assist non-Catholic clergy in their journeys home to full communion with the Catholic Church, from the beginning lay men and women began contacting us. Since their inquiries and conversions usually did not result in the loss of vocation or employment, their needs were not so acute, yet their reasons and desires for reception into the Catholic Church were just as strong. Moreover, their conversions did result sometimes in the same consequences and conflicts with family, friends, and even employers.

In the following pages, you will meet some of our friends who made the journey into the Catholic Church as laypeople. Most of them remained in the lay state after their conversion, while others later responded to the call of our Lord Jesus into ordained Catholic ministry.

The Prodigal Comes Home

by Rob Rodgers
former Anglican

Luke records a great parable of Our Lord in which many of us can probably see ourselves — the parable of the prodigal son. It was while reading this Gospel story nearly three years ago that I found my heart weeping at this parallel to my own dark past and glorious return to our Father's arms. You see, *I* was that ignorant, self-righteous son who had thought he needed nothing from the Father.

I once thought my life's destiny would be whatever I chose to make it. The laws of right and wrong, I insisted, could be twisted to fit *my* needs. When I was still young, I began to view faith as a threat to my freedom and as a result, my conscience became hardened to truth, to God, and to the difference between right and wrong.

Every Sunday, my parents took me to a place where I didn't want to be, a place where I didn't feel comfortable. I had been baptized in the Anglican faith, and I attended services until I was about nine years old. Finally, after I had put up enough of a fuss and my parents had lost sight of our need for the faith, I gained my "freedom."

It was a "freedom" I would abuse every chance I got for the next seventeen years. I put God out of my life. I recognized His presence only when necessary to please others, such as on occasions when I needed to talk about faith in order to be part of a conversation. But I was convinced that I didn't need God.

I took to this "free" lifestyle like bees to honey. Having pushed God out of my life, Satan was able to gain a great portion of my soul. Slowly my vision narrowed, my sense of guilt faded, and I lost any sense that my actions had consequences for which I was responsible.

I thought I was free! Deep inside, of course, I knew my "freedom" was only an illusion that would one day fade and I would be left to face the outcome of my choices alone and without comfort. Nevertheless, I still loved the illusion.

As the years went on, I took whatever I could get from the world. Work at our family business provided a seemingly endless source of money, which gave me a distorted sense of reality. I wanted to have my hands in everything I saw going on around me, and nothing was going to stop me.

In the eyes of my parents, I was a great son, but I had to work hard to keep them from suspecting otherwise. By the time I was in high school, I was deep into drugs, even selling them to friends. Alcohol also became an easy friend. Through these two tools of the Devil, my true identity was buried and I became another person.

I wore mask after mask so I could appear to be whatever the occasion called for. I had become a social chameleon. "Truth" to me was something I could fabricate. Nothing was sacred and nothing was beyond my twisting, if twisting it was to my benefit.

Whenever I found someone who loved me, I would appear to respond with genuine love on the outside. But inside, I was actually trying to calculate how much I could profit from the relationship. I gained trust through falsehoods and used it to my benefit. I quickly learned that I could take advantage of those who loved me to further my own agenda.

This abuse of love left a deep void in my heart, which I learned to bury through my addictions. On occasion, when I would allow my heart truly to love even a little, a glimpse of the truth would surface inside. The inner battle, to which I was otherwise blind, would manifest itself every once in a while, causing me to feel the true turmoil of my soul. In these moments, those who loved me would draw nearer to me, wanting to help. But the moment would soon pass, and I would return to my blindness.

My pit of despair was too deep to escape. I was helpless to crawl out of it on my own. I convinced myself that I was comfortable how I was living and safe in my false image of myself. I chose to know nothing else. Truth was something I feared. The dark had become a comfort for me.

There was no pain. Grief emerged only when I allowed the quiet voice inside to speak, urging me to start the long, impossible climb out of my pit. But hopeful moments like these would be quickly erased by my actions whenever I was under the influence of drugs and alcohol. I often publicly inflicted pain on myself. Any glimpses I had caught of the truth I quickly rejected as lies, while the lies I took as the truth.

Off to school and then London

The time came to leave my family for college, but instead of focusing on studies, I sought opportunities to boost my ever-growing ego. Soon, however, this ego suffered a terrible blow: I was on academic probation by the end of my second year.

Still, this wound to my selfishness was soon forgotten, buried beneath the usual addictions and lies. In the shadows of pleasure offered by the Devil, my eyes were blind to the truth about the road I was walking.

Finally, with the assistance of a family friend, I packed all my troubles into my car and moved west to begin a career in the hospitality industry. I felt free, because I felt I was leaving my problems behind. It would be just my best friend and I, off to start anew, to forget what had been and to find rebirth.

My new life, however, was short-lived. Within a few weeks, my ego unpacked itself and things turned out to be much the same as they had been before. Even so, I fooled myself into believing that the change of location had somehow altered who I was. I convinced myself to continue on this new road because I was a different person.

I felt somehow refreshed. My new friends thought I was a man of the world and open to the energies of life. I developed a drug-induced sensation of spirituality, a false kind of religion that many of our youth today embrace. For those who adopt this perspective, religion is whatever you make it; God is whatever you perceive Him to be, and salvation is not something to worry about.

Through what at the time seemed to be no more then a random roll of the dice, I was offered a great job at a hotel in London, which included supervising all in-room bars and private functions. This opportunity was like a dream come true: further travel, work at a top hotel, the exciting adventure of living in London, and full access to more alcohol than I had ever seen. I didn't hesitate to accept the offer. Full of even more pride than before, my ego was once again running the show. As I boarded the plane for England, I imagined how proud my family would be as they talked about me.

Leaving everything behind, I headed over the "great pond." Little did I know that this journey would change everything. It would stop me from running from the truth. It would shatter seventeen years of ignorance, seventeen years of lies. London would prove to be my hell, though in my blindness, I thought it was heaven.

Once there, I entered a new circle of colleagues and other acquaintances where morals were deeply in decay. The hospitality industry there was corrupt from top to bottom, seeming to center itself on my two addictions. Alcohol and drugs found their way into everything and everyone I knew. In a strange way, I felt at home, and in this home, I was king—or so I thought.

The Road to Damascus—Almost

My time at this hotel soon ended; corrupt business practices have a way of taking their revenge on you. Yet despite my deceit, despite my theft, *Someone* was there helping me struggle through the mud of my own doing. A management position at another well-known hotel became available, and my life shifted into high gear. I promised myself a new start. No more shifty handshakes, no more questionable transactions to speed that climb up the ladder, no more lies. But I soon fell on my face; the burden I was carrying was just too much. My addictions to alcohol and drugs were creeping into my professional life, and I was holding desperately onto a life that was founded on lie after lie. My weakness was beginning to show.

I still remember vividly the night—May 10, 1998—when, sprawled out on my back in misery, I had what was nearly a "Damascus Road" experience. I was utterly broken. I had traded all sense of morality and values for nights of female company; substance addictions were often my only nourishment; hatred governed my heart and left me helpless.

Yet evil has one great self-destructive fault: ignorance. That night, a crack appeared in the wall Satan had helped me to erect around myself. Through that crack, I curiously peered out into a light—a light so bright it dazzled my heart: the light of the Holy Spirit.

In one night, all the ignorance that had ruled my life began to dissolve. In its place was the truth that it had hidden from me—the life God could give me. He began to reveal to me the possibility of a life I had only dreamed of in the shadows of my mind.

I felt as though someone were taking a thirty-pound sledgehammer to my body. I was riddled with pain. My heart ached as the guilt of years now seized and broke its hardened shell.

My eyes saw and my being felt the pain that all my lies had caused me. My body felt as if it were being broken piece by piece. Yet as I was lying there shattered, confused, alone, and scared, the love of Jesus Christ—though I didn't know it was His love—raised me up in a way I had never before known. Warmth embraced me and comforted me. Hatred was swallowed up by grace. My ignorance gave way to curiosity, and my eyes were opened to the glory of life from God.

From Confusion to Rome

The next morning, I felt terribly confused about what had transpired. Had I lost my mind? Suffered a nervous breakdown? Experienced an acid flashback? Whatever had happened, when I looked into the mirror, I saw someone I hadn't seen for years, and I was frightened. I saw a young boy I thought I had left behind many years before.

Nothing made any sense. Everything, I felt, had changed. It was as if I had awakened in one of my dreams, yet this was reality.

Strangely enough, I wouldn't accept that Christ had come to me in the night. There was no way I was becoming Christian. Yet, my heart cried for this change, and a desire to search out the truth was engulfing me.

My mind became a sponge, soaking up everything I could learn that I thought might help me understand this new reality. I took a vow of chastity, gave up the bottle, and somehow rationalized that drugs would be my route to spiritual salvation (thus one of Satan's claws remained in my side). I began to read everything spiritual I could get my hands on, starting with Eastern mysticism and yoga. At one point, I almost entered a Buddhist monastery in southern England.

Next, I found myself exploring Judaism, especially the mystical strain known as Kabbalism. Finally, however, I went back to my scientific roots and there sought a logical explanation for what had happened in my life. In this way of thinking, there was no such thing as sin; my drug abuse was no hindrance to any kind of salvation; and I was relieved, since I could no longer count on alcohol to lean on.

I convinced myself that I had found what I was looking for. Everything made sense, I said, and with that I stopped, no more questioning the experience of that night. In fact, I began to explain it away—a mistake that allowed Satan to slip slowly back into my life. In time, I went back to alcohol and everything began to spin downward, though all the while I thought I was enjoying a wonderful life.

What I had experienced that memorable night transcended the logic of the mind, though I had tried to fit it into logical categories. What had taken place had been a miracle, but I now shrugged it off as an ordinary occurrence, a random chance. All the impact of that night seemed lost.

Meanwhile, while managing at the Ritz Hotel in London, I befriended Barry, the security manager. He would later be my Confirmation sponsor and is even now my mentor. Our luncheon talks became God's way of entering my life without my realizing it.

Slowly I began to reach out for the spiritual food Jesus Christ was offering me through Barry. Then, after several months, he invited me to attend a course at his parish. My heart jumped at the invitation, and a song came from my soul. I answered, "Without a doubt!"

I still remember that night as clearly as if it were just this morning. As I walked from the hotel to the Holy Apostles Parish, it seemed as if I were going crazy, as if I were on fire. My addictions had taught me to crave, but this was a kind of desire I had never known.

As soon as I stepped into the hall that night, *bam!* I felt inside the same sledgehammer that I had felt that night a year before. I cried like a baby separated from its mother. Then I met Miren, a woman who to this day is my spiritual mom.

Hers was a rare kind of love. She greeted me with the words "You're home!" It was a welcoming I shall never forget. Though she didn't know me from a stranger on the subway, yet she gave me the love I had always wished to find. I knew then that I was home, in my real home. The home I had run from in ignorance I now ran to in love.

Thirteen weeks went by as the course progressed, and each week I hounded Barry: "I want to be Catholic. I want to be Catholic!" But each time I pressed him, he replied simply, "Patience, Rob."

Finally, I was brought to the priest. He gave me a catechism and some writings by Thomas Merton, and we set a date for my first confession.

In the meantime, I was catechized one-on-one by an amazing son of God. Twice a week I met with Edward, a Jewish convert who was very orthodox in his teaching. A couple who became my spiritual parents, also very orthodox and deeply involved in the charismatic renewal, opened their arms to me as well. I was nurtured by them all, raised as a spiritual infant with the desire to praise the Lord with all my heart.

On to Zanesville

The date of my Confirmation was set for December 9, 2000. Two days later, I was to return to Canada for my first Christmas as a Catholic. It would also be the first Christmas with my family in four years.

My family eagerly waited. They loved the change in my life. I was clean and sober and once again living the moral life that my parents had modeled for me as a young boy. That Christmas was the greatest day of my life. In a river of tears, I received Holy Communion. I walked out into the world without the void in my heart that I had carried for so long.

The next day I completed an application to work with the National Evangelization Teams (NET). I had become involved with the Franciscan Friars of the Renewal while in London, and I immediately fell in love with their simplicity of life and devotion to serve others through Christ. When I told my family that I was leaving the hotel business and planning to do a year of missionary work in the United States with NET, my decision was met with some speculation and concern. But their hearts began to change as they saw the joy that now filled my life.

For nine months, I traveled across the United States, being fed daily with the gifts of the Spirit. My experience with NET peeled away layer by layer whatever film of my old life remained, and I was refined by the fire of love that burned in my heart. To all I met, I witnessed to the healing grace that had saved my life.

After my life on the road with NET, I returned to Zanesville, Ohio, with a woman who had stolen my heart so we could discern our course of life. Very happily, we were engaged on July 5, 2002. As we sought God about our future and learned to rest in Him, His grace presented an opportunity for me to work with the *Coming Home Network* and be spiritually fed as never before.

Today I recognize that so many different hands have formed my life, yet each has been guided by the one hand of God. He lifted me from the gutter, healed me of my addictions, and put life back into my spirit. He even touched my liver, damaged by alcohol abuse, and restored it to health. In all these ways, He gave me a will to live in a way I had never known.

In the mirror, I still see Robert Rodgers, once an alcoholic, a drug addict, a thief, a pathological liar, an abuser of every good thing that came into his life. I also see, however, a sinner who has been forgiven, a son of God who has come home to the arms of his eternal Father, a man who receives such remarkable life and love that it often seems like a dream.

The refrain of Psalm 118 is now the song of my heart each morning: "His steadfast love endures forever!" The first words from my mouth each day are spoken to the Lord: "Jesus, I love you." I am deeply grateful for the beauty of another chance, a chance to help others find the life I found through Christ our Lord. No day is a bad day, for Jesus Christ willingly went to the cross to die for me so that I could find true happiness. God bless and amen!

Originally published in the CHNewsletter *September 2002.*

Rob is a staff apologist and the coordinator of the Helpers Network *and Events for the* Coming Home Network. *Rob is also a retreat master for Catholic high schools in the area and is active in young adult and youth ministry. Rob, his wife Bernadette, and their daughter Josephina live near Zanesville, Ohio.*

Seeking the Answers to Life's Basic Questions

By Dr. Eduardo J. Echeverria
former Reformed Calvinist

"You made us for Yourself, and our hearts find no peace until they rest in You." In this statement, the philosopher-theologian St. Augustine of Hippo (A.D. 354-430) claimed that nothing less than God can completely satisfy the restless quest of man for peace—for the truth, for the good, for happiness. In other words, God is our ultimate fulfillment.

This is also the sentiment of the opening question and answer of the Baltimore Catechism: "'Why did God make you?' God made me to know Him, love Him, and serve Him in this world and to be happy with Him for ever in the next." However, I did not always know the answer to that question.

In 1950, I was born in Merida, the capital city of Yucatan, Mexico, the second of five children. When I was almost two years old, we left our Mexican roots and immigrated to the eastern part of the United States. For a short time, we lived in Manhattan but then moved up north to the Bronx. My Catholic parents were firm believers in the importance of Catholic education, so I spent my formative years at Our Lady of Lourdes grammar school and Immaculate Conception School, and then on to Mount St. Michael Academy, an all-boys high school run by Marist Brothers. I graduated in 1969.

I had been baptized, confirmed, and catechized a Catholic, yet I do not remember ever thinking seriously about personally turning toward God and away from sin by making a heartfelt commitment to Christ. I was like many teenagers: The Church's proclamation of the Gospel of Jesus Christ just did not seem relevant to my life. I never made a conscious choice to be an atheist; rather, I just assumed that the Church had nothing to say to me. Aside from the usual things, I lived my late teens in the "adversary culture" of the late 1960s—the Woodstock generation, the protests against U.S. involvement in Vietnam, and the counterculture's spiritual and moral critiques of the emptiness and inauthenticity of the established society.

Many of my boyhood friends were swept away by the drugs and music, the philosophy of "free love," absolute freedom, and self-expression. Thankfully, several close friends and I recognized that drugs, sex (and more sex), and rock 'n' roll were not the answer to life's meaning and purpose, and we resisted the dynamics of this culture.

In my resistance, I began to ask myself the questions, "Does God exist?" and "If He does, why did He make me?" Not remembering where to turn for answers, I began searching for direction to my life through the works of popular authors like Jean-Paul Sartre, Albert Camus, and Herman Hesse. It was the summer of 1970.

That summer, I made my first trip to Europe. In Amsterdam, a girl at a youth hostel told me about L'Abri Fellowship, a community in Switzerland where young people came from diverse cultures and religious backgrounds searching for answers to questions about God, man, and the meaning of life. I don't remember her telling me that L'Abri was an Evangelical Christian community, only that staying there was free for the first ten days. For a guy on a tight budget, therefore, L'Abri sounded like the place to be. Within a few days, I was off for Huemoz, Switzerland, a little village about seven miles up into the Swiss Alps near the city of Montreux, two hours from Geneva.

The first person I met at L'Abri was Os Guinness, whom I later came to know as a first-rate thinker and a deeply committed Christian. While he was deciding where I would stay, he gave me a copy of Francis Schaeffer's classic book, *The God Who*

Is There. Schaeffer, along with his wife, Edith, founded L'Abri Fellowship in 1955. You can imagine my surprise—more exactly, my bewilderment—when I learned that they had established L'Abri for the purpose of evangelizing people for Jesus Christ by demonstrating the character and reality of God by the way the community lived, taught, and prayed. The singularly unique purpose of this community was to present the Gospel of Jesus Christ as the answer to all of life's basic questions, and hence that nothing less than God, they claimed, could completely satisfy my restless quest for truth, for the good, for happiness.

After ten days at L'Abri, I responded by fleeing—not just the place, but more specifically, God. I rationalized leaving by telling others and myself that Christian faith required a demanding change of life that wasn't really for me. Thus, I left, hitchhiking with a friend to Rome.

God, however, was not going to let me get away that easily. Exhausted from hitchhiking and running out of money, I found myself a couple of weeks later unable to get into Spain without a visa. One night in a French town bordering Spain, I met two American guys. I began telling them about L'Abri and realized that I was persuading them to accompany me back. The L'Abri community, with genuine, Christian charity, welcomed me back.

From that moment on, I never looked back. I spent the rest of the summer there, and in time, I returned to Jesus. In faith through God's grace, I accepted the fundamental truth that the ultimate fulfillment of life to which God calls us is in Jesus Christ—the love of the Father manifested in the gift of the Son and communicated by the Holy Spirit. I now knew that God put me into this world to know, to love, and to serve Him. I discovered that this truth was not merely a matter of faith but—in contrast to those who said that there are no rational grounds for such believing—a reasonable assent of the mind. A Christian commitment involves accepting intellectually that certain things are true; that faith and reason are not antagonists but allies; that there are sound arguments for the reasonableness of the Christian faith. However, this was just the beginning of my journey home.

In the summer of 1970, I came wholeheartedly to acknowledge, assent to, and believe in Jesus Christ as my Savior and Lord. I responded in faith, repentance, and obedience to what I would later come to realize I had received at my infant Baptism some twenty years earlier. At that time, however, I did not see any essential connection between the sacrament of Baptism, spiritual rebirth, and salvation. In fact, Francis Schaeffer insisted that I be baptized again when I made my public confession of faith before the L'Abri community.

Being a neophyte, I trusted Schaeffer's judgment. He taught that Baptism as an external rite actually effects nothing and plays no role in determining our spiritual state before God in Christ. Years later, when I was more theologically mature, I realized that Schaeffer, a Presbyterian Calvinist, like the Roman Catholic, the Eastern Orthodox, the Anglican, and the Lutheran, understood the rite of Baptism to have some covenantal meaning. Still, he did not believe, what I later came to accept as the truth of Catholic teaching, that the act of Baptism itself actually effected the grace of regeneration, washing away the stain of Adam's original sin that we, as children of Adam, inherited.

Shortly after returning to the United States, I moved to Chicago with a good Christian friend I had met at L'Abri. My Christian experience at L'Abri had given direction to my life in more than one sense. It was there that I discerned my calling to the academic life, particularly to studying philosophy and theology. With two years of college work to finish, however, where was I to go?

Through this concatenation of Christian friends, I enrolled at Trinity Christian College in suburban Chicago in the fall of 1971. Once at Trinity, I was introduced to the neo-Calvinist Amsterdam school of philosophy and theology and began to study the great theological writings of Herman Dooyeweerd, Abraham Kuyper, Herman Bavinck, and G.C. Berkouwer. I graduated from Trinity in June 1973, having spent my last semester abroad in the Netherlands participating in a Trinity program at the University of Leiden. My plan was to do graduate studies at the Free University of Amsterdam, the bastion of the Amsterdam school of philosophy and theology. It was the summer of 1973, and I was now a committed Christian in the Reformed tradition of Dutch neo-Calvinism.

At this point in my journey home, I understood the one Christian faith to have many interpretations and expressions—Roman Catholic, Eastern Orthodox, Lutheran, Evangelical, etc.—but I had come to accept the Reformed tradition as the most authentic interpretation of the Christian faith. Central in this tradition were the writings of the Protestant reformer John Calvin (1509-64) and Abraham Kuyper (1837-1920), theologian, politician, and founder of the Free University of Amsterdam.

This tradition's unique understanding of the biblical themes of creation, fall, and redemption built upon the intellectual formation I had received at L'Abri. The world, including man and his works, is an actual manifestation and exercise of God's goodness and gift of creation. At the same time, there are also fallenness, evil, destructive powers, idols, and, yes, sin, as violation of the will and purpose of God. The whole of creation is fallen. Thanks be to God, however, His work of redemption was cosmic in scope, restoring life in its fullness and delivering the whole creation, including man and all his works—not the least of which is the life of the mind—from sin. Furthermore, God called us in Christ to be His co-workers by cooperating in His mission for renewal, for realizing His Kingdom, for making the world holy. In the phrase of Nicholas Wolterstorff, "neo-Calvinism is a world-formative Christianity, a tradition of holy worldliness."

After 8 years of being steeped in the Amsterdam school of philosophy and theology, I received my Ph. D. in September

1981. Still, I was restless. The liturgical life of the church in the Reformed tradition was deeply unsatisfying. My studies of the history of the Catholic Church led me to discover that the Church had an ancient liturgy that was rooted in her sacramental life, a life that was wholly biblical and evangelical, that is, flowing directly from the Gospel of Jesus Christ. I became convinced that the Reformed tradition wrongly rejected the Catholic Church's teaching about the sacraments, the liturgy—especially the sacrifice of the Mass—and her piety as it was chiefly expressed in the Council of Trent. This was a first but nonetheless decisive break for me with some aspects of the Reformed tradition.

Over the next eight years, I examined and found wanting other aspects of classical Reformed Protestantism, particularly the doctrines of *sola fide* and *sola Scriptura*. Through the writings of great men of faith like Thomas Aquinas, John Henry Cardinal Newman, and Pope John Paul II, I moved away from the Reformed tradition and became an Anglo-Catholic.

By fall 1991, I had held teaching posts in South Africa, the United States, and Canada, and by the next spring, everything in my mind and heart was converging to Rome. I was ready to heed Christ's call to embrace His Body, the Catholic Church, as the One True Fold—her antiquity; her unity; her orthodoxy; her Magisterium, or teaching authority, manifested in all teachings about faith and morals, that Christ had founded in Peter and his apostolic successors; her episcopal hierarchy; and her mission to teach all nations and to preach the Gospel to every creature so that all men may attain salvation, faith, Baptism, and the fulfillment of the commandments.

All of this I now accepted as wholly evangelical. As I put it to my last Anglican pastor, everything that drew me to Anglo-Catholicism was Roman Catholic in origin, and the Holy Spirit was now guiding me to accept the fullness of Truth in the Catholic Church. "Rome sweet home," to quote the title of Scott and Kimberly Hahn's popular book.

The Apostle Paul had written to Timothy that "the Church of the living God" was "the pillar and ground of the Truth" (1 Timothy 3:15). For twenty-two years of Christian searching, I had been trying to discover the truth about this Church revealed by God in His written Word. It was only later that I discovered a prayer of the Church that, using different words, accurately expressed my longing to come into a fuller knowledge of God in Christ. I record now in this chronicle the prayer for others who are searching for the truth about Christ's Church:

> Lord God, since by the adoption of grace, You have made us children of light: do not let false doctrine darken our minds, but grant that Your light may shine within us and we may always live in the brightness of truth.

I knew that the Christian life could only be grounded in authentic Christian doctrine, that is, in truth. St. Augustine, St. Thomas Aquinas, Newman, and Pope John Paul II had taught me this, as had Francis Schaeffer in my Christian experience. Thus, I could not accept, any more than Newman, the doctrine he called religious liberalism, namely, "that truth and falsehood in religion are but matter of opinion; that one doctrine is as good as another; that the Governor of the world does not intend that we should gain the truth; that there is no truth; that it is enough if we sincerely hold what we profess." These claims, as Newman saw, were incompatible with any recognition of the Christian faith as true.

In this light, I understood my conversion to be both a personal commitment and a free assent to the whole truth God has revealed about His Church. Significantly, this conversion was my response in faith and obedience to Christ's high-priestly prayer to the Father, "May they all be one, just as You, Father, are in Me and I am in You; so that they also may be one in Us, so that the world may believe that You sent Me" (John 17:21). The interpersonal communion of Persons that characterizes the love of the Father, the Son, and the Holy Spirit is the ultimate source of the Church's unity. So I now knew in truth that if I were to enter more deeply into the life of God, I must enter into fuller communion with the Church of Christ.

The ecclesiology of Vatican II is that the "Church [of Jesus Christ], constituted and organized in the world as a society, subsists in the Catholic Church, which is governed by the successor of Peter and by the bishops in union with that succession" (*Lumen Gentium*, No. 8). The Catholic Church, in a singularly unique way, is the fully and rightly ordered expression of the Church of Jesus Christ.

Vatican II also taught that all Christians, all those who are "in Christ," are truly, genuinely, but imperfectly, in communion with the Catholic Church. "[I]n some real way they are joined with us in the Holy Spirit, for to them also He gives His gifts and graces, and is thereby operative among them with His sanctifying power" (*Lumen Gentium,* No. 15). This very important teaching helped me to make sense of the "many elements of sanctification and of truth" that I found throughout my Christian experience—from L'Abri to the Reformed and Anglo-Catholic traditions of Protestant Christianity. Indeed, I now knew them to be gifts and graces that the Spirit of Christ used as instruments to bring me home.

At the same time, the teaching of Vatican II, recently reiterated in the *Catechism of the Catholic Church*, "does not treat these [elements of sanctification and of truth] as autonomous and free-floating," as Dominican Father Aidan Nichols puts it. "[R]ather do they derive from the fullness of gracious truth Christ has given His holy Catholic Church, and coming from that source, carry a built-in gravitational pull back—or on!—towards the Church's unity."

The inner dynamism of these gifts and graces toward Catholic unity, that essential mark of the Church as Christ willed her to be, is what brought me home. In this sense, my conversion essentially involved bringing to fulfillment in my own life a unity already given by God as His gift in founding His Church. In the spring of 1992, I became a member of Our Lady of Lourdes Catholic Church in Massapequa Park, Long Island.

For about three years after my return to the Catholic Church, I continued to teach at Molly College, a Catholic liberal arts college in Long Island founded by the Dominican Sisters of Amityville. I longed to be more directly involved in serving Christ and His Church, however. I could not imagine what He had in store for me. By January 1996, I was teaching philosophy at Conception Seminary College in Conception, Missouri. I rejoiced in God's blessing for this new opportunity to trust and serve Him.

The singularly most important thing about teaching at Conception Seminary College was being of service to Christ and His Church by helping the seminarians to discern, in the process of priestly formation, whether Christ was calling them to the sacramental priesthood. A priest is above all a faithful servant of Christ and a steward of the mystery of salvation, the new life of grace communicated by the Church in her sacramental life—the love of the Father manifested in the gift of the Son and communicated by the Holy Spirit, which is present fully and unsurpassably in Christ's redemptive sacrifice on the cross (1 John 4:9-10). My own contribution in this process of discernment was chiefly in the realm of philosophical formation, a critical and creative engagement with the history and problems of philosophy in the light of revelation.

So I found my way home by means of the gifts and graces of the Spirit of Christ. I have used the image of journeying home as the guiding theme in this chronicle of my return to the Catholic Church to describe my life's walk with God. Yet, the journey home has still not ended for me and all those who are, as the New Testament puts it, "in Christ;" that is, for all those who are in communion with the Body of Christ, the Church. We are the journeying People of God, the Pilgrim Church, and the Church promises to bring us to our home in heaven (Philippians 3:20; Hebrews 11:10, 13: 14). I have written in another place: "This eschatological hope also embraces the fallen creation, now redeemed in Christ and headed toward the fullness of the kingdom, which is the new heaven and the new earth (Revelation 21:1-8) realized in glory at the end of time."[1]

We have not yet reached our final destination, however. Meanwhile our present life is not a mere waiting room. As Christ's faithful people, we are called to announce and extend the kingdom here on earth. In the words of *Lumen Gentium*:

> The Church, consequently, equipped with the gifts of her Founder and faithfully guarding His precepts of charity, humility, and self-sacrifice, receives the mission to proclaim and to establish among all peoples the kingdom of Christ and of God. She becomes on earth the initial budding forth of that kingdom. While she grows, the Church strains toward the consummation of the kingdom and, with all her strength, hopes and desires to be united in glory with her King *(Lumen Gentium, No.5)*.

Thus, we are still on the road yearning to know the love of Christ, sharing in His glory, which surpasses knowledge, so that we may be filled with all the fullness of God, "with the joy native to the life of the Trinitarian Persons," as Father Nichols puts it, in our heavenly home (Ephesians 3:19).

Originally published in the CHNewsletter *Mar-Apr 1997.*

Dr. Eduardo J. Echeverria is a revert to the Catholic faith from the Reformed and Anglican traditions. He studied philosophy and theology at the Free University of Amsterdam. He is associate professor of philosophy at Sacred Heart Major Seminary in Detroit, Michigan.

---

[1] Eduardo J. Echeverria, "Nature and Grace: The Theological Foundations of Jacques Maritain's Public Philosophy," Journal of Markets & Morality, Acton Institute for the Study of Religion and Liberty, Vol.4, No.2, Fall 2001.

Home Again, Thanks Be to God!

by Lynn Nordhagen
former ex-Catholic Presbyterian

On January 24, the feast of St. Francis de Sales, I was received back into the arms of the Holy Catholic Church. Since I had made a profession of faith in the Presbyterian Church, I now made a renewed profession of faith in all the Catholic Church teaches. For this I chose to read the profession of the Council of Trent, since it spoke the truth concerning specific errors I had embraced. Then I received the sacraments of Penance, Confirmation, and Holy Eucharist. As I wrote to my friends in the *Coming Home Network*, "What can I say? It's all beyond words somehow. I feel *plunged* anew into sacramental graces. Drenched! Penance, Confirmation, and Holy Communion—all within the hour, and then a peaceful prayer time alone with Our Lord in the Blessed Sacrament. Visible, audible, touchable! 'This is what we proclaim to you: what was from the beginning, what we have heard, what we have seen with our eyes, what we have looked upon and our hands have touched—we speak of the Word of life' (1 John 1:1). Amen! I'll write more later, but right now, I'm more or less melted by love and speechless in the light of His grace."

Almost five years earlier, however, on April 5, 1992, after a full year of diligent study and faithful attendance, I stood before a Presbyterian congregation to make a profession of faith. I was making membership promises that included submitting myself to "the discipline and governance of the church." I joyfully wrote the date in my Bible. I was at the same time dedicating myself to serious study of God's revealed Word, in the classical

Reformed tradition, embracing all the "solas" of the Protestant Reformation: Faith Alone, Grace Alone, Scripture Alone, Christ Alone, and Glory to God Alone. I had studied and read until I became convinced of the truth of "TULIP," an acronym for the distinctives of Reformed theology.[1]

At that point, I had left the Catholic Church not just once but twice. I had grown up Catholic, before and during Vatican II. I enjoyed sixteen years of Catholic schooling, living close enough to walk to school all the way through college. Our parish was known in town, deservedly or not, as the "Holy Land" because of having the grade school, two convents, a high school, a Jesuit university, and a very high percentage of Catholic families in the neighborhood. I loved the Latin Mass, and in high school and college, I attended daily Mass and Communion. I was young enough to accept gracefully the changes of Vatican II, but not without some sadness. A wonderful Jesuit priest formed a group for a few of us interested high school students to study the documents of Vatican II. We loved our Church.

So how could I ever have left the Church I loved? Only for what I thought was more of God. The charismatic renewal came to our Catholic college campus, led by a Bible Belt Pentecostal preacher. Many of us were caught up in the emotional appeal of belonging to a group of Christians who were really excited about Jesus. Eventually the charismatic group split along Catholic/Protestant lines.

About the same time, I married one of the Protestant young men. For three years of our marriage, I remained Catholic, but I finally allowed myself to become disillusioned by the lukewarmness of so many cradle Catholics compared with the Pentecostal ardor in my husband's church. So in 1974, I gave up on Catholicism, and naively hoping that the Holy Spirit would

---

[1] TULIP stands for Total depravity, Unconditional election, Limited atonement, Irresistible grace, and the Perseverance of the saints.

soon unite all Christians anyway, I became very active in this independent charismatic church, attending at least five meetings a week.

Over the next ten years of raising our kids in this enthusiastic atmosphere, I nonetheless became very restless and increasingly sensitive to the frequent misrepresentations of what the Catholic Church actually taught. I perceived more and more differences between the teachings of the independent church and orthodox Christianity, and so in 1984, under the guidance of a loving priest, a former teacher of mine, I returned to the sacraments. This was a difficult time for my husband, who was concerned about my confusing the kids and about his responsibility as spiritual head of the family. The fundamentalist teaching on submission left no room for a wife to worship elsewhere. The pastor counseled me to submit by staying "under the umbrella" of my husband's spiritual protection, but I insisted that I must "obey God rather than men." Although my husband and I felt the pain of not being able to worship together, I also experienced the peace and joy of being home again in the Catholic Church.

I wish I could say that was the end of my wanderings. But there followed several very distressing years, including the serious illness of both my parents, my father's death, and a difficult year of classroom teaching in a Catholic school. I sought counseling and became involved in a "Catholic" meditation group, which taught "Christian Zen" and other mixtures of Eastern philosophy and religion.

I had been devotedly practicing this for some time when, through my kids' involvement in pro-life activities, I began conversing with a Protestant co-worker whose kids had also been arrested. We soon discovered a mutual interest in theology. I felt quite up to the task of arguing doctrine with a Calvinist, since I had actually paid attention during my sixteen years of Catholic schooling and had already had my "fling" with Protestantism. I felt secure in my Catholic faith, so I took on the apologetic challenge. Our lunchroom-table debate went on for a year and a half, but I, the Catholic, didn't win. I was not as prepared as I had thought. I had not really come up against the strong intellectual side of the Protestant Reformation before.

Now I was reading Martin Luther's *Bondage of the Will*, John Calvin on the Lord's Supper, G.C. Berkouwer on faith and perseverance, and many other Reformed authors. In addition, I listened to hundreds of theology tapes by R.C. Sproul and others. I was outnumbered and should have asked for help, but instead I looked critically at the New Age stuff I was involved in, saw the sheer volume of intellectual ammunition on the Protestant bookshelves, and became convinced that they had Scripture on their side.

I felt compelled to submit to the truth, and I started attending the Presbyterian Church in America (PCA), where I would later become a member. This involved more stress for my family, because I was rocking our boat again. I became very seriously concerned and argumentative about the doctrinal errors in the independent church where my husband and kids still attended. But over the next few years, my husband became satisfied that I was at least Protestant again, and we both made good friends in my Presbyterian church.

Even then, I grieved over giving up my belief in the Real Presence in the Eucharist, and I harassed my friend at work about talking me into the Real Absence. Eventually I made peace with the notion of a real presence being spiritually communicated to believers by the Holy Spirit in a special way during the Lord's Supper. But there was always that tug in my heart for the real thing. Still, if the Catholic belief was idolatrous, I had to reject it.

For five more years, I delved into Calvinism. It was very comforting to know that God was absolutely sovereign over human decisions, and to believe that as one of the elect I was perfectly sure of going to heaven, no matter what I did, since it ALL depends on God. I believed in predestination by God's decrees before the foundation of the world and that Christ died only for His chosen ones, because to think otherwise was to admit He was not in control of salvation. I was a convinced Calvinist who was determined to convince everybody else.

In April 1996, I read *Surprised by Truth* (Patrick Madrid, editor), the collected stories of eleven converts to Catholicism. I found myself saying, "You know that's probably true. You've ALWAYS known it." Another part of me would say, "Then how did you change your beliefs so thoroughly?" And "How can you even trust yourself to 'choose' any one belief system over another?"

I started reading and studying with renewed intensity. I read again John Henry Cardinal Newman's *Apologia Pro Vita Sua*. I read books on the Eucharist and on the papacy. I corresponded by e-mail with *Coming Home Network* members and other Catholic apologists.

A turning point came the day I finally realized I did not accept the principle of *sola Scriptura* any longer and told my pastor so, because then my whole orientation to authority changed. It was also very depressing and unsettling because I was still so unsure of many Catholic teachings. I became very fearful that this change would mean losing friends and upsetting family. I could not see how I was going to be sure of anything ever again, especially my own trustworthiness in decision-making. I identified with Newman saying in his *Apologia*, "I had been deceived greatly once; how could I be sure I was not deceived a second time? I then thought myself right; how was I to be certain that I was right *now*?"

Another crisis arrived a couple of months later when I started visiting the Blessed Sacrament to pray for enlightenment. I was unable in conscience to genuflect, because I didn't believe in the Real Presence. Then one day, I realized I didn't believe in His Presence in the Lord's Supper at the Presbyterian church, either. Immediately I felt an anguished doubt—He was nowhere on

Earth! Neither in the Catholic Mass, nor in the Protestant Lord's Supper. I was ALONE. I felt cut off from ANY communion. That Sunday, I passed up the elements at the Lord's Supper, then called and made an appointment with a Catholic pastor.

Doesn't it seem that the Catholic Church is never in a hurry? It seems the more impatient I was to know and decide, the more the priest advised me to slow down, to "make haste slowly." He assured me that things would all fall into place for me at the right time. It wouldn't necessarily be easy, he said, but I would know that it was right and that the time was right. How could I believe that all this exhausting effort was leading to something that was just going to "fall into place"? But after many months, when I was making a last ditch effort to find a livable compromise, one that would please my husband, myself, my family, and friends, things did fall into place. One day, prompted by the priest's gentle challenge about compromising, I knew what was right, and a great sense of relief came over me. I was ready for it not to be easy, just to be right.

It has been far from easy. I have felt overwhelmed and fearful, I have spent hours in desperate prayer, and I finally said many tearful goodbyes at my Presbyterian church.

One especially tough time was my meeting with the elders. I felt I had to honor the promises I had made to submit myself to their "discipline and governance," and I had tried to stay open and candid with the pastor all during the many months of study, indecision, and conflict. When I told him I had finally made the decision to reunite with the Catholic Church, he said the elders wished to meet with me to hear my thinking and to admonish me from Scripture.

I had told the pastor about St. Francis de Sales, who was bishop of Geneva, Switzerland, soon after the Reformation. As a young man, before he was made bishop, he was responsible for the conversion of thousands of Calvinists back to the Catholic Church. He won their hearts with his gentleness and persistence in teaching the truth. When they would not listen to his preaching, he wrote leaflets and slid them under their doors. He lived among them at great personal risk and won them by his love. I told the elders that I had decided to return to the sacraments on the day the Catholic Church celebrates the feast of this apostle to the Calvinists, January 24. I felt that this saint had reached down personally through space and time, through the communion of saints, to rescue one more little Calvinist. My meeting with the elders lasted almost two hours. After we had gone over most of the issues, the pastor read me their admonition.

On my way home, although it was late, I stopped to pray in the Blessed Sacrament chapel, and Newman's words expressed my feelings again:

Oh, my Lord and Savior, support me . . . in the strong arms of Thy sacraments and by the fresh fragrance of Thy consolations. Let the absolving words be said over me and the holy oil sign and seal me, and Thy own Body be my food, and Thy blood my sprinkling; and let my sweet Mother, Mary, breathe on me, and my Angel whisper peace to me, and my glorious Saints . . . smile upon me; that in them all, and through them all, I may receive the gift of perseverance, and die, as I desire to live, in Thy faith, in Thy Church, in Thy service, and in Thy love. Amen.

Originally published in the CHNewsletter *Mar-Apr 1997.*

Lynn was born and raised in Spokane, Washington, and graduated from Gonzaga University. She and her Protestant husband, Marvin, live in Chattaroy, Washington. They have four children.

Grace upon Grace

by Jeffrey Ziegler
former Presbyterian

What shall I render to the LORD
for all his bounty to me?
I will lift up the cup of salvation
and call on the name of the LORD.
Psalm 116[115]:12-13

What shall I render to You, O Lord, for all Your bounty to me? You created me out of nothing, You hold me in existence, You redeemed me by Your Son's Precious Blood, You adopted me in the sacrament of Baptism. You have given me an angel as a guide and protector and a Virgin Mother as an advocate and refuge. You have led me to the fullness of faith in the Catholic Church, and through her, You call me into an eternal communion of life and love with You. Truly I can justly thank You, O Lord, only by offering myself to You day by day in the Holy Sacrifice of the Mass, in union with the oblation of Your Son.

I did not exist, and then I came into being, and this was Your doing, O Lord. You loved me into existence when You infused an immortal soul into the body that my parents had procreated. And so I was conceived, a sinner who shared the taint of original sin merited by my first parents. You rescued me from the fate that befell so many hundreds of millions of my contemporaries—death from chemical or surgical abortion, death from the abortifacient Pill or IUD or Norplant or Depo-Provera, death from the burning of salt or the dismemberment of limbs. Through no merit of my own, You willed that I be born into a family where I was loved, in a place unafflicted by starvation or war. Six months after my birth, You baptized me, O Lord Christ, by means of a Presbyterian minister, and divine life flowed into my soul.

You allowed me to receive the rudiments of Christian formation at the Western Presbyterian Church (PCUSA) in Palmyra, New York. When I was in third grade, just before my family stopped attending church and I stopped attending Sunday school, I received from that church's minister a Revised Standard Version of the Bible that would play such an important role in later years. Because of the graces that flowed from my baptism, I never doubted the inerrancy of Scripture, for which I thank You, Almighty God.

That year I attained the age of reason and thus began the long train of sins, which You have forgiven in the sacrament of Penance and for which I must render an account at the moment of my death. And was there not something more involved than the world and the flesh—namely, the devil? Did I not tell a friend in fourth grade, in bizarre words that shock me as I recall them, that "Lucifer is the king of darkness, and I am the prince of darkness"?

Despite my sins, O Lord, You sought me out. At about the age of nine, I saw an advertisement in *TV Guide* for a television show devoted to the end times, and I watched that show. You inspired me to jot down the address at the end of that show and to write for further information. Thus I began to receive two pamphlets every month from the *Radio Bible Class*. I did not read the literature, but You moved me to keep it in a desk drawer.

As I passed through junior high school, I excelled in school, I excelled in athletics, and I became more deaf to my conscience. I thought only of myself and never of You. Once You spoke loudly to me through my conscience as I was about to commit a grievous sin against charity, but I chose to ignore Your voice.

At the age of thirteen, I became infatuated with a girl, and she did not like me. You inspired my mother (who probably saw my distress and wanted me to become more active outside of the home) to ask me either to attend Sunday school or to join the Boy Scouts; You gave me the grace to choose Sunday school. The teachers, a married couple, were evangelicals. They told me how to become a Christian, and on the afternoon of Sunday, September 25, 1983, I followed their instructions and those of the text we were using in that class. I confessed my sinfulness, my inability to save myself, my faith in the substitutionary atonement of Christ on the cross and my belief in salvation by faith alone. I accepted Your Son as my personal Lord and Savior.

You inspired in me, O Lord, an increasing hunger for Scripture and prayer. By Your grace, I delighted to memorize the Scripture passages quoted in my Sunday school text. I went on long walks, prayed to You, and at times knew the peace that only You can give. You led me to open up the desk drawer and devour the material from *Radio Bible Class*. I would read the epistles of St. Paul in that RSV Bible I had received years before, and I recall how deeply moved I was by his description of Christian family life.

And so the years of high school continued, and You were there as a provident Father. I read Scripture (all sixty-six books of the Protestant Bible in 1986), I prayed for others, I attended Sunday school, I went to church, I tried to lead others to You. I continued to read the material from *Radio Bible Class*; I bought several Bibles, *Strong's Exhaustive Concordance*, and many books by Evangelical authors. On occasion, I listened to *Focus on the Family*. I subscribed to the *Christian Herald* and *Christianity Today*. I imbibed the anti-Catholicism of much of my reading.

When I was about to sin, my evangelical mind told me that I was saved no matter what I did, but my conscience told me that I should not sin; often I rationalized and sinned.

My father supervised the book-review section of a secular newspaper, and You moved him to bring home books on religion for me to examine. One book he brought home was *Preaching the New Common Lectionary* (Abingdon), and by Your grace,

I used it as a basis of prayer. As I meditated on the Scripture readings for Sundays and feast days, I understood the importance of the liturgical year and the biblical basis of feasts like the Annunciation, the Visitation, the Presentation, and Epiphany.

During my last two years in high school, You led me to pro-life books, and my revulsion for the Roman Catholic Church was changed to a grudging tolerance, for I respected her biblical positions on abortion, divorce, and sexual morality. You allowed me to be moved by the attractive example of charity lived by a few large Catholic families that I knew. You permitted me to catch the flu during the winter of my junior year, and while ill, I turned on the television one Saturday afternoon and discovered Malcolm Muggeridge on *Firing Line*. He was a Catholic, and yet I thought, "This man must be a Christian."

You led me to the Middle English of *The Canterbury Tales*, and I was struck by its Christian ethos, even though it was written by a Catholic. You led me to *Aetemi Patris* and the prologue of the *Summa Theologica*, and I was struck both by the apparent arrogance of Leo XIII's authority and by the beauty and logic of the *Summa*'s prologue.

I was convinced I was fully a Christian, a member of the invisible Church of the saved; but You gave me the grace to try to discover which denomination was most biblical. (In conscience, I could not join the PCUSA because of its tolerance of abortion.) By Your grace, I would spend an hour or so each week in the church library reading about the various denominations; and there I read parts of Eerdmans' *Handbook of Christianity*. From that book, I copied a list of the major Christian authors throughout history—from Clement of Rome to Hans Küng(!)—and thought that perhaps they could help me in my search for the most biblical denomination.

I began my studies at Princeton University in September 1987. I joined Princeton Evangelical Fellowship; its leader told me that he would eventually introduce me to dispensationalist theology, which he said was more biblical than covenantal theology. I attended the Sunday services of the Presbyterian Church in America's congregation in town, and I loved the strong, biblical preaching of its pastor, an ex-Catholic. He told me that he would eventually introduce me to covenantal theology, which he said was more biblical than dispensationalist theology. You placed in my heart a hunger for the Eucharist, so I also attended Episcopal services on campus.

Father of mercies, by Your grace I recalled quotes from G.K. Chesterton's *Orthodoxy* that I had read the spring before in *Christianity Today*, and I borrowed the book from the campus literary. Every day after the conclusion of classes, I would read a chapter of it, and I loved it. Here, too, was a Catholic who seemed so Christian.

One day in September, I was sitting in a faculty department office, waiting to speak to a professor. You led me to pick up the campus newspaper, which I did not usually read because of its liberal bias, and I saw an advertisement for an Introduction to Catholic Teaching class taught on Wednesday evenings by Father C. John McCloskey III, a priest of Opus Dei who was then a chaplain at the Aquinas Institute (the name of the university's Newman Center); he is now the chaplain of Mercer House in Princeton. And so, by Your grace, I began to attend these short weekly classes in Murray-Dodge Hall in October. After one class, a thought came into my head that one day I might be Catholic; I developed a palpable revulsion at the idea.

That month, You moved me to borrow *Humanae Vitae* from the Princeton library (I was the second person to take it out—the first since 1968); I read it, and it made sense to me.

On Wednesday evening, October 21, You led Father McCloskey to invite me to his office and give me a copy of *Spiritual Journeys* (edited by Robert Baram and published by the Daughters of St. Paul) and a catechism written by, among others, then-Father Donald Wuerl. Like many evangelicals, I thought that the Church taught that all non-Catholics would go to hell. Preoccupied with this issue of salvation and convinced that C.S. Lewis was the epitome of both intellect and sanctity, I asked Father McCloskey, "How could a C.S. Lewis be in hell?" Father McCloskey patiently explained the Church's understanding of *extra Ecclesiam nulla salus* (no salvation outside the Church).

Fall break approached, and I stayed on campus to study. I often prayed in the Princeton University Chapel, a lovely neo-Gothic structure with stained-glass windows that portrayed figures as disparate as the archangels, St. Sebastian, Plato, John Calvin, and St. Thomas Aquinas; only an Anglican could have designed it. On Friday evening, October 23, You gave me the courage to pray in the Marquandt Transept of the University Chapel, where the Catholics had their daily Mass; it was the only part of the chapel with kneelers. Though I often knelt when I prayed in my room, I found it hard to kneel in a public place––like the sign of the cross, the practice reeked of Catholicism, ritualism, and salvation by works. As I sat alone in the chapel that Friday evening, part of me wanted to kneel to pray, and part of me did not. Then the kneeler in front of me came crashing to the floor. I looked around to see if any disapproving evangelical might be in the chapel; I saw none, and then I knelt to pray.

During that fall break, I spent much time each day studying material for my four classes—classical Greek, Latin, linear algebra, and ancient Greek literature—and I was also able to spend more time in prayer and spiritual reading. I read much of Father Wuerl's question-and-answer catechism, and most of the Catholic doctrines made sense to me. I started to read or reread the works from that Eerdmans list, beginning with the letters of St. Clement of Rome and St. Ignatius of Antioch. I was shocked to find that these two Apostolic Fathers not only mentioned but emphasized the real presence of Christ in the Eucharist and the necessity of submission to the hierarchy of bishops, priests, and deacons in order to maintain the unity of the Church. I was shocked because I thought these were post-Constantinian additions to the original Christian faith; now I saw that they were there at the close of the first century. And as I looked at the Greek text of St. Ignatius's letters, I saw that the bishops, priests (presbyters), and deacons of the Catholic hierarchy were nothing more than the development of the New Testament *episkopoi, presbyteroi,* and *diakonoi.*

During that break, I also began to consider what a wonderful thing it would be if all the Christians at Princeton could worship together in one church; for the first time, the divisions in Christianity disturbed me. Then a thought occurred to me that perhaps it might be God's will that all Christians worship together as Catholics—but I dismissed that thought, which I believe also caused me physical revulsion.

At the conclusion of the break, on Saturday evening, October 31, I did my laundry in the basement of Lourie-Love Hall, and You led me to pick up *Spiritual Journeys.* I became engrossed in the book, and story after story began to make a deep impression on me. Person after person converted to the Catholic Church after renouncing the private interpretation of Scripture and submitting his intellect to the Church's Magisterium. For the first time, I realized that when I read the Bible, I was interpreting it; previously, I had believed that I was merely absorbing its obvious meaning.

The clock of the tower of Nassau Hall tolled midnight, and I took a walk from my dorm room to St. Paul's Church on Nassau Street to the Aquinas Institute and back to Butler College. As I walked, You gave me the grace to think something like, "Here I am, Jeff Ziegler, seventeen years old, with my own propensities to sins X and Y, and breathing this Marxist, materialist, secularist air, conceiving that I can interpret Scripture; and there is the Catholic Church, with twenty centuries of never-changing but ever-developing interpretation of Scripture. Who am I to go against the Magisterium of the Catholic Church?" At that instant,

You gave me the grace to know the truth of the Catholic faith. I also knew that I could choose to accept or reject this grace. By Your grace, I chose to seek reception in the Catholic Church. I returned to campus as the clock struck one o'clock.

When I awoke the next morning, I did not go to the PCA service but instead attended Mass at the Aquinas Institute. I continued attending daily Mass and my instructions with Father McCloskey. On December 8, 1987, I made my first confession, was confirmed, and received my First Communion at the 7:30 p.m. Mass in the Princeton University Chapel.

"And from His fullness have we all received, grace upon grace" (John 1:16). Grace upon grace, a Blessed Trinity, grace upon grace! If any one of the events described above had not occurred, would I be a Catholic today? And You know, O Lord Christ, how utterly impoverished I would be without frequent encounters with You in Confession and Communion, how blind my intellect would be without the teaching of Your Vicar on Earth, the pope, and how tepid my heart would be without the graces granted through Eucharistic adoration and devotion to Our Lady.

What shall I render to the LORD
for all his bounty to me?
I will lift up the cup of salvation
and call on the name of the LORD.
Psalm 116[115]:12-13

Originally publlished in the CHNewsletter Jul-Aug 1997.

Jeff, who serves on the advisory board of the CHNetwork *and* Catholics United for the Faith, *teaches Latin and classical Greek at Thomas Jefferson Classical Academy in Mooresboro, North Carolina. He received his bachelor's degree in classics from Princeton University and his master's degree in sacred theology from the International Theological Institute in Gaming, Austria. He and his wife, Laura, have two daughters.*

You Are That Man

by Mark Connell
former ex-Catholic anti-Catholic Protestant

"I was born and raised in a Catholic home." This sentence, repeated in all too many "conversion stories," must be included in mine. It seems so much more tragic to preface a testimony with this sentence than to relay a happy conversion story that starts, "I was born and raised a staunch Calvinist, but then . . . " Why? Because when the story concerns a cradle Catholic, it signals that something was missing from what should have been the most wonderful, grace-filled Christian experience available on Earth.

Yes, the good news is that many of these Catholics are coming home! The disturbing news, however, is that these people once felt the need to leave the Church of their youth in order to recognize God's love.

Often, in an attempt to assuage the guilt of having left the Church over such issues as clerical abuse, lack of spiritual formation, or coldness in his or her local parish, an ex-Catholic will turn against the Church and become viciously anti-Catholic. This happened with me. I was not anti-Catholic when I left the Church, nor did I leave for any heavy doctrinal reason. I left for emotional ones. At the time of my departure, I was very pro-Catholic and longed for the Church to meet my spiritual needs, but I was angry that it wasn't.

I left the Church in 1992 to join a small, loving Protestant church. Eventually I would become an elder of this church, lead men's Bible studies, and host weekly prayer meetings. Independent of anything taught from the pulpit of this church,

I grew even angrier and proceeded to build a doctrinal "case" against Rome. Every evening, my grudge against the Church was hedging toward full-blown hatred as I reveled in the writings of professional anti-Catholics such as Dave Hunt and James G. McCarthy. Many a dark night slipped by as I continually "let the sun go down on my anger." Woe to the unprepared Catholic who crossed my path at this time! Woe to my Catholic family members! McCarthy and Hunt's books allowed me to build an airtight case against the Church, but I never considered that if air could not get in or out, neither could the Light. And so in the darkness of my prejudice, I grew as a misshapen plant. I bore bitter fruit on twisted branches.

I wrote anti-Catholic tracts and opened a post office box with the intent of distributing them. I spent long hours in the library researching local Catholic history in order to compile a "spiritual map" of my community. On a large street map, I marked the location of each Catholic church with an "X" (eight Xs in all). This mapping was done in order to target these Catholic churches for intense intercessory prayer campaigns. I was not praying for anything as noble as an increase in faith or vocations; I simply praying for all the Catholic churches in my community to be emptied. I went to many of these churches, anointed the buildings with oil, and prayed for the salvation of the members there.

Something Truly Miraculous

In the midst of all this, something truly miraculous happened. I heard a sermon by a Fundamentalist pastor who seemed to hate the Church as much as I did. In a pivotal moment of my spiritual life, I listened to him and comprehended fully what I had become. Suddenly, as when Nathan the prophet confronted the murderous King David, I could almost hear God say, "You are that man, Mark!" It was as if someone had held a mirror up to my face and I saw that I had become terribly disfigured. Hate had turned me into a monster. As I listened to this local anti-Catholic preacher,

I can vividly remember wondering what heaven would be like filled with only the "righteous" like him and me. I concluded that this kind of heaven would be a truly miserable and perfectly wretched place!

Within a month of hearing this sermon, I picked up a book by an "obscure" Catholic named Mother Teresa. *A Simple Path* challenged my whole conception of Christian service. Here was an elderly nun selflessly giving her whole life to Christ, but there was just one problem: She prayed the rosary! What was I to do? I knew that the rosary was an instrument used in "idolatrous" prayers to Mary; how could this woman serve God and Satan, too? For the answer, I turned to Dave Hunt's book, where he reassured me that "her [Mother Teresa's] evangelism leads no one to Christ . . . "[1] For some strange (and merciful) reason, I didn't buy Hunt's counsel this time. I began to wonder: *Am I just gathering around me a great number of teachers to say what my itching ears want to hear?* (cf, 2 Timothy 4:3)

I shared Mother Teresa's book with my pastor, a kind and compassionate man whom I still love deeply, and he was so moved that he preached a sermon on it. Contrary to Dave Hunt's assertion, people in this Protestant congregation were brought closer to Christ because of this nun's witness. Seeing this, I knew I had to radically alter my opinion of at least one Catholic, a tiny nun from Calcutta.

I was devastated by what I was discovering about my prejudices. The prospect that some of the very people I had been persecuting may in fact have been "saved" horrified me. I, of course, had no intention of going back to the Catholic Church, but at least I would be more charitable in my assessment of Catholics. Not wanting to concede too much, however, I resolved to reread Dave Hunt's book to see what I could salvage of my case against the Church.

---

[1] Hunt, Dave. (Eugene, Ore.:Harvest House Publishers, 1994), pg. 468.

Sola Scriptura: *Hunt or Luther?*

I started reading *A Woman Rides the Beast* for a second time, but this time something was different. Whereas in the past this book made me feel smug about my escape from the "Whore of Babylon," it now caused my case to collapse in ruins. This book is so internally inconsistent and mean-spirited, that I could only shake my head when I read it again. If Hunt had written in the same manner about the Jewish people, he would be termed an anti-Semite and featured on *Nightline*. Consider the following quote from his book: "Those conditioned to believe that wine had become Christ's blood were able to believe [Adolf] Hitler's myth of blood as well."[2] How could I be so blind to his prejudice?

As I studied this book, something else became apparent. In his rush to pummel Catholics, Hunt also wounded Martin Luther. With his assault on Luther's "heretical" belief in the real Presence, he shook my trust in *sola Scriptura*. Why? Because Luther and Hunt both believe that Scripture alone should be used to determine doctrine. Yet, while using Scripture, the two men were at opposite ends of the spectrum on what seemed to be a key doctrinal question: Is Christ physically present in the Eucharist? Hunt said this belief was "a fantasy" and "a hoax"[3] and cited many Scripture verses to support his belief. Luther disagreed, however, as he explained in *A Treatise Concerning the Blessed Sacrament and Concerning the Brotherhood*:

> There are those who practice their arts and subtleties to such an extent that they ask where the bread remains when it is changed into Christ's flesh, and the wine when it is changed into His blood; also in what manner the whole Christ, His flesh and blood, can be comprehended in so small a portion of bread and wine. What does it matter? It

[2] Ibid., pg. 377.

[3] Ibid., pg. 383 and 387

is enough to know that it is a divine sign, in which Christ's flesh and blood are truly present—how and where, we leave to Him.

Hunt claimed that Luther had been unable to jettison this belief from his Catholic upbringing. But Luther's writings clearly show that he used Scripture to support this belief, as is shown in the following quote from his Small Catechism:

> What is the sacrament of the Altar?
>
> Answer: Instituted by Christ Himself, it is the true body and blood of our Lord Jesus Christ, under the bread and wine, given to us Christians to eat and drink.
>
> Where is this written?
>
> Answer: The holy Evangelists Matthew, Mark, and Luke, and also St. Paul, write thus: "Our Lord Jesus Christ, on the night when He was betrayed, took bread, and when He had given thanks, He broke it, and gave it to the disciples and said, 'Take, eat; this is my body which is given for you. Do this in remembrance of me.'[4]

Hunt had a problem, and so did I. Using "Scripture alone," we had come to an impasse. *Sola Scriptura* did not seem to be a valid method for solving this important doctrinal dispute. Either Hunt was right or Martin Luther was right, or both were wrong. In any event, *sola Scriptura* had failed to weed out an error in doctrine. One or both were teaching a lie, but who? What Luther (using Scripture) saw as the body and blood of our Lord, Hunt (using Scripture) saw as a fantasy and heresy.

I saw that it ultimately came down to a standoff between Dave Hunt and Martin Luther's interpretations of Scripture. I started to wonder: *Am I just following the "traditions of men"*

---

[4] Tappert, Theodore G., trans. and ed. *The Book of Concord* (Philadelphia: Fortress Press, 1959), pg. 351.

by trusting Hunt, or am I following the intentions of Christ? This question started to burn inside of me. How would I resolve it?

Matthew 18: Our Lord's Instruction

I was dismayed to discover that I could not even bring this disagreement to "the church" as instructed by Jesus in Matthew chapter 18. In this discourse to His disciples, Jesus had outlined a three-step procedure to use if one had something against a brother, including the consequences if the brother would not submit to correction. I reasoned that Hunt's charge of heresy would qualify as having "ought against a brother." Jesus' solution was *not* to take this problem to the Scriptures (remember, that's how we arrived at this impasse) but instead to take it to "the Church." It suddenly became clear that I couldn't do this. Why not?

Well, quite frankly: To which Protestant church should I bring it? Dave Hunt's church? The Lutheran Church, which he had also charged with heresy? Or perhaps a "neutral" Protestant denomination like the Baptist church? If the Baptists, then which Baptist church? The Regular Baptists? The Southern Baptists? The American Baptists? To which one of the twenty-five thousand or so Protestant denominations should I bring it?

Which Protestant church would be given the final authority to cast one or both of these men out as "tax collectors and sinners"? And if they were cast out, what would stop them from simply starting up a new church, a church custom-tailored to their own particular teachings? The result could be denomination no. 25,001 and denomination no. 25,002 and a direct repudiation of Christ's command that this excommunication would be binding "in heaven and on Earth."

I began to see that in spite of the Protestant insistence on the Bible being the "court of last appeal," *sola Scriptura* was an unworkable doctrine. Without an authoritative Church with the authority to bind and loose (in heaven and on Earth), Jesus' solution for conflict resolution in the Church was ludicrous. I reasoned that Jesus loves us too much to give us worthless solutions; therefore, this authoritative Church must exist today, just as it must have existed from the time He issued the command. This Church also must have been exercising this authority throughout Christian history, definitively judging heresies such as Gnosticism and Pelagianism as being contrary to the truth.

I read the Church Fathers and saw that the belief in the Real Presence could be traced back to the early martyrs—the early Church consistently held that Jesus was really present in the Eucharist. From this discovery, I developed an intense hunger for the Eucharist that would not dissipate. I wanted to belong to a living Church tradition with a sense of being joined to a family that had its beginnings in the Upper Room and had continued to defend the Faith until this day.

During this time, I discovered that I didn't have to search for a church to weigh the merits of Luther's doctrine. Jesus Christ had already established a Church that had done just that. In the end, Dave Hunt had done what the Catholic Church had failed to do: He had destroyed my trust in *sola Scriptura*.

Implications

With these revelations came a necessary pruning. As branch after twisted branch of prejudice was lopped off, there was great pain and turmoil. I know that were it not for the love of my wife and the grace of God, I would not have survived the process. I did not want to leave the wonderful people at my church, and, as sad as it might sound, I did not want to leave the comfort of the dark little box into which I had tried to squeeze the richness of Christianity. On another level, I did not want to commit my life to a Church with which I was still angry. And to be even more honest, I did not want to eat the "wheelbarrows full of crow" that people would be lining up to feed me. Not surprisingly, this thinly veiled pride was the last obstacle to be overcome.

But I learned to lay my pride and anger aside as I prayed about Jesus' question in Luke 6:46, "And why do you call Me, 'Lord, Lord,' and do not do what I say?" I slowly came to the following conclusion: If someone is serious about obeying Christ, and if that person makes an honest and careful study of both Scripture and Church history, he or she will ultimately feel compelled to come into the bosom of the Catholic Church or suffer the utter misery of living a life of compromise.

My return to the Church happened on a quiet evening at the local monastery. There was no fanfare, no grand ceremony. I sincerely stated my intention to obey the teachings of the Church by making a profession of faith, and then I went to confession with my family. Together with our fellow Catholics, we received our Lord in the Blessed Sacrament during a public Mass. After a four-year rejection of the Eucharist, I could only weep. The sublime nature of the moment was heightened by the realization that this church was one of those marked by an "X" on my map.

On the edge of the woods near the monastery stands a statue of Jesus with arms outstretched. A detail of this statue had caught my attention while I was compiling my map two years earlier: The statue had no right hand. Such was my suspicion of the Church that this missing hand was proof to me of Rome's diabolical nature. The Bible had much to say about the importance of God's mighty right hand, and here was a symbol of the Catholic Church's negation of God's power. So, "X" marked the spot.

I pointed to the statue during one of my first meetings with the priest who brought me home. "See," I challenged, "Christ has no right hand!" Father Gabriel turned calmly toward me and said, "Mark, you are His right hand." My thoughts turned to Mother Teresa and my own stumbling journey to this place, and conviction followed. I had been so intent upon making God do my will that I hadn't even considered following Christ's insistent call to humble service. The sheer arrogance of my approach to "healing" the spiritual wounds of my community became brutally apparent. Now, whenever I leave Mass at this monastery, I see this statue that still challenges me to continue this lifelong process of dying to self.

Floating high above the Church of the Immaculate Conception, the symphony of bells calls the Catholics of this small Midwestern town to worship on this February morning. Far below the bell tower, the sanctuary slowly fills with people as I let my prayers ride upon the sound. It is a miracle that my wife and I are here today. A short year ago, I had told my Protestant pastor that I was going to pray for the Catholic people during Lent, that they would come to know the Lord. Now, here I am in this Church, eyes clouding with tears, heart filled with peace and wonder—a Catholic once again.

I have become graciously undone. All the things I thought I knew, all of my clever reasons for ridiculing these people, lie mercifully in ruins behind me. Heaped there also is my self-righteous facade, the victim of the truth. This morning, with nothing else to give God but my ragged self, I will offer that to Him again. In a short time, He will give Himself to my wife and me in a very real way. The priest will say, "The body of Christ," and we will say, "Amen!" We will proclaim what the Church has proclaimed for two thousand years: that Jesus is really and truly present in the Eucharist. Sitting here now, with the sounds and the sights of Catholicism above and around me, and with the expectation of the Eucharist before me, I am filled with awe. What a year. What a tumultuous and glorious journey.

As I write this, I am preparing for Ash Wednesday. Soon, the priest will place ashes upon my forehead as a symbol of repentance, death, and resurrection. As he inscribes a cross upon my forehead with an ash-blackened thumb, he will say something like this: "Repent and believe the Good News!" I will gladly bear upon my brow the symbol of our precious Savior's life-giving death. This will be the first time I will have participated in this solemn ceremony in five years. It will be nearly one year to the day since I voiced my commitment to pray for the Catholic people during Lent, that they might come to know the Lord. Isn't it amazing how God answers prayer?

Originally published in This Rock, *October 1997.*
Mark owns a business that supplies rock climbing equipment. He lives with his wife, Beth Ann, and son Nick in Utica, Illinois.

A Hop, a Skip, and a Great Leap

by Doug Trout
former ex-Catholic Evangelical Protestant

The Roman Catholic Church makes great claims of itself. By these, it distinguishes itself from other Christian traditions and communities in the world. Actually, many of these traditions consider these claims nothing short of audacious and a direct attack on orthodoxy. While some denominations may not be this aggressive in their denunciation of Rome, there is unanimous consent among Protestants and Evangelicals that the Catholic Church could not possibly be all that she claims to be.

I am thoroughly convinced that the reason for much of this dissent is ignorance rather than a true understanding of what the Catholic Church actually teaches.

I speak with experience in this matter. Even though I was raised in a Roman Catholic home, I didn't see religion as anything other than Sunday attendance at Mass. My neighborhood was predominantly Catholic, and yet I don't remember meeting anyone who seemed to be enthusiastic about the faith. As sad as it may sound, I don't recall hearing any Catholic outside the clergy even speak of God. Not only this, but they seemed rather uncomfortable to speak about their faith at all, as though it was a subject better left within the confines of church walls. Later in life, after having left the Catholic Church to become an Evangelical Protestant, I would often lament how terribly sad it was to see so many people apparently just going through the motions of Catholicism without having a living, vibrant relationship with Jesus Christ.

Now before I get a nasty phone call from one of my sisters, who will be upset with me because they don't understand how

I can say this, let me qualify my comments. Yes, my family did pray before dinner and ask God to bless our home, relatives, and friends. We were also encouraged to say our prayers at night before going to bed, at least when I was very young. My mother also had a crucifix on her bedroom wall. Beyond this, I don't remember any other religious discussion or influence in my home or among my Catholic friends. In a nutshell, every Catholic I knew seemed to be ignorant of his or her faith and indifferent toward the Church.

Now some of you may think I am being a bit harsh and unfair, but I can tell you that I have spoken with literally hundreds of Catholics who have had essentially the same experience. Many of them, unfortunately, either have abandoned Christianity altogether or have joined other Christian communities or sects whose theology and philosophy are in direct opposition to the Catholic Church. Still others remain Catholic and are practicing the ever-popular "cafeteria" Catholicism—a faith where they pick and choose the doctrines they wish to believe and submit to while discarding others as being irrelevant, out of touch, and impossible to live up to—a faith not in communion with the Catholic Church. This is a tragic situation that demands our attention.

I was a spiritually precocious child. Later on, when I entered high school, even though I was a lousy student, I had great interests in philosophy, psychology, and spirituality. I instinctively knew there was more to the meaning of life than what my experience as a Catholic had been. These were the only classes in school in which I excelled. By the time I was a senior in high school, I fancied myself a "free thinker" and loved to get into philosophical discussions of any kind. Without any strong Christian foundation, it was easy to divorce myself from organized religion of any kind and instead pursue "what was right in my own eyes."

In the mid-to-late seventies, drugs were easily accessible, and I soon fell in love with all of them. Most of my time was spent getting high and playing my guitar, preparing myself for what I thought would surely be my destiny: rock 'n' roll stardom. Eventually, drug abuse started taking its toll, and soon I was having a difficult time concentrating on anything. I became paranoid and felt hopelessly alone. Even though I was only sixteen years old, I had already burned myself out on dope.

It was at this time that I recall becoming aware that someone, or something, was trying to communicate with me. Somehow, I knew it was God. I soon started to hear the name Jesus in my head on a regular basis. This was very disturbing. I had stopped attending Mass a long time before and had distanced myself from any Christian influence. Deep in my heart, however, I felt Him calling me, and I knew He wouldn't stop. I can't explain the feeling very well, but I knew I belonged with Him. Sometimes I would cry, feeling like I was just incapable of responding. Instead, I kept avoiding Him, plunging myself headlong into a hedonistic lifestyle that wound up leaving me both morally and spiritually bankrupt. Yet, the void in my soul longed to be filled.

After graduating from high school, I joined the Marine Corps. There I ran into a good number of Christians who seemed peaceful and confident. I was jealous. I knew they were with the One Who wanted me, and yet I still would not heed His call. Many of these people challenged me to rethink Christianity. I started reading tracts and books on Bible prophecy that I found lying around the barracks, and as I became more exposed to the Bible, the louder the voice in my head became, pleading with my heart to embrace Christ. The modernist and pop-psychology arguments to which I had once appealed in forming my world-view were beginning to appear more and more like feeble, vindictive attempts to discredit religion and morality altogether. I could no longer find solace in them, and the temporal pleasures in life to which I had become captive were far too difficult to give up, so I proceeded on without Christ even as the voice kept calling.

After getting out of the Marine Corps, I joined a rock 'n' roll band and soon found myself back in the same burned-out condition. Knowing that much of my behavior was way out of sync with how God wanted me to live, I daily wrestled with my conscience, but the tugging in my heart only became stronger. I finally felt that I could not fight any more, and at the age of twenty-five, I decided to surrender my life to Christ.

I began attending an Evangelical Protestant fellowship, where I met people who were excited about their faith. They loved God and wanted to please Him in all areas of their life. They were moral and upright, encouraging me to seek and serve God with all my heart. Their example of holiness and piety prodded me into wanting that same kind of relationship with God in my own life. For this I am forever grateful.

I remained an Evangelical Protestant for ten years and was enrolled in seminary, pursuing my dream of becoming a pastor, when I met an old high school friend of mine. Mark, a lifelong Catholic whom I hadn't seen in years, had gone through a tremendous renewal experience. I, the Evangelical, was impressed with Mark's knowledge of the Bible, but I could not understand how anyone who had a "born again" experience could remain in the Catholic Church. I had never met a Catholic who knew much about the Bible, let alone could defend what I and the rest of Protestantism considered to be an unbiblical and indefensible theology.

I am forever indebted to Mark, who patiently listened to my arguments against Catholicism. His approach and attitude in refuting my arguments were gentle and thoughtful. I could tell that he was genuinely sincere about serving God with his whole heart and that he loved God. He was not out to win an argument; he was instead concerned with my very soul. I was impressed that not only did he have strong Biblical arguments to defend Catholicism but also that he loved God's Word and was a true student of it. He didn't pretend to have all the answers to my questions, but pointed me in the direction of people who did, eager to help in any way he could.

Through many long nights of study and prayer, I returned home to the Catholic Church in March 1997. Upon re-entering, I made a commitment to forever defend the Catholic Faith, to do whatever I could to help others understand the glory of the Church and to encourage others to do the same. It is in this spirit that I wish to present an explanation of what to me is the most convincing proof that the Catholic Church is everything she claims to be.

How Firm a Foundation

The Protestant Reformers, in the sixteenth century, staked their claims on what they called the two foundations upon which their renewal would stand or fall. These are *sola Scriptura*, the Latin term for "Scripture alone," and *sola fide*, another Latin term, for "faith alone."

In this article, we will be primarily concerned with the idea of "Scripture alone" theology.

This "doctrine," if you will, has some slightly different definitions depending on whom you're talking with, though all definitions share the same primary premise that the Bible alone is authoritative. In other words, the Bible alone is the sole rule of faith and practice for Christians and no one person or institution has the authority to bind the conscience of the believer.

As an Evangelical Protestant, I never questioned the validity of this doctrine. I had not expended much effort examining the far-reaching implications of the idea. It was taught to me as a matter of fact, without any air of controversy. Therefore, I had no reason or need to defend it. The thought of even entertaining Catholic thinking on this was so far from my mind that I never saw it as a viable option. The Evangelical view of history, the way I understood it, was that the true Church of Christ had always held to this principle and that it was not until the Catholic

Church had become corrupt and apostate that it was altered. I was told that the Protestant Reformers recognized this and restored the lost truths of the faith, rescuing humanity from hundreds of years of censorship and darkness.

This is not to say that I didn't struggle in looking for answers to the division among Bible-believing Christians. Actually, this was the one thing that most perplexed me when I first became an Evangelical. My enthusiasm for wanting to know everything I could about Christ and the Bible was all consuming. At the time, I was single and my social life revolved around the singles ministry at the church I attended. Here I met a great number of people who attended other churches but were coming to socialize. I can remember asking some of those people why they chose to attend other churches and not ours. I wondered what the differences were. How, I thought, could the Bible place such a premium on unity within the Body of Christ (Romans 12:4-5, Ephesians 4:4-6, 1 Corinthians 1:10, 12:12-13) while at the same time allow for so many differing interpretations? I was told that the appeals the Bible makes for unity did not mean that all Christians had to agree on every point of doctrine but rather share a basic understanding of the Christian faith. Often the person giving the answer would agree that the division among Bible-believing Christians was certainly a black mark upon the Church. However, this was easily explained away as a by-product of man's fallen nature. Sometimes this diversity was expressed as a strength rather than a weakness, because this kept man from being puffed up with knowledge. These matters were seen as "nonessentials" and allowed for freedom of conscience.

Over time, I grew to accept this line of thinking, feeling like Peter when he said to Jesus, "Where else can we go? You have the words of eternal life" (John 6:68). Even though I was never completely comfortable with this answer, I tried to shrug off the question as one of God's ways that my finite mind was incapable of understanding.

This question was reintroduced in my discussions with Mark. He asked me to explain how the Scriptures could claim the Church to be the "pillar and foundation of the truth" (1 Timothy 3:15) when churches have so many opposing positions on a wide variety of doctrinal issues. Remember, the dominant Protestant position is that the Body of Christ is made up of the true believers in Christ who are scattered throughout the world in various denominations. His argument was a strong one: How could Paul claim the Church to be *the very foundation of truth* and yet we hear so many different interpretations of what is true?

As an Evangelical, I was taught that sincerity does not equal truth—that a person could be very sincere and devout in his beliefs and still miss the boat because he was sincerely *wrong*. Yet all of a sudden, this seemed to be the very thing I had to accept if I was to continue in Evangelicalism. No post-Reformation denomination claims infallibility. Instead, Protestants believe that the dissension and division so prevalent within their ranks somehow forms a homogeneous gathering called the Church. This just didn't square with 1 Timothy 3:15.

This led me to a study on the issue of authority: Who had the authority to proclaim what the Bible taught, and upon what foundation is this authority based? How could I know that the Gospel I had received was the same Gospel of the Apostles? (Galatians 1:8) The Protestant Reformers' claimed that the Catholic Church was wrong in its interpretation of the Bible. The battle cry was "Scripture alone," but as was evident from the outset and glaring in their posterity, no consensus among them can be found. As I looked at the Reformers' claims, it seemed the height of hypocrisy for any one Reformer to tell people that all they needed was the Bible *alone* to give them understanding and yet proclaim from his pulpit how terribly mistaken others were when they disagreed with his interpretation. The numerous splits that occurred among the Reformers themselves, continuing to this day, suddenly made it clear to me that the single-mindedness of which the Scriptures speak of is impossible to maintain without a proper mechanism in place to provide the correct interpretation (1 Corinthians 1:10, Philippians 1:27-30).

I started again to look at all the verses of Scripture that had troubled me on this issue. In Matthew 18, Jesus told the disciples that if someone won't listen to the Church after repeated attempts to reconcile the matter, they must treat him as an outsider. My experience as an Evangelical was quite different from this. Often I would hear of people "church-hopping" because they had had a dispute with the leadership where they used to attend. I also knew of people who left churches over squabbles with fellow parishioners. Instead of following the suggestions in Matthew 18, they would just go off and find another place to fellowship until the next controversy occurred. This problem frustrates many pastors, but those who attempt to abide by the Scriptural mandate to execute church discipline are often accused of being dictatorial and harsh. They also risk incurring the wrath of other leaders within their congregation who might disagree and cause a greater split. I have seen this occur many times. Many of my friends who are pastors have related how impotent they feel in solving major disturbances authoritatively.

Jesus also told the Apostles in Matthew 18, "Truly, I say to you, whatever you bind on Earth shall be bound in heaven, and whatever you loose on Earth shall be loosed in heaven" (Matthew 18:18). I studied this phrase in great detail and realized that the Apostles had been commissioned with authority to legislate and regulate activity within the Church. This is literally what binding and loosing refers to in Matthew 18 (also Matthew 16:19). Jesus also told them that "he who hears you, hears Me, and he who rejects you, rejects Me" (Matthew 10:40, Luke 10:16). Jesus made it perfectly clear that their word is *final*, because their word is *His* word. The Kingdom of God is everlasting. In these passages, Jesus is commissioning the Apostles to administer the government of the kingdom. It only makes sense that since the kingdom is everlasting, the governing of that kingdom is also everlasting. The Evangelical and Protestant model of the Kingdom of God cannot stand, because no kingdom divided against itself can (Matthew 12:25)!

The mandate Jesus gave to His Apostles to govern the kingdom is without a doubt the most awesome responsibility given to the Church. And since it is a kingdom that cannot be shaken (Hebrews 12:28), it came with a promise. In Matthew 16:18, Christ tells the Apostles that "the gates of hell will not prevail against [the Church]." Hell could only prevail if it was successful in convincing the Church to implement and teach untruth, in effect taking a wrecking ball to the pillar and foundation of truth. In addition, Jesus promises that when the Holy Spirit comes, He will guide them into *"all the truth"* (John 16:12-15) and that He would never leave them desolate (John 14:15-18). The Bible and the Catholic Church both teach that it is not the integrity of men that keeps the Church from error but the promise of Christ.

The Apostle Paul demonstrates, in very practical ways, the understanding of the early Church in relation to this. One place he does this is in what I had considered the best proof text for the doctrine of *sola Scriptura*. In 2 Timothy 3:15-16, Paul tells Timothy that "all Scripture is inspired by God and profitable for teaching, for reproof, for correction, and for training in righteousness, that the man of God may be complete, equipped for every good work." Evangelical theologians and friends of mine will point to this and say, "See, Doug, it's all right here; this passage shows that we can rely on nothing but the Bible for our faith." The Bible often can say things we want it to say when we come to it with preconceived notions. Nowhere in this passage does it say that the Scriptures alone are authoritative.

Looking at the text again, but this time reading the two verses prior to 16-17 in the context of what Paul is saying, we see the fallacy in thinking this a proof text for *sola Scriptura*. Verse 14 begins, "But as for you continue in what you have learned, knowing from *whom* you learned it." Paul goes on in verse 15 to remind Timothy of his familiarity with the Old Testament Scriptures (at the time, of course, the New Testament did not exist) and their ability to *corroborate his teaching.* Yes, that's right; corroborate the apostolic message of salvation in Christ. For it is clear in the New Testament that the message of salvation was hidden until the Apostles were charged to reveal it (Matthew 28:20, Colossians 1:25-28, Galatians 2:7-8). The New Testament teaches that indeed the message of salvation is taught in the Old Testament, but hidden and never revealed without the authority of Christ and the Apostles (Matthew 11:27, Colossians 1:26, Ephesians 2:20-21, 3:5, Acts 10:34-43, 1 Peter 1:10-12, 1 Corinthians 2:6-12).

Look again at 2 Timothy 3:14. *It is not* an appeal for Timothy to look to the Scriptures alone for instruction but to regard them in light of his *instructor*, namely, Paul himself (cf. 2 Timothy 2:1-2). The Jews were using the Scriptures in an attempt to refute Christianity. If the Apostles could not appeal to their God-given authority in proclaiming the Gospel, then their teachings were nothing more than opinions and we would be free to disagree with them today. This, of course, is ridiculous.

In the same way, it would have been ridiculous to regard Timothy's teachings as *mere* opinion, as well as the teachings of those he was charged by the Apostle Paul to appoint as leaders after him.

Other passages that speak of authority are impossible to reconcile with *sola Scriptura.* Hebrews 13:17 says to "Obey your leaders and submit to them, for they are keeping watch over your souls as men who will have to give account; let them do this joyfully and not sadly, for that would be of no advantage to you." In this passage, one can see the writer being sympathetic to those struggling to submit. He's letting them know that if they have trouble agreeing with leadership, that these *leaders* will be held accountable, as if to say, don't worry, do *your* part, submit. However, at what point in the history of the Church did this command become optional?

The emphasis inherent in Protestant thinking is that individual fellowships and churches, even within many denominations, still maintain a great degree of autonomy from one another and therefore have the right to govern themselves. The concept of a familial, authoritative hierarchy is one that is impossible to reconcile with Bible-only theology and for this reason is carelessly overlooked. What is important to realize is that individual churches were never meant to be autonomous from one another, nor were they to govern themselves on their own. Again, this is clearly seen in the New Testament. When Paul appoints leaders in the churches he established, he didn't divorce himself from responsibility to lead them. On the contrary, he exhorts them to hold fast to the things he taught, and he visits them and appoints others to lead in his absence (2 Thessalonians 2:15, 2 Timothy 2:1-2, Titus 1:5-9). Not only this, but Paul himself submits to leadership (Galatians 2:1-3). The pattern for hierarchical authority is clearly established in the New Testament.

This pattern is also clearly seen in the Old Testament as well. In spite of the fact that God's appointed leaders at times were way off the mark both morally and spiritually, God never ordains anyone to start a reformed Judaism under the banner of *sola Torah* (for example, see 1 Samuel 1, 2, 19-31)

Jude also drives this point home. In Jude 11, he warns the reader not to error in the same way that Korah and his band of rebellious followers did. Jude is referring to Numbers 16. If you read the story, you'll find that Korah said nothing that would suggest his disapproval of Moses concerning orthodoxy. Korah's beef was that he wanted to know who put Moses in charge and why Moses thought he was so much better than everybody else, bossing them around the desert and so on. Hadn't God already made it clear that all the Israelites were a "kingdom of priests, a holy nation" (Exodus 19:6)? Who did Moses think he was to impose his will upon them? It didn't turn out well for Korah and his followers. Jude is giving a stern warning to New Covenant believers: Don't rebel against leadership.

Of course, all of these new insights were not very well received by my Evangelical friends.

Even in the face of the biblical evidence, they would tell me that the idea of a church hierarchy was contrived by the Catholic Church in order to maintain its political status, somewhere in the fourth or fifth century. They told me that the early church knew nothing of a pope or a Magisterium. Again, this is clearly not the case.

The patristic evidence supporting the Church's teachings on this is simply overwhelming. I was amazed to find throughout the writings of the early Church Fathers and their recognition of the Bishop of Rome as the supreme Bishop of the Church. Ignatius, an early Bishop of Antioch, ordained by John the Apostle, says that this Church holds the presidency over all the Churches (*Letter to the Romans*, A.D. 110). Many such statements are written throughout the first centuries of the Church. (A good source to look these up in is *The Faith of the Early Fathers*, a three-volume set edited by William A. Jurgens.)

As I studied the early writings of the Fathers, it also became clear that other doctrines concerning the Eucharist, communion of the saints, purgatory, Mary, and so on were not things invented by the Catholic Church in latter centuries but were evident from the beginning—part of the "deposit of faith," which was once for all delivered to the saints (Jude 3).

I am secure in my Father's house. I am daily filled with joy in knowing that the promise of Christ to lead His people into all the truth is being fulfilled in the Roman Catholic Church.

I will close with one of my favorite quotes from the great G.K. Chesterton, writing of the Catholic faith: "He has come too near to the truth and has forgotten that truth is a magnet, with the powers of attraction and repulsion . . . The moment men cease to pull against it [the Catholic Church], they feel a tug towards it. The moment they cease to shout it down, they begin to listen to it with pleasure. The moment they try to be fair to it, they begin to be fond of it. But when that affection has passed a certain point, it begins to take on the tragic and menacing grandeur of a great love affair . . . when he has entered the Church, he finds that the Church is much larger inside than it is outside."

My journey home to the Catholic Church reflects the sentiments expressed by Chesterton. Coming home to the Catholic Faith has not been easy. My wife still remains Evangelical and vigorously opposes my being Catholic. It has put a great strain on our marriage, and our future is unclear. Truth has been my desire from the time I first committed my life to the teachings of Christianity. As terrible as my circumstances may be, nothing can take away the gift I have received by the incredible grace of Jesus, the gift of the Church, made available to all who hunger for truth.

Originally published in the CHNetwork Journal *Apr-June 1998.*
Doug lives in Cleveland, Ohio.

How I Got This Way

By Chris Robinson
former Evangelical Protestant

Honest, I never meant to love the Catholic Church. I didn't even realize I had been reading Catholic books, until it was too late.

I think I was tricked by the One who has the most jovial disregard for human preference—the One who delights in surprising us, opening our eyes to bigger views of Himself, and taking us out of our comfort zones.

How on Earth did I get this way—relieved and grateful to be received into the Catholic Church?

Evangelicals expect Catholics to become Protestants, but not vice versa. They tend to look bewildered when they discover that, while I'm actively involved in an Evangelical congregation with my family, I've become a Catholic. They seem to feel awkward about further conversation. I've written this essay to answer the questions my Evangelical friends don't seem to feel comfortable asking.

My aim isn't necessarily to persuade anybody else but simply to describe what persuaded me—how my attitude and thinking changed. My conversion didn't come from reading a few pages, so it's also difficult to summarize in a few pages. I've tried to keep this shorter, nonetheless, by avoiding long explanations of what Catholics believe and why, and sticking to my own story.

The trek began quietly around 1987, when I accidentally recognized that some Catholics had a surprising level of spiritual depth. In many years as a committed Evangelical Christian, I had read the right books, listened to leading pastors, and had taken graduate-level classes in theology while my husband,

David, was in seminary. I taught inductive Bible studies, college-age Sunday school, and spent several years as a missionary. It was while we were missionaries in Egypt that I happened to read some older-than-Evangelical books that reached deeper into me than anything I had read before. I wanted to read more of those great old books—and then it dawned on me that those authors were all Catholic.

It stunned me to realize I had been learning from Catholics. Years ago, when I had gone to the Catholic Church with friends, I had been surprised by the beauty of the liturgy, the clarity of the Gospel, *and* the apparent disinterest of most of the people around me. I hadn't meant to be arrogant, but I had assumed the Catholic Church was spiritually wasted; otherwise, why had God brought about the Reformation? Yet *these* old Catholics had much to teach me!

I realized I was ignorant about Catholics. In some ways, it seemed as if Catholics and Protestants were all descendants from a generations-old family feud in which both sides of the family had gotten used to excluding each other and most didn't know much about the original dispute.

Questions sprouted. Are Catholics really Christians or not? Some Catholics sure seem to know Jesus; is that in spite of the Catholic Church? What keeps Catholics and Protestants apart? If Catholics aren't really Christians, I thought, I'd better find out and quit reading those old books!

So the first phase of exploration came partly from a desire to know whether Catholic books were really "safe" to read and partly from curiosity about Christian roots. But even more, I just wanted to know God better. If God was working in the Catholic Church but I failed to value it, then I must not know Him as fully as possible. If God had a Catholic side, I didn't want to be guilty of closing my heart to that part of Him. I had begun to have an uncomfortable hunch that God might not be as separated from Catholics as we Protestants were.

I started reading church history. My initial belief was, roughly, that over time the Catholic Church had become irredeemably corrupt and that by Martin Luther's day God had basically given up and started over with the triumphant Reformation.

History challenged that view, however. Indisputably, there were very serious problems within the Church of Luther's day. As a movement, however, the Reformation appeared to have had as many social and political motivations as spiritual ones. It was a tangled time. Holy leaders called for reform from within the Catholic Church, while others like Luther felt they had no choice but to jump ship. Theologically, Reformers differed from each other drastically about matters of doctrine and practice. The Reformation didn't seem so clean and pristine—so triumphantly directed by God—as I had thought. Luther's oft-quoted claim about plowboys being able to understand the Bible seemed to be contradicted by various Protestant leaders' inability to agree about very basic issues.

Reading beyond the Reformation . . . well, Protestant history seemed almost embarrassing, even when written by Protestants. Our track record over the centuries was no more stellar than that of Catholics. Besides all the doctrinal disagreements, virtually every sin and fault we criticized in the Catholic Church had been repeated in Protestant history. We hadn't purified ourselves by getting away from Rome; the problem remained within us. in the meantime, the Catholic Church had undergone many internal reforms about which Protestants tended to be oblivious. And it seemed clear that God continued to do wonderful things through faithful Catholics, although we Protestants usually didn't notice.

I hadn't grown up in a church-going family, but I had spent time in several denominations and independent fellowships. At times, with all the differing opinions, I had wondered what Jesus had meant when He told the Apostles that the Holy Spirit would guide them into all truth. Now I faced the puzzle: Protestant history didn't appear to validate a *sola Scriptura* (Bible alone) view.

Part of the legacy of the Reformation was Protestants splitting
again and again from people they disagreed with over the interpretation and application of the Bible. Yet, it couldn't be that God
had kept the roots of authority in the Catholic Church. . . .

I read some biographies of respected Christians, including
St. Francis of Assisi and John Hyde ("Praying Hyde"). While one
was Catholic and the other Presbyterian and they lived centuries
apart, I was struck by several similarities. Both were committed
to celibacy; both were men of deep prayer; both bore various
physical ailments with joy; both saw many instances of God's
miraculous intervention. Both seemed to have delighted God. I
could not overlook the fact, however, that St. Francis also had
all those very Catholic peculiarities like devotion to Mary, belief
in transubstantiation, and submission to the pope. I wondered if
maybe God wasn't offended by those Catholic peculiarities as
much as we Protestants were.

I moved on to explore Catholic beliefs. In addition to reading Protestant books about Catholic beliefs, I also actually read
Catholic books about Catholic beliefs. It disturbed me to see that
Protestant books consistently misrepresented Catholic teachings.
I had thought that Catholic "prayers to saints" were an ignorant
substitute for prayer to God, as if Catholics believe the saints are
equal to God or that God will not hear our prayers directly. I had
thought that the notion of the infallibility of the pope meant that
Catholics think that popes are sinless and that everything they say
is infallible. I had thought that the Catholic Church teaches that
we are saved by works, not by grace. Many Catholics also mis-
understand what the Church teaches about such things, but once
I realized what she actually teaches, I had fewer objections.

This brought on a sense of *déjà vu*. David and I were serving
as missionaries in a Muslim country. While our Muslim friends
generally loved to discuss religion, they never seemed able to
hear what we actually believed. They were sure they already
knew what Christians believed, and equally sure that Christians

were wrong. Yet when they stated what they "knew" Christians believed, it was quite distorted. It seemed that the same thing was true with Protestants regarding Catholic theology. Just as one couldn't learn about true Christianity by asking a Muslim—even one who claims to have been raised a Christian—it didn't seem that one could learn about Catholicism by listening to Protestants. Just as Muslims seemed predisposed not to truly "hear" what Christians believe, so Protestants seemed predisposed to misconstrue what the Catholic Church teaches. It is so hard for us to consider that the truth we have held may contain some error or at least may only be part of the picture.

So I tried to be open-minded as I considered the Catholic Church's viewpoints. I looked again at the Catholic belief in *sola verbum Dei*—the Word of God alone as authority, expressed through the Bible, through Sacred Tradition, and through the Magisterium, the living Church leadership.

It dawned on me that Protestant beliefs actually don't come solely from Scripture. Without admitting it, Protestants follow their own brands of Magisterium and Tradition—each group having its own authoritative voice in interpretation of the Bible, whether it's Tim LaHaye or R.C. Sproul or T.D. Jakes.

For example, Baptism: Is it a sign of individual faith, as believed by the Baptists, or a sign of the covenant, as Reformed folk believe? Should it be done by full immersion, as Baptists insist, or is it OK to sprinkle? The reason denominations disagree about this is that it isn't absolutely clear in the Bible. People hold to one view or another because they accept the voice of authority of their denomination, which is their form of "Magisterium," although they don't call it that.

When I married my Presbyterian husband, my church background had been basically Baptist. I eventually became reconciled to infant baptism because I learned that the earliest Christians practiced infant baptism. We didn't call it "the authority of Sacred Tradition," but it had made sense to me that the consistent practices of the earliest Christians must have been all right.

Another example I pondered: The doctrine of predestination is believed, with variations, by those in the Reformed faith. Predestination, however, is not taught clearly in the Bible. If it were, the shelves of theological libraries would not be filled with books on the topic of predestination vs. free will. If you asked people in our Presbyterian church, I expect almost everyone would say they believe in the doctrine of predestination—not because they fully understand it or can articulate much about it themselves, but because it's upheld by the denomination and articulated by smart guys like R.C. Sproul.

This mind-boggling notion came to me: The Catholic "distinctives" were not unbelievable, any more than Christian beliefs in general. They were just unfamiliar. They seemed unacceptable because I had been taught they weren't true. I already accepted teachings from the Bible that offended non-Christians. My submission to those teachings didn't come because they made total sense, but because I am convinced the Bible is dependable, I believe reality isn't limited to what I have personally experienced or what my little brain can comprehend. If the Bible clearly spelled out the Immaculate Conception, I would have believed it years ago, just as I believed in the Virgin Birth. I had changed my views on infant baptism due to Sacred Tradition: Could Sacred Tradition also change my views on Mary? It's no more difficult to believe in the Immaculate Conception, if one believes in the authority of the Church, than it is to believe in the Virgin Birth, based on the authority of the Bible.

I saw more parallels. It's no more difficult to believe in the Assumption of Mary than in the assumption of Enoch or Elijah. It is no more difficult to accept the Church's teachings about contraception than to accept the Bible's teachings about sexual morality in general. It is no more difficult to believe in the true presence of Christ in the Eucharist than to believe in the Incarnation.

Notice, I didn't say it's easy to believe any of this. It goes against my human grain to put my trust in miracles I can't absolutely prove, to live by extremely unpopular standards, or to submit to authority beyond my little self. Yet, ever since the Gospel first struck me as true, I recognized the importance of growing in my knowledge and practice of the truth, however inconvenient. One of my favorite Bible teachers was fond of saying that we should always live in obedience to our understanding of the Bible and that we should always hold our understanding of the Bible in an open hand for God to add to or correct. The question I now asked was whether authority rested solely in the Bible or whether the authority of the Word of God came, as Catholics claimed, through the checks-and-balances of the Bible, Sacred Tradition, and the living Magisterium.

Again, Protestant history made the latter view seem more reasonable. The Catholic Church had succeeded in growing past so many of its own sins and blunders, while Protestants kept dividing in reaction to sins and blunders. The Catholic Church maintained its stand on the authority of the Bible, while most denominations weakened on that issue as generations passed.

Some issues were not difficult for me. Early in my reading, it made sense to me that there is a major difference between worship and veneration. I didn't see any problem with veneration of Mary and the saints. I also found the basic idea of purgatory surprisingly easy to understand and amazingly biblical. The real issue was whether I could let go of the prejudiced assumption that, "This belief/practice couldn't be right because this is what Catholics think/do."

Gradually, with great uneasiness, I realized that Catholic theology made more sense to me than what I had learned as an Evangelical Protestant. I had quit "protesting"; I was a closet Catholic. I doubted myself: How could I be persuaded by ideas that didn't interest my Evangelical friends, let alone persuade them? Scariest of all, David hadn't shared my reading curiosity, hadn't experienced the paradigm shift, and now we didn't want it to be something that would divide us. In the first years of our marriage, we had been unified in our sense of calling. Now we didn't know what to do as missionaries since I had become Catholic-at-heart. David hadn't read along with me in history and Catholic theology; now he didn't want to read for the purpose of trying to talk me back into Protestant beliefs.

We ended up returning to the United States for a number of reasons, among them our inability to find an acceptable school situation for our growing daughters and, frankly, my own burn-out. Some people from the mission suggested that my interest in Catholicism had been a subconscious way of trying to escape the difficulties of our mission situation and that once we were home from the field, my subconsciously motivated interest would naturally decline.

The quandary did go onto the back burner for several years. It was not easy to re-establish life in the United States after spending our entire post-college adult life—a total of thirteen years—preparing and then serving as missionaries. We were, in a sense, "wounded soldiers," and it was disappointing that with few exceptions our Evangelical brothers and sisters were either too busy or felt too uncomfortable to help us heal. I got new insights into the story of the Good Samaritan when the people with the "right theology" tended to keep their distance from our pain.

In retrospect, I think most of us Christians tend to have seriously oversimplified views of how God works in ministry and through leadership. When we see troubles in Christian leaders that don't fit our beliefs/expectations, we tend to go into avoidance or denial. David and I had been Christian leaders as missionaries, and even though we weren't guilty of scandalous sin, we didn't seem like such heros anymore. Many people kept us at a distance because we didn't fit their expectations. I became disillusioned over God's permissiveness with all who call themselves Christians.

I recalled many examples of committed Christians who sought God's will and guidance, yet ended up doing all kinds of ill-advised things, ranging from the pathetic to the disastrous. This brought me deep anxiety. For several years, my experience encouraged me to be a deist; it was a major exercise in faith to trust that God was truly involved in Christendom. Yet, I couldn't help but believe in Jesus, so I couldn't pitch Christianity and settle into deism, much to my frustration. I spent several years on the edge of cynicism, seeking to be content with simply trusting God, emptying myself of expectations.

In June 1997, I somehow received grace to recognize my need to forgive the Evangelical "system" that had wounded me. It's a pivotal issue in the Christian life: our need to forgive other Christians who fall short and, beyond that, our need to be reconciled to God, Who doesn't go along with our naive expectations. Next, I realized it took the same kind of grace for me to forgive Evangelicals as it would take anyone to forgive the Catholic Church for her faults. Somehow I found myself with more courage to face how badly we sincere Christians botch things, and with clearer faith in God's ability to work beyond human and institutional flaws. It was all the more obvious to me that God had never lost the Catholic Church.

I guess my conversion happened in three general phases: First, my heart recognized God at work in the Catholic Church and was drawn to Him; second, my mind had to be satisfied that the theology was sound; third—again, a heart issue—I had some hard lessons to learn about God and reconciliation.

Interesting timing: Shortly after that, David asked if I would be interested in taking "whatever class people take when they want to become Catholics." I think he was hoping that more exposure to Catholics would disappoint me and I would finally let go of this inconvenient interest. My nervous phone call to the local parish church led to the discovery that our wonderful priest, Father David Dye, is also a convert from Protestantism. From

him, I learned about the *Coming Home Network*, a lay apostolate that helps non-Catholic clergy come home to the Catholic
Church. I don't know if you can imagine how alone I had felt in
this whole process, how I wondered at times if it was God drawing me or whether I had somehow "lost it." At least if I had lost
my mind and the Catholic Church looked like the true Church to
me, I wasn't entirely alone anymore!

The decision to become officially Catholic was still not a
painless one. For every other step of obedience to God, I had
received lots of encouragement and affirmation from many
Christians. I hadn't realized that approval had always been an
important part of the bargain for me until it was missing. There
were many reasons why joining the Catholic Church would be
impractical and difficult, but I didn't think ease and convenience
were supposed to be my criteria for deciding. I worried because I
did not want to divide my family, didn't want friends to feel hurt
or confused, and preferred to avoid misunderstanding and criticism. Yet, I also sensed that God wasn't worried—that He was
delighted and even amused.

It's a challenge to help Protestants understand, because Protestants change church membership for different reasons than I
did: usually because of disagreements, disappointment, or simply personal preferences—in doctrine, practice, or even music.
From that framework, my decision could seem like a rejection,
or worse, a rebellion.

But my entry into the Catholic Church came because of
what I grew to believe about God and about the nature of the
Church, how He works in and through little humans. It was a
response to the greatness and mystery of God—not a search
for greener grass but an acceptance of how big the lawn is.
At one point, our Presbyterian pastor told me, with characteristic warmth and concern, "We just can't let you do this.
We can't let you join the Catholic Church!" And I thought,
"The only way for me to not become a Catholic would be to

believe again that God is smaller and shrink my heart in the process."

The Catholic Church rejoices over God's work in Protestant congregations, although she considers their message incomplete. She sees them as part of God's family, as "separated brethren." The Gospel is powerful, and God blesses us as we submit to as much of it as we know. In contrast, many nominal Catholics do not know or live the fullness of the truth that the Catholic Church teaches. It was a Catholic convert, G.K. Chesterton, who wrote, "It's not that Christianity has been tried and found wanting, it's that it has been found difficult and left untried." It is left untried by non-Christians as well as many of us who call ourselves Christians, whether Catholic or Protestant.

In my case, joining the Catholic Church hasn't meant leaving my family's congregation. I participate in the Catholic Church on my own while continuing worship, fellowship, and service with my family. It might surprise people to hear that Catholic Church leadership encourages me to do this since my family is not Catholic. Father Dye even told David that if I get divisive, he will be David's advocate and get on my case.

The friends who have reacted most negatively to my news have been ex-Catholics or those married to ex-Catholics. They sincerely feel that they did not find God in the Catholic Church and instead experienced guilt, manipulation, dead rituals, legalism, and so forth. I understand the once-burned reaction. The irony is that I know folks from every imaginable Protestant background who express similar frustrations. Again, I perceive the problem is not with the Catholic Church itself but with human beings. Protestantism seems to me, to some degree, to be a quest for a congregation and leaders who will not disappoint.

We Christians so easily hurt each other as we stumble after Jesus; we can't survive if we don't practice reconciliation.

Well, that's my story of how I got this way, from Evangelical to Catholic. If my affiliation concerns you, perhaps you can be

comforted if you believe the Catholic Church hasn't done serious damage to folks like Blessed Mother Teresa and St. Francis
of Assisi. Whatever your opinion, I hope you will pray for me,
and I will pray for you: that we will follow Him with trust and
courage, as He calls us all to unity in Himself, to be His presence
on earth.

Post Script:

It's now seven years later, and it seems good to add a sort of
epilogue about what life is like for me several years after being
received into the Catholic Church.

In short, life is good! I have no regrets about accepting the
Catholic Church's invitation to come home. I'm grateful to be
able to receive the sacraments, and to be a part of that visible
as well as mystical Body of Christ which extends through the
centuries.

On the other hand, life is a little weird! It's somewhat inconvenient, but not oppressively so. At least weekly, I go to Mass by
myself. On rare occasions my husband or daughters come with
me, but they really don't "like" Catholic Mass, so it's usually just
me. Becoming Catholic was my decision, not theirs.

Also, at least weekly I attend worship services at the Presbyterian Church in America (PCA) congregation where my husband is now an elder. I do some volunteer work at my parish, but
most of my volunteer work is at my husband's church, and I look
for ways to serve where the doctrinal differences are not an issue. It's a congregation which has its flaws, like any community
of people, and I don't agree with everything, but I know God is
at work there and I'm happy to cooperate. As a couple, we have
a few acquaintances at my parish, but our social life is at his
church. I would like to grow deeper friendships with Catholics
but other time commitments limit that. My friends at the PCA
church are dear to me, and they are a lot of fun besides.

Our daughters are young adults now, and I grin as I say: having a mom who became Catholic doesn't seem to have confused or damaged them.

Catholics ask if my husband has any significant interest in Catholicism, and the simple answer is no, at least not so far. He serves well in the congregation where he's now an elder, and I think his impression is that God has enough for him there.

Catholics ask if my Protestant friends ask me about Catholicism, and the short answer is, not usually. Perhaps they are uncomfortable asking, perhaps they think I would be uncomfortable being asked, or perhaps (what I think is most likely) they just have enough on their minds already and it doesn't occur to them.

Still, over the long haul I've had many great conversations, as well as a few that didn't go well. A few people are positively curious about Catholicism; a few others have strong negative reactions to the subject.

Over many months, one Protestant friend asked me lots of good questions about my new Catholic faith, thought about the answers, and kept coming back with more good questions. I had the honor of being her sponsor a couple of years later when she decided to become Catholic, and not too long afterward, her husband took that step as well.

On the other side, there have been a few discussions in which I realized the other person perceived me as pushy and insensitive, when from my perspective I had only been speaking with enthusiasm about what is dear to me and had meant no judgment of them.

In all the years of my journey into the Catholic Church, there wasn't anyone trying to force it on me or actively convince me. I was curious about it, I asked questions, and along the way I met Catholics who warmly listened and responded. Since I've become Catholic, I love talking about my faith, I love being asked about it, and seeing people's surprise when they realize the Catholic faith is more beautiful and reasonable than they had realized. Sometimes

Catholics ask if I hear anti-Catholic teachings in my husband's church. The teaching pastors at my husband's congregation rarely say much about the Catholic Church in their sermons, but when they do, it's nearly always disappointing: a replay of misinformation passed to them by teachers they trusted. A few times over the years, I've approached them afterwards, sometimes face to face and sometimes in writing, to question and to offer more accurate information. These have been good conversations. Once I respectfully asked the senior pastor to consider halting attempts to represent what the Catholic Church teaches, unless or until he was able to put a significant amount of time into reading what she actually teaches and not books by Protestants about what she teaches. He didn't exactly grant my request, but it seemed like a good thing to ask.

What is it that helps people with significantly different viewpoints to hear each other and to be able to express their views without provoking the defensiveness of their hearers? I'm not really sure. The best I know is to avoid letting anything within myself prevent me from hearing another person, and to try to speak about my convictions in a way that communicates respect. One of the things I love about Blessed Mother Teresa is that people who disagreed with her beliefs still knew that she loved them. Blessed Mother Teresa, please pray for me, that the same can be said of me!

Originally published in the CHNetwork Journal *Jul-Dec 1998.*

Chris Robinson became a massage therapist in 1991, shortly after moving back to the U.S. from Egypt. She works with people from many different walks of life, including corporate executives, retirees, celebrities and monks. Her husband, David, is now an instructional technologist and their two daughters are on their way out of the nest. They live in metro Atlanta.

We Do Not Stand Alone

by Todd von Kampen
former Missouri Synod Lutheran

Well, this is going to be a great story, I thought.

I was in Denver's Mile High Stadium, and it was August 12, 1993. Ninety thousand young people from all across the globe, worked up to a fever pitch, erupted with thunderous cheers as they first spotted their hero: Pope John Paul II, just arrived to officially open World Youth Day.

My wife, Joan, was nearby with a group of Catholic young people from Scottsbluff and Gering, Nebraska, where we lived and worked at the daily newspaper. She was there as a participant, a cradle Catholic taking advantage of a once-in-a-lifetime opportunity to see her spiritual leader. I was plying my trade.

I jotted down impressions in my notebook as John Paul toured the stadium and began his greetings to the numerous nations represented in Denver. Nothing unexpected for a world leader, I thought, as the pope began greeting the non-Catholic Christians in the audience.

"Most of you are members of the Catholic Church, but others are from other Christian churches and communities, and I greet each one with sincere friendship," he said. "In spite of divisions among Christians, '*all those justified by faith through baptism are incorporated into Christ . . . brothers and sisters in the Lord.*'"

The Holy Father shook up my life in that moment. It may be difficult to understand why . . . unless you've grown up Lutheran.

I had just heard a statement echoing the key battle cry of the

Reformation, the one cited by Martin Luther and all Lutherans after him as the doctrine on which the Church stands or falls: "For it is by grace you have been saved, through faith—and this not from yourselves, it is the gift of God—not by works, so that no one can boast" (Ephesians 2:8-9, NIV).

And it had come from the *pope*—the successor of the man who excommunicated Luther nearly five hundred years before. Well-versed Catholics will recognize that John Paul merely quoted *Unitatis Redintegratio*, the Decree on Ecumenism from Vatican II. But I didn't know that. It was one of many things I didn't know—one of many things I wouldn't have believed only a few years before.

My mind raced back nearly six years to the day, back to the rectory at St. Agnes Catholic Church in Scottsbluff. I thought I wanted to marry Joan, but I had to be sure. I asked my most burning question point-blank to her pastor, Father Robert Karnish: "What is the way salvation is obtained?"

Without hesitation, Father Bob answered: "Faith in Jesus Christ, which is totally unmerited by us."

His answer backed up what Joan had been telling me—that she believed what I did when it came to justification. Because he answered that way, I stood before him to marry Joan a few months later.

And because the Holy Father said what he said at that moment in Denver, God eventually led me into the Catholic Church.

Scenes from a Journey

Every life's journey has its key scenes; its watershed events that set the course for all that follow them. Mine were placed roughly at five-year intervals from my Confirmation in my native denomination, the Lutheran Church-Missouri Synod (LCMS), on April 2, 1978, to my reconciliation with Rome on March 29, 1998.

To be specific, just five scenes form the backbone of my journey into the Catholic Church. My heart and mind are full of thoughts; my bookcase is bulging with books and magazine articles that multiplied as the journey went on. I could easily fill a special newspaper section—if not a full-length book—with the things that seem absolutely essential to understand how this born, bred and convicted conservative Lutheran ended up in the Roman Catholic Church!

However, throughout these five scenes, the issue of justification was there all the time. If you grow up in the LCMS and really believe what it teaches, it can't be otherwise. Of all the thousands of Protestant denominations, few are more dedicated than the Missouri Synod to preserving the original arguments with Rome—especially when it comes to justification, the article on which Luther said the church stands or falls.

To Catholics then and now, the key issue in the Reformation is authority—Luther's rejection of the doctrinal authority of the pope and the Magisterium of the Church. And, indeed, the continuing rejection of that authority is very important to Lutherans. It's not, however, the first issue they talk about.

Justification comes first—for Luther and the Reformers couched every disagreement in terms of their conviction that the Catholic Church doesn't believe that salvation comes through Christ's free gift, but from performing this sacrament, that rite, this prayer to Mary, that indulgence.

Almost any spiritual journey from Wittenberg to Rome—especially if it detours through Missouri—hinges totally on that conviction. Unless Lutherans perceive common ground with Catholics on justification, Catholics can't hope to get Lutherans to listen to the Church's views on authority, Mary and the saints, purgatory, and indulgences and the sacraments, especially the Eucharist. Unless the cornerstone of Lutherans' mighty fortress against Rome is removed, the rest of the wall won't fall.

Let's go back to the place where my fortress was built.

Scene 1, 1978: "We Knew What Was Right"

I was in a classroom in a Lutheran school in western Nebraska, not too long before my Confirmation. My pastor drew a diagram on a chalkboard to outline the differing beliefs on what happens when the Words of Institution are spoken in the Eucharist.

The Catholic section of the diagram said only "body" and "blood"; the Protestant section, "bread" and "wine." The Lutheran one linked "bread" to "body" and "wine" to "blood," showing Luther's belief in Christ's real presence "in, with and under" the bread and wine. Catholics believe in transubstantiation, Pastor said; Protestants believe the Eucharist is only a symbol. Both were wrong; Luther was right. This is where our synod stands.

Missouri is big on taking stands. The synod's founders were Saxon Germans who immigrated to America in 1839 rather than submit to the forced union of Germany's Lutheran and Reformed (Calvinist) state churches. The first LCMS president, the Rev. C.F.W. Walther, firmly believed in the doctrines espoused by Luther and his fellow German Reformers, especially as expressed in the Lutheran Confessions—the doctrinal statements adopted by Lutherans in the 1580 *Book of Concord.*

Walther's beliefs have been enshrined in the Missouri Synod since its founding in 1847. Article II of the LCMS Constitution makes it crystal clear what every member congregation must uphold: "the Scriptures of the Old and the New Testament as the written Word of God and *the only rule and norm of faith and of practice*" and the Lutheran Confessions "*as a true and unadulterated statement and exposition of the Word of God.*"

That constrains Missouri's members to stand firm against all who believe otherwise—even if they're in another Lutheran church body, even if they're part of the LCMS itself. During my childhood (I knew nothing of this before college), most of the faculty and students of the synod's flagship seminary in St. Louis walked out in 1974 after a majority of delegates to the previous year's LCMS convention declared they were drifting too far from Missouri's historic course and too close to liberal theology and its denial of scriptural authority. (A number of congregations followed them out and eventually joined two larger church bodies in the 1988 formation of the Evangelical Lutheran Church in America.)

These beliefs also commit the LCMS to the German Reformers' litany of objections to the Catholic Church's teachings: Catholics believe salvation depends on your works; they place the pope above the Bible; they pray to Mary and the saints; they believe in purgatory; they accept seven sacraments, not two; and, of course, they insist on this "magic show" called transubstantiation.

I absorbed all these objections, along with the absolute emphasis on justification by grace through faith as the chief cornerstone of Christianity. Christ died on the cross to save us from our sins. We're born sinful; there's nothing we can do to earn salvation. We are saved only through God's free gift of faith through Christ's sacrifice on the cross. And we need that free gift throughout our lives, for the Christian is both saint and sinner— always prone to fall into the trap of believing he or she can make it to heaven without God's help.

There was no doubt whatever in my mind about it—indeed, no one in my family doubted it. My Danish maternal grandmother summarized it best when recalling her own childhood a century ago: "We knew what was right, and it never occurred to us to do otherwise."

Which only more strongly poses the question: Given my background, how on Earth could I end up Catholic?

On one level, the answer is easy: It was God's grace. More to the point, He preserved me from the depth and intensity of the Missouri Synod's official feelings regarding the Catholic Church. For if you believe the Confessions are drawn from God's Word, you also commit yourself to believing "the pope of Rome and his dominion" (to quote a 1932 LCMS doctrinal statement) are the

Antichrist—Luther's incendiary charge against those who threw him out of the Church.

That simply wasn't part of my training. Young Missouri Synod Lutherans aren't taught the entire contents of the Lutheran Confessions. They are expected to read and master Luther's *Small Catechism*, which certainly includes the key elements of Lutheranism—the stress on justification, the views on the Real Presence. But you won't find the word "Antichrist"—or any anti-Catholic polemics—anywhere in it.

Though my pastor taught the theological differences with Rome, he didn't teach the polemics, and he didn't call the pope the Antichrist. And the standard LCMS Confirmation vow requires a new member to confess belief in Lutheran teachings "as you have learned to know it in the Small Catechism"—not the Confessions as a whole.

So I didn't carry all the anti-Catholic baggage into life as an adult Lutheran. But I believed the Missouri Synod's take on Rome's beliefs as firmly as Luther ever did.

Scene 2, 1983: Once Saved, Always Saved?

Fast-forward a few years. I was alone in a hotel room in Germany on the Fourth of July, the last day of a five-week tour with my LCMS college choir in honor of Martin Luther's five hundredth birthday. I was paging through my Bible, writing in my diary, looking for answers to reconcile what I believed about justification with what I'd witnessed among our group.

I had entered that school a year before with the intention of becoming a music teacher in LCMS high schools. The European tour changed my life. We sang in beautiful cathedrals, drank in the sights of our ancestral land and even sang a surreptitiously scheduled concert behind the Iron Curtain in a tiny, embattled church in Leipzig in what was then East Germany.

Those were the high points. They weren't why I was in that room.

Several of the choir members—people planning to be pastors, teachers, church musicians—largely abandoned the pretense of consistently living their faith while they were so far from home. Some of them drank to excess, which didn't help. But they also ridiculed those who suggested they weren't setting a good example.

And the leadership of the choir, all too often, sided with them.

We were all young; I know I didn't handle my own reactions as well as I should have. But the experience shattered my beliefs about who we were and what we were supposed to be doing. It wasn't that I expected people not to sin; I learned my Confirmation lessons too well for that. But these ministers-in-training not only were sinning . . . they didn't seem to care.

So there I was, trying to make sense of what had happened, asking myself: Was I wrong? I found myself in Paul's letter to the Romans, the epistle Luther used more than any other in building his theology of justification.

"What shall we say, then?" Paul wrote in Romans 6:1-2 (NIV). "Shall we go on sinning so that grace may increase? By no means! *We died to sin; how can we live in it any longer?*" He emphasizes and expands on the point in Romans 8:9: "You, however, are controlled not by the sinful nature but by the Spirit, *if the Spirit of God lives in you.* And if anyone does not have the Spirit of Christ, he does not belong to Christ."

Then, in Romans 8:12-14, Paul lays it on the table for Christians who are tempted not to live the life to which Christ has called them:

> Therefore, brothers, we have an obligation – but it is not to the sinful nature, to live according to it. For if you live according to the sinful nature, you will die, but if by the Spirit you put to death the misdeeds of the body, you will live, because those who are led by the Spirit of God are sons of God.

I wasn't wrong. Here was the proof in the Scriptures. We can't sin without consequences, even after we've been justified by grace through faith. God expects His people to shine their lights all the time, not just during the concert — to live their faith at all times, not put it away when it's time to have fun. To do otherwise — to sin and not care — is to throw away that undeserved gift of grace through faith in Christ.

At the time, that discovery saved me from total disillusionment in my Lutheran faith. It also started me down the road toward the Catholic Church — though it would be years before I understood how important, both personally and theologically, that moment would be.

I came home deeply conflicted about God's plan for me. I didn't think I could function in a ministry that appeared to tolerate such a gap between belief and practice. Then, quite unexpectedly, I got a call from the publisher of my hometown newspaper, for which I had written a column on high school activities. He wanted me to fill in for the rest of the summer for a sports editor who had suddenly quit.

I enjoyed it and found my niche. After I returned to college that fall, opportunities in journalism kept coming my way without my asking for them. After a month, I decided God was giving me a different mission. I transferred at semester's end to the University of Nebraska-Lincoln, home to one of the nation's best journalism programs. I've been a journalist ever since.

Scene 3, 1988: That All May Be One

Less than five years later, on May 28, 1988, I stood before a Catholic altar on my wedding day. Not only had God yanked my professional life in a different direction — He had sent me my life's partner from the most unexpected of directions.

My three years at UNL had been everything I hoped for — in every area but one. I was fortunate to land in an LCMS campus ministry full of young people who lived their faith amid the admittedly more hostile atmosphere of a secular university. I wrote for and eventually edited the monthly newsletter when I wasn't studying or writing for the main UNL campus newspaper, the *Daily Nebraskan.*

But I had hoped for, tried for, and frankly embarrassed myself in the quest to find a woman to share my life. Simply put, I crashed and burned. My last hope among the women I met at UNL faded for good soon after I left for my first job in North Platte, Nebraska.

Or so I thought.

Quite unexpectedly, a friendship with my copy desk chief at the *Daily Nebraskan*—Joan Rezac—began to blossom. I nearly missed the signals when she started hinting she was interested in something more—but I came to my senses just in time. On April 5, 1987, I asked her on the phone: "Are we moving beyond a friendship?"

"I'm glad you called," she said. "The thought had crossed my mind!"

Right then, I knew—absolutely *knew*—the search was over. I can't explain why, and I didn't tell Joan until much later. But the phone calls and trips back to Lincoln for dates proved it. Here was a fellow journalist who loved music and seemed to understand me better than anyone ever had.

I can't do justice in this short space to how perfectly Joan fit into my life—other than to say I've never doubted in the years since that phone call that she was, and is, God's precious gift to me.

But she was Catholic. *Catholic.* Why, God—why did you send me a CATHOLIC? This surely can't work—can it?

We started working on the answer only a few weeks into our relationship. I gave her a copy of Luther's *Small Catechism*, while she gave me a catechism she had studied from in her Confirmation class. Naturally, as a good Missouri Synod Lutheran who knew Catholics were wrong, I figured I had the tools to wake Joan up. If we were to have a future as a couple, I had to.

During those first few months, I tried hard and long but there was only one problem: It made her a stronger Catholic. I was the one who had to adjust.

I attended church with her occasionally, heard Mass in the vernacular, saw Communion given in both kinds. She told me how Vatican II had broadened the Church's approach to other faiths. I read that Catholics were finding that Luther's teachings weren't as un-Catholic as they had thought. And on justification? Joan said she believed that works, while they don't save us, let our faith shine through.

In other words, this Catholic Church was . . . so to speak . . . more Lutheran than I imagined. It was my first clue that I had been viewing Rome through a distorted mirror—the one held up by my Confirmation instruction. Though Vatican II had happened a decade before that, the Rome that I was taught as a young Lutheran was the Rome of 1517—at least in the way Rome presented itself at that long-ago time. Something was different.

I could not escape that fact as Joan and I debated the spiritual issues that summer of 1987. It wasn't an easy ride, to be sure. Sometimes it seemed that Joan and I were speaking different languages. I certainly didn't believe all that stuff about Mary, the saints, purgatory and the sacrifice of the Mass, though I was hearing things here and there that gave me pause.

Nevertheless, we came through that time closer than ever. And Father Karnish's straight answer to my straight question about justification helped convince me that Joan and I could function as a Christian couple. If the priest who helped form Joan's faith was saying the same thing she was, we could grow in faith together as husband and wife.

However, finding some points of agreement with Catholics wasn't enough for me to become one—though we did get married at St. Agnes. We resolved to attend each other's churches regularly, minister together where we could and let God tell us whether He wanted us to join one or the other or remain in both.

I needed more proof that the Catholic Church I was hearing about from Joan and Father Karnish was the Church that really existed.

It took me ten years to be convinced.

Scene 4, 1993: The Surprising Pope from Poland

The moment in Denver when I heard those astonishing words from the pope happened almost halfway in between those ten years. It came at a time when our marriage was full of spiritual blessings and professional challenges—but it seemed that we were destined to be a two-faith couple.

Joan had taken Lutheran Confirmation classes in Des Moines, where we moved after our marriage. But she just wasn't inspired to join. Something would be missing, she said—something she couldn't put into words. So after we moved to Scottsbluff in 1991, I entered an RCIA class at St. Agnes, intending to stop before the point that I would have to commit myself to join.

Again, I was surprised at the level of agreement I was finding between the two faith traditions. I remember thinking that I could be comfortable at St. Agnes—but something kept gnawing at me. You see, I had started RCIA instruction in Des Moines, but left after two weeks. That priest seemed to doubt the essence of Christian faith—Catholic, Lutheran, or otherwise.

So I asked St. Agnes' new pastor, Father Charles Torpey: Could he guarantee me that I would hear the same message about Catholicism in another parish or another diocese?

No, he said.

He was merely reflecting the varying interpretations of Vatican II that have plagued the Church for most of the years since the Council. But for me, at that time, Father Torpey's answer stopped me cold. I was used to hearing pretty much the same Lutheran doctrines from one Missouri Synod congregation to the next. Even though I was comfortable with what Joan believed, her family believed and her parish believed, without the guarantee I sought, I simply assumed the Catholic Church as a whole couldn't possibly believe as they did.

A year later, John Paul II shook up that assumption in Denver.

As Joan and I had our second child and then moved back to North Platte, the pope kept doing things I couldn't ignore. The year after World Youth Day, the Vatican released the English translation of the *Catechism of the Catholic Church*. Though I didn't read it cover to cover until after I joined the Church, its release was a profound event—the beginning of order from the chaos of the varying interpretations of Vatican II.

Then John Paul issued *Ut Unum Sint*, the great 1995 encyclical on ecumenism in which he urged Protestants and Eastern Orthodox alike to join Catholics in restoring the Church's unity. A year later, the Holy Father went to Paderborn, Germany, and directly urged Lutherans and Catholics to look at the complete picture of Luther and the Reformation and approach their five hundred year feud in a different way:

> Luther's thinking was characterized by considerable emphasis on the individual, which meant that the awareness of the requirements of society became weaker. Luther's original intention in his call for reform in the Church was a call to repentance and renewal to begin in the life of every individual.
>
> There are many reasons why these beginnings nevertheless led to division. One is the failure of the Catholic Church . . . and the intrusion of political and economic interest, as well as Luther's own passion, which drove him far beyond what he originally intended into radical criticism of the Catholic Church, of its way of teaching.
>
> We all bear the guilt. That is why we are called upon to repent and must all allow the Lord to cleanse us over and over.

After nearly a decade of study and close observation of Catholicism, I could take the pope's words and sentiment for what they were. The messages I first heard in 1987 had been confirmed week in and week out from Catholic pulpits. I had absorbed the wonderful liturgical music coming from Catholic composers. I prayed for unity in God's Church more strongly than ever.

And yet . . . I remained confirmed in my Lutheran thinking. When it came to Mary, the saints, purgatory and so on, I had searched in vain for a response to Luther's ancient challenge: Prove it to me from Scripture!

In mid-1997, we moved to Omaha. As always, I started looking for an LCMS congregation to join. I found one I thought I liked—one that did contemporary music, one that had people I had known from other parts of Nebraska. But something wasn't right. Something kept gnawing at me, preventing me from becoming an official member of the congregation. I didn't know what it was.

That Christmas, we received a gift from Sister Mariette Melmer, a cousin of Joan's mother and a Notre Dame sister based not far from our new home. (The Lord called her home in August 1999.) She told Joan she thought we would find it interesting. Joan started reading the book, then passed it on to me. It was *Rome Sweet Home*, Scott and Kimberly Hahn's story of their journeys from Presbyterianism into the Catholic Church.

It wasn't a perfect fit; I was a Lutheran reading an ex-Calvinist's conception of what Luther believed. And yet . . . here were all these Scripture passages addressing the differences between Lutherans and Catholics. Hahn was pointing to Scripture. And he was making sense—for instance, his connection of purgatory to passages I had never paid attention to before, like 1 Corinthians 3:12-15:

If any man builds on this foundation [of Christ] using gold, silver, costly stones, wood, hay or straw, his work will be shown for what it is, because the Day will bring it to light. It will be revealed with fire, and the fire will test the quality of each man's work. If what he has built survives, he will receive his reward. If it is burned up, he will suffer loss; he himself will be saved, but only as one escaping through the flames.

As so many ex-Protestant converts have said . . . I knew I was in trouble. It was time to answer the questions once and for all. I was driven by something the pope had written in *Ut Unum Sint*:

In the first place, with regard to doctrinal formulations which differ from those normally in use in the community to which one belongs, it is certainly right to determine whether the words involved say the same thing. . . .

In this regard, ecumenical dialogue, which prompts the parties involved to question each other, to understand each other and to explain their positions to each other, makes surprising discoveries possible. Intolerant polemics and controversies have made incompatible assertions out of what was really the result of two different ways of looking at the same reality.[1]

I couldn't pass up that challenge. It called on skills I use all the time as a journalist—the translation of the jargon of doctors, lawyers, school administrators, etc., into language common people can use. After ten years of virtual dual membership in the Catholic Church and the LCMS, I believed I knew both sides' theological languages well enough to test it.

The twenty-year journey was entering its final phase.

---

[1] Pope John Paul II. *Ut Unum Sint* (Boston: Pauline Books and Media, 1995), no. 38.

Scene 5, 1998 – Amid the Crumbled Fortress

Just over a month later, on February 1, I stood over the dishes in the sink, looking out at the winter night. The tears kept coming. I knew I had run out of arguments. The walls of my mighty Lutheran fortress lay in ruins around my feet. I knew I had to become Catholic.

I was nearing the end of the second draft of what had become a forty-page paper, a conversation with myself about my journey. I had pored through Internet pages, haunted the libraries of our city and a nearby Catholic university and raided bookstores in my quest.

The pope had been right. On several critical issues, Lutherans and Catholics indeed said the same thing in different ways. With others, it had been less a matter of giving up Lutheran beliefs than coming to understand how Catholic they really were. And with the rest—Catholics simply had the more convincing case.

Naturally, justification was the first issue. As I sorted through a decade's worth of evidence, I found I had no doubts left: On this most important issue, Lutherans and Catholics were arguing over style—not substance. And after five hundred years of diatribes by both sides, both faith traditions are beginning to understand that at last!

Over time, I had come to understand that two questions govern our lives as Christian believers: "How are you saved?" and "OK, you're saved—now what?" The first refers to the moment and means of salvation; the second, to our spiritual journey from the moment of salvation until death. Just as Paul did throughout Romans, we must ask and answer *both* questions together to understand the entire picture of salvation.

Lutheran sermons typically focus on the first question, while Catholics concentrate on the second. Consequently, each thinks the other doesn't answer the key question. Lutherans assume Catholics believe our totally undeserved gift of God's grace is *not* the *sole* means of our salvation—but the very beginning of the Council of Trent's Decree on Justification freely confesses our utter dependence on God:

> If anyone shall say that man can be justified before God by his own works which are done either by his own natural powers, or through the teaching of the Law, and without divine grace through Christ Jesus: let him be anathema. (Canon 1)
>
> If anyone shall say that without the anticipatory inspiration of the Holy Spirit and without His assistance man can believe, hope and love or be repentant, as he ought, so that the grace of justification may be conferred upon him: let him be anathema. (Canon 3)

For their part, Catholics assume that "faith alone" means Lutherans believe that "once saved, always saved." Paul didn't believe that, as we have seen. Christ didn't teach it, either, as we see in Matthew 7:21: "Not everyone who says to me, 'Lord, Lord,' will enter the kingdom of heaven, but only he who does the will of My Father who is in heaven."

We *are* totally dependent on God for our salvation, Catholics teach, but we can throw it away. How? By willfully returning to a life of sin and assuming we're saved anyway! Thus, the *Catechism of the Catholic Church* teaches: "Mortal sin . . . results in the loss of charity and the privation of sanctifying grace, that is, of the state of grace. If it is not redeemed by repentance and God's forgiveness, it causes exclusion from Christ's kingdom and the eternal death of hell" (CCC, No. 1861).

So . . . do Lutherans believe you can throw your salvation away? The Lutheran Confessions say: *Yes!* One of the most unequivocal statements to that effect can be found in the Apology of the Augsburg Confession, where Luther's right-hand man, Philip Melanchthon, writes about Paul's statement that "if I have a faith that can move mountains, but have not love, I am nothing" (1 Corinthians 13:2):

In this text Paul requires love. **We require it, too.** We have said above that we should be renewed and begin to keep the law, according to the statement (Jeremiah 31:33), "I will put my law within their hearts." **Whoever casts away love will not keep his faith, be it ever so great, because he will not keep the Holy Spirit.** (Apology, IV, 219)[2]

Now we've reached the common ground. Recall that many English translations render the "love" of 1 Corinthians 13:13 ("And now these three remain: faith, hope and love. But the greatest of these is love") as "charity" (in Greek, *agape*; in Latin, *caritas*). Charity is an *active* love of both God above all things and our neighbor as ourselves; as such, it's considered by Catholics as the greatest of the "theological virtues" (which also include faith and hope). It's what following through on our faith—the Catholic concept, much maligned by Lutherans, of "faith fashioned by love"—is all about.

Lutherans speak of these issues under another name: the "third use of the Law," as found in the 1580 Formula of Concord:

> The law has been given to men for three reasons: (1) to maintain external discipline against unruly and disobedient men, (2) to lead men to a knowledge of their sin, (3) after they are reborn, and although the flesh still inheres in them, to give them on that account a definite rule according to which they should pattern and regulate their entire life . . .
>
> We believe, teach and confess that the preaching of the law is to be diligently applied not only to unbelievers and the impenitent but also to people who are genuinely

[2]Related thoughts elsewhere in the *Book of Concord* may be found at: Augsburg Confession, VI, 1-2; Apology, IV, 348-350; Apology, XX, 13; Smalcald Articles, III, III, 42-45; Formula of Concord, Epitome, III, 11. All citations are from *The Book of Concord*, ed. Theodore G. Tappert et al (Philadelphia: Fortress Press, 1959).

believing, truly converted, regenerated, and justified through faith.

For although they are indeed reborn and have been renewed in the spirit of their mind, such regeneration and renewal is incomplete in this world. In fact, it has only begun, and in the spirit of their mind the believers are in a constant war against their flesh (that is, their corrupt nature and kind), which clings to them until death. (Formula of Concord, Epitome, VI, 1, 3-4a)

Put another way: The Law—loving God with all your heart, soul and mind and your neighbor as yourself—doesn't cease to apply to you once you're saved. The commandments of the Law tell believers what they ought to be doing *as a matter of course.* If Christians aren't doing good works and don't care, how can anyone tell they are saved? Indeed, how can they themselves expect to see heaven with such an attitude?

That's what James was getting at when he wrote that "faith without works is dead" (James 2:26). But it's also what Catholics mean when they speak of justification as a process—one that lasts until God calls us home. If we freely sin and don't care, we fall into the category of those who "have shipwrecked their faith" (1 Timothy 1:19). But we have the sure promise in 2 Timothy 2:11-13 that "if we endure, we will also reign with Him" and that "if we are faithless, He will remain faithful, for He cannot disown Himself"!

This is the common ground of the *Joint Declaration on the Doctrine of Justification*, the breakthrough agreement between Catholics and many Lutherans (though not the Missouri Synod) signed in Augsburg, Germany, on Reformation Day 1999. It declares that the signatories consider its contents to "encompass a consensus on *basic truths* of the doctrine of justification."

Its key passage answers both of our key questions of the Christian life: *"Together we confess: By grace alone, in faith in*

Christ's saving work and not because of any merit on our part, we are accepted by God and receive the Holy Spirit, who renews our hearts while equipping and calling us to good works" (Joint Declaration on the Doctrine of Justification, No. 15).

Does that seem familiar? It should. It's anchored not only in Ephesians 2:8-9—the "justification in a nutshell" passage that Lutherans cite so often—but also verses 10 and 11, which Catholics insist must not be forgotten: "For it is by grace you have been saved, through faith—and this not from yourselves, it is the gift of God—not by works, so that no one can boast. *For we are God's workmanship, created in Christ Jesus to do good works, which God prepared in advance for us to do.*"

One must emphasize that the Joint Declaration speaks of shared *"basic* truths, " not total agreement. The two faith traditions are still seeking common ground on *how* we live out our faith, *how* we know what God expects us to do and *how* He gives us the grace to do it through Word and Sacrament—in essence, all the remaining points at issue between Lutherans and Catholics.

But it's clear that Catholics and Lutherans—in two different ways, just as John Paul II perceived—agree on what one might call "the circle of eternal life," one that begins and ends with God.

The circle works like this: God, through Christ's death for our sins, alone makes our salvation possible—but we have to accept His gift of faith, and we absolutely *must* live that faith by following God's commands, lest we lose the Holy Spirit and the salvation that Christ earned for us. ***But . . .*** we *cannot* follow through and we *cannot* accept the gift of faith—or, put in the passive form that Lutherans prefer, the reception of faith by us cannot take place—unless God alone gives us the ability to do so. So, in the end, ***we are totally dependent on God!***

The belief that Catholics and Lutherans somehow disagreed on that was, and is, the cornerstone of the typical Lutheran's mighty fortress against Rome. Once the cornerstone was removed from my wall, the other bricks began to collapse.

I began to perceive other similarities between Catholics and Lutherans that hadn't occurred to me before—most notably on the two key ingredients of the Church's authority: the relationship between Scripture and Tradition and the question of infallibility.

Luther, of course, set the tone for Protestants everywhere with his emphasis on *sola Scriptura*—the Bible as the sole authority. But John Paul II changed the tone of the debate in *Ut Unum Sint*, defining the question in dispute as "the relationship between Sacred Scripture, as *the highest authority in matters of faith*, and Sacred Tradition, *as indispensable to the interpretation of the Word of God*."

Compare that to Article II of the LCMS Constitution. It's the same order of primacy! Catholics indeed look first to the Scriptures—but they interpret those Scriptures in the light of the teaching they uphold as directly passed on from the apostles, the Church Fathers, and the ecumenical councils. And in Missouri's universe, at any rate, the Lutheran Confessions have the same relationship to Scripture. They define how the LCMS reads and lives its faith.

In other words, *sola Scriptura* is nothing more than a phrase or slogan. It can't be anything else as long as a group of Christians follows a particular set of teachings, whether it comes from Luther, John Calvin, John Knox, or John Wesley.

In that case . . . which side has the better case for its Tradition? Lutherans—who kept much of the Catholic Tradition but based the rest of their teachings on the interpretations of a handful of sixteenth century men? Or the Catholic Church, which can do what Luther could not—cite the Scriptures in defense of its authority to pass on and interpret the faith?

It isn't that the LCMS *in practice* denies the connection between Scripture and Tradition. It's a question of *which* tradition it accepts. The issue of infallibility is much the same. The LCMS believes the Holy Spirit guides its officers and pastors (its Magisterium, if you will) and its triennial conventions (its ecumenical councils) in deciding doctrinal issues.

Again, which has the better scriptural case for its authority? I concluded that Rome had a convincing case — and Missouri, by its own preferred standard, had none. Once I realized that, the other issues between Lutherans and Catholics were much easier to deal with.

There were other areas in which it appeared that Lutheran practice mimicked Catholic reality. Luther may have reduced seven sacraments to two by his own definition — and yet Lutherans hold Confirmation, Matrimony, Holy Orders, Confession, and absolution (in the corporate sense, anyway) and pastoral care of the sick (parallel to Anointing of the Sick) in high esteem. In each, they believe God blesses His people as the pastor proclaims God's Word. And isn't that the essence of the "means of grace" that explains the basic act of both Baptism and the Eucharist — the application of God's Word to visible elements to impart His grace?

Coupled with my new scriptural proofs and my conclusions on Catholic authority, the sacraments proved easier to deal with than I thought. I had had the flow all wrong. The sacraments weren't obstacles to our reaching God. They were means for God to reach us!

Much the same may be said of Mary and the saints. I didn't expect those issues to fall as easily as they did. But both are linked to one question: Do Lutherans believe the "communion of saints" unites the saints in heaven and on Earth in one Body of Christ? And if it does, why would we not seek the aid of the Christians who have gone before?

Lutherans will admit that the saints in heaven, including Mary, pray for the saints on Earth. Unfortunately, they don't believe *we* can pray to *them*, asking them to pray for us. But that ignores Paul's observation that "the eye cannot say to the hand, 'I don't need you!'" (1 Corinthians 12:21a, NIV).

We ask our fellow living Christians to pray for us in time of trouble. The Catholic Church invites us—though it doesn't *demand*—to likewise seek the prayers of the blessed dead. Christ remains the one Mediator, but He makes use of whatever mediums He wishes to draw us to Himself—including our fellow members of the Body of Christ.

As for Mary, I found the case for Catholic dogma bolstered by a most unexpected source: Luther himself. Evidence can be found in his writings that he believed in all the Marian dogmas of the Catholic Church—Mary was Mother of God, was perpetually a virgin, was immaculately conceived and assumed into heaven. Most astonishingly, the founder of this church that disdains praying to Mary invokes her intercession at the beginning and the end of his 1521 commentary on the Magnificat!

It's quite another thing to equate Mary or the saints with God or to expect them to accomplish specific *things* for you. Luther was adamant in opposing that thinking—but so is the Catholic Church. Pope Paul VI clarified the point for Catholics when he cautioned that veneration of Mary and the saints must be done within the context of "a rightly ordered faith"—one that looks to Christ as the sole source of salvation and grace.

This space, of course, is too limited to cover all the Catholic-Lutheran issues, let alone all the evidence I found for the Catholic position. One more subject, however, needs to be covered. Ultimately for me, it came down to the Eucharist.

The dispute over the sacrifice of the Mass wasn't the obstacle I expected it to be. The Church does not see it as a *repetition* of Christ's sacrifice—as Luther and the Reformers perceived the Catholic position—but as the *one single sacrifice* presented again to us, a re-presentation of Calvary every time we "do this in remembrance of Me." (The late LCMS theology professor Arthur Carl Piepkorn—a key player in the first U.S. Lutheran-Catholic dialogues in the 1960s—wrote of the Eucharist in eerily similar terms.)

That brought me to the transubstantiation issue, the fate of the bread and wine after the Words of Institution. I had come a long way by following the pope's advice. I had had to give up very little of my Lutheran way of thinking. But transubstantiation couldn't be resolved as two different approaches to a common belief. I was back to the diagram Pastor had put on the chalkboard twenty years before: Either the bread and wine are still there—or they aren't.

So I went to Luther's 1520 treatise *The Babylonian Captivity of the Church*, the work that defined his views on transubstantiation and redefined the sacraments. I had been struck by an oddity: Catholics and Lutherans appealed to the same Scripture passages and emphasized a plain, literal reading of the text. There must be something more to Luther's position.

There was. Luther wrote:

Does not Christ appear to have anticipated this curiosity admirably by saying of the wine, not *Hoc est sanguis meus*, but *Hic est sanguis meus?* . . . That the pronoun "this," in both Greek and Latin, is referred to "body," is due to the fact that in both of these languages the two words are of the same gender. *In Hebrew, however, which has no neuter gender, "this" is referred to "bread,"* so that it would be proper to say *Hic* [bread] *est corpus meum.*

Ninety-nine percent of the time, Luther bases his theology on the original Bible languages—Greek and Hebrew, not Latin. *But not here.* He's objecting to the Latin translation—the translation of the Church whose authority he was rejecting. He was dismissing the original translation, the Greek, because it agrees with the Latin. And he's appealing to a different language entirely—Hebrew, which he assumes Christ spoke at the Last Supper (modern scholars believe it more likely was Aramaic)—to undermine the transubstantiation doctrine which he associated with Rome's supposed corruptions of the faith.

My hands shook as I read that passage for the first time. I thought: *But that's wrong! He can't do that!*

I was back in my professional realm. I don't know Greek . . . but I'm a writer, and I can research. I spent the next day ransacking the library and the Internet, finding the exact Greek words and learning how the Greek language treats pronouns. When I was done, the evidence was overwhelming: In the language used by the New Testament's divinely inspired authors, Christ's "this" *cannot refer to anything other than "body."* (A straight-across reading of the Greek in an interlinear New Testament reinforces the point: *"This is the body of Me."*)

In other words . . . Rome was right, and Luther was wrong. I no longer had a case against joining the Catholic Church.

Prayer for Unity

I was received into the Church and took Communion with my wife for the first time less than two months later. Our oldest son, Jonathan, made his First Communion in December 1998 and was confirmed in 2004. Our second son, Joshua, made his First Communion in 2001, and we have been joined by two little ones, Benjamin and Annetta—our first children born with us all united in the Catholic Church.

I can't begin to express the joy of being fully spiritually united with my wife and children—not to mention all the Catholics whose quiet witnesses and utter lack of pressure unquestionably were God's instruments on the way to Rome.

There has been pain, too, and that isn't an unfamiliar story to Christians who have reconciled with Rome. It's one thing for Catholics to ask forgiveness for the events of centuries ago. It's another for Eastern Orthodox and Protestants of all stripes to grant it and to issue their own apologies—to put aside the pain and the polemics and humbly, sincerely, thoroughly explore how it all happened, how the other side thinks and what God is saying to His people in these increasingly faithless days.

Pope John Paul II and now Pope Benedict XVI (his longtime aide, Cardinal Joseph Ratzinger) have called on Catholics to work for the unity of the Church—to join Christ's high-priestly prayer that we all may be one. I pray that Rome and Missouri in particular may be led to forgive each other, to look toward God and His Word with truly unbiased eyes and ask whether they're meant to remain divided. They share far, far more than they know.

After John Paul spoke his astonishing words in Denver, I heard Irish recording artist Dana sing the World Youth Day 1993 theme song for the first time. It quickly took root in my heart because of its echo—whether intended or not, I don't know—of Luther's alleged "Here I stand" statement at the Diet of Worms. It seems an appropriate way to end this tale:

We are one body, one body in Christ,
And we do not stand alone,
We are one body, one body in Christ,
And He came that we might have life . . .

Originally published in the CHNetwork Journal *Jan-June 1999.*

Todd von Kampen is a journalist living in Omaha, Nebraska. He was baptized and confirmed in the Lutheran Church-Missouri Synod, to which he belonged until he was received into the Catholic Church on March 29, 1998. Todd, Joan, and their children (Jonathan, Joshua, Benjamin, and Annetta) are members of the Church of the Blessed Sacrament in Omaha.

And the Two Shall Become One

by Tim and Mary Drake
former Lutheran

Courtship: Her Side

We met and began dating as freshmen in college. At the time, I had a poor understanding of my faith. I felt that there were more similarities than differences between our denominations.

We both believed in the Trinity and in Jesus Christ. We could share some common prayers. We both believed in the importance of church attendance and in raising our children to be Christians. I wasn't sure whether the difference in our denominations mattered.

When my mother expressed her concern over Tim's faith, I shared with her that although Tim was Lutheran, he had more of a relationship with God than any of the Catholics I had dated. They were "Catholic" in name only. Tim, however, took his faith seriously.

His Side

I grew up surrounded largely by Lutherans. Aside from an occasional Catholic wedding, I was not exposed to Catholic traditions. I remember finding the wedding Masses long, the kneeling odd, and the church decorations ornate. Somehow, however, I acquired the usual prejudices against Mary, the pope, and confession.

At the age of ten, standing in a hallway on my first day in a new grade school, I met the first Catholic I ever truly got to know. Mark and I became best friends. At that age, religion wasn't something he and I discussed, but as our relationship developed, we couldn't help but recognize the differences in our lives. Mark and I spent as much time as we could at each other's houses and on a few occasions attended each other's churches.

One night while I was staying over at his home, I discovered a laminated prayer card from Italy sitting on his nightstand. It was a prayer card of St. Joseph. I found the artwork and the prayer to be quite beautiful. After I told him how much I admired the card, he gave it to me.

After high school, Mark, the prayer card, and I journeyed to the same college. In college as in high school, I used the St. Joseph prayer card in times of special need. As an intercessor, Joseph never seemed to fail.

It was at college that I met Mary. Mary and I lived on the same floor of our dormitory, and we became friends. We enjoyed going on walks with each other, talking for hours on end, and simply being with each other. By the end of our freshman year, we began dating.

Our courtship lasted four years. In Mary's junior year, she decided to live off campus in the Newman Catholic Campus Ministry Center. Partly in response to her decision and partially out of my own desire to learn more about my faith, I decided to live in the Lutheran Campus Ministry *Christus House*.

This move opened us up to discussing matters of faith more seriously. I was as committed in my Lutheranism as Mary was in her Catholicism. As resident peer ministers, we participated in joint retreats, prayed together, and took part together in Wednesday evening vespers.

I found the faith of Mary's family, their devotion, and their traditions particularly attractive. They were truly a holy family; it showed in their faithful attendance at Mass every Sunday and in how they prayed together. I found myself drawn to Mary and her family. It was here that I first gained a respect for Catholicism.

Engagement: Her Side

Prior to and following our engagement in November 1988, Tim and I began to talk more seriously about our respective faiths. We took a premarital inventory and went through a marriage preparation course in the Catholic Church. I was grateful that Tim respected my desire to use Natural Family Planning in our marriage.

Tim did have a hard time, however, understanding the Church's desire that couples raise their children as Catholics. I worried about our children and wondered what church they would attend. Not having any hard answers to that question, we trusted that God would show us His way.

His Side

As an interdenominational couple, we struggled with the questions all such couples face. What church would we attend? How would we raise our children?

We found comfort in the similarities and often prayed the *Our Father* together. We wrestled with the issues, and occasionally we argued. Slowly we began to realize that we could, if we remained respectful, work through it.

During marriage preparation the priest asked us whether we were willing to raise our children as Catholics. This promise was one I found difficult to understand. I felt slighted, as though Catholics thought my denomination was somehow inferior to or less important than theirs.

I thought to myself, *What if I don't want to raise our children Catholic?* I certainly didn't want to say yes to something I wasn't sure I wanted to do. Reluctantly, I agreed. Although we didn't have all the issues worked out, we were married on July 8, 1989.

Marriage: Her Side

We were married on a hot Minnesota summer day. The service was a mixed ceremony at St. Eloi's Catholic Church in my hometown of Ghent, Minnesota. We decided not to have a Mass so that Tim's side would not feel left out. Tim's Lutheran campus pastor gave the homily, while our priest co-celebrated.

I particularly remember the *Our Father*. Tim and I were gathered in a circle near the altar, holding hands with our wedding party, the pastor, and priest. In a wonderful display of ecumenism and unity, dear Father Bernie Schriner asked that everyone hold hands, even across the aisles. A college friend sang a moving rendition of the prayer.

Toward the end, overcome with emotion, Father Schriner shouted "Everyone!" and together everyone sang, "For Thine is the kingdom, and the power, and the glory forever. Amen." There wasn't a dry eye in the place.

After our wedding, as before, we would sometimes attend our churches separately. At other times, we would attend one or the other together, or sometimes we would attend both churches each Sunday. We both found it difficult to do this. Although I had been brought up in Catholic grade school, I didn't understand my faith well enough to be able to explain to Tim why we had to go to both.

We continued to struggle with the issue and attended both churches until sometime in 1993. We had just moved into our first home in St. Paul, and Tim found it more convenient to attend St. Columba Catholic Church just three blocks away from our home.

Around this time, I began praying for Tim's conversion. I didn't know whether it was the right thing to do, so I would utter this prayer: "Lord, I don't know whether this is Your will. If Tim could be converted, that would be great. Whatever You think is best, Lord."

His Side

It was so hot on the day we married that my brother, Jeff, my best man, Mark, and I had to stand in the Catholic school's walk-in freezer to keep cool before the service. What struck me about the day is that it would be one of the few times in our lives when all those we cared about would be gathered together with us to help us celebrate our love for one another.

After our wedding, we struggled with Sunday services, vacillating between attending Mary's church, mine, or both. I found it frustrating to attend both of our churches each Sunday morning. Often the readings would be the same.

It was difficult to watch Mary receive the Eucharist while I remained behind in the pew. I imagined how hard it would be to watch my family go up for Communion without me. The words spoken by the congregation in Mass—"Lord, I am not worthy to receive You, but only say the word and I shall be healed"—both irritated me and gave me hope. I felt that because I was Lutheran I was not deemed "worthy" to receive what Christ offered for all. I took hope, however, in the fact that Christ would "say the word" and heal me.

Over time, I grew disillusioned with the Lutheran parishes we attended. The teachings of the church seemed to vary greatly depending on the pastor. Mostly out of convenience, I started attending church with Mary and forgoing a Lutheran Sunday service, reserving attendance at Lutheran services for only special occasions such as Christmas and Easter.

The real crack in my Lutheran shell came, however, early in the 1990s as the Evangelical Lutheran Church in America began changing doctrine with regard to sexuality and abortion. The denomination even began funding pastors' abortions through their medical insurance coverage. And abortion was an issue I could not compromise on.

The Catholic Church taught that abortion was always wrong,

while the ELCA had started teaching that it was an unfortunate but necessary fact of life for some women. Suddenly, being Lutheran meant more to me than sitting in a pew. Ultimately, it meant believing everything that the Lutheran Church believes and teaches.

Thus began my walk down the road leading elsewhere. I was certainly attracted to Catholicism, but I had many questions and doubts. What I needed in my life was a fellow convert with whom I could dialogue.

My wife, Mary, and friend Mark had embraced Catholicism because they were born into it. I desperately needed to talk to someone who had come to it on his own. God provided exactly what I needed, but in a most unusual way.

Conversion: Her Side

During the summer of 1993, while walking home from church one morning, Tim expressed his potential desire to learn more about Catholicism. I was both shocked and excited. At the same time, I was cautious. I didn't want to say too much.

I kept my distance and feared getting involved because I didn't want him to feel pressured. I knew that if I pressured him, he would resent it later on. I knew that it had to be his free decision. I didn't want Tim converting because of me. I offered to be his sponsor and he accepted, and I began praying more.

His Side

I had been wrestling with the idea of conversion, but what I needed more than anything was a fellow convert with whom I could talk. The Holy Spirit would answer that prayer in a most unusual way.

In 1992, at the age of twenty-five, I came to learn about the family I didn't know I had. I also learned that because of the circumstances of my conception, my father had wanted me aborted.

To say that such news was shocking is an understatement. Learning the truth turned my whole world upside down. It threw everything I thought I knew into question. Yet learning that truth led me to a far greater truth.

The greatest blessing was learning of my half brother Rich, whom I had never met. I gave Rich a call and we spoke for a long time, agreeing to meet at a nearby restaurant. I was nervous about our meeting and didn't know what to expect. As I walked into the restaurant that evening, there was no denying who my brother was. We shared an undeniable resemblance.

Meeting him was like looking into a mirror and seeing myself thirteen years later. As we sat eating our hamburgers and comparing stories, the waitress asked, "Are you guys brothers?" Here we were, meeting for the first time in our lives, and a stranger could see the resemblance. We laughed, thinking, *"If you only knew!"*

In that meeting with Rich, a unique and inseparable bond was formed. We each felt more complete. Yet our bond is one that is more than genetic.

As we sat talking, I learned that Rich had converted to Catholicism at age eighteen. Not only had I gained the convert I needed to talk with, but I had also gained a brother. Like me, he had grown up Lutheran. His sharing his story with me propelled me to learn more. The Holy Spirit had placed him in my life exactly when I needed him.

Not long after I met Rich, a couple of other events pointed me toward the Church. The new *Catechism of the Catholic Church* was published, and we purchased a copy. I liked having it around because it seemed to have answers for so many of my questions. It also impressed upon me the validity of having all that the Church believes in a single source. It gave meaning to the statement "one holy, Catholic, and apostolic Church."

Also at about this time, Mary's church, St. Columba's, started perpetual Eucharistic adoration. Feeling the need to pray more and not fully understanding the meaning of the Blessed Sacrament, I signed up to pray an hour each Sunday evening.

Unfortunately, the RCIA program at our local church left something to be desired. Had it been for RCIA alone, I never would have converted. So I'm grateful that a friend offered to go with me to a thirteen-week "Fundamentals of Catholicism" class at a nearby parish.

The class was taught by an orthodox, faithful, and humble priest capable of handling any question put to him. It didn't take long for the Holy Spirit to work within me. An audiotape by former Protestant minister Scott Hahn and the book *Surprised by Truth* further propelled me toward the decision I knew I had to make.

Incredibly, the issues with which I had long contended were no longer issues. They had melted away. I felt as if I had been infused with a knowledge and acceptance of the Church and her teachings.

I learned that asking the Blessed Virgin Mary or the saints to pray for me was no different than asking a friend to pray for me. I understood the Church's respect for the sanctity of all human life and its teaching on the selfishness of contraception. I came to know the differences in belief about the Eucharist and why non-Catholic reception of our Lord's body and blood implies a unity among Christians that has not existed since the Reformation.

I wanted our family to be one spiritually. I was on the road to reconciliation.

Confession was my last major obstacle, more out of fear than any lack of understanding. It was difficult to overcome the Lutheran belief, as Martin Luther had put it, that we are "dung heaps covered with snow." My teacher-priest compared the Lutheran concept of forgiveness to typing with an old typewriter. If a sin were like a mistake, you could white it out, but you would always know that the mistake had been made.

In contrast, he compared the Catholic idea of forgiveness to using a computer. Confession, he explained, was like hitting the delete key. Once the key was struck, you would never be able to tell the mistake had been made. If this was true, I felt that confession had to be an utterly powerful and freeing sacrament given by Christ to His Church.

On Ash Wednesday, I was moved to go to confession. Compiling a laundry list of twenty-seven years' worth of sin was a very humbling experience. The Cathedral of St. Paul seemed an appropriate place for the sacrament.

There, I poured out the sins of my life and was filled with the grace that accompanies the sacrament. It wasn't a lightning bolt of grace, striking me suddenly, but rather a gradual appreciation of the sacrament and its graces. After confession, things moved quickly.

Converting is a covenant you enter into with God. Like marriage or parenthood, it is one of those things you can't really try out beforehand. Once I decided to convert, there was no going back. It was all or nothing. Either I accepted the Church and her teachings, or I wasn't Catholic. There was no room to pick and choose.

RCIA and the Fundamentals classes were very much like marriage preparation coursework and Engaged Encounter. There was only so much prayer, reading, discussion, and discerning I could do. My intellect could only take me so far. Eventually my heart had to follow.

Through adoration of the Blessed Sacrament, I had acquired an unquenchable hunger for the Eucharist. Truly, I was in love with God and was being moved to take a childlike leap. I didn't have all the answers. I didn't know where it would lead. But I had to trust in God. As the Church teaches, some things have been and will continue to be a mystery. This is what faith is.

I was unable to wait until Easter to convert. My heart had been opened to the truth. To delay converting felt like denying

God. On March 19, 1995, the feast day of St. Joseph, gathered with my friends and family and Mary as my sponsor, I professed my belief in the Holy Catholic Church and all her teachings, was confirmed, and accompanied Mary to the Lord's table for the first time since we had begun dating ten years earlier.

I can now look back on these remarkable events and clearly see the hand of God in their timing. Had I not learned the truth about my family, not only would I still be living without knowledge of my father or my half brothers but I also probably never would have met my biological father before his death, and I might not have come into the Church.

New Life: Her Side

It is a sad statement about my Catholic education that I grew up so ignorant about my faith. In some ways, I was not taught my faith; in other ways, I took my faith for granted. I made no effort actively to learn more about it.

I now realize how thankful I am that Tim converted. The questions that Tim raised through his Fundamentals class inspired me to learn more. His questions and reading taught me things I never knew.

Tim shared with me what he was learning, and he taught me the true differences between Lutheranism and Catholicism. Tim's conversion was a great blessing to me. I am a more faithful Catholic because of it.

I'm also thankful that the Spirit moved Tim to convert when he did. Though he didn't convert in order to make our family life easier, his conversion did in fact make it easier, especially in raising children. It is an incredible blessing to be a family strong in one faith. It helps to make our decisions easier. We feel more united in how we discipline and raise our children, and we share common friends who feel strongly about their faith as well.

His Side

Although I believed in Christ, my faith did not hold the fullness of truth so beautifully expressed in Christ and His Church. Therefore, through my conversion, 1 Corinthians 7:14 was fulfilled: An unbelieving husband was sanctified by a believing wife.

Even more miraculously, God took my love for Mary, combined it with my love for Him, and created new life, not only within me, but within us. Just weeks after my conversion, after a long struggle with infertility, my wife and I learned we were expecting a child. Our joy was compounded in discovering that the timing would be near the timing of Christ's own birth; we felt closer than ever to the Holy Family when we learned that our due date was Christmas. Elias Joseph Drake was born on December 27, 1995.

It used to be that both the Lutheran denominations and the Catholic Church seriously cautioned against mixed marriages because of the potential "danger of loss of faith." While I understand their caution and the potential that mixed marriages have for causing pain, I marvel at the joy that Mary and I now share. In the end, our own mixed marriage strengthened not only my faith but Mary's as well.

Originally published in the CHNewsletter *May 2002.*

Tim is the Culture of Life editor and features correspondent with the National Catholic Register. *He is also editor of the books* There We Stood, Here We Stand: Eleven Lutherans Rediscover Their Catholic Roots *(First Books, 2001) and* Saints of the Jubilee *(First Books, 2002). His most recent book is* Young and Catholic: The Face of Tomorrow's Church. *Tim and Mary live in St. Cloud, Minnesota.*

From One Worldwide Church to the True One

by Dan Severino
former ex-Catholic member of
the Worldwide Church of God

I was born, baptized, and catechized a Catholic. When my parents married, my father was nominally Catholic and my mother consequently converted, taking on the sole responsibility for the religious formation of us children. I don't remember how faithfully we attended Mass, but I do remember going to Sunday school regularly. Though I wasn't a devoutly religious child, I was always inclined toward God. I wanted to please Him, so I made a conscious effort to obey my parents and tell the truth. I tried to read the Bible but didn't understand it, so my interest waned. I remember being inspired for a time by my First Holy Communion and Confirmation to participate regularly in the sacraments and daily devotions.

During those childhood years, my mother became a captive audience to radio and television evangelists. Then shortly after my Confirmation, she decided to become a member of the Worldwide Church of God (WCG). I was content being Catholic, and if my dad had been more devout, I probably would have stayed, but I wasn't strong enough or equipped to go against my mother's direction.

Since the Worldwide Church of God isn't a well-known denomination, it's likely that few readers have met a member or convert from this sect. We should begin by giving a little of the background history of this group.

The WCG today is a much different organization than it was in the mid-sixties when I began attending with my mother.

Herbert W. Armstrong founded it, believing that he had been called by God to restore the Gospel that had been lost since the first century. Under his leadership, the WCG espoused an eclectic mix of doctrines. The central definitive doctrine was the observance of Saturday as the seventh-day Sabbath. The members of the WCG also held to the sacred calendar of the Jewish people, celebrating the Days of Unleavened Bread by removing all leavened products from their homes. Christmas and Easter were not observed because they were not biblically ordained festivals. Members also followed the dietary restrictions of the Jewish people and did not eat pork products. We would diligently read the ingredients of items such as bread and crackers to make sure they were made with vegetable shortening and not animal fats.

Prophecy and the return of Christ were always on the forefront of the church's teaching and evangelization. Mr. Armstrong and his son, Garner Ted, spoke daily on their radio program, *The World Tomorrow*. The program got its name from the expected thousand-year reign of Christ that included a worldwide secular utopia. Many sermons on prophecy were preached. The Catholic Church was looked upon with great suspicion. Part of the prophetic package included the belief that the United States and Great Britain were the descendants of Israel, and therefore the Old Testament prophecies that mentioned Israel were thought to be speaking to our nations.

There was no belief in the Trinity. God the Father and God the Son were separate beings, with the Holy Spirit being only the power of God. The WCG held to *sola Scriptura*, but not to *sola fide*. A Christian was required to keep the Ten Commandments for salvation—if one didn't keep the seventh-day Sabbath, one couldn't be saved. Members of the WCG were discouraged from reading materials from other religious organizations, for fear one might become victim to the devil's clever arguments. The WCG also believed in divine healing and preached that reliance on the medical profession was a sure sign of a lack of faith.

When I graduated from high school, I was accepted into the WCG's own Ambassador College. This beautiful campus in Pasadena, California, was a combination of restored millionaire mansions and elegant new structures. My four years at Ambassador College provided many great memories. Culturally, it was a very rich experience. Many world leaders and other influential people were invited to speak before the student body. Upon graduation, many students went into the WCG ministry. My talents, however, were musical, and though the dean of faculty encouraged me to remain as a part of the music faculty, I chose to return home to Pennsylvania where I continued my musical studies. There I became involved in the local WCG congregation and even did some preaching.

After Mr. Armstrong's death in 1986, his handpicked successor began a series of changes that rocked the WCG, causing it to split into different factions (though schisms had been regular during my thirty-plus years in the WCG). These changes included a gradual openness to more traditional Christian doctrines such as the Trinity as well as a relaxation of the WCG's strict Sabbath rules. I was always one to support the leadership of the WCG, so when the church changed its attitude toward doctors, I had no difficulty following along. Hadn't St. Luke been referred to as the beloved physician? When WCG changed its views on the nature of God, softening its literal interpretation of the anthropomorphic descriptions of God and becoming more Trinitarian, I again found no problem in this.

In the spring of 1995, the WCG split into two separate groups. Those holding to the traditions of Mr. Armstrong called themselves the United Church of God (UCG); those who agreed with the changes instituted by Mr. Armstrong's successor stuck with the WCG. My wife and I stayed with the WCG; my mother went with the UCG. It was a difficult time. Everyone had longtime friends who were now separated because of differing understandings. Every faction claimed loyalty to Mr. Armstrong.

Many members became bewildered over what to believe; many quit religion altogether.

Those who stayed with the WCG, however, felt a tremendous excitement. They felt they were relieved of the burdens of the Old Covenant. The WCG took to a traditional Protestant view of justification by faith. The WCG didn't go so far as to say faith alone, and this is where a new round of debate began. The range of belief available in Protestantism concerning justification, or almost any issue, is quite large. Various church leaders leaned toward Calvinistic theology, while others were more Arminian. Some took up the motto "No creed but Christ." Some believed that the Bible was totally without error; others leaned toward the position that only the principles concerning salvation were without error. I mention this for two reasons—because of the liquid nature of the WCG at this time and because I could finally study theological issues on my own in good conscience. Since the WCG had a range of beliefs on most issues, I felt free to study and come to my own conclusions. So, I began reading various schools of thought.

Yet another big change in the WCG was the introduction of the worship leader. This was done to follow the pattern of successful contemporary Protestant churches. Success was defined as those with strong growth in membership numbers. It was a large responsibility and one that couldn't be taken lightly. The success of the service was determined by the success of the worship leader. In time, I was in charge of our congregation's worship activities and all our worship leaders. The WCG provided an Internet discussion group, where all worship leaders in our worldwide congregations could share and debate ideas.

Not being satisfied with contemporary Christian worship, I began looking at alternatives. Liturgy soon became a major part of our Internet discussions. Since the Protestant world accepted Advent, I began to develop an Advent program for our local WCG congregation. Some WCG members still didn't feel comfortable with Christmas, so we just called it Incarnation Day.

I became more and more interested in liturgy. Since I was classically trained in music and not inclined toward contemporary Christian music, I developed a strong interest in religious music of the past. At first, it was the hymnody of the church in its Protestant tradition. This led me to the Masses of Bach, Beethoven, and Schubert. Finally, I became exposed to the wonderful liturgical works of the Renaissance, Gothic and medieval styles of music. My wife and I loved a CD of the chants of St. Hildegard von Bingen. As you can see, my musical exploration brought me in closer and closer contact with Catholic culture.

At this same time, we were talking on our Internet forums about how often we should participate in the Lord's Supper (the Eucharist). Our old WCG tradition was to take it only once a year. Most thought we shouldn't celebrate it too often because we would begin to take it for granted. My theological research at this time was making me aware that even the Protestant Reformers (Martin Luther and John Calvin) believed that the Lord's Supper should be taken weekly. My religious sentiments naturally inclined me to awe and great reverence for God. Contemporary Christian music and contemporary Christian churches were missing something. The awe and reverence were replaced with a shallow emotionalism that just didn't ring true. Something was missing, but I didn't know what it was.

I thought if I would just go back far enough in time, I would find out where and why things got off-track. I was becoming increasingly dissatisfied with the WCG. My studies were taking me farther back in history, and the WCG was bringing me current Protestant thought that I just couldn't accept. My local WCG pastor recommended that I just keep my mind on Christ and not let these things bother me. That answer wasn't satisfactory. There was a hunger for more. I wanted the truth.

One evening while driving home from work, pondering my quest for the truth, knowing I would eventually leave the WCG, the thought came to me, "Before you die, you're going to become Catholic again." I didn't reject the thought, but I thought I would first become some type of conservative Protestant.

This was the light bulb moment for me. This was the moment that I needed to finally consider what the Catholic Church had to say in defense of her theological positions. The doctrine of justification by faith alone wasn't a return to the theology of the early Church as I had always assumed. It was a theological idea formed to assuage the guilty conscience of a talented but troubled Augustinian monk. Upon further study, I found that what Luther taught wasn't a return to the ancient belief of the Church but actually a new doctrine.

Shortly before this time I finally found a book that might answer my questions on the worship of the early Church. It was *The Lamb's Supper: The Mass as Heaven on Earth* by Dr. Scott Hahn. I remember listening a couple of months before on our local Christian radio station to an interview with Dr. Hahn and his conversion to the Catholic Church. The specific details of the conversation escape me, but I remember his enthusiasm. At the time, I was not aware of any Protestants converting to the Catholic faith. I assumed it was always Catholics becoming Protestant. This was a "hmmm" moment. *The Lamb's Supper* was a captivating read. I read it in one day. Dr. Hahn's book convinced me of the importance of the Eucharist in the early Church and therefore of its necessity today. His enthusiasm expressed in his writing is infectious, and it gave me a strong shove in the direction of Catholicism. But then I thought of the complexities that this drastic of a change would bring to my personal life, so I backtracked a bit. Even so, I held onto the central importance of the Eucharist. Since I was in charge of leading our worship, I thought of ways of bringing the Eucharist weekly to our local WCG. Our pastor told me that the people were not ready for such a drastic change. It wasn't the direction of the WCG, and I should just forget about it.

Learning to *think* Catholic takes time. On this, God allowed me to struggle. One day while studying, I concluded that the Catholic Church was the most biblical of all churches. Unfortunately, this made me try for a while to become a Bible-alone Catholic. This works well for the Real Presence in the Eucharist, baptismal regeneration, or the sacrament of Reconciliation. In my mind, the Catholic scriptural position on these doctrines was far more persuasive than any Protestant position. To understand the Marian doctrines, one must think Catholic. One must accept the scriptural approach of St. Augustine that the New Testament is concealed in the Old and the Old Testament is revealed in the New. To do this, one must accept Tradition, and to do this, one must give up being a Bible-alone Catholic. This requires a real paradigm shift and takes a while to accomplish.

I was finally ready to seek out a priest. I thought we should call the local priest and talk to him in the privacy of our home. My wife called. She said we wanted to return to the Catholic Church. He said, "Mass is tomorrow at 9:00 a.m. See me after Mass." Whoa! I didn't feel that ready. But the next morning we arrived at St. Matthias Parish in the little town of Evans City, Pennsylvania. We entered the church, made the sign of the cross (for the first time in about thirty-five years), and sat way in the back. I was very nervous and mentally uncomfortable. At the first sight of the huge cross in this little rural church, I was repelled. It was too personal, too vivid, and too real.

As the Mass progressed, I became more and more uncomfortable. I didn't know what to make of these feelings. I was confused. After the Mass, the priest invited us to his rectory to talk. My wife and I were so nervous we could barely make an intelligent conversation. After leaving, we shared our experiences and discovered that we felt the same way. After meditating on the experience, I knew I wasn't ready immediately, but I also knew that according to all my study, the Catholic Church was the Church established by Jesus. I had to follow my head in spite of my conflicted feelings.

My wife and I decided not to tell anyone in our WCG church about visiting the Catholic priest and attending Mass. One of the unusual things about being in the WCG at this time was that a good percentage of the people would visit other Protestant churches and tell of their positive experiences. However, no one talked of going to a Catholic Church. Membership in our local WCG congregation, which was about eighty-five after the major split in 1995, fell to about forty a year later and was only in the mid-twenties in the summer of 2000. Since WCG members believed that Christians could be found in any Christian church, there was no compelling reason for many to stay. Loyalty to the WCG wasn't high. Some resented the WCG for the whiplash caused first by believing they were the only true church and then by being told there were Christians everywhere where people believed in Christ as their personal Savior.

I finally came to the conclusion that perhaps God wanted me to really want to come back to the Catholic Church. It was like God was saying to me, "You left Me for thirty years, and you want to just hop in a pew like nothing happened! Not so easy, Dan."

In my studies, I became more convinced of the doctrinal truth of Catholicism. But the fear of repeating the experience of our first Mass was haunting. What if it would happen again? I didn't know much about limbo—but I felt as if I was living in it.

One evening during this time, we were having a Bible study at our home. I was absent due to my work, but my wife was there. The minister made it a point to talk about the imputation of righteousness and not infusion. My wife just sat there and let the minister talk. After this, we knew we were reaching critical mass. A decision needed to be made. We did the only thing we knew to do. We prayed. We decided we had to face our fear and go to a

Mass. After this Mass, I was much more comfortable and so was my wife. My wife and I made our plan to let the people know we were going to return to our Catholic roots.

We met with our local priest who then made all the arrangements to have our marriage sacramentalized. On Saturday, August 26, 2000, we were married in the Church and then together received the sacraments after an almost thirty-five-year absence. We drove to our honeymoon destination, and the first question we asked the motel owner was "Where's the nearest Catholic Church where we can attend Mass?" We've been living happily ever after.

Originally published in the CHNewsletter *November 2002.*

Dan now runs a music store. He lives with his wife Pauline and their two children (Daniel and Karen) in Evans City, Pennsylvania.

Preaching Christ Crucified

By Daniel Ali
former Muslim

In 1959, I was born into a Muslim family in Kurdistan in northern Iraq. I was the fifth child of a large family. The Arab culture and the religion of Islam were the dominant influences, overshadowing the three other nations in Iraq, the largest of which are the Kurds. I began the formal study of Arabic at the age of twelve. By the time I was sixteen, I was writing poetry in Arabic, some of which was published as early as 1976.

My political activities in the Kurdish opposition against Saddam Hussein spanned most of my adult life in Iraq. Saddam Hussein, in one of his many attacks on the Kurds, forcibly moved large populations from their homes, banishing them to other parts of the country, to grab and secure his control over the Kurdish oil fields. Thus began in 1975 my active effort to free the Kurds and unite them politically. For this, I suffered jail and torture a number of times at the hand of Saddam. My close encounters with death were seen as "luck" when armies invading Kurdistan took the lives of my fellow fighters. Numerous times God saved me from death: by a judge's decree, by the chemical bombs raining down upon the Kurds, by near-drowning, and serious wounding. However, I did not then recognize that it was the hand of God.

I continued in my freedom fighting, often spending months in the mountains suffering cold and hunger, raw fear, and my people's utter abandonment by the nations of the world. In 1988, I saw my most loved friends die in the horrors of the chemical attack on the town of Halabja. I came to understand the frailty of every man in his sin and the utter hopelessness of life without God's intervention and protection.

Since the early stages of my life, I was interested in Christian ways of life due mainly to my earliest memories of our Christian neighbors, many of whom were beautiful examples of Christ's love. Remembering them leaves me with the precious realization that God was calling me to Him, even from my childhood.

One day, an Armenian Christian chanced to give me a book on the martyrs of the early Church. I read it and was inspired to live and die for the freedom of my people, the Kurds. I had a voracious appetite for reading during my youth and read widely in theology, philosophy, and history. I became fluent in English, reading Voltaire, Hegel, and Dickens, to name a few. Eventually I went on to avidly study the giants of the Christian faith, St. Thomas Aquinas among them. By consistent investigation and comparison of Islamic and Christian theology, I came to recognize the truth of Christianity in early 1982. But this remained an intellectual acknowledgement only. I recognized that Jesus was the Messiah, but I did not know Him personally.

After the Persian Gulf War, I married Sara, an American Christian, telling her that I believed Jesus was the Messiah but admonishing her that she was not to try to convert me to her religion. I did this despite the fact that I did profess to believe that Jesus is the Messiah. Muslims understand these terms quite differently than do Christians. She knew this was a solemn agreement, and for the next two years, we endured all the storminess of an intercultural and interreligious marriage. Through the many arguments and bitter disagreements, I slowly came to see that Sara constantly forgave me, loved me, and wanted me more than she wanted her own way. Unbeknownst to her, she was the living testimony of the Person of Christ in our marital struggles. Eventually, I began getting up at night to secretly read the New Testament. I was coming ever closer to the Lord as I met with Him secretly in His holy Word, the Bible.

We came to the United States early in 1993 and continued a small business Sara operated at the time. I had studied Islamic and Christian theology for most of my life. This study took me on a journey that led me finally to Jesus Christ, whom I intellectually recognized as the Messiah. Even at this point in my life, however, I did not make the final commitment of baptism.

One day, I was approached by my dentist, Doc Blevins, who prayed with me and eventually brought me to faith in Christ during the summer of 1995. I was baptized into the Body of Christ on September 17, 1995. Everything was changed. I began immediately to tell my Muslim friends why I had converted and made great efforts to evangelize them. I studied the Bible until I could quote chapter and verse and began to witness to everyone who would listen. Many did listen, intrigued by this Kurdish convert with so much enthusiasm for Jesus and the Bible. I knew that I now had what was needed for my entire nation, indeed for all of the Muslims and the unreached world. I had the Gospel and nothing could keep me from sharing it!

For the next year or so, I read for hours every day, witnessing to hundreds of customers at work and finding that I had a gift to bring people to faith in Christ or to get them to be once again active in their faith. In my small business, in our neighborhood, among strangers and friends, I found nothing worth speaking of anymore but Jesus Christ. It has now been eight years; during that time, the Lord has used my witness to win many people to Himself, some of them Muslims, some of them backsliders and some of them atheistic fence-sitters. "Whoever is ashamed of Me and of My words . . . the Son of Man will be ashamed of when He comes in His Father's glory" (Mark 8:38).

Soon after my baptism, Sara and I began a neighborhood Bible study for anyone from any denomination who would come. To this Bible study came a nine-year-old neighbor boy, Joe Sobran, who would read questions and answers from his Baltimore Catechism. Sara and I were shocked at the unique questions and were floored by the simple and profound answers in the back of each chapter. Little Joey did not give up, asking us why we were not Catholic. He would plant seeds every time he spoke to us of the faith.

One evening, Sara and I were watching television and happened upon EWTN at the exact moment of the Consecration where the priest was elevating the Host. We were shocked by this simple and beautiful respect for Jesus. Then the priest elevated the chalice, in its ornate beauty. The priest's vestments had a beauty that showed that only the best we can offer is good enough for God. Sara and I suddenly understood that the beauty in the Catholic Church was there because it was truly the HOUSE of GOD.

In 1996, Sara and I were introduced to the late Catholic theologian, Father William G. Most, who taught us Catholic theology. He generously gave time every Sunday for a year and a half to bring these two fundamentalists around to joining the Catholic Church. We were received into the Catholic Church July 13, 1998 at a special Mass.

Before Father Most died in January 1999, he and I discussed forming a forum in which Christians and Muslims could dialogue. Father Most was a great encouragement in the founding of the Christian-Islamic Forum as well as in the way he lived his last months. It was an eternal blessing to have sat at his feet and learned the Catholic faith.

After the death of Father Most, I carried on my life's mission of reaching Muslims. Early in 2001 after returning with some friends from a pilgrimage to Rome, I begin the work on the legal framework for the non-profit Christian-Islamic Forum, Inc. On August 13, 2001, the Christian-Islamic Forum officially came into being.

The very first introductory meeting of our new organization was to be held at Holy Spirit Catholic Church in Annandale, Virginia, on, of all dates, September 11, 2001. As you can imagine, this meeting did not happen due to the terrorist attack against our country. The conclusion Sara and I drew from the horrific events was that God was telling everyone it was time to pay attention to the Muslims. Either they were going to aggressively "evangelize" the West through their various forms of jihad or we were going to have to evangelize them with the Good News of Jesus Christ. I've been called on to speak numerous times since the tragedy. These talks have been about the realities of Islam, their strategies for converting us to Islam, and what we can do to successfully be heard and received by them. In the past, Christians have depended on the Bible to evangelize Muslims. This strategy has been largely unsuccessful because Muslims believe that Christians and Jews corrupted the Bible. We are developing a method to reach out to Muslims using only their sources, the Qur'an, Mohammed's Tradition, etc. All of us in the West are having to study now and learn to engage a religion and a culture completely foreign to Judeo-Christian culture, and the events calling for this have an urgency to them we ignore at our peril.

May God guide and empower us for this task by the power of the Holy Spirit and the grace of His Son, our Lord Jesus Christ.

Originally published in the CHNewsletter April 2003.
Dan is a convert from Islam and founder of the Christian Islamic Forum.

Welcome to the Universal (Catholic) Family of God

by Dr. Jeff Schwehm
former Jehovah's Witness

And everyone who has given up houses or brothers or sisters or father or mother or children or lands for the sake of my name will receive a hundred times more, and will inherit everlasting life (Matthew 19:29).

My short life before the JWs

I was born in the Catholic town of New Orleans, Louisiana. My father's family was Catholic, and my mother's family was Lutheran (Lutheran Church-Missouri Synod). My mother was the spiritual leader in the family. My father was not a practicing Catholic by the time I came along. I can remember attending kindergarten and Sunday school at the Lutheran church. My mother taught Sunday school to the little kids and was room mother for my kindergarten class. The Lutheran church and my mother taught me to love the Bible and Jesus. I knew that I had been baptized when I was a baby and that Jesus loved me. I remember church being a fun place to attend and to be with my mother and the rest of her side of the family. This all changed when my maternal grandmother died when I was about five years old.

Being a JW

Within a year after the death of my grandmother, my mother stopped going to the Lutheran Church and started attending the Kingdom Hall of the Jehovah's Witnesses. During this time, my father would periodically take us kids to Catholic Mass, where we would all fall fast asleep. There was no Catholic Sunday school and I really didn't understand what was happening there. I had no idea that my mother was no longer attending the Lutheran church, so I begged to go back to that church.

Eventually, my father started attending the Kingdom Hall of the Jehovah's Witnesses, and within about three years, my father, his parents, and one of his sisters left the Catholic faith and became Jehovah's Witnesses (JWs).

From the time I was five until I was around twenty-five years old, I was a Jehovah's Witness. As a Jehovah's Witness, we attended five meetings a week. There was no worship service. All of these meetings were classes designed to teach you how to convert others to the faith, and I got really good at doing this. I started going from door to door with Watchtower literature when I was six years old and gave my first sermon in front of the congregation when I was eight. By the time I was nineteen, I was giving presentations at conventions of JWs with over two thousand JWs in attendance.

After high school, I became a pioneer minister of the JWs, which means I spent a thousand hours a year going door to door. Eventually, I was invited to serve at the World Headquarters of Jehovah's Witnesses in Brooklyn, New York, which is where I met my wife, Kathy. I spent a year there.

Kathy's story

Kathy was raised a Catholic but was never satisfied. When she was older, she asked her very devout Catholic mother if she could explore other denominations. Her mother allowed it. Kathy spent time in Pentecostal, Baptist, and Presbyterian churches. However, none of these completely satisfied her. During this time, Kathy continued to attend CCD (children's instruction) classes.

Eventually, her mother started studying with the Jehovah's Witnesses. This greatly upset Kathy since she was required to sit in on the study. Kathy would ask questions and even tell her CCD teacher what the Jehovah's Witnesses were teaching her, but the CCD teacher could not teach the Catholic faith very well. Kathy eventually began to accept the Jehovah's Witnesses' teachings as truth.

Kathy's stepfather, mother, and brother also became Jehovah's Witnesses. Kathy's brother Scott served at the World Headquarters in New York, and it was on a visit to the headquarters that she met me.

Doubts as a Jehovah's Witness

I do not have time to explain ALL of the doubts that I had as a Jehovah's Witness. However, I can tell you that I had doubts about the faith and I believe my hope was that in serving at the headquarters that somehow these doubts would go away. Fortunately, they did not.

The main doubt I want to talk about, which really changed my view of God and my relationship to Him, occurred after Kathy and I had been married for a few years and I was starting to become inactive as a Jehovah's Witness. You see, by this time I had left the World Headquarters and started college. Kathy was working in downtown New Orleans. I would get done with my classes on Fridays by two p.m. and then go to the theology section of Loyola University's library for hours and just read. Mostly I read the books written by ex-Jehovah's Witnesses who were now Protestants.

The main teaching that I doubted at this time was the view of salvation. Jehovah's Witnesses say that only 144,000 people will go to heaven and live with Jesus for eternity—only these 144,000 people are adopted Sons of God. (In fact, we referred to these people, who were mostly leaders in the faith, as "Christ's brothers.") The rest of the Jehovah's Witnesses are taught that they will live forever in paradise on Earth someday. These people are not Christ's brothers but merely friends of Jesus. The friends of Jesus are taught that they must prove their faithfulness to God by cleaning up the Earth after Jesus returns and kills all non-JWs, and then after one thousand years of working themselves back to perfection, they will be tested again by Satan. If they pass this last test, then they can live forever in paradise on Earth.

This teaching seemed wrong to me after I prayed one night to the Lord and asked Him to reveal to me what He wanted me to know. I opened my Bible and read the entire book of Romans from cover to cover. The following Scripture sums up what God said to me that night:

> For those who are led by the Spirit of God are children of God. For you did not receive a spirit of slavery to fall back into fear, but you received a spirit of adoption, through which we cry, "Abba, Father!" The Spirit bears witness to our spirit that we are children of God, and if children, then heirs, heirs of God and joint heirs with Christ, if only we suffer with Him so that we may be glorified with Him" (Romans 8:14-17)

God told me that He wanted me to be His Son. He wanted to adopt me.

As a Jehovah's Witness, I had been taught that I could never be a Son of God and that I could never, even with lots of hard work, be a full member of God's family. I would never be able to see God. He would always be this holy other person from whom I would always be separated, even if I got to live for all eternity.

Years passed after seeing this. After I finished college, Kathy and I moved to Arkansas so that I could go to graduate school. I devoted all of my time to my graduate studies and left God behind, or so I thought. We lived for a couple of years in, as Kathy describes it, "spiritual limbo," where I even questioned God's love for me. Like the Israelites, I had a short memory of all the blessings God had given to me, one of His children who did not know Him very well.

However, God allowed me to get in touch with numerous Christians—mostly Protestant—on the Internet during this time, and our discussions were very helpful. At some point, Kathy and I both expressed our belief in God and our desire to worship with other believers. Around this time, I began doing doctrinal research and discovered that the mainline churches represented the historic Christian faith much better than the Jehovah's Witnesses did. (The Jehovah's Witnesses deny Jesus' divinity and reject the majority of the key doctrines, such as the Trinity, immortality of the soul, and the existence of hell, that most people consider Christian.)

Kathy and I wanted to find a church to attend and I had been speaking with my Lutheran relatives, so we decided we should attend a Lutheran church. Eventually, we started attending a church in Arkansas that belonged to the Lutheran Church-Missouri Synod. We joined that church about a year before I finished graduate school, and in January 1999, I started teaching at Concordia University in Seward, Nebraska. After we arrived in Nebraska, Kathy and I—in spite of being shunned by many of our Jehovah's Witnesses friends and relatives— thought we were finally home. God, however, wanted to give us so much more.

When we first moved to Seward, the Mormons had just started building a church in town. They had been visiting many of the Lutheran parishioners, so the local Lutheran church decided to teach a Sunday school class on the teachings of the Mormons. One of the comments the pastor leading the discussion made was that the church that Jesus founded would always exist and never be destroyed. He made this point because the Mormons teach (as do the Jehovah's Witnesses) that the early church went apostate sometime in its history and that God chose Joseph Smith (the Jehovah's Witnesses would say Charles Russell) to restore His true Church on Earth. He quoted this passage: "And so I say to you, you are Peter, and upon this rock I will build My church, and the gates of the netherworld shall not prevail against it" (Matt. 16:18).

I was sitting next to Kathy, and I took out a piece of paper and asked the question, "If this is true, then what was Luther doing when he broke away from the Catholic Church?" In other words, what is the difference between what Luther did and what Joseph Smith did and what Charles Russell did?

It was also roughly during this time that I started to try to share my newfound Christian faith with some friends of mine who had just recently left the Jehovah's Witnesses. I would try to demonstrate to them that certain teachings like the Trinity, immortality of the soul, and so on, were the true doctrines of the Christian faith. I would use the Bible to try to "prove" it to them. Their response was, "How do you know your interpretation is correct, since when we were JWs we would interpret those verses 180 degrees in the opposite direction?"

So, I said to myself, "I bet there were other writings from Christians who were around during the time of the Apostles who could shed light on what the early church really believed." So I started reading the early Church Fathers. Justin Martyr soon became one of my favorites. I especially liked the way he described how early Christians worshipped. I thought, "Wow! Christians have been worshipping like the Lutherans worship for centuries."

Eventually, I started reading books on the development of the New Testament and why the Catholics have those extra books in their Old Testament Bibles. I also wanted to know if the early Church *really* believed Jesus to be God. I was shocked at the answers I was getting to these questions.

First, I read some letters that were written around 107 A.D. by a Christian bishop, Ignatius of Antioch. In his letters, he talked about the real presence of Christ in the Eucharist and referred to Jesus as God. However, he also described the early Church as "Catholic" and he said, "The true church is the church where the bishop is."[1] I thought to myself, "O my God, the early Church had a hierarchy!!!!!!!!!"

I also read a book written by a third-century bishop named Eusebius on the history of the Christian Church. Eusebius described the early Church in such a way that I could see that it looked a lot like the Catholic Church, the main difference being that the Catholic Church of today is a lot bigger.

I even read a church history book in which the Protestant historian admitted that the Church used apostolic succession—although he did not call it that, but he described how apostolic succession operates—to fight heresies in the second century.

I discovered that if it were not for the Catholic Church, I would have no idea what books belonged in the New Testament because the Church decided that for me at the end of the fourth century after Christ!

God must have wanted us badly.

Now, you would think that with all of this data I would have become Catholic right then. The answer is no. About this time, I happened to become reacquainted with a friend from high school named Jim. Today, he is Father Jim and a Catholic priest. Father Jim is also a convert to the Catholic Church. He was raised Presbyterian.

Father Jim and I would have deep conversations on religious history and agree pretty much all of the time. Father Jim would say that I was more Catholic than some of his own parishioners, and I would always respond, "But I'm not ready to swim the Tiber yet." He would then say, "What does the Holy Spirit have to do, whack you over the head with a two-by-four?" Finally, Father Jim challenged me to read the *Catechism of the Catholic Church* and said that if I found anything wrong with it to let him know, and if I didn't then I would know what I had to do.

---

[1] *Letter to the Smyrnaeans,* 8:2.

So, during the summer of 2002, I finished reading the *Catechism of the Catholic Church* and some other books, written by converts to the Catholic Church. God finally found his two-by-four.

At the beginning of this story, I quoted Matthew 19:29, which says those who leave family for Jesus will receive more in return. Well, that is what God hit me with over the head. Here I thought I was already an adopted son of God as a Lutheran Protestant Christian—and I was—but I was still not a full member of the family. There was—as God revealed to me—something missing.

For example: "When Jesus saw His mother, and the disciple whom He loved standing near, He said to His mother, 'Woman, behold your son!' Then He said to the disciple, 'Behold, your mother!' And from that hour the disciple took her into his home" (John 19:26, 27).

You see, Jesus wanted to give me a new mother, His mother. My mother, Eve, had said yes to Satan and no to God. Mary had said yes to God. In addition, my own mother, Susan, has never forgiven me for leaving the JWs, and my relationship with her has been strained. (The Jehovah's Witnesses shun people who leave the faith.) Here Jesus wants to give us His mother because in reality all of us are "the disciple that Jesus loves."

In Romans 8, which we read earlier, Jesus wants me to share in His inheritance. Because of this, I can call God "Daddy," which is what *"abba"* means.

In Matthew 25:31-46, Jesus tells me that He is my brother. Jesus identifies Himself as a brother to suffering humanity.

There were fifteen hundred years of Christian brothers and sisters whom I had never been introduced to who were just waiting to meet me. For example, in Hebrews, chapters 11 and 12, the writer reminds us that from Enoch (an Old Testament prophet) to the present day, there is a great cloud of witnesses (saints), older brothers and sisters, cheering us on and praying for us so that we will make it one day into God's house in heaven.

God's two-by-four was to introduce me to His entire family and say, "I want you to be a part of all of this."

After finding a new job and watching the amazing way in which God converted my wife, I had the privilege to be sealed through the sacrament of Confirmation into "God's Universal Family," the Church, during Mass at the Feast of the Descent of the Holy Spirit, known as Pentecost. As I confessed the faith of the Church that Christ founded through the words of the Nicene Creed during that Mass, I could hear with my ears those same words coming from the people in the pews in the cathedral. I also knew through faith that the angels and saints in heaven were confessing those words with me. For me, whenever I go to Mass, it is a huge family reunion that is beyond the limits of space and time and unites heaven and Earth together as we all worship our wonderful Father in heaven.

Originally published in the CHNewsletter *April 2004.*

Jeff has a Ph.D. in chemistry from the University of Arkansas. He and his wife Kathy live in Sheboygan, Wisconsin where he is assistant professor of Biochemistry at Lakeland College. Jeff and Kathy work with an apostolate called the Fellowship of Catholic Ex-Jehovah's Witnesses: *www.catholicxjw.com.*

A Twentieth-Century Centurion Swears Allegiance to Christ

by Msgr. Stuart Swetland
former Evangelical Protestant

From my Navy days fighting terrorism in the Middle East through my years debating politics at Oxford, Christ called me ever closer to His Church and finally into His priesthood.

June 14, 1985, began as a routine day at sea for the crew of the USS Kidd. Having just completed some joint naval exercises, we were in the Aegean Sea, en route to a port visit in Haifa, Israel. I was standing watch as the duty officer.

Suddenly, the calm of the day was interrupted by reports that an American passenger plane, TWA Flight 847 out of Athens to Rome, had been hijacked to Beirut by two members of the radical terrorist group Islamic Jihad. On board were more than 150 passengers, mostly Americans — including five Navy divers. Petty Officer 2nd Class Robert Stethem would soon be tortured and shot in the head.

President Ronald Reagan planned to take decisive action. In less than forty-eight hours, we were off the coast of Beirut. Before long, other ships and Special Forces — including the then-secret Delta Force — began to join our growing flotilla.

My role was initially to serve as landing officer for the helicopters using our flight deck. But two hours before we were to launch, the captain summoned me into his cabin. He told me that a team of Navy SEALS was going to create a diversion ashore, drawing the enemy's fire before swimming out to sea. I was to command a small boat to pluck them from the water at high speed. The captain told me we would probably come under heavy fire and that the chance of casualties was greater than fifty/fifty.

I chose the best unmarried men I could find for my three-man crew; then I prepared. I had been briefed on events in Beirut. I knew what the terrorists had done to Petty Officers; a great anger began to take hold of me. My anger gave way to hatred—hatred toward the cowardly thugs who had killed my shipmate. I was glad I had been chosen for this mission, even though it put my life in danger. I wanted to kill the terrorists who had killed Stethem.

We launched our operation at midnight, but immediately everything was put on hold. I found out later that President Reagan was waiting for further intelligence on the location of the hostages. He didn't want to leave any American behind. For the next two hours, we sat in the water, circling at our launch positions, waiting for the "go" command.

I pray the hate out of my heart

Then I did what I think every soldier, sailor, Marine, or airman has done throughout history: I prayed. There are no atheists in foxholes. A recent convert to Catholicism, I had learned to pray the rosary by reading the works of St. Louis Marie de Monfort, and it had been the one form of prayer I had always been able to use under any circumstances. It did not fail me that evening.

As I prayed, the words of the Our Father struck me as never before: "Forgive us our trespasses, as we forgive those who trespass against us." *Forgive?* How could God possibly ask me to forgive the thugs who had tortured and killed a brave American sailor?

My mind drifted to the sorrowful mysteries. Jesus being crucified: "Father, forgive them," He exclaimed as the nails pierced His sacred flesh. I thought of His admonition from the Sermon on the Mount: "Love your enemies." How could God demand this? Surely this teaching had exceptions. As we circled in the choppy ocean waters off Beirut, I rediscovered what I already had come to know and believe: The Gospel of Jesus Christ is true, and it does not admit of exceptions.

If I had died that night, my salvation would have been in jeopardy. I had hated those terrorists from my heart. I wanted them dead. I didn't just want to protect and free innocent hostages (a worthy effort where one can accept the death of an aggressor as an unintended consequence). I wanted to send the hijackers and their accomplices to hell.

If I had died in that state, hell is where I would have found myself.

However, the "go" command never came. Before sunrise, President Reagan aborted the military operations, and negotiations eventually led to the release of the remaining hostages.

Thanks be to God! For that night, floating in the darkness off the coast of Beirut, I had another conversion: I learned the meaning of mercy, forgiveness, and love. In those hours, God gave me the actual grace—the supernatural power—to help me let go of my hatred and wrath.

Nevertheless, I relied on another grace that night: the grace I had received in becoming Catholic. This grace allowed me to know and to believe in the truth of the teaching of Christ and His Church. In those moments before battle, if I had for a moment doubted that the Word of God as revealed in Scripture and Tradition was true, I believe I would have resisted God's call to "love your enemies," probably the most difficult command in Scripture. Without the faith to believe that the teachings of Christ and His Church are infallibly true, I would not have had the courage to change that evening.

God's grace not only saved me from myself that evening; this conversion from hatred to love—one of many in my life—brought me closer to discovering my call to the priesthood.

"Why did you become Catholic?"

The day that I was received into full communion with the Catholic Church was the most joyful day of my life. At the Easter Vigil in 1984, in the small chapel of Oxford University's Newman Center, I was confirmed and received the Eucharist for the first time. The moment I received the Host, I know that I was being united with Jesus Christ in every possible way: physically, spiritually, emotionally, and intellectually. I knew that I was following the will of the Father more closely than I ever had before.

But becoming Catholic was about the last thing I had expected to do while at Oxford.

Often when someone asks me why I became a Catholic, I answer with a clever line stolen from some famous convert. A favorite is G.K. Chesterton's quip, "To get my sins forgiven." Another favorite is the short affirmation, "Because it's true."

Sometimes it's more an accusation that a question. If the person asks, "Why did you become a *Catholic?*" with the emphasis on *Catholic*, he has a problem with the Church. If the emphasis is on *you*, he's usually an intellectual elitist who believes that no educated person would become (or remain) Catholic. If the emphasis is on *become*, the questioner finds it possible that a person raised in the Church would remain in it but inconceivable that someone with my background would choose to *become* Catholic.

I love to challenge such prejudices, because I too once held them. When I "went up" to Oxford, as the English say (the expression assumes that everyone is coming from London, thus going "up," north, to Oxford), my religion could have best been described as lapsed Protestant with strong anti-Catholic biases. In many ways, I was a functioning pagan steeped in all the fashionable ideas of modern American ideology. Politically and economically, I was a conservative with a libertarian tendency. I was a pretty typical product of my background.

A born-again conservative in revolutionary times

I was born on May 15, 1959, in Pittsburgh, Pennsylvania, the youngest of three children. My parents were and are devout Christians, and I was baptized a Lutheran soon after birth. When I was three, my parents moved to rural northeast Pennsylvania. There wasn't always a Lutheran church close at hand in those parts, so for the next decade, I attended Methodist and Baptist churches as well—each Evangelical, with a strong sense that the Bible was literally and inerrantly true. My family attended church every Sunday morning, participated in Sunday school (where my parents often assisted or taught), frequently attended midweek services on Wednesday nights and encouraged prayer and Bible study at home.

At the age of six or seven, I committed myself to a personal relationship with Christ, as much as one can as a small child. I deepened this commitment at twelve, when, as a member of a Baptist community, I was re-baptized. A few years later, when a Lutheran community began in our small town, I again recommitted myself when I was confirmed as a member there.

On each of these occasions, I was truly converting in the sense of going deeper into my relationship with Christ. I was really "growing in the Lord," a process that I believe parallels our Lord's own growth in "age and grace and wisdom." This ongoing conversation is a necessary part of spiritual maturity.

But there was something missing. As I grew spiritually, I began to question many things. From my earliest memories, I have always been fascinated with moral questions, especially those that touch on economic and political issues. Perhaps this is because I grew up during the revolutionary times of the late 1960s and early 1970s in a house with a politically active conservative Republican father. (My earliest political memory is of my dad's bumper sticker in 1966: "Don't blame me. I voted for [Barry] Goldwater.") My elder siblings and my dad argued constantly about Vietnam, the draft, the voting age, women's rights, civil rights, and a host of other issues.

Looking for the right answers

It was natural for me to search for answers to the questions that were being argued daily on television, in the newspaper, and at our dinner table. Having been taught to search for the truth in the Bible, I began to study it to find out the "right answers."

Even in my late teenage years, I questioned what seemed to be contradictory answers to the most basic questions from people who all claimed that God loves us and had given us the truth in Scripture. My mother and sister were working hard for women's rights because they saw the biblical truth that all people were created in the image and likeness of God and thus deserved equal respect. As an educator and administrator, my mother was a pioneer for women in leadership roles, although she never received the same pay as her (often less-qualified) male counterparts. But many Evangelicals condemned her and others like her for failing to be "submissive" according to their readings of St. Paul's epistles. Devout Christians read the same texts and came up with opposite conclusions!

On many issues, from the sublime (the meaning of Holy Communion) to the ridiculous (whether men could wear their hair long), I found believing Christians at odds, despite their reliance on the same Bible. Who was to decide among them? How could I decide what was right?

From the Naval Academy to a "peace church"

If I had stayed in my rural hamlet, these issues might never have been enough to cause me a crisis of faith. But the larger world beckoned. Partly because I wanted to get a free, high-quality education, partly because my parents had instilled in me the important notion of service and partly for the prestige of it all, I entered the United States Naval Academy (USNA) as part of the Class of 1981. Those in the admissions office informed my parents that they did not think I could handle the academy academically and not to expect much.

Born stubborn, I needed to hear no more. I threw myself into my studies (majoring in physics) and graduated first in my class, winning a Rhodes Scholarship in my senior year.

My time at USNA, however, was not good for my faith. During my plebe (freshman) year, I searched for a place of worship. The naval chaplaincy provided a generic Protestant service that I enjoyed but didn't find comforting or challenging. I began to look for a "civilian" church to attend. I was in for a shock. When I attended a Lutheran church in the Annapolis area, I was greeted coldly. After a couple of weeks, they told me I wasn't welcome back if I was in uniform — that the congregation was a "peace church" that had taken an anti-war stance during the Vietnam conflict. Since plebes had to wear their uniforms, I couldn't attend this church.

This rejection left me reeling. My home community had celebrated my military scholarship and sent me forth with a blessing — and here were members of the same denomination, reading the same Bible, condemning me for being in the service. Who was right? How could I know?

The crucible of doubt

Being a typical eighteen year-old, this was all I needed to quit practicing my faith. For the next four years, I was, at best, an irregular churchgoer. I stopped praying, and instead I threw myself into my work and studies. I did not resolve these faith issues; I just bracketed them, dismissing Christianity as a religion that was hopelessly confused.

When I arrived at Oxford in October 1981, I had an opportunity to study beyond my technological background. Former Rhodes

Scholars from the Navy, including Admiral Stansfield Turner and Secretary of the Navy James Woolsey, had convinced me to study P.P.E. (politics, philosophy, and economics) at Oxford. I decided that this was the time to search for answers to the ethical and moral questions that had always interested me. In fact, my tutors at Oxford challenged me to do just that.

Among the first books they had me read were René Descartes' *A Discourse on Method*, *Meditations on the First Philosophy,* and *Principles of Philosophy*. Descartes challenges the reader to place all of his beliefs in the "crucible of doubt." This methodological doubt means that one should question why he holds any and all beliefs, even belief in the existence of God, in creation, and in himself. Through this method, Descartes reaches his famous *"Cogito ergo sum"* — "I think, therefore I am," as the basis for a philosophical argument for the existence of God and the universe. I set about applying this method in my life.

Radical doubt is dangerous. By rejecting all received wisdom and tradition, you place yourself in an intellectual void. Only later would I understand that we are not isolated atoms but, rather, beings born for and in community. We need to remain connected to that communion with the living and the dead and with the wisdom of the ages. As Chesterton said, "Belief in tradition is just applying the principles of democracy to the dead."

I confront Christianity's claims

Having begun to ask myself (and others) to justify all beliefs — moral, intellectual, and religious — I soon found myself face to face with the basic claims of Christianity. I could no longer simply bracket them.

There God's grace worked in me, especially through certain Christians He placed in my life. As I began my studies at New College in Oxford, a group of young men and women, several of them believing Catholics, befriended me. During our next three years together, their influence, their patience, and especially the witness of their lives helped lead me into the Church.

Having inherited all the anti-Catholic prejudice of a typical Evangelical Protestant, I resisted what was becoming plain to me — that there is a wisdom in the teaching of the Catholic Church that is explainable only by its greater-than-human inspiration. As I searched for answers to the questions my tutors asked me, I kept finding that the best—the most reasonable, well articulated, and convincing—responses came from the Catholic Tradition. The writings of the saints (especially St. Augustine and St. Thomas Aquinas and those influenced by them, such as John Henry Cardinal Newman, Elizabeth Anscombe, and John Finnis) were superior to those proposed by other sources. It seemed to me that Catholic thought about social questions—for example, the issues for war and peace (especially the just-war tradition)--was clearer and better thought-out than the other arguments I was studying. At first, I thought this was a coincidence; as time went on, I could not deny that something different was behind the writings of these men and women.

On my own, I began to examine the basic assumptions of the Christian Faith. First, did Jesus exist? Yes, this is well documented. Next, is He who He says He is? I must admit that I agreed with C.S. Lewis's ideas that He was either "liar, lunatic or Lord." But how could I judge the authority of His claims?

The key question: Did Jesus really rise?

After much thought and study (and just a little prayer--to this stage I wasn't yet seriously praying), I decided that the central claim of Christianity is the claim of Jesus' bodily Resurrection. The truth of the biblical witness seemed to me to hinge on this claim. So how should one judge the authenticity of the Resurrection?

I tried to approach the biblical texts like other ancient texts. At this time, I was also reading Julius Caesar and Thucydides for their insights into military strategy and tactics. Most thinkers readily accepted these texts. Was Scripture less trustworthy?

The text I first found most compelling was 1 Corinthians 15. Here St. Paul tells of all those who had seen and experienced the risen Lord: more than five hundred witnesses, many of whom were still alive when Paul wrote the letter (about twenty years after the events). This letter seems to be an authentic testimony to the truth of the bodily Resurrection of Jesus. The hundreds of witnesses lend credibility to Paul's own experience of the risen Lord. If these others had not really experienced the convincing proofs of Jesus' Resurrection, Paul would quickly have been seen as a fraud.

As I studied more, I was startled by the overwhelming evidence for the Resurrection, especially in the life of the early Church. Almost to a person, those first believers went to a martyr's death for their firm and certain belief in the Resurrection. No other explanation made sense of the data. That Jesus really had not died? No, the medical evidence in John's Gospel of "blood and water rushing from His side" shows that He really died. Plus, even a cursory reading of Roman history shows that no Roman soldier would so botch a crucifixion as to allow a condemned man to survive.

No, for anyone "with eyes to see and ears to hear," the accounts of the Resurrection and the lives of the men and women who had witnessed the life, death, and Resurrection of Jesus were convincing evidence of the authenticity of the Resurrection.

The Church's teachings all ring true

In addition, there were existential, subjective reasons for me to believe. Throughout my sojourn away from practicing Christianity, I had never been comfortable in denying what I had experienced in prayer and worship as a child. On some level of my being, I knew that I had encountered the living God in my life. I could not "unhear" that Word that had spoken to my heart as a child. Now my mind was united with what I knew connaturally in my heart all along: that Jesus is our risen Lord!

With this rediscovery, I began studying the Scriptures closely, looking for a community of believers in which to worship. I found one in an Evangelical Anglican Church in Oxford. However, after a few months of worshiping there, I found I needed more than just that wonderful community's charismatic preaching and singing.

I now *really* knew, on an adult level, that the Scriptures were true. I wanted to find a community that also believed this and was trying to live it daily. I also wanted to answer the many ethical, moral, and political questions that still intrigued me.

As I studied and prayed more, I kept encountering the issues that divided Catholics and Evangelical Protestants. I read of how Jesus commissioned His Apostles to forgive sin in John 20:22-23, but where and how was this power exercised today in the community? Scripture talked about anointing the sick in James 5:14-15, yet only Catholics seemed to take this text seriously. What Jesus said about Holy Communion seemed very straightforward to me, especially in John 6, yet Evangelicals speak of the Lord's Supper as only symbolic. The Scriptures talked about the transformative power of God's grace, so that one can speak like St. Paul of total transformation of oneself to become "another Christ," but Evangelicals believe that Christ's righteousness merely covers our sinful nature instead of transforming it. Sacred Scripture speaks of the intercession of the heavenly host on behalf of God's people on Earth, but only Catholics prayed to the saints and angels as intercessors and friends.

Then there were the moral teachings of the Church, which seemed to make more sense to me each day. As I examined the alternatives, secular and religious, no other ethical system had the same internal consistency and tight argumentation that I found in the Catholic moral tradition of natural law. In addition, the Catholic moral tradition answered the question of how to decide moral issues—by appealing to the teaching authority given to the Apostles and to their successors (the Magisterium of the Church). This teaching authority made sense of God's love and desire to lead His children into all truth.

Still another influence was the example of the Catholics I knew as friends, who lived their faith with a peace and joy about them that I didn't find elsewhere in the world. In fact, it was a peace and joy that "surpassed all understanding." I knew that I needed and desired that same peace and joy.

I sense the Real Presence

I began seeking private instruction in the Faith from Oxford's Catholic chaplain. For two-and-a-half years, he patiently met with me each week as I struggled to learn what the Catholic Church teaches. I examined every aspect of the Faith that I could handle. I attended lectures on questions of faith and morals held around the university. I visited with Father Thomas More Mann, a saintly Franciscan who introduced me to a side of the Church entirely new to me: its outreach to the poor and vulnerable. I began to pray seriously and to attend Mass each day. I loved to pray before and after Mass in the chapel in front of the tabernacle.

Growing up, I had been exposed to different theologies of the Eucharist. To the Baptists and Methodists, it was only a symbolic remembrance. Lutherans believed in "consubstantiation": Jesus is present "with" (con) the substance of bread and wine, but only in its "use" at Communion. The elements remained bread and wine at all times. In fact, I once watched my Lutheran pastor return extra Communion hosts to the bag for a later use after they had been consecrated. When I questioned him about this practice, he told me that they were no longer consecrated because Jesus was present only in the "use." When I pressed him to explain how this was possible and how this squared with Jesus' own words "This is My body; this is My blood," he told me that it was a mystery that we couldn't hope to understand.

As I prayed in the chapel, day in and day out, I had a very real sense of Jesus' abiding Presence in the place. When I finally got to the Church's teachings on the Eucharist, I grew excited: I had been experiencing the Real Presence in my own private prayer in the chapel.

The Church is a truth-teaching thing

Once I became conceptually aware of what I had connaturally experienced with the Eucharist, I began truly to hunger and thirst for our Eucharistic Lord. Before I could receive Him, however, I had to be able to say that I believed what the Catholic Church believed. So I redoubled by efforts to study the teachings of the Church, trying to come to terms with them, particularly her sexual ethic, which seemed so idealistic. It was beautiful but seemed impossibly demanding.

By this time, my friends knew I was examining questions of the Faith. I was trying to see whether I could accept every aspect of the Church's teaching. My friend Dermot Quinn, however, pointed out the futility of this approach. Even if I could study every detail of every teaching and come to say honestly that I agreed with the Church, this would not make my faith truly Catholic. What made a person Catholic, Dermot insisted, was not just belief that the Church taught the truth in matters of faith and morals, but the belief that the Church is a "truth-teaching thing." In other words, the most important question I had to answer was "Is the Catholic Church who she says she is?" Is she the Church founded by Jesus Christ, containing all that Christ's believers need for their instruction and sanctification?

If I believed this, I should be (had to be!) Catholic. If I did not, it really didn't matter whether I happened to agree with particular Church teachings.

The choice before me was clear. I had come to believe that the Church was who she claimed to be. The fact that I still had difficulties with some of her teachings didn't really matter. As

Newman said, "A thousand difficulties do not make for one doubt." I didn't doubt that the Church was the Mystical Body of Christ extended through space and time. I was confident that the Church's teachings in faith and morals were true even if I didn't fully understand why they were true, because I believed that God had endowed His Church with a special charism of the Holy Spirit that ensured that her authentic teachings in matters of faith and morals are, at least, not false. So I was ready to be received into full communion.

I knew then, as I know now, that my life as a Catholic would partly be spent in coming to a better understanding of my faith. I would need to do theology ("faith seeking understanding") to know and live the truth better.

This point needs to be emphasized: If God truly loves us, then He must ensure that we have a way of knowing what He is like and how we are to live. A loving father wants to be known by his children and teaches his children how to live and how to love. Any father who didn't would be negligent. I had come to know and experience that our loving Abba is no "reclusive" father. He has provided us, His children, with a way to know how we should live. The teaching office of the Church ensures that in every age we have access to the fullness of truth that has been revealed to us in Jesus Christ, who empowers the Church's official teachers, the bishops in union with the Bishop of Rome, to teach with a greater-than-human authority in the areas of faith and morals. He does this out of love for His children. Like all children, however, we must attentively listen to our Father and seek to understand His teachings if we are to live them out.

It is also very important for us to have confidence and trust in this function of the Magisterium of the Church. This is especially true when it comes to accepting *and living* the difficult and demanding teachings of the Gospel. When faced with temptation, often coupled with intense emotions, we have a tendency toward rationalization. In such difficult times, we must have at least moral certitude about the teaching authority of the Church. One of the great injustices that dissenting theologians, pastors, and teachers have done to God's people is to place uncertainty in people's minds, doubts about Church teachings and even about the very authority of the Church to teach. This makes it easier for us to use our difficulties and doubts as excuses not to live up to the demands of the Gospel.

Answering the call planted in my heart

That June night in 1985 off the coast of Beirut, I needed certainty that God did in fact demand that I love my enemies. I needed confidence that God's promises to me would be fulfilled. I needed to know that God's grace was sufficient for me to follow the Gospel's call to love. Without this confidence, I could well have lost my soul.

Once received into the Church, I was soon back in the Navy, serving as a line officer aboard frigates and destroyers. I found it challenging to try to live as a devout Catholic in the military. It was particularly difficult not to be able to attend daily Mass. At sea, we would often go two months without seeing a Catholic chaplain or making a port visit. Nonetheless, I was determined to serve the Lord as I served my country. It was the height of the Cold War, and it was easy to see that the Soviets and their empire needed to be contained. As I was soon to learn firsthand, innocents needed protection throughout the world, especially from the threat of terrorism that was (and is) affecting so many.

Throughout my time of service, but especially after the events of the summer of 1985, an old desire began to re-emerge in my soul. When I was five or six, if you had asked me what I wanted to be when I grew up, I would have said a minister. Of course, I had put away such "childish thoughts" as I grew, especially in light of my struggle with faith. But now they began to re-emerge. I discussed these feelings with spiritual advisers, who recommended that I wait three years after my conversion before acting on them. Converts often can be overly zealous when it comes to their desire to serve the Lord.

I loved the Navy. But over time, I became more and more convinced that God was calling me to a higher form of service: the priesthood. I wanted to share with others the joy I had experienced—the joy of knowing God's forgiveness, the joy of receiving Him in the Eucharist, and the joy of knowing the truth revealed to us in His Word. I resigned my commission in order to enter the seminary, was ordained a priest on May 25, 1991, and have had the honor to serve most of my priesthood as a Newman Center chaplain.

As a "Newman convert" myself, I feel right at home in this capacity. Each day God challenges me to go deeper into the mystery of His love. In hindsight, I see my life as a constant call to just such an ongoing conversion. At times, I'm faithful to this call, and other times I fall far short of a proper response to His grace. What has been true all through my life is that the Lord continues to be "kind and merciful to me, a sinner." My greatest joy as a priest is sharing that kindness and mercy with others—even with my enemies.

Originally published in the CHNewsletter *June 2004.*

Msgr. Swetland is the Catholic chaplain and director of the Newman Foundation at the University of Illinois at Urbana-Champaign.

From Baptist, to Mormon, to Catholic Priest

by Father Steve Seever
former Mormon

If you had told me less than ten years ago that I would be an ordained deacon in the Catholic Church preparing for priesthood in just over a year, I would have told you to go have your head examined. I was Catholic, and I went to church, but the priesthood was far from my mind. It wasn't even on the radar screen.

Twenty-five years ago, if you had told me that I would be Catholic, I would have considered it about as possible as my becoming the highest-paid sports star in history. In fact, I would have given you my testimony of Joseph Smith and the Book of Mormon and would have assured you without the slightest hesitation that Smith was a true prophet, that the Book of Mormon was Scripture superior to the Bible, and that I would never have anything to do with the Church of the Devil, which had removed many "plain and precious things" from the Bible and was responsible for the complete disappearance of the truth from the Earth.

Given the fact that I now wear clerical and Roman collar, it's obvious that I've had a change of heart about as radical as what it would take to make Marie Osmond a card-carrying member of the Communist Party.

I've been around church for as long as I can remember. I'm the adopted son of two Southern Baptists. I went to church from the time they could carry me — three times a week — twice on Sundays and once on Wednesday nights. I went to Sunday school from age five until my late teens. Every Sunday we went to church and the message was always the same — give your heart and life to Jesus. One day, in late March or early April 1970, I responded to that message and was baptized just a couple of weeks later. Since I was never good at sports, and because of that had few friends, I retreated to books as a way of escaping and creating my own pleasant world. My mom had taught me to read, and I had read on my own since age three, always above my age level. Now that I had a new faith, I started to read about it. On the day of my baptism, my parents gave me a brand-new King James Bible. I started reading that and any other book about Christianity that suited me.

Later, in junior high school, I made the acquaintance of some Mormons. They were only too happy to find out about my interest in religious topics and provided me with all the reading material I could carry. I was enthralled by the story of Joseph Smith's first vision. Like Smith, I had become disenchanted with the church I was in. The cliques in the youth group and the inability of many of its members to really live a Christian life had caused me to be open to anyone who had answers that would produce the change of life that I was sure Jesus wanted. Smith was only fifteen at the time of his vision—just three years older than me. To me, this proved that a teenager could have a life-changing experience of God. Certainly, the Mormons I knew lived clean lives and seemed to know the Bible better than I did.

The more I read, the more convinced I became, and I wanted to be baptized as a Mormon. My parents wouldn't hear of it. Still, I would sneak away on my bike on Sunday afternoons to the local Mormon Church just to be around my newly adopted faith. My Baptist friends called Mormonism a cult, which compelled me to learn more so I could defend my faith and prove them wrong. Soon I could twist the average Baptist around my little finger in a debate. When I finally grew tired of studying the doctrine of the Mormon Church, I started reading its history. That was the big "mistake." The more I read the history of Mormonism, written by men like Joseph Smith and Brigham Young, the more convinced

I became that something was wrong. The history of the Mormon Church I had been taught was far from the history written by the men who lived it. Someone, somewhere, had lied.

Now I was angry with God and thought He had let me be deceived. For several months, I couldn't go to church anywhere, nor could I pray. But I could and did continue to read Mormon history, just to make sure I wasn't missing something that would put it all back together. I stumbled one day upon a statement by one of the early Mormon leaders who had said that the only possible choices were Mormonism or the Catholic Church. I also met and began a dialogue with Dr. Walter Martin, a Baptist minister and author of *The Kingdom of the Cults*. Dr. Martin showed me that the beliefs of Mormonism had been held by others in the early Church and had been refuted by the early Church Fathers, so I began reading the Fathers. I quickly found out that Walt was right, but also that the Fathers weren't "Baptists." Their beliefs sounded very "Catholic" to me—especially concerning the Eucharist. One day, I went to Mass with two Catholic friends, and two days later, they took me to the rectory of the church to meet the priest. So began my friendship with Father Richard Engle and my journey home to the Catholic Church.

I had told God several times in anger that if He wanted me to trust Him, He'd have to provide answers to my questions so that I'd never be deceived again. I felt that if I could just get past different interpretations of the Bible, I would be OK. In the conversations that followed with Father Engle, he encouraged my reading of the Fathers. What a sneaky priest! Father Engle wasn't afraid of an ex-Mormon challenging him and was very warm in his presentation of the faith and let me proceed at my own pace. I think now that if anyone other than Father Engle had answered that door, I would not be Catholic today. After about six months, he called me one evening and asked if I was interested in becoming Catholic. By that time, I had become convinced that the early Church was Catholic, and I was drawn more and more to the beauty of the Eucharist and impressed by the witness of the early martyrs. So, in October 1981, I took the plunge and became Catholic.

In 1985, I met a girl whom I married a year later. She was an ex-Catholic who attended a Methodist church, and we were married there. I grew lax in the practice of my faith—due in part to a hasty marriage that began to fall apart in the second year. For six more years, we tried to keep the marriage together, and I even attended church with her, though I knew that there was something "different." In 1994, the marriage fell apart, and we were divorced.

For several weeks, I hung around, just licking my wounds and began to get depressed. One day, I felt the impression to go pray at St. Teresa's Retreat Center as I was driving by. I don't remember how long I was there, but when I got up, I knew I needed to go back to church. That next Sunday, I headed back to church and began to fall in love all over again—this time with the Mass. It quieted my soul. This was what had been missing—a personal encounter with Jesus in the Eucharist. The more I went to Mass, the more I fell in love with it and the more I desired to know about the Faith.

In 1995, I got involved in RCIA at my parish, and this program fueled not only my intellect but also my desire to pray, resulting in conversion. In 1997, I entered Ohio Dominican University to study theology and philosophy with the hopes of becoming a pastoral minister at a parish. The more I studied and prayed, the more I felt attracted to the priesthood, but I simply chalked it up to too much misguided zeal. So many people, including my pastor, kept encouraging me to the priesthood that I could no longer ignore the thoughts. I finally decided to open myself to the possibility, and for a year and a half, I sought advice and counsel, prayed and met with the vocations director. I entered the seminary in August 2001 and was ordained a transitional deacon on March 4, 2004, by Bishop James Griffin of the Diocese of

Columbus, Ohio. It's truly been an amazing "journey home", one that I never thought I'd take and that proves the truth of the old saying, "God writes straight with crooked lines"—in my case, very crooked lines.

Originally published in the CHNewsletter *August 2004.*

Father Seever was received into the Catholic Church in October 1981. On June 25, 2005, he was ordained to the Catholic priesthood and now serves the Church in the Diocese of Columbus, Ohio.

From Evangelical to Evangelical Catholic

By Jason Shanks
former Evangelical Protestant

For the first two years of my college education, I had a girlfriend. Faced with the obvious long-term implications, I began wrestling with the question, "What in God's eyes defines two people as married?"

Looking for answers, I sat down with the leader of an "interdenominational" Protestant organization on campus and asked, "Why must we be married in a church? Why cannot a couple just declare that they are married in their dorm room? Where in Scripture does one find the vows? Where in Scripture does it say that we need to exchange rings?"

His response shocked me: "Nowhere in Scripture does it require vows or say that one has to be married in a church." He suggested I might consult with another pastor but, in his opinion, a couple need only be married by the Justice of the Peace to be married in the eyes of God.

A bit taken away, I asked, "Then why do most Christians get married in a church with vows? Why do they exchange rings?" But even before he answered, I had answered my own question: "Because it's tradition." Later, I argued the point with my family. "TRADITION!" I couldn't believe it. The ring on the finger of the Protestant pastor I so admired was not the product of "Bible alone" theology but of tradition, and a Catholic one at that!

Although none that I knew would ever acknowledge it, I had discovered that Protestants held to a tradition not found in the Bible. Starting here, I began to see the inconsistencies of

Protestantism. My "Bible alone" theology had broken down. (Later I would realize that I was arguing for marriage to be recognized as more than a couple's mutual agreement but as a sacrament.) Therefore, here my investigation began: at the sacrament of Matrimony.

The next point in my move toward Catholicism was the disunity of Christianity. During my junior year, my best friend and mentor stepped into my life, Biff Rocha. Biff was and is a great man to whom I owe so much of my life. He really put me back together for I had hit rock bottom emotionally and spiritually. He was Catholic and was there to answer many of my questions.

For spring break, we decided to go to Washington, D.C. During our long drive there, I noticed a very interesting thing. On every intersection there were four different churches, one on every corner. The denominations ranged in name and most of the major ones were represented. Some were break-aways from the same denomination to become, for example, the second or third Baptists, Methodists, etc. In the midst of all this disunity, I sometimes noticed that the Muslims had a Mosque or the Buddhists a temple. Eventually I became so disturbed that I turned to Biff who was driving and said, "I don't think Christ wanted this." How had it gotten this way? But I filed these thoughts away and moved on with the trip.

Once back at Miami University, sitting in a Bible study, one of the members made the comment how we are totally, one hundred percent evil—that we can do no good. My knee-jerk response was, "Well, then why are we having a Bible study? If I am totally, one hundred percent evil, than any interpretation I derive from Scripture will be evil, too. Wouldn't it be better for me not to study the Bible than to make it evil?" I was so upset. I later learned that this concept is called "total depravity."

I remember returning to my room and, seeing my roommates, exclaiming, "That's it. I am throwing everything and anything I have learned about Christianity out and starting over. I'm going to find the truth no matter where it takes me."

Since I was going to stay in Oxford, Ohio, for summer session, as was Biff, I asked him if he wanted to read and research together all summer. Therefore, we did. I read dozens of books — he would point me in a direction and I would read, but he would not give me the answers. He wanted me to find it for myself.

So I started with the Reformation. *Why had we broken away?* I read Martin Luther, John Calvin, and other reformers. I narrowed the Reformation down to five crucial issues: faith alone, Bible alone, grace alone, Christ alone, and indulgences. I knew through my reading that the Catholic Church of today agrees that the way indulgences had been sold during Luther's time was wrong. The Council of Trent corrected this abuse and confirmed that to a certain extent Luther was justified in his anger.

I then learned that the Catholic Church agrees with grace alone and Christ alone. So, the last two remaining issues were faith alone and Bible alone. I discovered that Mary, the communion of the saints, purgatory, Eucharist, and Confession were not issues of the Reformation! Martin Luther believed in the veneration of Mary, held to the Real Presence in the Eucharist, and retained the sacraments of Baptism and Confession. So, I ignored these issues, even though I did have some strong objections to them at the time, but these weren't the reasons the Reformers broke away.

Faith alone and the Bible alone became the focus of my research. These issues are crucial in any investigation into the Church. After reading the Epistle of James and reading Martin Luther, I knew that faith alone could not be correct. It was not an either/or between faith and works, but a both/and. Faith and works are two sides of the same coin. The Catholic Church rejects works *alone* just as much as she rejects faith *alone*. Nowhere in Scripture does it argue for faith alone but for an "obedient faith," a faith that works itself out through love. You cannot have one without the other. Even though "alone" is not present in the original Greek text of Romans 3:28, Luther added it in his German translation because he said it was implied. James, The only place in Scripture where faith *alone* is mentioned is James 2:24, "See how a man is justified by works and not by faith alone."

Don't panic, this isn't advocating a work alone position, but a faith and works position. I realized that to "accept" Christ we have to do a work. It may be minimal, it may be small, but we have to "do" something. We have to say a prayer, ask Him into our lives. Our faith leads us to action, and our action increases our faith. After reading Luther, I concluded that many Protestants today would disagree with him. He thought that all we need to do was "believe." He also said, "We are a dunghill covered with snow"—total depravity before John Calvin said it. Faith alone, therefore, was for me no longer an issue. Luther was wrong.

The next issue was Bible alone. I found that Protestants actually do not practice it. The marriage issue showed me that. Even though there were many non-biblical traditions in the Protestant world, they still claim that the Bible is the final authority.

My mind began to overflow with other pertinent questions: How did we get the Bible? Where did the canon come from? Where in the Bible does it say the Bible is the final authority? Where in the Bible does it define the specific list or canon of books to be included? What did the early Church do before the canon was defined? Did they pass things on orally? Was it the Church who gave us the Bible or the Bible that gave us the Church? Why do Protestants accept such doctrines as the Trinity, for example, which are not spelled out in Scripture? There were many heresies in the early Church regarding the divinity of Jesus and the Trinity, all based on different interpretations of Scripture, and it wasn't until the Church councils of the fourth and fifth centuries that the orthodox doctrines we now hold were defined.

If Scripture is so easily interpreted, then why was there such a catastrophic division amongst Christians in 1054 A.D. over the Holy Spirit? Where in the Bible does it say one needs to "accept" Jesus Christ as "your personal savior"? It doesn't. According to the New Testament, the early Church brought people into relationship with Jesus through Baptism. Baptism was the means to salvation (1 Peter 3:21). Where does the Bible say we must go to church on Sundays? It doesn't. It was the bishops of the early Church that changed the primary day of Christian worship from Saturday to Sunday. The celebrations and holidays that most Christians observe today are not in Scripture; they were established by the Church. This is the reason the Jehovah Witnesses don't celebrate holidays or, along with the Seventh-day Adventists, go to church on Saturdays like the Jews.

I, also, began to see the ramifications of Bible *only* thinking. Luther believed that every person was his own priest, "the priesthood of all believers," and as such could interpret Scripture for himself. He believed that the Holy Spirit would lead all men to the same truth. Later, however, he was upset when this didn't happen. Among other things, disputes arose amongst his followers and the other Reformers over whether infants could be baptized. I began to see how this emphasis on private interpretation has led to the widespread disunity that now exists amongst Christians. Without a trustworthy, Spirit-led authority structure, there is chaos.

Even though I was coming to accept Catholic conclusions, I found myself in, what we call in the *Coming Home Network*, "no man's land." After concluding that I no longer agreed with Luther's reasons for breaking away, I realized that I could not remain a Protestant, but I was certainly not ready to become a Catholic!

So, I thought I'd go back to the writings of the Apostles and early Church fathers in the hope of finding a simpler church unencumbered with traditions and rituals. I went back expecting to find a Protestant Church, but, boy, was John Henry Cardinal Newman right when he wrote, "to become deep in history is to cease to be Protestant." When I read the fathers of the Church, I realized that they were celebrating the Mass; they believed in the Eucharist; they had Confession; and they were anointing the sick. I discovered that they believed in the primacy of Peter and they were appointing priests. They weren't setting up a Protestant church, but a Catholic one.

Uh, oh! I had concluded that I would never be a part of any denomination or church, yet here I was confronted with the fact that I might have to become Catholic.

The icing on the cake for me was John chapter 6. Now as I read it I was reading with different eyes. I asked the question, "What did the people present think Jesus was saying? Did they think He was speaking with symbolic language?" No, his Jewish audience and most of His disciples left him as He repeatedly said, "You must eat my flesh and drink my blood to have eternal life." If He was only speaking figuratively, then why did most of those present consider his words a very hard teaching a kin to cannibalism? I realized that the Catholic Church was being more faithful to Scripture. They were not reading into it. They were being systematic and consistent in their theology. And, it was here I decided that to remain Protestant was not being true to myself. In mind and spirit I had become Catholic.

I can remember the reaction of my friends when they returned to school for our senior year. Many were not pleased; one in particular rebuked me. For me, however, ridicule and taking a stand for what I thought to be true was nothing new. Later on, all my friends came to support my decision even though personally none of them agreed with my conclusions. Now as a Catholic leader within an interdenominational campus Christian organization, I began to see things in a different light. The usual jokes about Catholics no longer went unnoticed.

I wanted to be confirmed in my senior year, but my schedule would not allow it. After graduation, I lived with my parents for a year, and started attending RCIA at the local Catholic parish. Every Sunday at Mass, I would watching the people take the Eucharist, and yearned for the day when I, too, could partake. I also ached to be reconciled with God and His Church.

And I couldn't wait to experience the great release of Confession. My first confession was an amazing experience! The priest was awesome. It is enough for you to know that for sometime I had felt much guilt, sadness, and pain for the many sins of my life. In the confessional, as the priest absolved me of my sins, I felt the hug of God. I was forgiven. I walked out and sat in a pew crying for joy. From the moment I left the confessional that day, my pain was over. I was reconciled!

And so on Easter 1999, I was confirmed in the Catholic Church. I received the Eucharist for the first time and cried at that as well.

That next summer, I went down to visit Biff in Houston, Texas. We decided to go to Confession. I had either never listened, forgotten, or was never taught how to do it properly. My initial confession experience was more informal and laid back. It had been like having an accountability partner. But this priest wanted it to be formal and I didn't know what I was doing. He proceeded to yell at me within the confessional for not knowing what to do. I left and felt so mortified I couldn't attend Mass. Instead, I went to a quiet area and pleaded with the Lord: "Is this what you have called me to? Why this? Where are You in the midst of this Church?" You see, I knew the Church of the books. I knew the Church by reading the Saints and Church Fathers; I now was discovering the Church as it is today.

Then God in His mercy reminded me of the reasons I had converted. They had not been for issues for making me feel better but for issues of truth. I remembered the Eucharist and the truth of John 6. I knew there was work to be done and I had hoped to help.

Please know that since then I have met and worked with many incredible men and women of God in the Catholic Church, people who sincerely desire Him and yearn to bring Him into the lives of others. The Church doesn't teach pro-choice, although some people choose to believe it. The Church doesn't teach the use of artificial birth control, although some people choose to do so. The Church doesn't teach being apathetic towards ones faith, although many people are. As in many Protestant churches, the people don't always do or follow what their church believes or teaches. As Pope John Paul II was constantly challenging Catholics, we need to open our hearts and minds to Christ.

Biff describes Protestants and Catholics in terms of weight lifting, which has helped me. He said that the Protestants have a dumbbell and are using that dumbbell for all it's worth. They are using it hours on end, once or twice a day, and they are showing results. The dumbbell represents the Bible. Catholics have a full weight facility with machines, weight benches, the full regiment! And while some are showing growth many are taking their weight facility and training for granted. Now, would it be better to make Catholics reduce down to a dumbbell? No, it would still remain on the rack. It would be better to take the Protestant working the dumbbell and give him or her a whole work out facility. The Catholic Church is where the fullness of the faith resides. This is where the abundant life is to be found, whether some people take advantage of it or not.

Let truth be your search, if you let truth be your guide, I believe you will one day be Catholic. And I will be there to welcome you home. You may not know this yet . . . but you will.

May the grace of God, the love of Christ, and the fellowship of the Holy Spirit be with you now and forever, Amen!

Originally published in the CHNewsletter *February 2005.*

Jason is the pastoral assistant at St. Mary of the Assumption Church in Columbus, Ohio, where he lives with his wife, Melissa. He is completing a master's in theology at the Pontifical College Josephinum with a concentration in evangelization. Jason also hosts a website devoted to evangelization: www.seekmission.com.

Appendix A

Resources for the Journey Home

The following list of books is provided to help those on the journey understand more clearly the various dogmas, practices, and customs of the Catholic Church. The sad reality is that too few Protestants have actually read books written by Catholics about the Catholic Church. They have relied too often on books written by people who have only seen the Church from the outside or have left the Church sometimes with great bitterness and anger. But is this reliable? If you were a Methodist wanting Catholics to understand the basics of the Methodist faith, wouldn't you want them to read books written by sincere Methodists? For this reason we present the following list of Catholic books produced by sincere Catholics who love the Church and love the Lord who established Her.

This is in no way a comprehensive list. Rather it represents our personal choices of books that the staff and members of the *Coming Home Network International* have found particularly helpful. The two main criteria for these choices were: 1) faithfulness to the historic magisterial teachings of the Catholic Church and 2) ease of understanding.

Apologetics

Armstrong, Dave. *A Biblical Defense of Catholicism* (Manchester, N.H.: Sophia Institute Press, 2003). Dave Armstrong focuses on those issues about which Catholics and Protestants disagree the most: the role of the Bible as a rule of faith, whether we are justified by faith alone, whether doctrine develops, what the Eucharist really is, veneration of Mary and prayer to the saints, the existence of Purgatory, the role of penance in salvation, and the nature and infallibility of the papacy.

Armstrong, Dave. *The Catholic Verses* (Manchester, N.H.: Sophia Institute Press, 2004). Armstrong here explains ninety-five key Bible passages that confound all who would use Scripture to criticize the Church and Her doctrines.

Chesterton, G.K. *The Everlasting Man* (San Francisco: Ignatius Press, 1993). Considered by many to be Chesterton's greatest masterpiece, this is his comprehensive view of world history as informed by the Incarnation. Beginning with the origin of man and the various religious attitudes throughout history, Chesterton shows how the fulfillment of all of man's desires takes place in the person of Christ and His Church.

Flaherty, Regis. *Catholic Customs* (Ann Arbor, Mich.: Servant Publications, 2002). Sacraments and sacramentals. Feast days and fasts. Rosaries, novenas, and stations of the cross. These and many other traditional practices of the Catholic faithful receive a fresh look in this book.

Hahn, Scott and Leon Suprenant. *Catholic For A Reason: Scripture and the Mystery of the Family of God* (Steubenville, Ohio: Emmaus Road Publishing, 1998). A collection of essays by Scott and Kimberly Hahn, Jeff Cavins, Tim Gray, Curtis Martin, and others on the Eucharist, Mary, purgatory, justification, and more. Each is presented in the context of Scriptural exegesis and through the paradigm of the Church as God's covenant family.

Hahn, Scott and Leon Suprenant. *Catholic For A Reason II: Scripture and the Mystery of the Mother of God* (Steubenville, Ohio: Emmaus Road Publishing, 2000). A follow-up to the above volume examining the scriptural basis for the Church's teaching on Mary.

Hahn, Scott and Leon Suprenant. *Catholic For A Reason III: Scripture and the Mystery of the Mass.* (Steubenville, Ohio: Emmaus Road Publishing, 2004) A follow-up to the above two volumes examining the inexhaustible beauty and mystery of the Mass. Each chapter lends unique insight into topics such as "The Mass and the Synoptic Gospels," "The Eucharist in the Apostolic Church," and "The Mass and Evangelization."

Jaki, Stanley. *Newman to Converts* (Pinckney, Mich.: Real View Books, 2001). A unique collection and study of the instructions Newman gave in letters to potential converts. Newman's emphasis on such "conservative" notions as the obviousness of the four Notes of the Church, a Church which, in his eyes, was the one true fold of salvation, should prove uncomfortable to today's proponents of dubious innovations in Catholic ecclesiology.

Kresta, Al. *Why Do Catholics Genuflect* (Cincinnati: Servant Books, 2001). Mary and the other saints, the Eucharist and the confessional, popes and purgatory, mortal sin and holy water. Are you puzzled by all this Catholic stuff? This book answers in clear, concise terms many of the most common questions asked about the Catholic Faith.

Longenecker, Dwight. *Challenging Catholics: A Catholic-Evangelical Dialogue* (London: Paternoster Press, 2001). This book helps Catholics and Protestants understand each other better, and provides a good starting point for discussing the Catholic faith with Evangelical Christians. *Challenging Catholics* complements the work which has gone on in official talks.

Longenecker, Dwight. *More Christianity* (Huntington, Ind.: Our Sunday Visitor, 2002). This is an obvious pun on C.S. Lewis's famous book. The theme is that Catholicism is not different from other strands of Christian belief; it is simply fuller and richer. Why have 'mere Christianity' when you can have 'more Christianity'?

Keating, Karl. *Catholicism and Fundamentalism* (San Francisco: Ignatius Press, 1988). This book, which effectively refutes the common fundamentalist misconceptions of and attacks on the Catholic Church, has served as the initial stepping stone for many modern converts.

Keating, Karl. *What Catholics Really Believe* (San Francisco: Ignatius Press, 1992). Here are fifty-two answers to common misconceptions about the Catholic Faith that are held by many Catholics and Protestants. Drawing upon Scripture and the Catholic Tradition, Keating not only shows the logical errors in these positions but clearly spells out Catholic teaching and explains the rationale behind frequently misunderstood doctrines and practices.

Key, Paul R. *95 Reasons for Becoming or Remaining Catholic* (Zanesville, Ohio: CHResources, 1998). Paul Key, a former Presbyterian pastor of eighteen years, shares his ninety-five reasons for becoming and remaining Catholic, including biblical, intellectual, philosophical, historical, practical, institutional, spiritual, marital, familial, and Eucharistic reasons.

Nevins, Albert J. *Answering a Fundamentalist* (Huntington, Ind.: Our Sunday Visitor, 1990). Each of the sixteen chapters focuses on dispelling common fundamentalist misunderstandings about the Catholic Faith through logic and reasoning rooted in Scripture and Apostolic Tradition.

Apostolic Succession

Kocik, Thomas M. *Apostolic Succession in an Ecumenical Context* (New York: Alba House, 1996). A thorough and enjoyable study of the historical roots and current implications of apostolic succession.

Canon of Scripture

Short treatments on the Canon can be found in some of the stories in *Surprised by Truth* (Patrick Madrid, ed.). (See under *Testimonies of Converts*).

Catholicism: Basic Stuff

Foy, Felician A., and Rose M. Avato, eds. *Our Sunday Visitor's Catholic Almanac* (Huntington, Ind.: Our Sunday Visitor, 1997). Published yearly, this is a must desk reference book. Probably the most complete one-volume source of facts and information on the Catholic Church.

Stravinskas, Peter M. J. *The Catholic Encyclopedia* (Huntington, Ind.: Our Sunday Visitor, 1995). A thorough one-volume compendium of everything Catholic.

Catholicism: Selected Official Church Documents

Catechism of the Catholic Church (Rome: Libreria Editrice
    Vaticana, 1994). This is the first universal catechism since
    the Council of Trent in the sixteenth century. This is the
    standard source for learning dogma for the post-Vatican II
    Catholic. Everyone should have one at home.

The Companion to the Catechism of the Catholic Church (San
    Francisco: Ignatius Press, 1994). A convenient compendium
    of all the texts referred in the footnotes of the new
    Catechism.

Denzinger, Heinrich. *The Sources of Catholic Dogma*, tr. by Roy
    J. Deferrari of the thirtieth edition of Denzinger's *Enchiridion
    Symbolorum*. (New York: B. Herder Book Co., 1957). The
    standard source of official documents used by Catholic
    theologians. Difficult to obtain today but can sometimes be
    located in libraries or used-book stores.

Flannery, Austin O.P., ed. *Vatican II*. Two vols. (Northport, N.Y.:
    Costello Publishing Co., 1987). The official documents of
    the Second Vatican Council with many other magisterial
    pronouncements.

Trouve, Marianne Lorraine ed. *The Sixteen Documents of Vatican
    II* (Boston: Pauline Books and Media, 1999). The Ecclesial
    Classics series presents essential documents on topics of
    vital importance to the life of the Church today. Each volume
    is dedicated to a particular theme and includes explanatory
    introductions to the texts. This volume contains the following
    Vatican II documents: Constitution on the Sacred Liturgy,
    Decree on the Media of Social Communication, Dogmatic
    Constitution on the Church, Decree on the Catholic Churches

of the Eastern Rite, Decree on Ecumenism, Decree on the Pastoral Office of Bishops in the Church, Decree on the Adaptation and Renewal of Religious Life, Decree on Priestly Training, Declaration on Christian Education, Declaration on the Relation of the Church to Non-Christian Religions, Dogmatic Constitution on Divine Revelation, Decree on the Apostolate of the Laity, Declaration on Religious Freedom, Decree on the Mission Activity of the Church, Decree on the Ministry and Life of Priests, Pastoral Constitution on the Church in the Modern World.

The following Vatican documents and encyclical letters by Pope John Paul II are extremely important for understanding the essential issues facing the modern Church. They may be accessed at www.vatican.com.

Dominus Iesus: On the Unicity and Salvific Universality of Jesus Christ and the Church (Congregation for the Doctrine of the Faith. Boston: Pauline Books & Media 2000). This document is a theological and doctrinal explanation of the necessity of Jesus Christ and the Catholic Church for the salvation of man. It also discusses non-Catholic churches and how they relate to the salvific mission of the Catholic Church.

Dominum et Vivificantem: On the Holy Spirit in the Life of the Church and the World (Boston: St. Paul Books and Media, 1986).

Redemptoris Mater: On the Blessed Virgin Mary in the life of the Pilgrim Church (Boston: St. Paul Books and Media, 1987).

Christifideles Laici: The Lay Members of Christ's Faithful People (Boston: St. Paul Books and Media, 1988).

Veritatis Splendor: The Splendor of Truth (Boston: St. Paul Books and Media, 1993).

Tertio Millennio Adveniente: On the Coming of the Third Millennium (Boston: St. Paul Books and Media, 1994).

Ut Unum Sint: On Commitment to Ecumenism (Boston: St. Paul Books and Media, 1995).

Catholicism: Surveys of Church Teachings

(Many of the specific topics in this resource list are treated in these surveys.)

Adam, Karl. *The Spirit of Catholicism* (1954. Reprint, Steubenville, Ohio: Franciscan University Press, 1996). A classic study of the essence of Catholicism that is well worth reading.

Baker, Father Kenneth. *Fundamentals of Catholicism*, three vols. (San Francisco: Ignatius Press, 1985). A thorough discussion of all the major teachings of the Catholic Church in a very readable and conversational style.

D'Ambrosio, Marcellino. *Exploring the Catholic Church: An Introduction to Catholic Teaching and Practice* (Ann Arbor, Mich.: Charis Books, 2001). *Exploring the Catholic Church* is a primer on selected essential Catholic beliefs and practices. It deals with topics such as what does it mean to be a Catholic, the importance of the sacraments of Baptism and Confirmation, understanding the Mass, dealing with sin, and Mary and the saints.

De Lubac, Henri. *Catholicism: Christ and the Common Destiny of Man* (San Francisco: Ignatius Press, 1988). This book and the following one represent classic Catholic teaching by an eminent French Jesuit who was one of the premier theologians of the twentieth century. Challenging material but well worth the effort.

De Lubac, Henri. *The Splendor of the Church* (San Francisco: Ignatius Press, 1988). Like the previous volume, this book is richly grounded in the Church Fathers.

Gibbons, James Cardinal. *The Faith of Our Fathers* (Rockford, Ill.: TAN Books and Publishers, Inc., 1980). A classic study first published in 1876 that reads as freshly as if it were written today. Cardinal Gibbons was one of America's greatest bishops.

Howard, Thomas. *On Being Catholic* (San Francisco: Ignatius Press, 1997). In this very unique book, Dr. Howard gives lay meditations on Catholic teaching and practice, opening up in practical and simple terms the richness at work in virtually every detail of Catholic prayer, piety, liturgy, and experience.

Lawler, Ronald, Donald W. Wuerl, Thomas Comerford Lawler, eds. *The Teaching of Christ: A Catholic Catechism for Adults* (Huntington, Ind.: Our Sunday Visitor, 1991). A cooperative work by a large number of faithful Catholic scholars, this is more than a catechism. This invaluable tool is a precise and clear presentation of a complete vision of Catholic faith and life.

Kreeft, Peter. *Fundamentals of the Faith* (San Francisco: Ignatius Press, 1988). In this helpful book by a prolific convert to the Catholic faith, Dr. Kreeft considers all the fundamental elements of Christianity and Catholicism, explaining, defending, and showing their relevance to our life and the world's yearnings.

Newman, John Henry Cardinal. *An Essay on the Development of Christian Doctrine* (1878. Reprint, South Bend, Ind.: University of Notre Dame Press, 1986). Newman's classic study in which he set out to prove that the Anglican Church was the "via media" or middle way between the Catholic Church and Protestantism, but in the process became convinced that the fullness of the deposit of faith as delivered by Jesus to His apostles can be found only in the Catholic Church. This book has proved a great source of inspiration and conviction for many a convert.

Ott, Ludwig. *The Fundamentals of Catholic Dogma* (Rockford, Ill.: TAN Books and Publishing, Inc., 1960 fourth ed.). The translation of a popular pre-Vatican II theology text that was standard in the German-speaking Church. Pithy but an excellent reference manual.

Schreck, Alan. *Basics of the Faith: A Catholic Catechism* (Ann Arbor, Mich.: Servant Books, 1987). A highly readable guide to the basic teachings of the Catholic Church.

Schreck, Alan. *Catholic and Christian: An Explanation of Commonly Misunderstood Catholic Beliefs* (Cincinnati, Ohio: St. Anthony Messenger Press, 2004). An extremely well written explanation of the most frequently misunderstood Catholic beliefs.

Schreck, Alan. *Your Catholic Faith* (Ann Arbor, Mich.: Servant Books, 1989). A concise, question-and-answer Catechism that is particularly helpful for parents trying to teach their children the basics.

Sheed, Frank. *Theology and Sanity* (1947. Reprint, San Francisco: Ignatius Press, 1978). One of Sheed's most popular books, this is the ideal volume for helping the layman accept a more active role in the Church by showing him the practical aspects of theology and the role it has in the life of Christian believers.

Trese, Leo. *The Faith Explained* (1959. Reprint, Manila, Philippines: Sinag-Tala, 1995). A concise and straightforward account of Catholic teachings. The author illuminates the central elements of the Catholic faith in a lively, clear, and direct style. Updated to include changes since the Second Vatican Council, this is an increasingly popular book for giving classes on basic Christian doctrine, as well as for personal study by interested non-Catholics.

Celibacy of the Clergy

Cochini, Christian. *Apostolic Origins of Priestly Celibacy*, tr. by Nelly Marans. (San Francisco: Ignatius Press, 1990). The definitive scholarly examination of the topic of clerical celibacy in the first seven centuries of the Church's history.

Stravinskas, Peter M. J. *Priestly Celibacy: Its Scriptural, Historical, and Psychological Roots* (Mt. Pocono, Pa.: Newman House Press, 2001). The practice of celibacy has come under attack at various times throughout history, and sometimes the debates have obscured the great value celibacy is to the individual practitioner and to the Church. An excellent collection of essays on the gift of celibacy for clergy and laity alike.

Christian Living

Benedict XVI, *God and the World: A Conversation with Peter Seewald* (San Francisco: Ignatius Press, 2002). As Prefect of the Congregation for the Doctrine of the Faith, Joseph Cardinal Ratzinger, now Pope Benedict XVI, gave an interview with Peter Seewald. In this meeting that took place over three days at the Benedictine Abbey of Monte Cassino, the future pope answered a stimulating, well-prepared series of wide-ranging questions on profound issues. He responds with candor, frankness, and deep insight, giving answers that are sometimes surprising and always thought provoking.

Benedict XVI, *Truth and Tolerance: Christian Belief and World Religions* (San Francisco: Ignatius Press, 2004). Is truth knowable? If we know the truth, must we hide it in the name of tolerance? Cardinal Ratzinger, now Pope Benedict XVI, engages the problem of truth, tolerance, religion, and culture in the modern world. Describing the vast array of world religions, Ratzinger embraces the difficult challenge of meeting diverse understandings of spiritual truth while defending the Catholic teaching of salvation through Jesus Christ.

Hahn, Scott, *First Comes Love: Finding Your Family in the Church and the Trinity* (New York: Doubleday, 2002). Using the idea of the family to explain Catholic thought about the Trinity, Hahn shows the divine reality found in the relationship between the Father, and the Son, and the Holy Spirit, as well as the nurturing embraces of Mary, the Mother of all Christians.

Nordhagen, Lynn. *When Only One Converts* (Huntington, Ind.: Our Sunday Visitor, 2001). Here is found a candid collection of conversion accounts where only one member of a couple wanted to become Catholic, revealing the stresses this caused in their marriage and how they coped or even *grew* spiritually.

Shaw, Russell. *To Hunt, To Shoot, To Entertain: Clericalism and the Catholic Laity* (San Francisco: Ignatius Press, 1993). This important book probes the theological and historical roots of clericalism that have affected the Catholic laity, along with contemporary expressions of clericalism in today's Church.

Church Fathers (Selections of Texts)

Bennett, Rod. *Four Witnesses* (San Francisco: Ignatius Press, 2002). What was the early Church like? Author Rod Bennett shows that, contrary to popular belief, there is a reliable way to know. Four ancient Christian writers—four witnesses to early Christianity—left us an extensive body of documentation on this vital subject, and this book brings their fascinating testimony to life for modern believers. With all the power and drama of a gripping novel, this book is a journey of discovery of ancient and beautiful truths through the lives of four great saints of the early Church—Clement of Rome, Ignatius of Antioch, Justin Martyr, and Irenaeus of Lyons.

Bettenson, Henry, ed. *The Early Christian Fathers* (New York: Oxford University Press, 1986, eighth impression). The writings of the Fathers of the early Church are of particular importance to anyone who wishes to understand Christian doctrine. This book illustrates the process of development in Christian thought, life, and worship during the period which culminated in the acceptance of the Christian faith by the Emperor Constantine, and the meeting of the Council of Nicaea in AD 325.

Bettenson, Henry, ed. *The Later Christian Fathers* (New York: Oxford University Press, 1970). This and the preceding volume are chronologically arranged with a topical index in each volume.

Jurgens, William. *The Faith of the Early Fathers.* Three vols. (Collegeville, Minn.: The Liturgical Press, 1970). A rich source of quotations from the Fathers that is enhanced by a systematic doctrinal index at the end of each volume.

Russell, Claire. *Glimpses of the Church Fathers* (London: Scepter Press, 1994). A very thorough and handy one-volume selection of the writings of the Fathers of the Church arranged chronologically and topically.

Church History (Catholic historians)

Belloc, Hilaire. Belloc is a forgotten gem of English literature. A close friend of G.K. Chesterton, Belloc was at one time considered the rising star of English writers. However, as his writings became more candid defenses of the Catholic Church, he became less and less popular until today he is almost forgotten. Every one of his books is a powerful correction for the revisionist histories so many of us received not only in our Protestant seminaries but in American public schools. The following books reprinted by TAN, Rockford, Il., are all excellent reads giving the Catholic perspective particularly on the English Reformation:

> *Europe and the Faith*
> *The Crusades*
> *How the Reformation Happened*
> *Characters of the Reformation*

The Great Heresies
Survivals and New Arrivals

Bokenkotter, Thomas, *A Concise History of the Catholic Church* (New York: Doubleday, 1990). Meticulously expanded and updated for the new millennium this popular history of the Church originally published in 1979 offers a short but insightful history of the Catholic Church from the earliest times to the twentieth century. Long a mainstay for scholars, students, and others looking for a definitive, accessible history of Catholicism, it has now been meticulously expanded and updated for the new millennium.

Bouyer, Louis. *The Spirit and Forms of Protestantism* (Princeton: Scepter Publishers, 2001). A French Lutheran convert to Catholicism and leading authority on liturgical and devotional theology, Bouyer makes a powerful case for the chief principles of the Reformation—*sola gratia*, *sola fide*, and *sola Scriptura*—and then argues why the Reformation "spirit" cannot be sustained. This book remains among the most incisive looks into the main difference between Catholicism and Protestantism.

Carlin, David. *The Decline and Fall of the Catholic Church in America* (Manchester, N.H.: Sophia Press Institute, 2003). David Carlin, a professor of sociology at the College of Rhode Island, has written a new and incisive version of "decline and fall," this time analyzing the present condition of the Catholic Church in the United States. Though this book is blunt and honest, and sees few bright spots in the contemporary scene, it represents a frank analysis of the present extremely weak leadership and condition of the Catholic Church in the United States. However, the book is more than an analysis of the Catholic Church in America. Carlin understands that to see the problems of the Church in the United States, it is necessary to go back to take a look at the condition of the Protestant churches, at the effects of Vatican II, at the rising and practically dominant secularism that pervades the country.

Crocker, Harry W. *Triumph: The Power and the Glory of the Catholic Church* (New York: Three Rivers Press, 2001). Readers need to know the story of the Catholic Church but balk at opening those multi-volume Church histories. Crocker has written a book that solves the problem. In *Triumph,* he has told 2,000 years of Catholic history in fewer than 500 highly readable pages. The book has all the virtues of a good novel while packing an enormous amount of information.

Eusebius of Caesarea, *The History of the Church*, tr. by G. A. Williamson. (London: Penguin Books, 1989). Bishop Eusebius, (ca. A.D. 260-339), a learned scholar who lived most of his life in Caesarea in Palestine, broke new ground in writing *The History of the Church* and provided a model for all later ecclesiastical historians. In tracing the history of the Church from the time of Christ to the Great Persecution at the beginning of the fourth century and ending with the conversion of the Emperor Constantine, he tried to show the purity and continuity of the doctrinal tradition of Christianity in its struggle against persecutors and heretics, and supported his account by extensive quotations from original sources to a degree hitherto unknown.

Hogan, Father Richard M. *Dissent from the Creed* (Huntington, Ind.: Our Sunday Visitor, 2001). An easy-to-read history and explanation of false teachings from the time of the Ascension to the present.

Laux, Father John. *Church History* (Rockford, Ill: TAN Books, and Publishers, Inc., 1989 ed.) A thorough and thick one-volume classic presentation of the history of the Catholic Church written expressly for students and for adults.

Marty, Martin E. *A Short History of American Catholicism* (Tyler, Tex.: Thomas More Publishing, 1995). A useful and sympathetic overview by one of the leading Protestant observers of the religious scene. Marty's usual light touch does not fail him as he limns the possible and promising at the beginning of Catholicism's next half millennium in North America.

Maynard, Theodore. *The Story of American Catholicism* (New York: The Macmillan Company, 1942). An out of print gem but well worth the search. Essentially a retelling of American history filling in the many Catholic gaps left out by historical revisionists.

Schreck, Alan. *The Compact History of the Catholic Church* (Ann Arbor, Mich.: Servant Books, 1987). A lively and readable introduction to the life of the Church throughout the ages.

Weigel, George. *The Courage To Be Catholic: Crisis, Reform, and the Future of the Church* (New York: Basic Books, 2002). A masterful short history of the priestly sexual abuse scandal that erupted in recent years. However, the book is more than that. It is also an acute analysis of the history of various aspects of the Church in the United States since the close of the Second Vatican Council.

Eschatology

Currie, David. *Rapture: The End-Times Error That Leaves the Bible Behind* (Manchester, N.H.: Sophia Institute Press, 2003).

More than a critique of faulty end times beliefs, *Rapture* is a detailed excursion through the difficult and controversial passages of the Bible used by certain Protestants to produce belief systems that are not only quite modern, but also incompatible with Catholic teaching.

Thigpen, Paul. *Rapture Trap* (West Chester, Pa.: Ascension Press, 2001). Paul Thigpen, Ph.D., lays out in clear, simple terms the biblical foundations of Catholic teaching on the close of the age—the "end times." Along with Scripture, he draws from Tradition, the Catechism of the Catholic Church, Church history, and contemporary experience to reveal the shortcomings of the rapture doctrine and the larger tangle of twisted religious teachings to which it is tied.

Olson, Carl. *Will Catholics Be Left Behind* (San Francisco, Ignatius Press, 2003). This timely book, written by a former Fundamentalist, is a thorough critique of the popular Fundamentalist notion of the "Rapture"—the belief that Christians will be removed from earth prior to a time of Tribulation and the Second Coming. It examines the theological, historical, and Biblical basis for "premillennial dispensationalism," the belief system based around the Rapture and popularized in the best-selling *Left Behind* books. Written for both the layperson and the serious student, this book combines an engaging, popular approach with detailed footnotes and exhaustive research.

The Eucharist

Gaudoin-Parker, Michael. *The Real Presence through the Ages* (New York: Alba House Press, 1993). Selections from Church documents from the early Christian centuries to the present, with informative introductions.

Groeschel, Father Benedict J. *In the Presence of Our Lord: The History, Theology, and Psychology of Eucharistic Devotion* (Huntington, Ind., Our Sunday Visitor, 1997). Well-written book with excellent references and documentation. It thoroughly explains historical foundations and evolvement to current practices. This book stands out as being a great information resource on a subject that has many devotional books. It is solidly in-line with the Magisterium as are all of Fr. Groeschel's books.

Hahn, Scott. *The Lambs Supper: The Mass as Heaven on Earth* (New York: Doubleday, 1999). Each time we celebrate Mass we enter into the heavenly liturgy, which is so powerfully and beautifully described in the Book of Revelation. The Lamb's Supper will help you understand the Book of Revelation in light of the Mass.

O'Connor, James. *The Hidden Manna: A Theology of the Eucharist* (San Francisco: Ignatius Press, 1988). A must-read, in-depth presentation and commentary on substantial excerpts from the major sources of the Church's Tradition, focusing on the Real Presence, extending all the way back to apostolic times.

Ryland, Ray. *Transubstantiation* (Zanesville, Ohio: CHResources, 2002). A beautiful little booklet explaining in an understandable manner the true Catholic doctrine of the real presence of our Lord Jesus Christ in the Holy Eucharist.

Shea, Mark P. *This Is My Body: An Evangelical Discovers the Real Presence* (Huntington, Ill.: Our Sunday Visitor, 1992). This is My Body is a popular apologetic written in terms engaging and accessible to Evangelical Protestants. Shea treats standard misconceptions and objections to the teaching on the real presence of Jesus in the sacrament of the Eucharist, showing most to be simple errors in logic or ironic oversights in scriptural exegesis.

Justification

Akin, Jimmy. *The Salvation Controversy* (San Diego: Catholic Answers, 2001). A serious work on faith versus works, penance, purgatory, indulgences, and more. Questions relating to salvation, especially faith versus works, but also penance, purgatory, indulgences, and free cooperation with God's grace, have been sore points in the dialogue between Catholics and Protestants.

Decree on Justification Council of Trent. The Council of Trent, meeting on and off from 1545 to 1563 in the Alpine Italian town of Trent, was the Catholic Church's response to the challenge presented by the Protestant Reformation. Its doctrinal decrees touch on many of the controversial topics debated during the times such as justification, the Eucharist, and the other sacraments. Many of the doctrinal teachings of this ecumenical council are intended as definitive dogmatic pronouncements and as such are regarded as infallible.

Liturgy

Aquilina, Mike. *The Mass of the Early Christians* (Huntington, Ind.: Our Sunday Visitor, 2001). Here is revealed the Church's most ancient Eucharistic beliefs and practices. Using the words of the early Christians themselves, from many documents and inscriptions, Aquilina traces the history of the Mass from Jesus' lifetime through the fourth century. The Mass stood at the center of the Church's life, evident in the Scriptures as well as the earliest Christian sermons, letters, artwork, tombstones, and architecture. Even the pagans bore witness to the Mass in the records of their persecutions.

Howard, Thomas. *Evangelical Is Not Enough* (San Francisco: Ignatius Press, 1984). Thomas Howard describes his pilgrimage from Evangelicalism to liturgical Christianity. He soon afterwards became a Roman Catholic. He describes Evangelicalism with great sympathy and then examines more formal, liturgical worship with the freshness of someone discovering for the first time what his soul had always hungered for. This is a book of apologetics without polemics. A persuasive account by a former evangelical of the liturgical riches of ancient catholic worship.

Jungman, Josef A. *The Early Liturgy: To the Time of Gregory the Great*, tr. by Francis A. Brunner. (South Bend, Ind.: University of Notre Dame Press, 1959).

Stravinskas, Peter M. J. *The Bible and the Mass* (Ann Arbor, Mich.: Servant Publications, 1989). This work examines and explains the parts of the Mass, giving scriptural references and explanations for the various actions and prayers. Each chapter ends with study questions geared toward group discussion. This is perfect for Bible study, theology class, or prayer group, or simply to deepen your own understanding of the Church's highest form of prayer, the Eucharistic sacrifice.

Mary and the Saints

Breen, Sr. Eileen. *Mary the Second Eve: Selections from the Writings of John Henry Newman* (Rockford, Ill.: TAN Books and Publishers, Inc., 1982). This booklet demonstrates that today's Marian doctrines—including the doctrines of the Immaculate Conception and the Assumption—are firmly rooted in the teachings of the early Church. It shows that these teachings are based on Sacred Scripture and on the testimony of the Fathers, and therefore are not something invented later by the Church.

Hahn, Scott. *Hail, Holy Queen* (New York: Doubleday, 2001). Everything we know and believe about Mary is rooted in what we know and believe about her Son. This book explains from Scripture why Mary, the Queen Mother, is an integral part of Christ's kingdom.

Howell, Kenneth. *Mary of Nazareth* (Santa Barbara, Calif.: Queenship Publishing, 1998). Dr. Howell's *Mary of Nazareth* will lead you through the relevant Scriptures about Mary and will help you understand how intimately bound to one another Jesus and Mary are. It will explain how troubling Catholic doctrines of Mary are rooted in biblical testimony. This scriptural meditation will touch your mind and heart as you enter into the beautiful life by which Mary gave the world its Redeemer. Most of all, you will discover how Mary is a key instrument in bringing about that unity for which Jesus her Son prayed.

Howell, Kenneth. *Meeting Mary: Our Mother in Faith & Study Guide* (San Diego: Catholic Answers, 2003). Just as the mother is at the center of the family, so Mary is at the center of every Catholic's daily life—yet her role is often misunderstood. In this learning guide, Dr. Howell describes the central importance of Mary to not only every Catholic, but every Christian. He explains the reasons behind the four Marian dogmas and discusses the Marian apparitions at Guadalupe, Lourdes, and Fatima—and what those apparitions mean for all of us.

Madrid, Patrick. *Any Friend of God's Is a Friend of Mine: A Biblical and Historical Explanation of the Catholic Doctrine of the Communion of the Saints* (San Diego: Basilica Press, 1996). A short but lucid explanation of how Catholics and Protestants differ in their understanding of the communion of the saints.

Miravalle, Mark I. *An Introduction to Mary* (Ann Arbor, Mich.: Servant Books, 1990). This book is most helpful in clearing up many misconceptions about the Catholic Church's teachings on Mary.

Moral Theology

May, William E. *An Introduction to Moral Theology*, revised edition. (Huntington, Ind.: Our Sunday Visitor, 1994). In this fine textbook, you will find carefully documented, footnoted, and indexed what the Church teaches, why it is obligated to do so, and why its members are obligated to examine and to apply that teaching.

Novels

Grodi, Marcus C., *How Firm a Foundation* (Zanesville, Ohio: CH Resources, 2002). Stephen LaPointe believed in Jesus. For him, the Bible was the only sufficient, firm foundation for his life. He wanted to obey God in all things and had given up a career to become an ordained minister. He loved to preach the Word and knew that one day he would stand before God, accountable for everything he preached. However, there was one problem: How could he be certain that what he was preaching was true?

Papacy

Butler, Scott, Norman Dahlgren, and David Hess. *Jesus, Peter, and the Keys: A Scriptural Handbook on the Papacy* (Santa Barbara, Calif.: Queenship Publishing Co. 1996). An extensive collection of exegetical and historical sources that bear on the Petrine doctrine. This book contains most of the important data that any view of the papacy must explain.

Jaki, Stanley L. *And On This Rock*. Second Edition (Manassas, Va.: Trinity Communications, 1987). Father Jaki puts these words of Christ into their full biblical perspective and geographical context, offering the reader a novel insight into the primacy of Peter.

Jaki, Stanley L. *The Keys of the Kingdom* (Chicago: Franciscan Herald Press, 1986). Here Father Jaki gives a thorough analysis of historical, biblical, patristic, and medieval texts on the keys of the kingdom.

Ray, Stephen K. *Upon This Rock: St. Peter and the Primacy of Rome in Scripture and the Early Church* (San Francisco: Ignatius Press, 1999). Ray, a former Baptist, goes through the Scriptures and the first five centuries of the Church to demonstrate that the early Christians had a clear understanding of the primacy of Peter in the see of Rome. This book contains the most complete compilation of Scriptural and Patristic quotations on the primacy of Peter and the Papal office of any book available.

Soloviev, Vladimir. *The Russian Church and The Papacy* (San Diego: Catholic Answers, 2001). Pope John Paul II has introduced Soloviev, a spiritual genius and profound religious thinker, to contemporaries in his encyclical "*Fides et Ratio*" ('Faith and Reason') as an illustrious Christian thinker and declaring his work "prophetic". As editor, Father Ryland admirably captures the central themes of Soloviev's work, which shook the foundations of anti-Catholic Russian Orthodoxy, with three simple propositions: 1) Jesus Christ instituted the universal jurisdiction and infallible teaching authority of the papacy as a perpetual gift to His Church; 2) Apart from the papacy, the Eastern Churches will always remain what they are now: ethnic, national churches, totally independent and disunited; and 3) Only in union with Rome can the separated Eastern Churches become truly Catholic.

Prayer and the Rosary

Belmonte, Charles and James Socias, eds. *Handbook of Prayers* (Princeton: Scepter Press, 1992). A helpful compilation of Catholic prayers, devotions, and blessings.

Chautard, Dom Jean-Baptiste. *The Soul of the Apostolate* (1907. Reprint, Rockford, Ill.: TAN Books and Publishers, Inc., 1977). A powerful, life-changing book that was the bedside reading of many popes. This classic underscores the importance of the inner life of prayer as the foundations for all acts of service.

De Sales, Frances. *Introduction to the Devout Life* (New York: Doubleday, 1989). Written precisely for the laity, this made St. Francis de Sales (1567-1622) perhaps the first spiritual writer to compose a treatise of lay spirituality. As he stated in his preface, those who have written previously on the spiritual life have done so for the instruction of persons who have given up association with the world or they have taught a spirituality that would lead persons to do so. The intention of St. Francis, however, was to give spiritual instruction to those who remain in the world, in their professions and in their families, and falsely believe that it is impossible for them to strive for the devout life.

Dubay, Thomas. *Fire Within* (San Francisco: Ignatius Press, 1989). This book synthesizes the teachings on prayer of the two great doctors of the Church, St. John of the Cross and St. Teresa of Avila, along with the teaching of Sacred Scripture. The teaching that Fr. Dubay synthesized, however, is not collected from Teresa and John for contemplatives alone. It is meant for every Christian and is based on the Gospel imperative of personal prayer and the call to holiness.

Garrigou-Lagrange, Reginald. *Christian Perfection and Contemplation* (Rockford, Ill.: TAN Books and Publishing, Inc., 2003). *Christian Perfection and Contemplation* is an entire treatise on the operation of grace in the spiritual life that clearly and skillfully explains the great principles of the spiritual life according to St. Thomas Aquinas and other sterling Catholic Sources.

Garrigou-Lagrange, Reginald. *The Three Conversions in the Spiritual Life* (Rockford, Ill.: TAN Books and Publishing, Inc., 2002). All Catholics should go through three "conversions" in their spiritual life—but many do not, and thus remain spiritually stunted all their lives. Here, Fr. Garrigou-Lagrange—perhaps the greatest theologian of the twentieth century—explains the classic Catholic traditions on the spiritual life from Scripture, the Fathers, St. Thomas Aquinas, St. John of the Cross, and St. Catherine of Siena. He explains the Purgative, Illuminative, and Unitive Ways, plus Luther's errors on spirituality.

Guardini, Romano. *The Art of Praying* (1957. Reprint, Manchester, N.H.: Sophia Institute Press, 1994 ed). Where did you learn to pray? At your mother's knee? In first grade? Since then, your understanding of the world has matured immeasurably. Has your understanding of prayer also matured, or (like most of us) do you simply say your prayers, year after year, as you were taught so long ago? No wonder we have so many erroneous notions about prayer. No wonder our prayers are still far from what they should be. Only God's grace could perfect your prayers overnight, but in this helpful book, you'll find hundreds of practical ways you can immediately improve your prayers and grow closer to God.

Guardini, Romano. *The Rosary of Our Lady* (1955. Reprint, Manchester, N.H.: Sophia Institute Press, 1994). A spirit-filled explanation of the rosary that will lead you to a deeper experience of grace. Probably best read after learning to pray the rosary.

à Kempis, Thomas. *The Imitation of Christ, tr. by Joseph N. Tylenda.* (1418. Reprint, New York: Vintage Books, 1998). For almost six hundred years, this gentle book, filled with the spirit of the love of God, has brought understanding and comfort to millions of readers in over fifty languages, providing them with a source of heart-felt personal prayer. These meditations on the life and teachings of Jesus, written in times even more troubled and dangerous than our own, have become second only to the Bible as a guide and inspiration.

Richard, Thomas. *Ordinary Path to Holiness* (New York: Society of St. Paul, 2003). This work provides an overview of this traditional Catholic spirituality which has been tested and proven in the crucible of the lives of the saints. Understanding this traditional Catholic spirituality will give the reader powerful insights into his or her personal pilgrimage. This book is an invaluable aid to that understanding.

Scanlan, Michael. *Rosary Companion* (Steubenville, Ohio: Franciscan University Press, 1993). A simple, very practical aid to understanding the scriptural background to the rosary.

Teresa of Avila. *Interior Castle*, tr. by E. Allison Peers. (1577. Reprint, New York: Doubleday, 1989). This is one of the most celebrated books on mystical theology in existence. It is the most sublime and mature of Teresa of Avila's works, and expresses the full flowering of her deep experience in guiding souls toward spiritual perfection. In addition to its profound mystical content, it is also a treasury of unforgettable maxims on such ascetic subjects as self-knowledge, humility, detachment, and suffering. Above all, however, this account of a soul's progress in virtue and grace is the record of a life — of the interior life of Teresa of Avila, whose courageous soul, luminous mind, and endearingly human temperament hold so deep an attraction for the modern mind.

Therese of Lisieux. *Story of a Soul*, tr. by John Clarke. (1897. Reprint, Washington: ICS Publications, 1996). This story, the humble, simple, and joyful acknowledgement of God's mercy and love in St. Therese's own uncomplicated life, captured the interest and attention of its readers from the first time it appeared in print. In fact, we can say that St. Therese's book, like the simple and direct message of the Gospels, can be the source of a deep and religious inspiration for those who read it.

John of the Cross. *The Collected Works of Saint John of the Cross*, tr. by Kieran Kavanaugh and Otilio Rodriguez. (1591. Reprint, Washington: ICS Publications, 1996). The fourth centenary of the death of St. John of the Cross inspired this revised edition of the English translation of his writings. The result is an edition that preserves the true meaning of the great mystic's writings, presents them as clearly as possible, and at the same time gives the reader the doctrinal and historical information that will lead to a deeper understanding and appreciation of the teachings of the mystical Doctor. Included in *The Collected Works* are St. John's poetry, *The Ascent of Mount Carmel*, *The Dark Night*, *The Spiritual Canticle*, and *The Living Flame of Love*, as well as his letters and other counsels.

The Reformation

Adam, Karl. *The Roots of the Reformation*, tr. by Cecily Hastings. (New York: Sheed & Ward, 1951). An unbelievably powerful 94-page candid summary of the issues that led to the Reformation and their implications for today.

Belloc, Hilaire. *How the Reformation Happened* (Rockford, Ill.: TAN Books and Publishers, Inc., 1992). A enjoyable and eye-opening presentation of a Catholic perspective on the English Reformation.

Daniel-Rops, Henri. *The Catholic Reformation*. Two vols., tr. by Audrey Butler. (New York: Image Books, 1963).

Daniel-Rops, Henri. *The Protestant Reformation*. Two vols. (New York: Image Books, 1963). A classic retelling of all the issues, people, and events of the Reformation period.

Sacraments

Gray, Tim. *Sacraments in Scripture* (Steubenville, Ohio: Emmaus Road Publishing, 2001). Delves into the biblical origin for each of these masterpieces of God's love. The author guides readers through the Gospels, showing Christ's deliberate acts to inaugurate these sacred signs as the foundation of the New Covenant. Perfect for individual or group study. Each chapter ends with a section of questions for review.

Hahn, Scott. *Swear to God: The Promise and Power of the Sacraments* (New York, Doubleday, 2004). Dr. Hahn explores the richness of Christ's sacraments—their doctrine, history, symbols, and rituals.

Hahn, Scott. Lord Have *Mercy: The Healing Power of Confession* (New York, Doubleday, 2003). Dr. Hahn gets to the heart of the matter of Confession: how it is anticipated in the Old Testament, how it is presented in the New Testament, and how necessary it is for the spiritual life today.

Stravinskas, Peter M. J. *Understanding the Sacraments* (Ann Arbor, Mich.: Servant Publications, 1984). The single shortest and best study guide on the sacraments, offering clear and faithful Catholic teaching in chapters on each of the seven. Everyday examples and anecdotes enliven the text. An introductory chapter explains the meaning of the word "sacrament," while the closing chapter tells you how to recover a sense of the sacred in the liturgy and how to receive God's healing through the sacraments.

Wuerl, Donald. *The Church and Her Sacraments* (Huntington, Ind.: Our Sunday Visitor, 1990). A brief but lucid explanation by the Bishop of Pittsburgh.

Sacramentals, Customs, and Traditions

Dues, Greg. *Catholic Customs and Traditions: A Popular Guide* (Mystic, Conn.: Twenty-Third Publications, 1990). A simple, clear, concise presentation of common Catholic customs.

Richter, Klemens. *The Meaning of the Sacramental Symbols, tr.* by Linda M. Maloney. (Collegeville, Minn.: The Liturgical Press, 1990). A comprehensive examination of the symbols of worship, tracing their origins, what they have meant through the ages, and whether their meaning is clear for Christians today.

Sacred Tradition

Shea, Mark P. *By What Authority? An Evangelical Discovers Catholic Tradition* (Huntington, Ind.: Our Sunday Visitor, 1996). Interspersed with his own journey from Evangelicalism to the Catholic Church, Mark Shea skillfully explains how and why Sacred Tradition occupies a central role in divine revelation.

Scriptures and Scripture Studies

One of the most common requests we receive is for recommendations for reliable Scripture translations, commentaries, and Bible studies. Unfortunately, too many of the notes in many Catholic study Bibles present hypothetical, higher-critical opinions in a matter-of-fact way, giving lay readers the idea that these opinions are accepted facts. The following translations and commentaries avoid this speculation as well as the influence of modern political correctness.

The Catholic Answer Bible, New American Bible (Huntington, Ind.: Our Sunday Visitor, 2002). Designed for readers of every age, this innovative Bible contains twenty-two full-color inserts featuring forty-four of the most common questions asked about the Catholic faith.

The Holy Bible, Revised Standard Version Catholic Edition (1966. Reprint, San Francisco: Ignatius Press, 1994).

The Navarre Bible Commentaries (Dublin, Ireland: Four Courts Press, 1992). These New Testament commentaries contain both the Latin and the RSVCE texts accompanied by running commentary.

Barber, Michael. *Singing in the Reign* (Steubenville, Ohio: Emmaus Road Publishing, 2001). Discover the secret riches of the Psalms. Christians know the Psalms, sing the Psalms, and pray the Psalms, yet believers have lost the big picture — the single sense that unites all the Psalms as one coherent book.

Epie, Chantal. *The Scriptural Roots of Catholic Teaching* (Manchester, N.H.: Sophia Institute Press, 2002). This book is a comprehensive and user-friendly guide that shows you where to find all the Church's major teachings in Scripture — especially the ones that non-Catholics most often contradict. Epie reveals the Scriptural foundations of all the most important and most often controverted teachings of the Church: the source of Divine Revelation, the founding of the Church by Christ Himself, His establishment of the Sacraments as means of grace, and the importance of devotion to Mary and the saints.

Fuentes, Antonio. *A Guide to the Bible* (Dublin, Ireland: Four Courts Press, 2002). A guide that will provide readers with an overview of the Bible and make it easier for them to see the gradual unfolding of the biblical message. The author, who teaches Scripture at Navarre University, Pamplona, describes the aim of the book as being: "to provide short commentaries on the various books of the Bible, commentaries written for the general reader, the type of reader who is not interested in detailed exegesis but, rather, wants to know what God is saying in the Bible, and what was the social context in which each book was written."

Graham, Henry G. *Where We Got the Bible: Our Debt to the Catholic Church* (1911. Reprint, San Diego: Catholic Answers, 1997). This classic work traces the origin and preservation of sacred Scripture. It also includes the conversion story of the author, who converted from Calvinist ministry to Catholicism. This is a two-in-one book that exonerates the Catholic Church from the charge of neglecting the Bible, while also showing the truth of the faith that can be discovered even by someone reared in a society burdened with anti-Catholic prejudice.

Gray, Tim. *Mission of the Messiah* (Steubenville, Ohio: Emmaus Road Publishing, 1998). *Mission of the Messiah* is a compelling new study of the Gospel of Luke that presents the messianic mission of Jesus as the fulfillment of Old Testament prophecy. This book is a must for anyone whose heart is burning to know and love Christ more profoundly.

Hahn, Scott. *A Father Who Keeps his Promises* (Cincinnati: St. Anthony Messenger Press, 1998). Dr. Hahn focuses the reader on the "big picture" of Scripture: God's fatherly plan in making and keeping covenants with us throughout salvation history—so that we might live as the family of God.

Hahn, Scott and Curtis Mitch. *Ignatius Study Bible.* (San Francisco: Ignatius Press, 2005). Based around the Revised Standard Version Catholic Edition, the six volumes in this Study Bible present a penetrating study of the Gospels, Acts, and Romans, with fresh insights from contemporary scholarship all the way back to the Church Fathers. Each volume includes ample notes, word studies, charts, a cross-reference, study questions, and topical essays covering authorship, date, place, structure, and themes.

Madrid, Patrick. *Where is that in the Bible* (Huntington, Ind.: Our Sunday Visitor, 2001). When non-Catholics start quoting Bible verses to "prove" that Catholic teachings aren't biblical, reach for this powerful Bible-based explanation and defense of the Catholic Faith! *Where Is That In the Bible?* shows you how to deflate standard objections to Catholicism and how to use Scripture to bring people into, or back into, the Church.

Oatis, Gregory. *Catholic Doctrine in Scripture* (Zanesville, Ohio: CHResources, 2003). This is a compendium of Scripture verses, topically arranged and easy to use, which illustrate the scriptural affirmation of Catholic teachings. The book provides chapter and verse, plus the actual biblical text for each reference on over fifty-five key topics including apostolic succession, intercessory prayer, indulgences, the Holy Eucharist, Confession, and many more. Allows the reader to instantly find all verses related to key areas of the Faith.

Ponessa, Joseph and Laurie Watson Manhardt. *The Gospel of John* (Steubenville, Ohio: Emmaus Road Publishing, 2005). The Gospel of John is a natural starting place in the "Come and See" series and an excellent introduction to Bible study in general. Its easy-to use, workbook format makes this study ideal for use in the classroom, in home study, or in parish catechesis. The "Come and See" series is the answer for those seeking quality Bible study materials that draw from the richness of Catholic Tradition—the teaching of the Church Fathers, the prayers of the saints, and the Catechism of the Catholic Church.

Ponessa, Joseph and Laurie Watson Manhardt. *Prophets and Apostles* (Steubenville, Ohio: Emmaus Road Publishing, 2004). This book combines the "old" and the "new" — covering eleven prophets of the Old Testament and five apostles of the New Testament. Richly supplemented by passages from the Catechism of the Catholic Church, various prayers of the saints, helpful memorization tools, and questions for reflection, this book takes a refreshingly direct and engaging approach to the study of Scripture.

Shea, Mark P. *Making Senses Out of Scripture* (San Diego: Basilica Press, 1999). A wonderfully helpful guide for reading the Bible according to the Church's living Tradition. It skillfully draws on the riches of the Catholic Faith and communicates Her deep truths very clearly, yet it is written with a witty and winsome style that makes the book as accessible to the beginning student of Scripture as it is to the advanced.

Spiritualities in the Catholic Church

Aumann, Jordan. *Christian Spirituality in the Catholic Tradition.* (San Francisco: Ignatius Press, 1985). A broad survey of how different Catholic orders (groups) have lived out the Gospel of Jesus Christ.

Aumann, Jordan. *Spiritual Theology* (Chicago: Christian Classics, 1980). A perceptive survey of spiritual growth from one of the leading spiritual theologians in the Catholic Church.

Testimonies of Converts

Baram Robert, ed. *Spiritual Journeys toward the Fullness of Faith* (Boston: Daughters of St. Paul, 1988). Twenty-seven men and women share their faith journeys home to the Catholic Church.

Barres, Oliver. *One Shepherd, One Flock* (San Diego: Catholic Answers, 2000). Most conversion books contain multiple stories. *One Shepherd, One Flock* contains just one, and it's like no other. The first part is taken from the diary Oliver Barres kept *before* becoming Catholic. You travel with him from disagreement to assent—no other conversion story can match this. The second part defends the Catholic beliefs Barres once found indefensible.

Cavins, Jeff. *My Life on the Rock: A Rebel Returns to the Catholic Faith* (West Chester: Ascension Press, 2000). The dramatic conversion story of Jeff Cavins is the true and bittersweet story of an emotional and spiritual search for peace in a chaotic world. Jeff's story recounts his early Catholic upbringing, rejection of the Faith, ordination as a Protestant minister, and finally his return home to the Catholic Church. It definitely was not a smooth trip: he went toe-to-toe with his own father and three Bishops in his search for truth.

Chervin, Ronda, ed. *The Ingrafting* (New Hope, Ky.: Remnant of Israel, 1993). The accounts contained in *The Ingrafting* have been chosen from among many stories of Jews who each year recognize Jesus as the Messiah of Israel and the Catholic Church as the true Church of the true Messiah. They span a century, and include the story of a Chasid from the mountains of Hungary, born in 1899, as well as that of a young man from Los Angeles, baptized in 1984.

Connor, Charles. *Classic Catholic Converts* (San Francisco: Ignatius Press, 2001). *Classic Catholic Converts* presents the compelling stories of over twenty-five well-known converts to Catholicism from the 19th and 20th centuries. It tells of powerful testimonials to God's grace, men and women from all walks of life in Europe and America whose search for the fullness of truth led them to the Catholic Church.

Currie, David. *Born Fundamentalist Born Again Catholic* (San Francisco: Ignatius Press, 1996). A book written as an explanation to family and friends about why David became a Roman Catholic. Currie presents a very lucid, systematic, and intelligible account of the reasons for his conversion to the ancient Church that Christ founded. He gives a detailed discussion of the important theological and doctrinal beliefs that Catholics and Evangelicals hold in common, as well as key doctrines that separate us, particularly the Eucharist, the Pope, and Mary.

Drake, Timothy. *There We Stood, Here We Stand: Eleven Lutherans Rediscover Their Catholic Roots* (Bloomington, Ind.: First Books Library, 2001). These thought-provoking testimonies by eleven former Lutherans reveal how far the Lutheran Church has strayed from Luther. They include moving stories from four former female pastors, three former pastors, and others. Their intensely personal stories address the differences between Lutheranism and Catholicism, differences so profound that they have led many into the Catholic Church.

Hahn, Scott and Kimberly. *Rome Sweet Home* (San Francisco: Ignatius Press, 1993). Scott and Kimberly's moving testimony of the grace and the trials that led Scott in 1986 and Kimberly in 1990 from Presbyterianism to the Catholic Church. One of the most well publicized conversion stories in the late twentieth century.

Howard, Thomas. *Lead, Kindly Light* (1994. Reprint, San Francisco: Ignatius Press, 2004). Well-known Catholic convert, writer and English professor Thomas Howard tells his own story of his personal spiritual journey from Evangelicalism, through Anglicanism, into the Catholic Church. Howard cleverly weaves anecdotes with doctrines as he retraces the steps of his fascinating spiritual search and journey to Rome in the spirit of John Henry Newman.

Longenecker, Dwight. *Path to Rome* (Leominster, England: Gracewing, 2004). A collection of English conversion stories.

Madrid, Patrick, ed. *Surprised by Truth* (San Diego: Basilica Press, 1994). This is the first of a series of modern conversion accounts that are both packed with biblical, theological, and historical proofs for Catholicism and at the same time very winsome and entertaining.

Madrid, Patrick, ed. *Surprised By Truth 2* (Manchester, N.H.: Sophia Institute Press, 2000). This collection of testimonies by people who've found new life in the Catholic Church is one of the most potent weapons for the Faith ever crafted! These authors don't just tell their stories—they also give you an insider's view of the fatal weaknesses in the creeds and belief systems that beckon unwary Catholics every day: Fundamentalism, New Age paganism, Mormonism, materialistic hedonism, and many others.

Madrid, Patrick, ed. *Surprised by Truth 3* (Manchester, N.H.: Sophia Institute Press, 2002). These stories will remind you of the critical truth that all converts know but most others forget: churches must not be judged by the weakness of their members, but by the truth of what they teach. The closer these former Protestants looked at Catholicism, the more they found that Christ's truth is taught in its fullness only in the Catholic Church. No wonder this book is a convert maker!

Merton, Thomas. *The Seven Storey Mountain* (1948, Reprint, Orlando, Fla.: Harcourt Trade Publishers, 1998). A modern-day *Confessions of Saint Augustine*, *The Seven Storey Mountain* is one of the most influential religious works of the twentieth century. A classic of a secular man turned Trappist monk.

Moss, Rosalind, ed. *Home at Last: Eleven Who Found Their Way to the Catholic Church* (San Diego: Catholic Answers, 2000). Eleven distinct and often startling accounts of conversion. The contributors to this book were Anglican, Presbyterian, atheist, Lutheran, Jewish, Baptist, Pentecostal, agnostic- but now they are Catholic.

Newman, John Henry. *Apologia pro Vita Sua* (1880. Reprint, London: Penguin Books, Ltd., 1994). This classic narrates the conversion of one of the greatest English cardinals in the nineteenth century. The *Apologia* is Newman's account of his religious life. He tries to show the reader how his doubts about the Anglican Church began and how he gradually converted to Roman Catholicism. He describes his involvement in the Oxford movement which was meant to explain the theology of the Church of England and as he wrote tracts on the subject, he became less and less convinced of their truth. He says that the things that he had thought separated him from the Catholic Church became less and less important. The book was intended as an answer to charges that he was a Catholic all his life and had been trying to subvert the Church of England from within.

Pearce, Joseph. *Literary Converts* (San Francisco: Ignatius Press, 1999). *Literary Converts* is a biographical exploration into the spiritual lives of some those figures. More specifically, it takes us on a journey into the deepest beliefs of some of the greatest writers in the English language: Oscar Wilde, Evelyn Waugh, C.S. Lewis, Malcolm Muggeridge, Graham Greene, G.K. Chesterton, Dorothy Sayers, T.S. Eliot and J.R.R. Tolkien.

Ray, Stephen K. *Crossing the Tiber* (San Francisco: Ignatius Press, 1997). A moving account of the conversion of an evangelical, thoroughly documented with over 400 biblical and patristic quotations and commentary.

Appendix B

*How to become a member of
the Coming Home Network International
and support its work*

There are three types of membership in the *Coming Home Network International*:

Primary Membership is for former clergy and their families who are somewhere along the journey into the Catholic Church.

Secondary Membership is for laity of other traditions and fallen-away Catholics, who again are somewhere along the journey into the Catholic Church.

Tertiary or associate membership is for Catholic laity, priests, deacons, religious, bishops, and even cardinals who support the *CHNetwork* in their prayers and generous contributions.

Members are encouraged to form local fellowship groups for prayer, fellowship, and small-group studies of Scripture or Church teachings, as well as for reaching out with the truth of the Catholic faith to friends and relatives outside the Church.

The goal of the *CHNetwork* is to assist the Catholic Church in fulfilling her mission of evangelization and call for Christian unity, as most recently proclaimed by Pope John Paul II in his 1995 encyclical *Ut Unum Sint*.

One of the strongest desires of all members of the *CHNetwork* is to help all Catholics appreciate the wonderful faith they have always had and sometimes take for granted.

How Can I Help?

There are several ways in which you can support the work of the *Coming Home Network International:*

• **Become a member of the *CHNetwork*.** As a member, you receive the newsletter and information about how to connect with others around the world who are on the journey. You also can attend regional retreats, gatherings, and pilgrimages. An annual suggested donation of $35 helps cover the costs of printing and mailing the newsletter plus other administrative and apostolic expenses.

• **Pray for the *CHNetwork*,** its staff, and members. All members are encouraged to pray regularly for all the needs of the *CHNetwork* and to present these needs at least one hour each month before the Blessed Sacrament.

• **Make a contribution to the *CHNetwork*.** The *Coming Home Network International* is a nonprofit Catholic lay apostolate, solely funded through the contributions of its members and friends. All donations are tax-deductible and greatly appreciated.

• **Tell others about our work and encourage them to support it.** Let your priest and bishop know about our apostolate. Often when clergy of other traditions become interested in finding out about the Catholic faith, they do not know where to turn. We want to help them.

• **Distribute our brochures, newsletters, resources, and even a copy of this book to clergy and laity of other traditions.** Most members of other traditions have been misinformed about the teachings of the Catholic faith. Following the model of St. Francis de Sales who committed his life to bringing thousands of Calvinists back to the Catholic faith, we believe the loving communication of the truth will win hearts back to the Church.

• **Schedule one of our staff members or a member of the *CHNetwork* to speak at your parish or at a conference.** Marcus Grodi as well as other clergy and lay converts on our staff, board of directors, or in our membership are experienced speakers and enjoy sharing their conversion stories as well as other topics to strengthen the faith of Catholic laity.

• **The *Coming Home Network International*** depends almost entirely on gifts from individuals like yourself to continue our work. Your generous donation allows us to provide financial and spiritual assistance to those seeking the truth of the Catholic Faith.

How Can I Become a Member?

If you are interested in becoming a member of the *CHNetwork,* complete the survey on the following page and return it to the address below. A $35 annual donation is requested to cover the costs of printing and mailing the newsletter, as well as other administrative and apostolic expenses.

The Coming Home Network International
P. O. Box 8290
Zanesville, OH 43702-8290
Phone: 1-740-450-1175

CHNetwork **Membership Survey**

Name: _____

Address: _____

City: _____ State: _____Zip: _____

Country: _____

Phone: (home) (___)_____(cell) (___)_____

(work) (___)_____ (email)_____

Denominational Information:
     In which denomination were . . .

                 You   Your Spouse

Baptized: _____

Date baptized: _____

Place baptized: _____

Previously member: _____

Seminary & degree: _____

Ordained: _____

Date ordained: _____

Place ordained: _____

Ordained by whom: _____

If you are now Catholic, when & where were you received
     into the Church:

Date received:_____

Place received: _____

Current Occupation: _____

Children: (Names, age & current denomination)

_____

_____

_____

_____

_____

_____

_____

Please describe your present relationship to the Catholic Church: (use additional paper if needed)

_____

_____

What is your spouse's relationship to the Catholic Church: (use additional paper if needed)

_____

_____

Can we release your name to other CHN members looking for fellowship? ☐ YES ☐ NO

The Coming Home Network International
P. O. Box 8290
Zanesville, OH 43702-8290
Phone: 1-740-450-1175
http://www.chnetwork.org